THE PRINT TRADE
IN IRELAND

A DICTIONARY OF THE PRINT TRADE IN IRELAND
1550-1775

ROBERT MUNTER

FORDHAM UNIVERSITY PRESS
New York
1988

© Copyright 1988 by FORDHAM UNIVERSITY
All rights reserved.
LC 88–80279
ISBN 0–8232–1200–9
First edition

Printed in the United States of America

TO
PUTSY

CONTENTS

Abbreviations and Short Titles   ix

Introduction   1

The Dictionary   11

Bibliography   315

ABBREVIATIONS AND
SHORT TITLES

Bentham, *Abstracts*   Sir William Bentham, *Genealogical Abstracts of Prerogative Wills*, PROI.

BL   British Museum Library.

Cal. Anc. Rec. Dublin   J. T. Gilbert, *Calendar of the Ancient Records of Dublin*, 1889.

Caulfield, *Cork Council Book*   R. Caulfield, *The Council Book of the Corporation of the City of Cork*, 1876.

Craig, *Bookbinding*   Maurice Craig, *Irish Bookbinding, 1600–1800*, 1954.

Crosslé, *Prerogative Wills*   Phillip Crosslé, *Copies of Prerogative Wills*, RIA, Dublin.

Dictionary 1557–1640   H. G. Aldis et al., *A Dictionary of Printers and Booksellers in England, Scotland and Ireland, and of Foreign Printers of English Books 1557–1640*, 1910.

Dictionary 1641–67   H. R. Plomer, *A Dictionary of Booksellers and Printers who were at work in England, Scotland and Ireland 1641–1667*, 1907.

Dictionary 1668–1725   H. R. Plomer, *A Dictionary of the Printers and Booksellers who were at work in England, Scotland and Ireland from 1668 to 1725*, 1922.

Dictionary 1726–75   H. R. Plomer et al., *A Dictionary of the Printers and Booksellers who were at work in England, Scotland and Ireland from 1726 to 1775*, 1932.

Dunton, *Dublin Scuffle*   John Dunton, *The Dublin Scuffle*, 1699.

Evans, *American Bibliography*   Charles Evans, *American Bibliography: a chronological dictionary of all books, pamphlets, and periodicals published . . . 1639 down to . . . 1820*, 1941–59.

Gilbert, *History of Dublin*   J. T. Gilbert, *A History of the City of Dublin*, 1861.

Guild Records   *Records of the Guild of St. Luke the Evangelist*, Sidthorpe and Sons, 33 Molesworth Street, Dublin.

Madden, *Irish Periodical Literature*   R. R. Madden, *Irish Periodical Literature, from the End of the 17th Century to the Middle of the 19th Century*, 1867.

Munter, *Handlist*   Robert Munter, *A Handlist of Irish Newspapers, 1685–1750*, 1960.

Munter, *Irish Newspapers*   Robert Munter, *The History of the Irish Newspaper, 1685–1760*, 1967.

Phillips, unpublished thesis   J. W. Phillips, "A bibliographical inquiry into printing and publishing in Dublin during the eighteenth century," 1953, unpublished thesis, TCD.

PROI   Public Record Office, Ireland.

RIA   Royal Irish Academy, Dublin.

Strickland, *Irish Artists*   W. G. Strickland, *A Dictionary of Irish Artists*, 1913.

TCD   Trinity College, Dublin.

Thrift, *Freemen*   G. Thrift, *Roll of Freemen City of Dublin 1468–1485, 1575–1770*, 1919.

Vicars, *Index of Wills*   Sir A. Vicars, *Index to the Prerogative Wills of Ireland, 1563–1810*, 1897.

Young, *Belfast Town Book*   R. N. Young (ed.), *Town Book of the Corporation of Belfast, 1613–1816*, 1892.

Introduction

BETWEEN 1907 and 1932 there were published five dictionaries* which together listed all the known printers and booksellers who were at work in the British book trade between the years 1457 and 1775. More than fifty years have passed since this series was completed and, quite naturally, a great deal of information has been acquired concerning the men and women involved. With few exceptions—the supplemental list of Scottish printers and booksellers published by *Studies in Bibliography* in 1959 and 1961—much of this information has been scattered through diverse journals, pamphlets, and monographs; some quite rare, some long out of print. Moreover, there have continued to exist sources pertaining to the print trade that have been inadequately investigated or simply ignored: for example, the records of the stationers' guild of Dublin.

The present work therefore seeks to do three things: (1) to record the names, places of business, and periods of activity of numerous stationers not previously listed in the published dictionaries, (2) to correct, clarify, and augment many of the existing entries from these dictionaries, and (3) to broaden the perspective from the book trade to the print trade, thereby including more representatives of the general profession. The result is a single volume that includes all of the aforementioned that pertains to printing in Ireland from the earliest known work in 1550 to 1775.

Additional information on the print trade of Ireland necessitated a new dictionary, and the contributions of various historians, antiquarians, bibliographers, and others have made it possible. Prominent among these was the persistent detective work of E. R. McC. Dix, the many contributions of Séamus Ó Casaide, La Tourette Stockwell, Phillip Crosslé, Mau-

---

*E. Gordon Duff, *A Century of the English Book Trade*, 1905; H. G. Aldis et al., *A Dictionary of Printers and Booksellers in England, Scotland and Ireland, and of Foreign Printers of English Books 1557–1640*, 1910; H. R. Plomer, *A Dictionary of the Booksellers and Printers who were at work in England, Scotland and Ireland 1641–1667*, 1907; H. R. Plomer, *A Dictionary of the Printers and Booksellers who were at work in England, Scotland and Ireland from 1668 to 1725*, 1922; and H. R. Plomer et al., *A Dictionary of the Printers and Booksellers who were at work in England, Scotland and Ireland from 1726 to 1775*, 1932.

rice Craig, and Francis O'Kelly (who left so many valuable notes). Some had their work privately printed, for some it remained in notebooks or unfinished manuscripts, but many published their findings in various journals, proceedings, and periodicals in the *Irish Book Lover, Notes and Queries, The Library,* and the like. I have made full use of all of this material.

In addition to drawing on the work of others, for nearly forty years I have been collecting information from yet other sources, from advertisements and sales catalogues, from the imprints in almanacs, broadsheets, directories, and sheet music, from manuscript collections in various Irish depositories, from parish registers, records of wills, the registry of deeds in Dublin, and, of utmost importance, from the unpublished records of the Guild of St. Luke the Evangelist, which included the stationers of Dublin.

There are thirteen volumes of these guild records, covering the life of that body from its founding in 1670 to its dissolution in 1841. They include such information as the names of the brethren, dates of their admission to the guild, the offices they held along with details of election divisions, the bylaws passed, and various agreements and orders deemed sufficiently important to have been entered in the order book. There are as well complete minutes for the years 1695 to 1841 (some six volumes), Master and Treasurer accounts for the years 1720 to 1833 (with a few omissions), a book of enrollment of apprentices (an earlier book apparently having disappeared), plus a few miscellaneous items.

Through the utilization of all of these diverse sources it was possible to identify many previously unknown stationers, some who proved to have been quite prominent in the profession. Most of those discovered, however, were the more obscure tradesmen, foreigners, and particularly intruders (those who practiced their trade in defiance of the guild). The obvious imprints identifying the printer and publisher or the advertisement of a bookseller were not the only leads to the stationers of the day, for a subscriber's list that revealed the provincial purchase of twelve copies of some Dublin publication might well make known a Londonderry bookseller, or a signature on a petition objecting to the lowering of duties on foreign paper might indicate a papermaker.

But it was the Guild of St. Luke records that yielded the most information concerning the practitioners of the print trade and also disclosed something of the profession's structure. The guild was chartered in 1670 by Charles II in a patent granted to six cutlers, four painter–stainers, and two stationers. Each of these three trades was known as a faculty, with the odd combination of occupations undoubtedly due to each being too small to function on its own. Although united in a guild organization, a member could not practice another faculty's trade nor could he move from faculty to faculty.

There were two forms of membership in the guild, free (or full) brothers and quarter brothers: there were no brethren at large until the late eighteenth century when an occasional honorary membership was allowed. Free brothers were those admitted to full participation in guild governance and to the practice of their trade without restriction. There were various ways to become a free brother but the most usual was for a person to serve a seven-year apprenticeship, be recommended by the master he had served, be approved by the Council of the House, and thus gain "freedom by service." If your father was a guild member when you were born, upon reaching adulthood (at times this appeared to be age twenty-five), you could gain "freedom by birth." Finally, if a person could demonstrate skill in some aspect of the stationer's calling—perhaps gained in England, a foreign country, or through some irregular training —he could petition to be admitted "free by special grace."

Quarter brothers were so named because they had to pay quarterly dues in order to practice their trade, but they could not vote or hold any office in the guild. Journeymen often found it cheaper and less burdensome to remain as quarter brothers. Occasionally women, never allowed full freedom, were carried as quarter brothers. Officially, all brethren had to be Church of England members. This was never strictly enforced, however, and consequently Catholics and dissenters were often allowed as quarter brothers, as were the occasional Huguenot refugees. From 1680 hawkers (street vendors) were brought in as quarter brothers and were additionally licensed as to what (chapbooks, broadsheets, newspapers) and where they might "hawk." The majority of hawkers were indigent Catholics, and the relatively little interest the guild took in their existence is reflected in the casual record-keeping of their activities. In 1691 intruders were allowed to join as quarter brothers regardless of proof of training. Apparently, the guild had found it too difficult to prevent them from working.

Having three different occupations represented in the guild necessitated devising some method to share the governance of the body. The original charter, subsequent bylaws, and later simply tradition guaranteed that each faculty would be equally represented in office-holding regardless of their numerical importance. Even when the stationers numerically dominated they were not able to control guild functions. The faculties rotated the important offices of Master and the two Wardens and held an equal number of seats in the legislative branch, the Council of the House. Elections were held yearly in August, with those elected taking office on St. Luke's Day, October 18. Each free brother had a vote and, although the candidates for each position had to come from the faculty whose turn it was to hold office, all faculties voted for each position.

The Master was the head of the guild and its official spokesman. He made expenditures on behalf of the body, presided over meetings, and was always prominent on ceremonial occasions. Masters were always elected from Warden peers—that is, those who had served a term as Warden. The Wardens assisted the Master, but the bylaws were silent as to their duties. Actually, the Wardens appear to have carried out much of the guild business themselves—the budget, accounts, and preparation for the quarterly meetings of the full hall.

Masters and Wardens were aided in turn by the Council of the House, which was composed of elected representatives, originally seven from each faculty and, after 1683, nine from each. Election to the Council was for life, membership ending only by resignation, death, or extreme misbehavior. Wardens were rarely elected if not already members of the Council. If for some reason a non-member was elected, he would invariably be elected to the Council with the first vacancy from his own faculty. The Council met privately to consider the business agenda for the quarterly full house meeting. The quarter days were originally the second Monday before the quarterly assemblies of the city. In 1702 this was changed to the first Tuesday of January, April, July, and October, and in 1813 again changed to the first Thursday. The Council also examined all credentials of prospective members and gave final approval to the admittance of both full and quarter brothers.

Besides Master, Wardens, and Council, there were two lesser officers, the Beadle and the Treasurer. The Beadle was a sort of formal secretary who called meetings, served official notices, and so forth, while the Treasurer kept tally on all funds, income from dues, rentals, and fines, as well as all disbursements. Although re-elected annually, it was usual for a person to serve as Treasurer for several years.

As for the functioning of the guild, information is quite scanty on its efforts to police the trade of the three faculties and to supervise training and quality of production, supposedly their primary task. The impression is that they were generally ineffective. The attempts that were made to regulate trade were restricted to Dublin and never extended to the provinces. The guild either had very little power to enforce the decisions of the hall or they made relatively little effort to do so. Perhaps the division into three faculties weakened the guild's control. The stationer's faculty never demanded the registry of intended publications, which led to constant squabbles among members over ownership rights, all of which compacted with the persistent controversy over the pirating of English titles. Printers and publishers produced books, pamphlets, and on occasion newspapers without imprints, which made any guild supervision awkward.

Probably the guild's major failing was that it was never able to control the large number of intruders. The existence of many Catholics and Protestant dissenters, particularly in Dublin, made this very problem the more complicated. The unofficial toleration, the shunning of overt persecution of either of these two groups meant that they were left quite free to conduct their businesses while being denied access to the guild; those allowed membership as quarter brothers would hardly feel a strong allegiance. In 1719 the guild made a short-lived effort to police intruders, but to little avail. Again in 1755 and 1756, they established a committee to deal with the non-guild practitioners, which also came to nought. Seemingly in both instances, the guild either quickly lost interest or found the problem too formidable. In 1793 Catholic membership as free brothers was finally allowed, and although several Catholics took advantage of this new law, by this date the guild had become more a social club than a guardian of guild crafts. Membership remained important only in that it allowed a role in city government.

As valuable as the guild records are, they are as well most frustrating. The record-keeping itself was generally sloppy and haphazard; some entries, obviously erroneous, were never corrected. The great variation in the spelling, often phonetic, of the members' names made tracking them difficult. (But how could it have been otherwise in an age given to indifferent spelling, when a printer could set his own name in type three different ways in a single issue of a newspaper: Pew, Pugh, and Pue!) The brethren were seldom identified by faculty, so that there is no distinguishing the painter Wilson from the stationer Wilson from the cutler Wilson. Within the stationer faculty, it is equally hard to determine who followed what line, bookbinder, printer, or bookseller.

Indeed, identification outside of the guild records of those that followed the various stationers' specialties is not easy. Papermakers seldom kept a shop in town, they placed advertisements infrequently, and they did not always have a recognizable watermark. When by some good fortune a master papermaker becomes known, we still learn nothing of his apprentices or journeymen. Papermakers were rarely guild members, and few would have considered them even stationers. Thus we have no record of any attempt to round up papermaker intruders.

Bookbinders are equally hard to discover, even if they were guild members. Except for the occasional master, few bookbinders signed their work. A bid to bind some government journals often provides the sole key to a bookbinder's existence. They were often dealers in old books as well, and further frustration for the researcher attends the bookbinder's economical practice of using the same labels for both parts of this business. Engravers too produced their maps and frontispieces without signatures and, as with bookbinders, only by comparison of style or technique can we get a clue as to the craftsman responsible. Typefounders and press makers could prove to be the most phantom of all.

For all the limitations of the guild records, they are a goldmine of biographical information while providing numerous sidelights on the petty quarrels and the more serious concerns of the membership. No single source was more useful in compiling the information for this dictionary and, when combined with the material from other sources, has made possible a much broader study of the Irish print trade.

The present dictionary has 957 entries, 579 of which are not contained in the earlier dictionaries. Thirty-seven entries remain unchanged, while 344 are entries in the former publications but have been altered here in various ways: by extension of the dates of activity; by the listing of new places of business; by the addition of new information on trade, political, or religious affiliations; or by the complete elimination of an entry found to be bogus. The discrepancy in total number is due to the occasional discovery that two earlier entries were actually references to one person or that some entries were composed of two different individuals' work.

The form of the entries generally follows the pattern established in the earlier five dictionaries. Nevertheless some explanation of terms and format seems necessary. Print trade is used in the title because it is more reflective of the profession overall than is book trade, since what is included is far more than simply the business of books. Intimately associated in the stationers' realm was such diverse work as broadsheet and newspaper production, almanac and directory publication, and the printing of mezzotint engravings. For all those practitioners of the print trade, the word stationer is employed as a generic label, an all-encompassing connotation being suggested rather than the narrow definition of bookseller, publisher, and some fixed shop. Perhaps such usage is not altogether satisfactory, but it falls not far short of the way the word was used in the guild records.

The specific entries began by giving the full name of the stationer. The spelling of names, as with spelling in general, being so delightfully anarchic, necessitated some limitations in listing the many possible variants. Only the different spellings that the individual himself employed with some consistency, or those repeatedly used in the guild records, have been given.

Following the name appears the individual's occupation, his specialization within the stationers' trade. The divisions include bookseller, bookbinder, engraver, papermaker, printer, publisher, and typefounder. If his specific calling is unknown, he is listed simply as a stationer. The categories of music printer, music seller, press maker, or print seller have not been used. Persons who followed any of these latter trades are listed in the dictionary only when they practice one of the other branches of the print trade.

Although publisher has been retained as one of the divisions of the profession, it remains an unsatisfactory label. Nearly all booksellers were on occasion publishers as well, as were various printers and engravers. The term as used in the entries thus has been restricted to those who practiced some other specialty of the trade as well, while the rare individual who served only as a publisher for, say, an almanac, or those who saw but one or two publications through the press, have not been listed.

Next appears the towns, business addresses, and the dates of activity at each location. In an entry where the individual worked in various locations, dates are given in parentheses for the time of residence in each town or place of business. If only a question mark appears, it means just that, dates unknown; if a question mark follows the date, it implies some doubt. A final date, not in parentheses, provides the total of all years in the trade. As with personal names, there were many random and idiosyncratic spellings of place names—Blew Boar or Blue Boar, Key or Quay, Nicholas Street or St. Nicholas-street, Cork or Corke—and here I have taken the liberty of using the most common, accepted form of the day.

The information provided within the entry covers a series of subjects: dates of apprenticeships, memberships, and offices held in the guild (with the dates used for office-holding being the year following the August election); religious preferences; any political involvement of note or criminal persecutions suffered; and various personal, marital, and business relationships with other stationers. Unlike the earlier dictionaries, there are no separate entries for partnerships or companies—such as Phineas Bagnell & Co. The reason involves the difficulty of defining or identifying such partnerships. Seldom is there any evidence of actual written contracts, and although close cooperation might exist between various stationers over a period of years, more often than not associations or coteries were ephemeral, many times having been formed for but one publishing project.

For those entries where there is a dearth of information, I have attempted to list all the extant prints or publications bearing the individual's colophon. For the more prolific stationers, this is impossible. Therefore, what is provided is a sample of the more representative work or a culling from the more significant productions. Also recorded is such information as an individual's being the first printer in a town or the publisher of its first newspaper; the first to employ Irish, Hebrew, or Greek type; or the first woman to be carried as a quarter brother by the guild. On occasion a brief explanation of trade disputes is offered—the controversy over the pirating of Richardson's *Sir Charles Grandison* or the conflict over rival editions of Prévost d'Exiles' *Dean of Coleraine*. To describe the Wood's Half-penny or the Charles Lucas affairs, however, is certainly beyond the scope of this dictionary.

Documentation within the entries has been kept to a bare minimum. It is primarily employed where there has been some prior question or dispute about an individual's activity, or where there has been some major alteration or emendation of previously published information. For example, the earlier entry for Richard Pue is divided here into two individual entries, Richard Pue father and son, and the two Thomas Watsons earlier cited have been identified here as the same individual, and thus both have been documented.

In all of the dictionaries previously published, the editors conclude their preface or introduction with the self-acknowledgment of the shortcomings and incomplete nature of their endeavors. The present work readily admits as much: no such compilation can ever be definitive. Information about many individuals is yet wanting, knowledge of their doings but vague, and thus the plea must be repeated for present and future scholars to continue their efforts that they may provide corrections and additions to these works.

THE
DICTIONARY

A

ACHESON (**ROBERT**), printer in Dublin, 1768–75. He was apprenticed to Oliver Nelson (q.v.) in 1761, was admitted free of the guild by service in 1768, and paid quarterage through 1775 (*Guild Records*).

ADAMS (**J.**), bookseller in Coleraine, 1747–48. Sole reference: he was listed in the colophons as one of the provincial sellers of Exshaw's *London Magazine*.

ADAMS (**JAMES**), printer in Dublin, d. 1767. Sole reference: in 1767 his will was proved in the Diocesan Court in Dublin (*Dictionary 1726–75*).

ADAMS (**ORION**), bookbinder, printer, and publisher in Dublin, Cope Street, 1766–67. He worked in Oxford (?), Chester, Birmingham, etc. from 1726 to 1797 in a long itinerant career (*Dictionary 1726–75*). He was in a brief Dublin partnership with Thomas Ryder (q.v.), jointly printing and publishing plays and operas and Forman's *A Defense of the Courage, Honour and Loyalty of the Irish Nation*, 1767. Adams purportedly drew Ryder "into several disagreeable engagements, encumbered him with partnership debts, of many of which he was totally unacquainted, till Mr. Adams treacherous flight from Ireland" (Sequin's *Hibernian Magazine*, Jan. 1773).

ADEY or EDY (**SAMUEL**), bookbinder and publisher in Dublin, Copper Alley, 1683–1703. He served as a journeyman to John Blakesley (q.v.) in 1683, was recorded as "In Eng'd" in 1684, and again listed as a journeyman from 1686 to 1688. By 1694 he had his own bookbinding business and in 1695 published Henry, Bishop of Killaroo's *A Sermon Preached in Christ's-Church*. In 1704 he is listed as "In Jamaica" (*Guild Records*).

AFLECK, AFFLECK, FLECK, or FLEAKE (JOHN), bookseller in Dublin, (1) the Key, Bride Street (1704?–16); (2) Buchanan's Head, Damask Street, near George's Lane (1716–21). 1696–1721. He served as a journeyman to Patrick Campbell (q.v.) from 1696 to 1704?, and was admitted free of the guild in 1709 (*Guild Records*). He broadened his activities to selling "Books, Lands, Houses, Pictures and Household Goods &c. by Auction," and likewise helped "People to Money on Security" (*Dublin Courant*, 31 Aug. 1720). His business ventures failed in 1721, and in 1723 he petitioned for relief as an ancient freeman of the city and was granted a small pension, paid through 1736, in which year he nevertheless died in poverty (*Guild Records*).

ALEXANDER (JOHN), printer in Strabane, 1771–90. He was the first printer in Strabane and published its first newspaper, *The Strabane Journal, or the General Advertiser*. He died in 1790 and left a will which was proved (Rep. D. K., PROI, 56, 1931).

ALLEN (GEORGE), bookbinder, bookseller, and publisher in Dublin, the Two Bibles, Dame Street, 1773–89. He was apprenticed to Abraham Bradley (q.v.), was admitted free of the guild by service in 1773, and paid quarterage through 1789 (*Guild Records*). He published devotional works and in 1774 several of the plays of Shakespeare: *Antony and Cleopatra, As You Like It, Hamlet, Richard III*. He died in 1795.

ALLOTT (THOMAS), stationer in Dublin, 1640s? "Administration of the goods of Thomas Allott, late of Dublin, Stationer, deceased was granted to Ferdinando Blaker of Dublin Gent. next-of-kin of said deceased. 1 June 1643" (*Dublin Grant Book*).

ANBUREY (WILLIAM-SHAW), printer and publisher in Dublin, (1) Abbey Street (1727–29); (2) Capel Street (1729–30). 1727–30. He published the ephemeral *Anburey's Weekly Journal* (three issues in March 1727). Worked in partnership with James Watts (q.v.), and in 1730 they printed James Delacourt's *Art of Beauing*. In 1730 he was prosecuted for libeling a fellow of Trinity College: Anburey allegedly "Printed the said Libels and sold them . . . to disperse in the Streets" (*Dublin Intelligence*, 21 Mar. 1729/30), and consequently dropped out of business.

ANCKETILL (MATHEW) *see* Mathew Ankettele

ANDERSON (JAMES), stationer in Belfast, 1661–? He was listed as a stationer, and sworn free of the city of Belfast (Young, *Belfast Town Book*).

ANDERSON (JOHN), bookseller in Six Mile Cross, 1751. Sole reference: he was listed in the colophon as one of the provincial sellers of Clarks's *Brief Survey of Principles Maintained, by the General Synod of Ulster*, 1751.

ANGEL (JOHN), bookbinder in Dublin, 1775. Sole reference: in 1775 he received a disbursement from the Commons for binding books in connection with the Stamp Act (*Commons' Journ. Ire.*, ix, app. p. ccclxxv).

ANKETTELE, ANKETTEL, or ANCKETILL (MATHEW), printer in Armagh, 1774–77. He was apprenticed to Oliver Nelson (q.v.) in 1751 and was admitted free of the guild by service in 1774 (*Guild Records*). He was apparently working in Armagh in 1777 (*A Short History of the Ancketill Family* . . . Compiled by one of its members. Belfast, 1901).

ARCHBALD (JOHN), papermaker in Dublin, Usher's Quay, 1773–88. His mill was in Tallaght, County Dublin, where he succeeded Pierce Archbald (q.v.). In 1773 he signed a petition to the Irish House of Commons objecting to the removal of duties on foreign paper (BL, 1890.e.5. (232)).

ARCHBALD (PIERCE), papermaker in Dublin, Usher's Quay, 1761–76. His mill was in Tallaght, County Dublin. His relationship to John Archbald (q.v.) is unknown.

ARCHER (JOSEPH), papermaker in Dublin, Hammond Lane, 1768–75? "Having served His Majesty for several Years in the Quality of Lieut. and on the Reduction of the Regim't he belonged to applied himself to the paper making business," he petitioned for freedom by composition and was admitted free of the guild in 1768, paid quarterage through 1770, and was then listed until 1775 as "in country" (*Guild Records*).

ARCHER (PATRICK), papermaker in Dublin, Cook Street, 1767. His relationship to Joseph Archer (q.v.) is unknown.

ARMITAGE (THOMAS), bookseller and publisher in Dublin, (1) Draper's Court, near Nicholas Gate (1759–70); (2) Crampton Court (1771–76). 1759–76. In 1767 he was auctioneer for the Dublin Sheriff's sale of the stock in trade of Robert Bell (q.v.), and in 1773 he signed a petition to the Irish

House of Commons objecting to the removal of duties on foreign paper (BL, 1890.e.5. (232)). He published editions of Sterne's *Sentimental Journey*, 1775, and *Tristram Shandy*, 1776.

ARMSTEAD (JAMES), stationer in Dublin, the Rose and Crown, Dame Street, 1676. He was recorded as a journeyman to William Norman (q.v.); later in the year he was listed as "gon" (*Guild Records*).

ASHBURN (ARCHIBALD), stationer in Ireland, 1714? "Mr. Andres Hind, a broken Master printer in company with Archibald Ashburn, journeyman, came to York 13 Dec. 1714 from Ireland" (Gent, *Life of Thomas Gent*).

ASHWORTH (DANIEL), papermaker in Dublin, 1719–23? He built a new paper mill at Templeogue, County Dublin, 1719: "Whereas the City of Dublin hath for many ages passed been seized and possessed of a watercourse taken out of the river Dodeer [sic], and now beginning at the weir at the foot of Ball-ruddery-hill, between a house now called Ashworth's new paper-mill..." (6 Geo. I, c. 16). The plant, "A very good large Double Paper Mill with 2 Flats and a large Dwelling House," was for sale by 1722, and continued advertised through 1723 (*Dublin Intelligence*, 14 Apr. 1722, 11 May, 27 Apr. 1723). It apparently was purchased by Thomas Turner (q.v.).

B

BABE (HENRY), printer in Dublin, the Yellow Lyon, St. Thomas Street, opposite the Bank (1730–38). 1711–38. He served as a journeyman to Stephen Powell (q.v.) from 1711, and had his own printing business by 1730. He printed several religious works and topical polemics, in one of which he libeled Sir John Freke and Ensign John Cook, Babe being exposed by Richard Dickson (q.v.) as "a miscreant, well known, tho' as a Blind, he has signed his Name to the said Paper. E. B. [Edward Bate (q.v.)]" (*Dublin Intelligence*, 19 Dec. 1730). Adjudged guilty, he was committed to Newgate Prison, but was at work again in 1736, printing *The Doway Catechism, in English and Irish*....

BACON (THOMAS), bookseller, printer, and publisher in Dublin, Bacon's Coffee House, Essex Street, 1736–42. He first styled himself an auctioneer, branched out as a press corrector and as a bookseller by 1739, and then joined the stationers' guild as a printer in 1741 (*Guild Records*). He had a short, mercurial career in the trade, founding the *Dublin Mercury*, succeeding Richard Reilly (q.v.) as printer to the Dublin Society and, as well, printer of the official newspaper, the *Dublin Gazette*, in 1742. He printed various works from medical texts to naval treatises, then in 1742 became involved in a factional dispute over the publishing of Richardson's *Pamela*. To compete with George Faulkner's (q.v.) pirated edition, Richardson sent Bacon sheets for the 3rd and 4th volumes which the latter sold at a lower rate, this to the broad accusations of assisting the London press to destroy the Dublin. Later in the year when Bacon brought out a translation of Prévost d'Exiles' *Dean of*

Coleraine, an opposing consortium of printers joined Faulkner in publishing a rival edition at a ridiculously low price which apparently ruined Bacon: by 1743 he was reported "having failed in his circumstances and . . . gone aside." In 1754, in an appendage to volume 8 of his *Grandison*, Richardson made a cryptic reference to Bacon's being "now in orders," and in the following year the latter died a pauper.

BAGGOT or BAGGOTT (Henry), stationer in Dublin, 1755–70. Sole reference: he was recorded as paying fees as a quarter brother from 1755 to 1770 (*Guild Records*).

BAGNELL (George), bookseller, papermaker, printer, and publisher in Cork, (1) opposite the Exchange Coffee House (1755–57); (2) Castle Street (1757–68). 1755–68. He was in partnership with Phineas Bagnell (q.v.) (their relationship is unknown). Together they printed and published numerous works, including the 7th edition of Temple's *History of the Irish Rebellion*, and they did considerable printing for the Cork Corporation from 1758 (Caulfield, *Cork Council Book*). About 1762 they built or acquired a paper mill at Ballyrosheen [Riverstown], County Cork. In 1763 they petitioned the Irish House of Commons for encouragement, claiming to be the first "to have brought the manufacture of paper to any degree of perfection in that part of the kingdom." Their watermark is known. George died in 1768 (*Freeman's Journal*, 22 Mar. 1768).

BAGNELL (Phineas), bookseller, papermaker, printer, and publisher in Cork, (1) Castle Street (?–1751); (2) opposite the Exchange Coffee House (1751–57); (3) Castle Street (1758–82). 1751?–84? He was apprentice to Abraham Bradley (q.v.) in 1740, but was never admitted free of the guild (*Guild Records*). He was first mentioned as a bookseller in 1751, and for the next thirty years remained exceedingly active in the trade. In 1755, in partnership with George Bagnell (q.v.) (their relationship is unknown), he acquired the rights to George and James Knight's (q.v.) *Cork Evening Post*. About 1762 the partners also built or acquired a paper mill at Ballyrosheen [Riverstown], County Cork. From the death of George Bagnell the business imprint read Phineas Bagnell and Co., and over this was printed and published many works, including King's *State of the Protestants* and the *Political Works of Charles Lucas*. In 1771 Phineas took George and James Knight into partnership to publish the *Cork Evening Post*, in 1777 he bought them out again, and in 1781 the Knights in turn purchased the Bagnell interest in the paper. Phineas then joined James Baldwin in publishing the *Volunteer Journal or Independent Gazetteer*, but by the end of the year ill health forced Phineas to retire from the printing and publishing business and the Knights leased his Castle Street premises (*Volunteer Journal*, 23 Dec. 1782), although he was to continue his interest in paper manufacturing for at least another two years. Perhaps he had taken a son or another relative into partnership in 1778, for the Cork Corporation payments from 1771 to 1778 were made to Phineas Bagnell, while those for 1778–80 were to "Messers. Bagnell" (Caulfield, *Cork Council Book*).

BAGNELL (GEORGE), bookseller in Clonmel, 1720. Sole reference: an advertisement in 1720 listed Bagnell as taking subscriptions for a printing of "Sixteen sermons . . . by Increase Mather D. D. of Boston in New England" (*Dublin Courant*, 4 July).

BAINE or BAIN (JOHN), typefounder in Dublin, 1747–49. Baine's career spanned many years: in Scotland (1742–47), in Dublin (1747–49; perhaps longer), and finally ending in America (1787–90). In 1742 he and Alexander Wilson established a type foundry in St. Andrews, in 1744 removed to Glasgow, and from there did considerable business in Dublin—furnishing most of the Dublin printers with their type—so considerable that Baine moved to Dublin in 1747 to represent the firm. "Whether Baine set up a foundry in Dublin, or was merely an agent for the sale of the Scottish-made type is not known" (*Biblio. Soc. Ire.* ii, no. 2). By 1749 the partnership had dissolved, and nothing is known of Baine's activities until after his emigration to America about 1786. Here he established the first type foundry in Philadelphia in 1787 (*Dictionary 1726–75*).

BAMFORD (JONATHAN), stationer in Dublin, 1755–56. In a committee report of 1756, on quarter brothers behind in their dues, he is recorded as owing more than a year's fees, "a great arrears. A Journeyman to be watched by way of a hint to his faculty" (*Guild Records*).

BANFIELD (RICHARD), stationer in Dublin, 1716–18. In 1716 he paid an intrusion fine of £4 9s 8d, and again appeared on the list of intruders for the year 1718 (*Guild Records*).

BARBER (GEORGE), stationer in Dublin, 1729–35. He was summoned as an intruder in 1729, sworn as a quarter brother in 1730, and paid quarterage through 1735 (*Guild Records*).

BARBER (GEORGE, Mrs.), stationer in Dublin, 1736–39. For three years "Widow Barber" continued to pay dues to the guild at the same rate as her husband, George (q.v.) (*Guild Records*).

BARDIN (JAMES), bookseller in Cork, Chequer Lane, 1740–? In 1740 he advertised "A Curious and exact Print of the Rev. Jonathan Swift DSPD is to be sold at Mr. James Bardin's" (*Dublin News Letter*, 2 Dec.). In 1791 there was a reference to the "dwelling House of the late **J.** Bardin, bookseller" (Caulfield, *Cork Council Book*).

BARDIN or BARDEN (JOHN), bookbinder in Dublin, 1735–46. He was admitted to the guild as a quarter brother in 1735, as a free brother in 1743, and paid quarterage through 1746 (*Guild Records*).

BARRON (NICHOLAS), stationer in Dublin, 1670–79. He was admitted free of the guild in 1670 and paid quarterage through 1679, his name being crossed out in the 1680 Council list (*Guild Records*).

BARRY (EDWARD or EDMUNDOS), stationer in Dublin, 1671–79. He was admitted free of the guild in 1671 and paid quarterage through 1679. Entries for 1672 and 1675 named Barry as one of two members specially exempt from having to serve, if elected, as officers of the guild (*Guild Records*). An Edward Barry printed in London in 1681 (*Dictionary 1668–1726*).

BATE or BEATE (EDWARD), printer and publisher in Dublin, George's Lane, 1729–51. In 1728 he married the daughter of Stephen Powell (q.v.), and the latter's widow a year later deeded to Bate all of her husband's printing equipment upon condition that he pay her son Samuel Powell (q.v.) £100 and provide for herself "sufficient meat, drink, washing and apparell for her life" (*Reg. of Deeds*, Dublin). Bate printed and published many works, particularly supplying the flying stationers of the city; D'Assigny's *A Serious Enquiry into the present Decay of Freemasonry in the Kingdom of Ireland*, 1744, Harris' *Hibernica*, 1747, and Spratt's *New Book of Masonic Constitutions for Irish Lodges*, 1751. He was frequently involved in controversy, over the 1744 factious war concerning editions of Sale's *Universal History*, and in 1749 was ordered to attend the House of Commons for printing the polemics of Charles Lucas (*Commons' Journ. Ire.*, v, 12). He died in 1764 (*Freeman's Journal*, 13 Nov.).

BATES (CHARLES DAVID), printer in Dublin, 1774. He was admitted free of the guild by special grace in 1774, and in the same year was recorded as the printer to the guild's "Committee of the Free Press" (*Guild Records*).

BEALE (CALEB), papermaker in Cork, 1769–? He was in partnership with Samuel Neale (q.v.) (*Library*, Mar. 1958). They had a paper mill at Spring-hill [adjoining Riverstown], County Cork (*Irish Book Lover*, vol. 1, no. 3).

BEAN (P.), printer in Dublin, (?). Sole reference: he was referred to as a mid-eighteenth-century Catholic printer of devotional books and chapbooks (Phillips, unpublished thesis).

BEARD (Mr.), bookseller in Cork, 1744–45. Newspaper advertisements list Beard as taking subscriptions for the George Faulkner (q.v.) edition of Sale's *Universal History* (*Dublin Journal*, 25 Sept., 18 Dec. 1744; *Pue's Occurrences*, 12 Jan. 1744/45).

BEARD (THOMAS), engraver in Dublin, 1728–30. Stated to have been the first to practice the profession in Ireland: "If any gentlemen have a fancy for a private plate (in Mezzotint) they may have it done at a very reasonable rate by Thomas Beard of London" (*Dublin Intelligence*, 1 Mar. 1728/29). He produced a series of prints sold by various booksellers in Dublin, but appears to have been employed largely by Thomas Wilkinson (q.v.). He left Dublin shortly after 1729 (Strickland, *Irish Artists*).

BEATE (EDWARD) *see* Edward Bate

BEATTY (EDWARD), bookbinder and publisher in Dublin, (1) Fownes Street (1745–73); (2) St. Andrews Street (1774–92). 1745–92. He was apprenticed to William Crofton (q.v.), was admitted free of the guild by service in 1745, and paid quarterage through 1792. He was an active guild member, serving as Warden in 1752, Master in 1760, and on the Council from 1762. In 1773 he contributed to a subscription for a monument to Dr. Charles Lucas (*Guild Records*). In 1780 he joined several other stationers in publishing Young's *Tour of Ireland*.

BEATTY (JOHN), bookseller and publisher in Dublin, 1775–1831. He was apprenticed to James Williams (q.v.), admitted free of the guild by service in 1775, paid quarterage at least through 1792, paid arrears in 1831, served on the Council from 1786 to 1795, and was listed as "dead" in 1832 (*Guild Records*). He was admitted free of the city in 1776. He occasionally joined other Dublin stationers in publishing, e.g., Lewis' *Candid Philosopher*, 1778, and Young's *Tour of Ireland*, 1780.

BECKET (T.), bookseller in Dublin 1741. Sole reference: he was stated to have been in partnership with Peter de Hondt (q.v.) in 1741 (Phillips, unpublished thesis).

BELL (ROBERT), bookseller and publisher in Dublin, (1) Cork Hill, opposite Lucas' Coffee House (1759–62); (2) Stephen Street, opposite Aungier Street (1763–67). 1759–67. He was admitted to the guild as a quarter brother in 1759 and paid quarterage through 1766 (*Guild Records*). He published a Glasgow-printed edition of Thomson's *Seasons* in 1760, and from 1762 advertised book auctions "at his Great Auction-Room" (Book Sale Catalogues, 1762–66). On the death of the editor Walter Harris (q.v.), Bell and John Fleming (q.v.)

acquired from the executors the remaining sheets of Harris' edition of Ware's *Works*. The two partners reprinted the prefaces, issued a new title-page dated 1764, and published it as their own edition. Such practices perhaps led to Bell's business failure, for his stock-in-trade was sold for bankruptcy by the Dublin sheriff in 1767. By 1773, however, Bell was at work in Philadelphia, Pennsylvania, where he enjoyed a prosperous career as auctioneer, bookseller, printer, and publisher, with a long list of imprints to 1784 (Evans, *American Bibliography*).

BENNETT (GEORGE), bookseller, printer, and publisher in Cork, 1715–47. He published a newspaper, the *Idler*, 1715, reprinted the London *Free Holder*, 1716, and printed *A Tutor to Arithmetick*, 1719, and the *Cork News Letter* from 1723 to 1725. In 1723 he and a Mr. Wilson bound 234 copies of the Bible for the City of Cork, and in 1734 he was appointed to execute all printing that should be wanted by that City (Caulfield, *Cork Council Book*). From 1719 he was a continuous subscriber to Dublin publications: Fiddes' *Theologia speculativa*, 1719, Defoe's *The Compleat English Tradesman*, 1726, Keating's *History of Ireland*, 1723, etc., and by 1725 he was described as "the leading bookseller in the City of Cork" (*Dublin Weekly Intelligence*, 17 Apr.). He was a member of the Cork Corporation, Mayor of the city in 1724, and Alderman from 1725 to 1743. He died in 1747.

BENNETT (GEORGE II), bookseller in Cork, 1762. Sole reference: he was mentioned in the subscribers' list in 1762 as Alderman George Bennett, having taken sixteen sets of George Faulkner's (q.v.) second edition of Swift's *Works*.

BENSON (THOMAS), bookseller and publisher in Dublin, Shakespeare's Head, Castle Street, 1726–31. He was apprenticed to Eliphal Dobson (q.v.), was admitted free of the guild by service in 1726, and paid quarterage through 1731 (*Guild Records*). He published Ramsey's *Travels of Cyrus* and Richard Savage's *The Bastard, a Poem*, 1728, and Charles Coffey's *The Beggar's Wedding, A New Opera*, 1729. In 1729 he also advertised the London pirated edition [Overton and Hoole] of Brooking's map of Dublin (*Dublin Weekly Journal*, 15 Feb.). Possibly in 1730 he took over the management of the Templeogue Spa in Rathfarnham. A publication, *The Templeogue Ballad*, was "Printed at the Cherry-tree, Rathfarnham, 1730 and dedicated to the Worthy Manager, Mr. Benson" (Halliday Pamphlets, v. 96, RIA). Cherry Tree was the name of the house on the other side of the Dodder River from the Spawell.

BENTLEY or BENTLY (JOHN), bookseller, bookbinder, and publisher in Dublin, (1) the corner of St. Nicholas Street, over against the Thosel (1681–99); (2) over against the Four Court door, Christ Church Yard (1700–12). 1681–1712. He was admitted free of the guild in 1681 and continued an active member, serving on the Council in 1691, as Beadle in 1692, and as Warden in 1689 and 1690 (*Guild Records*). He published various pamphlets, as in 1685 *A Full and true Account of the taking of the late Duke of Monmouth* (in competition with Andrew Crook's [q.v.] and Samuel Helsham's [q.v.] *A True Account of the taking of James late Duke of Monmouth*) and *An Account of the Proceedings of the Two Houses of Parliament now assembled in England*. However, his "principle Business is Binding. . . . He is a very honest Man, but has met with misfortunes in the World, by thinking some others as honest as himself" (Dunton, *Dublin Scuffle*). He died in 1712.

BENTLEY or BENTLY (NATHAN), bookseller in Dublin, 1707–18. He was admitted free of the guild by service in 1707 and paid quarterage through 1718. He was nominated for Warden in 1714 (*Guild Records*).

BESTICK or BESTIC (JOHN), papermaker in Dublin, 1771–73. He was admitted free of the guild by composition in 1771 but paid no quarterage (*Guild Records*). In 1773, as a papermaker, he signed a petition to the Irish House of Commons objecting to the removal of duties of foreign paper (BL, 1890. e.5. (232)). He died intestate in Lucan in 1790 (*Dublin Grant Book*).

BEWSHER (WILLIAM) *see* William Brewsher

BINAULD (WILLIAM), bookseller and publisher in Dublin, the Bible, Eustice Street, 1712–32. He was admitted free of the guild by petition in 1712 and paid quarterage through 1724, though he continued in business to 1732 (*Guild Records*). He was a French Huguenot, a former tutor (he claimed to have been tutor to Samuel Molyneux), and one of the earliest editors and press correctors in Ireland. He advertised his business "to those that have a mind. . . . Where they will be supplied with all sorts of French and Latin Books" (*Dublin Courant*, 2 Jan. 1722/23). Mainly he sold classics and continental imports, like the Dutch edition of Rapin's *History of England*. He and Eliphal Dobson (q.v.) published a folio Bible, printed by Aaron Rhames (q.v.) in 1714, and declared it "A thing never before undertaken in this kingdom" (*Dublin Gazette*, 20 Oct. 1713); Archbishop King thought it "very faulty" (Mant's *History*). He died intestate in 1732 (*Dublin Grant Book*), his stock being sold at auction.

BINNS (THOMAS), stationer in Dublin, the Rose and Crown, Dame Street, 1698–1700. He was a journeyman to William Norman (q.v.). Perhaps he was enrolled with the guild as a result of a decree in 1698 ordering "that all persons of this Guild do enter theire severall respective Journeymen &

Bind and Enroll y Apprentices within ten days" (*Guild Records*).

BIXOU or alias TABB (L.), printer in Limerick, on Ball's Bridge, 1722–23. In 1722, in partnership with Samuel Terry (q.v.), he reprinted the second book known to have been published in Limerick, *The Libertine School'd*, 1722, and in 1723 he printed *A Sacramental Cathechism.*

BLACK (JOHN), bookbinder and printer in Dublin, 1774–82. He was admitted free of the guild by special grace in 1774, paid quarterage through 1782, and was listed in the Clerk's list as dead in 1789 (*Guild Records*). He married Elizabeth Booth in 1785 (*Dublin Grant Book*), and possibly thus was associated with William Booth, a Dublin bookbinder in the 1780s.

BLACKSLEY (JOHN) *see* John Blakesley

BLADEN (WILLIAM), printer and publisher in Dublin, Castle Street, 1631–63. His early career from 1612 was spent in London as a bookseller until he was appointed a factor in Dublin for the Irish "stock" of the London Company of Stationers (*Dictionary 1641–67*). He was admitted free of the city of Dublin in 1631, served as Sheriff in 1636, as an Alderman from 1642 to 1663, and as Mayor in 1647. He purchased from the London Company of Stationers their Irish privileges for £2,600 in 1638, became the King's Printer in 1641, and during the Commonwealth the state printer. He printed and published various works but most of his printing was official, with numerous contracts under the Commonwealth—e.g., *Laws and Ordinances of Warre: Established for the better Conduct of the Armie*, 1652 (*Commonwealth Council Books*). He printed and published Ireland's first newspaper, *An Account of the Chief*

Occurrences of Ireland, Together with some Particulars from England, 22 Feb. 1659/60. He died in 1663.

BLAIR or BLAIRE (BRYCE or BRICE), bookseller in Belfast, 1710–19. He was advertised as a bookseller taking subscriptions for various Dublin publications: the *Tryal of Doctor Henry Sacheverell*, 1710, Temple's *History of the Irish Rebellion*, 1712, and Fiddes' *Theologia speculativa*, 1719 (*Dublin Intelligence*, 24 June 1710, 28 Oct. 1712, 14 Nov. 1719; *Dublin Courant*, 31 Jan. 1719/20).

BLAKESLEY or BLACKSLEY (JOHN), printer in Dublin, 1677–88. He was admitted free of the guild in 1677, paid quarterage through 1688, served as Beadle in 1677, and on the Council in 1683 and 1684. He was listed as "gone" in 1687 and as "mort" in 1689 (*Guild Records*).

BLOW (DANIEL), papermaker, printer, and publisher in Belfast, 1747–78. "Last Tuesday, Mr. Daniel Blow of Belfast, printer, was married to Miss Molly Saunders, an agreeable young lady with a hansome fortune" (*Dublin Courant*, 6 Feb. 1746/47). He was the son and partner of James Blow (q.v.), and was named executor of the father's will (Bentham, *Abstracts*). He operated a paper mill in County Antrim, which in 1750 received an award from the Royal Dublin Society for the encouragement of home industry. He also printed and published extensively including almanacks, plays, and, in partnership with H. B. P. Grierson (q.v.), an edition of the Bible, 1765.

BLOW (JAMES), bookseller, papermaker, printer, and publisher in Belfast, 1694–1758. From 1694 to 1705 he was associated with his brother-in-law, Patrick Neill (q.v.), and from 1747 was in partnership with his son Daniel (q.v.). He became

Belfast's most prominent stationer, frequently taking subscriptions for Dublin publications, as well as printing and publishing broadly on his own. The majority of his work was theological in nature, including the New Testament, with Neill sometime between 1694 and 1705 (no copy is known to survive), the Bible, with George Grierson (q.v.), 1714, and another edition alone, 1751, as well as a *Church Catechism* in Irish, 1722. He had a paper mill in County Antrim: in 1745 and 1746, the *Belfast Courant* was said to have been printed on paper from this mill (Young, *Belfast Town Book*). He died in 1759, leaving his estate to his son Daniel.

BLYTH (**JAMES**), printer in Londonderry, 1773–77. In 1773 he joined George Douglas in printing and publishing the *Londonderry Journal and Donegal and Tyrone Advertiser*. He also printed, on his own, *Two Sermons*, 1776, and a pamphlet, 1777.

BOLTON (**ROBERT**), printer in Dublin, at Milton's Head, Skinner Row, 1749. He was a journeyman to Oliver Nelson (q.v.) (*Guild Records*); "employed . . . to take Care of printing the Dublin Courant" (*Commons' Journ. Ire.*, v, 36).

BOND (**HENRY**), papermaker in Ireland, 1730s? Sole reference: a notice in the *Dublin Gazette* read "Prisoner for debt in Waterford Gaol to take benefit of Act for relief of insolvent debtors [11 Geo. II, c. 116] . . . Henry Bond, papermaker" (27 May 1738).

BOND (**THOMAS**), printer in Dublin, the Post Office Coffee House, Fishamble Street, 1700–24. He was listed as an intruder in 1701 and 1702, admitted free of the guild by service to Patrick Campbell (q.v.) in 1704, and paid quarterage through 1724 (*Guild Records*).

BONHAM (**George**), bookbinder, bookseller, printer, and publisher in Dublin, (1) at Horace's Head, William Street (1774); (2) 42 Dame Street, opposite Fowne's Court (1775–78?); (3) 68 South Great George's Street (1784–1802). 1771–1804. He was apprenticed to George Exshaw (q.v.), admitted free of the guild by service in 1771, paid quarterage through 1804, served as Warden in 1802, and was listed as dead in 1817 (*Guild Records*). He was admitted free of the city in 1776. In 1775 he apparently purchased the shop of Samuel Powell (q.v.) from Powell's daughter Sarah: in Bonham's publication of Edward's *Larger Course of Arithmatic*, 1776, he described himself as "successor to the late S. Powell." He printed music, Young's *Tour of Ireland*, 1780, tendered for the binding of the Parliamentary *Journals*, 1785, was printer to the Royal Irish Academy in 1788, and engraved music plates for their *Transactions* in the 1790s.

BOOKSELLERS (**The Company of**), booksellers in Cork, 1768–73 (*Dictionary 1726–75*).

BORDINS (**James**), bookseller in Dublin, 1740. Sole reference: he was listed as one of the booksellers offering "A Curious and Exact Print of the Rev. Doctor Jonathan Swift DSPD" (*Dublin News Letter*, Dec. 1740).

BOUCHER (**William**), printer in Dublin, 1774–85. He was apprenticed to John Mitchell (q.v.) in 1765, and was admitted free of the guild by service in 1774. In 1766 he signed a guild petition against journeymen's combinations. He died about 1785 (*Guild Records*).

BOUFFARD, BOUFFAR, or BOUFFUS (**Isaac**), bookseller in Dublin, 1699–1705. He was a French Huguenot refugee, admitted to the guild as a quarter brother in 1699, paid quarterage through 1705, and was listed as "gon" in 1708 (*Guild Records*).

BOURKE (THOMAS), printer in Waterford (1643–46?) and Kilkenny (1648–49?). 1643–49? He was the first printer in Waterford, and served there as printer to the Catholic Confederation from 1643 to 1646. Most of his work was proclamations, declarations, and various Catholic polemics like *A Remonstrance of Grievances*, 1643, but he also printed *Alexipharmacon, or a Sovereign Antidote against a Virulent Cordiell*, 1644, and an almanac, 1646. By 1647 he had moved with his press to Kilkenny and again printed various publications for the Supreme Council. Nothing more is heard of him after the Cromwellian conquest.

BOWES (PHILIP), bookbinder, bookseller, printer, and publisher in Dublin, (1) Cook Street, opposite Bridge Street (1741–44); (2) Church Street, between the Bridge and the end of Pill Lane (1744–72). 1741–72. As a Catholic he was admitted to the guild as a quarter brother in 1741 and paid quarterage through 1764. An entry in the Council list of 1756 labeled him "a papist and pirate" (*Guild Records*). Most of his work was devotional tracts and chapbooks, like the pamphlet *A Papist Misrepresented and Represented*, 1750. In 1755 he pirated Patrick Lord's (q.v.) edition of O'Conor's *Case of the Roman Catholics*.

BOWES (RICHARD), printer in Dublin, 1771 (*Dictionary 1726–75*). This is undoubtedly a spurious entry. Two imprints bear his name: *A Candid Appeal to the Public*, 1771, "Printed by Richard Bowes in Church Street," and *A Postscript to the Candid Appeal to the Public*, n.d., "Printed by Richard Bowes, in Church Street near the old Bridge." Both are satires on a

Gorges Edmond Howard, Esq., and internal evidence suggests their being fictitious imprints.

BOYCE (J.), printer in Dublin, Dick's Coffee House, Skinner Row, 1701. In 1701 he printed *Family Hymns*.

BOYCE (WILLIAM), printer in Dublin, Mary Lane, 1772. In 1772 Administration (Intestate) was granted of his personal estate by the Diocesan Court, Dublin (*Dictionary 1726–75*).

BOYLE (WILLIAM), bookseller in Cork, 1712. Sole reference: an advertisement in 1712 listed Boyle as taking subscriptions for a printing of Patrick Campbell's (q.v.) edition of Temple's *History of the Irish Rebellion* (*Dublin Intelligence*, 28 Oct.).

BRADLEY (ABRAHAM), bookbinder, bookseller, printer, and publisher in Dublin, (1) the Golden Ball and Ring, opposite Sycamore Alley, Dame Street (1729–37); (2) the Two Bibles, Dame Street (1744–83). 1729–83. He was apprenticed to George Risk (q.v.), was admitted free of the guild by service in 1729, and paid quarterage through 1783. He served the guild as Warden in 1743, as Master in 1748, and on the Council from 1747. Seven apprentices trained under him, six of whom became successful stationers (*Guild Records*). He was a prominent bookseller from 1730 (advertising as well a variety of medicinal drugs), and from 1733 published alone or in partnership numerous works, including music printing, and, with George Ewing (q.v.), the second Irish edition of Shakespeare's *Works*, 1739. He succeeded Samuel Fairbrother (q.v.) as King's Stationer in 1749, which post he held until 1780, and from 1751 to 1777 he was printer to the House of Commons. In the latter capacity he printed the *Journals* for the sessions from 1753 to

1775. As King's Stationer he was nominally in charge of parliamentary binding, and as such he was called the most "resourceful and imaginative bookbinder who ever lived" (Craig, *Bookbinding*).

BRADLEY (HULTON), bookseller and publisher in Dublin, King's Arms and Two Bibles, Dame Street, 1758–1800. In 1751 he was apprenticed to his father, Abraham Bradley (q.v.), never took his freedom of the guild, but practiced. Among his publications were Epictetus' *Works*, 1759, Kennett's *Romanarum antiquitatum notitia: or, the antiquities of Rome*, 1767, and Pope's *Works*, 1770.

BRADLEY (JOHN), bookbinder in Dublin, 1748–88? He was apprenticed to his uncle, Abraham Bradley (q.v.), was admitted free of the guild by service in 1748, and paid quarterage through 1786. He served on the Council from 1780, was marked on the Clerk's list as dead in 1787 but appeared again without note on the 1788 list (*Guild Records*).

BRANGAN (THOMAS), printer in Dublin, (1) the Printing House, New Row (1713); (2) Arran's Quay (1714–16); and in Limerick, the Duke of Marlborough's Head, Key Lane (1716). 1713–16. In 1713 he printed the *Trial of E. Terrel* (an infamous priest-catcher, executed in 1713 "for having several wives" [*Whalley's News Letter*, 3 Oct. 1713]), and a broadside poem by Sir Richard Steele in 1714. In 1716 he printed the short-lived *Limerick News Letter*, the first newspaper in that town (Munter, *Handlist*), and in the same year printed R. Buggin's *The Inchanted Garden: A Vision*.

BRAY (DAVID or JOHN), stationer in Dublin, standing near Essex Bridge, 1728–32. A David Bray was listed as a quarter brother in 1728 and as a full brother in 1729, a John Bray was listed as a full brother in 1730 and 1731, and a Bray (no Christian name given) was listed as a full brother in 1732 (*Guild Records*).

BRENT (JOHN), printer in Dublin, (1) Capel Street (1687–91?); (2) the Post Office Coffee House, Fishamble Street (?–1697); (3) back of Dick's Coffee House, Skinner Row (1697–1701). 1687–1713. In 1687, as a printer, he witnessed the will of William Hatton (q.v.) (Crosslé, *Prerogative Wills*). Possibly he was in Cork in the early 1690s, for in 1691 he printed two pamphlets for David Jones (q.v.), Edward Wetenhall's *Pastoral Admonitions* and a sermon, the colophon of the latter stating "Cork, Printed by John Brent, for David Jones, Bookseller." He was admitted to the guild in 1692, paid quarterage through 1706, was listed as "In England" in 1709, and again paid quarterage from 1711 to 1713. In 1699 he served as Beadle (*Guild Records*). In 1695 he printed for the City Corporation (*Cal. Anc. Rec. Dublin*), and from 1697 to 1701 he worked in a loose partnership with John Brocas (q.v.) and Stephen Powell (q.v.). They printed broadly, including William Barton's *Psalms*, 1698, one of the earliest Irish publications to include music printing, and during Dunton's visit to Ireland they became his printer. Dunton characterized Brent as a "Scrupulous, Honest Conscientious Man, and I do think, a True Nathaniel. . . . He's perfect Innocence, yet a Man of Letters; he knows no harm, and therefore contrives none" (*Dublin Scuffle*).

BREWSHER or BEWSHER (WILLIAM), bookbinder in Dublin, 1761–1803. He was apprenticed to Edward Beatty (q.v.), was admitted free of the guild by service in 1761, and paid quarterage through 1788. He served as acting Beadle in 1788 and as Beadle in 1790. He apparently left no dependents, for his quarter salary due at his death in 1804 was paid to the past year's acting Beadle (*Guild Records*).

BRICK (S.), bookseller in Dublin, 1737. Sole reference: an advertisement in 1737 listed Brick as taking subscriptions for a printing of Thomas Bacon's (q.v.) *A Complete System of the Revenue of Ireland* (*Dublin News Letter*, 4 Jan.).

BRIDGES (F.), bookseller in Cork, 1737. Sole reference: an advertisement in 1737 listed Bridges as taking subscriptions for George Ewing (q.v.), George Risk (q.v.), and William Smith's (q.v.) proposed edition of Virgil's *Works* (*Dublin News Letter*, 16 Feb.).

BRIEN or BRYAN (WILLIAM), bookseller in Dublin, Dame Street, near Crow Street, 1744–72. He was apprenticed to Robert Owen (q.v.), was admitted free of the guild by service in 1745, and paid quarterage through 1757. He served as Warden in 1756 and was carried on the Clerk's list until 1772. In 1773 he was recorded as "not in business" (*Guild Records*). He died in 1797 (Crosslé, *Prerogative Wills*).

BROCAS (JOHN), printer and publisher in Dublin, (1) the Post Office Coffee House, Fishamble Street (1696–97); (2) the back of Dick's Coffee House, Skinner Row (1687–98); (3) School House Lane (1698–1711). 1696–1711. He was admitted free of the guild in 1696, paid quarterage through 1711, served as Warden in 1705, and on the Council from 1705 to 1711 (*Guild Records*). He was recognized as one of the finest craftsman in his trade: Dunton described him, writing "no Man in the Universe, better understands the Nobel Art and Mystery of Printing, than John Brocas in Skinner Row" (*Dublin Scuffle*). He first published jointly with Cornelius Carter (q.v.) in 1696, and was associated with John Brent (q.v.) and Stephen Powell (q.v.) from 1697 to 1701. In 1700 the partnership published some of the first music printing in Ireland, William Barton's *Psalms*, "adapted to the Church tunes." Brocas first printed on his own in 1698, and in 1700 he published one of the earliest plays in Ireland, Phillip's *St. Stephens' Green or the Generous Lovers*. In 1702 he published "by Authority" a short-lived newspaper, the *Dublin Castle*, and from 1705 to 1707? the *Flying Post or the Post Master* (Munter, *Handlist*). In 1703 he was called before the Irish House of Commons for printing, with James Malone (q.v.), the proscribed *Memoirs of King James II*; he apologized, was fined, and released (*Commons' Journ. Ire.*, ii, 389).

BROCK (**STEARNE or STERNE**), bookseller and publisher in Dublin, (1) Essex Street, near Essex Quay (1729–34); (2) the Stationer's Arms, Castle Street (1735–36); (3) Dame Street, at the corner of Crow Street (1736–37). 1729–37. He was apprenticed to Edward Hamilton (q.v.), was listed as an intruder in 1729 and 1734, was finally admitted free of the guild by service in 1735, and paid quarterage through 1737 (*Guild Records*). Possibly he succeeded Ferdinando Davys (q.v.) in Essex Street, and in 1734 he took over the shop of Jane Dobson (q.v.). In 1734 he published the posthumous sermons of Dr. Samuel Clarke and sold the sheets in England for 1*s* 6*d* (as against a sheet charge of £2 for the English edition). As a consequence, James Knapton, the publisher of the English edition, was one of those who petitioned the English House of Commons for an alteration of the copyright act of 8 Anne (*Commons' Journ.*, xxii, 400). In 1734 Brock jointly published, with Abraham Bradley (q.v.) and Thomas Moore (q.v.), Gay's *The History of the Most Illustrious House of Nassau*, and in 1736 he published alone *A General History of China*. He died in 1737.

BROGAN (**J.**), bookseller in Athlone, 1747. Sole reference: advertisements in *The London Magazine*, Jan. 1746/47 and Apr. 1747, printed for Edward and John Exshaw (q.v.), listed Brogan as one of the provincial sellers of the journal.

BROOKS (JOHN), engraver in Dublin, Sir Isaac Newton's Head, at the Corner of the Blind Quay, Cork Hill, opposite Lucas' Coffee House, 1733?–46. He reintroduced mezzotint engraving into Ireland, not practiced since the departure of Thomas Beard (q.v.) (Gilbert, *History of Dublin*). For some time he was associated with Andrew Miller (q.v.), and he left for London in 1746 (Strickland, *Irish Artists*).

BROWN (LEONARD), bookbinder in Dublin, 1748–50. He was admitted to the guild as a quarter brother in 1748 and paid quarterage through 1750 (*Guild Records*).

BROWN (THOMAS), stationer in Dublin, 1686–88. He was listed as a journeyman to Mathew Gun (q.v.) from 1686 to 1688, but with no record of quarterage payments (*Guild Records*).

BROWNE (S.), bookseller and publisher in Dublin, 1765. Sole reference: the colophon in Goldsmith's *Memoirs of a Protestant condemned to the Galleys of France, for his Religion,* 1765, listed it as being printed for William Fleming (q.v.) and S. Browne.

BROWNE or BROWN (THOMAS), bookseller, printer, and publisher in Dublin, (1) the Three Candles, High Street (1730?–40); (2) the Bible, High Street (1740–59). 1718–59. A Catholic, he was admitted to the guild as a quarter brother in 1718 and paid quarterage through 1759. In 1725 he complained that his quarter rate was "too much for him in regard to his business" (*Guild Records*). However, in 1740 he took over the shop and stock of Luke Dillon (q.v.) (*Dublin News Letter*, 7–11 Oct. 1740), and through printing "a great Variety of Books in the Country Trade and furnishing Country Chapmen and others Wholesale and Retail at reasonable Rates," was reputed to be quite wealthy by 1750. He printed Isaac Butler's *Almanack*, 1740, and in 1744 and 1745 possibly was in partnership with John Fleming (q.v.), for a list of booksellers taking subscriptions for George Faulkner's (q.v.) edition of Sale's *Universal History* reads ". . . T. Brown and J. Fleming, High Street" (*Dublin Journal*, 25 Sept. 1744, 12 Jan. 1744/45). He died in 1759.

BROWNING (EDMUND or EDWARD), bookseller in Cork, 1762–74. He contracted, on a yearly basis, to supply the Cork Council with "English and Irish Newspapers and votes of the House of Commons," from 1762 to 1774 (Caulfield, *Cork Council Book*).

BROWNRIGG (JOHN), bookseller in Dublin, 1722–24. He was admitted free of the guild in 1722 and appeared on the Clerk's list through 1724, possibly holding an honorary membership (*Guild Records*).

BRUCE (WILLIAM), bookseller and publisher in Dublin, Blind Quay, 1725–38. He was in partnership with his cousin, John Smith (q.v.), from 1725, when the latter's father, William Smith (q.v.), temporarily quit business (Lepper and Crosslé, *History of the Grand Lodge of Free and Accepted Masons of Ireland*). They advertised "Books newly arrived from England, Holland and France . . . a Variety of Maps, Prospects of Buildings, Copper-Plates, Mezotints" (*Dublin Weekly Journal*, 3 July 1725), and published Dobb's *Essay on the Trade . . . of Ireland*, 1729, Burnet's *History of his Own Time*, 1730, and *Debates of the British Parliament*, 1737. The guild twice listed Bruce as an intruder, 1729 and 1734, demanding his appearance, but there was no record that he ever did so (*Guild Records*).

BRUEN (M.), bookseller in Boyle, 1747. Sole reference: advertisements in *The London Magazine*, Feb. 1746/47 and Apr. 1747, listed Bruen as one of the provincial sellers of the journal.

BRYAN (BENJAMIN), stationer in Dublin, (1) the Rose and Crown, Dame Street (1677); (2) (?). 1677–78. He was a journeyman to William Norman (q.v.) in 1677 and, upon discharge from Norman, to John Blakesley (q.v.) in 1678 (*Guild Records*).

BRYAN (JOHN), stationer in Dublin, 1680–86. He was listed as a stationer in 1680 and 1681, in 1683 as an intruder to be brought before the guild, in 1683 and 1684 as "a stationer in Engd," again listed in 1685 and 1686, and in 1687 last referred to as "gon" (*Guild Records*).

BRYAN (WILLIAM) *see* William Brien

BUCKLEY (RICHARD), bookseller in Dublin, High Street, 1729–54. He was admitted to the guild as a quarter brother in 1729 and paid quarterage through 1754 (*Guild Records*). "Monday last died Mr. Richard Buckley in High Street, a man of Good Character" (*Pue's Occurrences*, 8 Feb. 1754/55).

BUCKLEY (RICHARD, Mrs.), bookseller in Dublin, High Street, 1754–57. She was the wife of Richard Buckley (q.v.), and one of three women to appear for the first time, 1754, among the quarter brothers of the guild. From 1754 to 1757 she continued the same quarterage payment as her husband, being listed as Mrs. Buckley in 1754 and as "widow Buckley" in 1756 and 1757 (*Guild Records*).

BUCKRIDGE (EDMUND), papermaker in Ireland, 1692? In 1692, in partnership with George Eagar (q.v.) and William

Sutton (q.v.), he obtained a King's letter granting an Irish monopoly of fourteen years for the making of "all sorts of coloured papers" (*World's Paper Trade Review*). There is no evidence that the three ever acted on their patent or even came to Ireland from England.

BUNTEEN or BUNTING (William), bookseller in Sligo, 1710–13. An advertisement in 1710 listed Bunteen as taking subscriptions for a printing of the *Tryal of Doctor Henry Sacheverall* (*Dublin Intelligence*, 24 June and 1 July), and in 1713 as selling Richardson's edition of the *Book of Common Prayer*, ". . . all in Irish and English, the Elements of the Irish Language being added to every one of them" (*Dublin Gazette*, 11 July).

BURKE (Martin), printer and publisher in Galway, Back Street, 1769–79. He printed and published *Burke's Connaght Journal* from 1769 to 1779 (Madden, *Irish Periodical Literature*).

BURNE (Owin), printer in Dublin, the Churl, Cook Street, 1754. Sole reference: in 1754 he printed *A Full and True Narrative of a most Cruel . . . Murder . . . of James Eyre Weeks.*

BURNETT (George), bookbinder, bookseller, and publisher in Dublin, Abbey Street, 1768–1802. He was admitted free of the guild in 1768, paid quarterage through 1802, served as Warden in 1795, and on the Council from 1782 (*Guild Records*). In 1780, with a large coterie of stationers, he jointly published Young's *Tour of Ireland*, and in 1799 *Pizarro, A Tragedy*, ". . . as performed at . . . Drury-lane . . . adapted . . . by Richard Brinsley Sheridan" (*Dublin Journal*, 11 July). He died in 1803.

BURROUGHS (Edward), papermaker in Dublin, Engine Alley, near Usher's Island, 1767–1800. In 1767 he took over Thomas Slator's (q.v.) paper mill at Templeogue, Country Dublin; his watermark is known. He was neither a quarter brother nor a free brother of the guild, but the guild allowed Thomas Paine, first apprenticed to Slator, to complete his apprenticeship with Burroughs (*Guild Records*). In 1773 he signed a petition to the Irish House of Commons objecting to the removal of duties on foreign paper (BL, 1890.e.5. (232)).

BURROWS or BURROUGHS (Henry), bookseller in Dublin, Hendrick Street, 1753–84? He was apprenticed to Thomas Thornton (q.v.), was admitted free of the guild by service in 1753, and paid quarterage through 1784. In the 1787 Clerk's list he was marked "dead," but was listed again in 1789 without comment (*Guild Records*). In 1754 he subscribed to twelve copies of Peter Wilson's (q.v.) publication of Kennedy's *Modern Elements of Numeral Arithmetic*.

BURTON (John), bookseller and printer in Dublin, 1752–80. There are only vague references to this stationer in the guild records. He paid a franchise fine in 1752, and twice stood candidate for Treasurer, in 1755 and 1764 (*Guild Records*). In 1761 Dillon Chamberlain (q.v.) and Samuel Smith (q.v.) advertised an edition of Sterne's *Tristram Shandy*, noting "A Pyratical Edition of the above work being advertised to be published in a few Days, (printed in the BURTON manner) . . ." (*Dublin Journal*, 14 Feb.). In 1780, Burton is listed among the publishers in George Bonham's (q.v.) edition of Young's *Tour of Ireland*.

BURY (A.), bookseller in Drogheda, 1747–49. Advertisements in the *London Magazine*, from Jan. 1746/47 to Dec. 1749, listed Bury as one of the provincial sellers of the journal.

He also took subscriptions for "Number VIII" of *A New Life of William III* (*Dublin Courant*, 9 Jan. 1746/47).

BUSTEED (**GEORGE**), printer and publisher in Cork, (1) Castle Street (1764–66); (2) Paul Street (1766–68). 1764–68. He printed and published the *Cork Chronicle or Universal Register* from 1764 to 1768, and printed for the Cork Corporation from 1766 to 1768 (Caulfield, *Cork Council Book*). He retired from business or possibly died in 1768.

BUSTEED (**JOHN**), printer and publisher in Cork, (1) Paul Street (1768–?); (2) Castle Street (?–1776); and in Ennis, Church Street, 1778–? 1768–80? Probably he was the son or brother, and successor, of George Busteed (q.v.). He continued publication of the newspaper, calling it the *Cork Chronicle or Free Intelligencer*, 1769–72. In partnership with W. Sargent (q.v.) he published the *Hibernian Morning Post or Literary Chronicle*, 1773–76. Busteed also printed for the City Corporation from 1768 to 1776, the last payment record having a note adding "that John Busteed be no longer employed for printing, and the taking his newspaper discontinued" (Caulfield, *Cork Council Book*). In 1778 he was in Ennis in partnership with George Trinder, where they jointly published the *Clare Journal*, the first newspaper and the first printing in that town. In 1780 they published Lloyd's *Short Tour, or, An Impartial and Accurate Description of the County of Clare*.

BUTLER (**ISAAC**), bookseller and publisher in Dublin, St. Patrick Street, 1721–56. He was admitted to the guild as a quarter brother in 1727—being listed as an "almanack compiler"—and paid quarterage through 1731 (*Guild Records*). In 1721 he published his first almanac, *Butler's Advice from the Stars*, and in 1731 he acquired the rights to *Whalley's Almanack*, which he probably had been compiling since 1726 (see

Mary Whalley). The first known edition of Butler's version, advertised as "John Whalley's successor," was published by Samuel Fuller (q.v.) (*Dublin Weekly Journal*, 16 Oct. 1731), and continued through 1756. In his last edition, titled *Gentlemen and Dealer's Almanack*, Butler as well composed the first index of Dublin streets, lanes, public buildings, etc. (Peter Wilson [q.v.] independently compiled an alphabetical listing of street names from Rocque's 1756 map of Dublin later in the same year.) At times Butler was employed by the Physico-Historical Society of Dublin as a botanist, and by the Dean of St. Patrick's as a historian of the Cathedral. "A Student of Astronomy and Botany . . . and well skilled in the Occult Sciences," Butler left his autobiography, and in 1755 died aged 66.

BUTLER (JOHN), bookseller, printer, and publisher in Dublin, (1) York Street (1750–51); (2) the old Exchange, Cork Hill (1751–85?). 1750–83. He was admitted free of the guild by petition in 1752 but paid no quarterage. He was listed by the Clerk through 1772, in 1773 as "not in business" and in 1774 as "not in Trade," but was listed again in 1783 (*Guild Records*). He printed, with Richard James (q.v.), the *Dublin Gazette* from 1750 to 1753, and in 1753 printed and published Aheron's *Treatise of Architecture* (*Dublin Journal*, 27 Nov. 1753). In 1775 he received a disbursement from the Commons in connection with the Stamp Act (*Commons' Journ. Ire.*, ix, app. cclxxv). He died in 1790.

BUTLER (MICHAEL), printer in Kilkenny, High Street, 1758–79. No imprint with his name is known, but he may have been included in that of "Edward Crofton and Company" (q.v.) (*Dictionary 1726–75*). He was the brother-in-law of Edmund Finn (q.v.). Butler died in 1779 (*Kilkenny Parish Records*).

BUTLER (NICHOLAS), engraver in Dublin, upper Blind Quay (1767). 1763–67. In 1763 he was awarded a premium by the Dublin Society for "new designs in Copper plates," and in 1767 was in partnership with Patrick Fitzpatrick (q.v.) (Strickland, *Irish Artists*).

BUTLER (PETER), engraver in Dublin and Cork, 1753–82. In 1753 he was awarded a premium by the Dublin Society, in 1774 he engraved Connor's *Map of the City and Suburbs of Cork*, and in 1782 a prize-plate for books for the Rev. Giles Lee's school (Strickland, *Irish Artists*).

BUTLER (THOMAS), bookseller in Dublin, the Green Door, Ross Lane, near Bride Street, 1744–46. He was apprenticed to John Watson (q.v.), was admitted free of the guild by service in 1745, but paid no quarterage (*Guild Records*). In 1744 he advertised "Thomas Butler, Bookseller (who served his apprenticeship to Mr. John Watson, and served Mr. Samuel Fairbrother and Mr. Richard Gunne, Booksellers as shopkeeper). Has opened a Shop at the Green Door, in Ross-lane near Bridestreet, the house where the sign of the Whip and Spur was kept" (*Dublin Gazette*, 10 Apr.). From 1744 to 1746 he was listed among those taking subscriptions for George Faulkner's (q.v.) edition of Sale's *Universal History* (*Dublin Journal*, 25 Sept. 1744; *Pue's Occurrences*, 5 Jan. 1744/45; *Dublin Courant*, 7 Jan. 1745/46).

BUTREE (JOHN), bookseller in Dublin, near the Barrack, 1766 (*Dictionary 1726–75*).

BYRN (JAMES), printer in Dublin, (1) Thomas Street, near Francis Street, or, in Thomas Street, opposite the Market House (1748–53); (2) the Spinning Wheel, at the corner of Kezar's

Lane, Cook Street, or, the Spinning Wheel, Cook Street, opposite Bride Street (1753–73). 1748–73. He was listed as an intruder in 1754 and 1755, admitted to the guild as a quarter brother in 1756, and paid quarterage through 1764 (*Guild Records*). He printed the first Irish edition of Henry VIII's *Defense of the Seven Sacraments*. In 1740 he printed some of Sir Richard Cox's pamphlets in the Charles Lucas (q.v.) controversy, *The Cork Surgeon's Antidote against the Dublin Apothecary's Poysen*, nos. 1, 5, 6, and 7. In 1753, for James Eyre Weeks, a Country Party advocate, Byrn printed one of two rival editions of the *Dublin Spy*, referring to his opponent Thomas Hutchinson's (q.v.) newspaper as the "Counterfeit Spy." Hutchinson countered with the warning, "The HEAD of the PRESS in Thomas street is desired when he publishes his own Faetid Lucubrations, such as Dying Speeches and Hymns, ushering his Friends to the Gallows, to put his own proper Name to the Imprint" (*Dublin Spy*, 13 Aug.). In 1773 Byrn signed an appeal for assistance on behalf of reduced tradesmen (*Public Journal*, 27 Aug.). He died in 1802 (*Dublin Evening Post*, 20 Apr.).

BYRNE (GEORGE), engraver in Dublin, Fishamble Street, 1758?–77. He engraved Rocque's *Map of the County and City of Kilkenny*, 1758, Nevill's *Map of the County of Wicklow*, 1760, several plates for Wilson's *Dublin Magazine*, 1762, 1763, and worked for Exshaw's *London Magazine*, 1777. He died in 1791 (Strickland, *Irish Artists*).

BYRNE (THOMAS), printer in Dublin, 1773–1800. He was admitted free of the guild by special grace in 1773, "being the son of Matthew Byrne who was a Freeman of the City," and paid quarterage through 1788. He served as Warden in 1786 and on the Council from 1788 (*Guild Records*). In 1822 he died in New York (*Limerick Chronicle*, 9 Oct.).

C

CADDELL (ROBERT), bookseller in Dublin, 1708–15. He was apprenticed to John Ware (q.v.), admitted free of the guild by service in 1708, and paid quarterage through 1715. He served briefly as Warden in 1715, being replaced in April for having "removed out of town" (*Guild Records*).

CALWELL or CALDWELL (JER.), bookseller and printer in Waterford, Broad Street, 1747–67? He did a good deal of printing, chiefly small books, and many of his imprints are undated (*Dictionary 1726–75*), but he did publish a list of his stock for sale in 1750. Certainly he was in business in 1765, and the *Waterford Mail*, 3 Sept. 1824, referred to a *Caldwell's Waterford Mercury* for 1767 as the first newspaper published in that town.

CAMMELL (PATRICK) *see* Patrick Campbell

CAMPBELL (ALEXANDER), printer in Dublin, the Time, on the lower end of Cork Hill, 1718. He was a journeyman to Thomas Hume (q.v.) (Gent, *Life of Thomas Gent*).

CAMPBELL (CHARLES), printer in Dublin, (1) 20 Dame Street (1770–79); (2) 11 Trinity Street (1779–?). 1770–80. He petitioned the guild to be admitted by composition, but was admitted without fine upon paying the usual fees (*Guild Records*). In 1778 he succeeded H. Powell as printer of the *Dublin Evening Post*.

CAMPBELL or CAMMEL (PATRICK), bookseller and publisher in Dublin, (1) the Rose and Crown, Dame Street (1676–?); (2) Christ Church Yard (1683–90); (3) Castle Street (1692–95); (4) the Blue Bible, Skinner Row (1695–1702); (5) the Bible, on the Blind Quay, near Cork Hill (1705–15); (6) the lower end of Cork Hill (1716–20). 1676–1720. He was a journeyman to William Norman (q.v.) in 1676, and possibly later to George Foster (q.v.). He was a quarter brother in the guild in 1677, a free brother in 1683, and sworn in 1692, when he altered his name from Cammell. He was elected Warden in 1710, but refused to serve: his being a Presbyterian led to challenges whenever he stood for guild office (*Guild Records*). A contentious stationer and a militant Whig, he fled Ireland during the life of the Patriot Parliament but was back in Dublin by 1692. He was involved in a series of controveries for the rest of his life. Dunton, during his visit to Ireland, carried on a hate affair with Campbell over rival book auctions, claiming that the latter had ordered the press closed to him (*Dublin Scuffle*); as Dublin's first book auctioneer, Campbell had held auctions from early 1698 at least. Also in 1698, Campbell, along with Jacob Milner (q.v.), affixed the title-page and preface of Cocker's popular text to Hodder's *Arithmatick*, in order to sell a large stock of the latter they had on hand. Brought before the guild, they were forced to destroy the editions (*Guild Records*). In 1702, Campbell's support of the trustees for the forfeited estates of Ireland led to a prolonged pamphlet war. During the troubled years, 1710–14, he was subject to constant government harassment. Indicted for printing *Queries to the New Hereditary Rights Men* and *St. Germain's Letter found at Douay*, he was tried and acquitted (*Dublin Intelligence*, 12 May 1711). In 1715 he was again tried at the King's Bench, and in 1719 he was involved in a dispute over rival editions of Fiddes' *Theologia speculativa* (*Dublin Courant*, 11 Nov. 1719). Throughout his career he published many works on contemporary issues, but various lives, histories, and religious tracts as well. He died in 1720.

CANON (GILBERT), bookseller in Newry, 1710. Sole reference: advertisements in 1710 listed him as one of the provincial booksellers taking subscriptions for a Dublin edition of the *Tryal of Doctor Henry Sacheverell* (*Dublin Intelligence*, 24 June and 1 July).

CARBARY (MICHAEL), papermaker in Dublin, 1773. Sole reference: in 1773 he signed a petition to the Irish House of Commons from papermakers objecting to the removal of duties of foreign paper (BL, 1890.e.5. (232)).

CARPENTER (DANIEL), printer and publisher in Newry, (1) Canal Street (1761–?); (2) Sugar Island (1770?–90). 1761–90. He was the first printer in Newry and published that town's first newspaper, the *Newry Journal*, from 1761. In the same year he printed and published Stackburn's *Life of our Lord* and continued as an active stationer publishing mostly religious tracts, to his last known imprint, Blair's *Sermons*, 1790.

CARR (THOMAS), bookseller, printer, and publisher in Dublin, Silver Court, Castle Street, 1712–28? He was admitted to the guild as a quarter brother in 1712, paid quarterage through 1718, and was listed again in the Master's accounts in 1720 (*Guild Records*). A J. Carr, in Silver Court, Castle Street, printed *A New Epilogue Spoke and Sung by Polley Peacham at her Benefit Play: The Way of the World*, n.d. (Mrs. Sterling, who played Polley, had her benefit 11 April 1728 [Stockwell, *Dublin Theatre and Theatre Customs*]). He might be the same as Thomas Carr, and perhaps served as a journeyman to Richard Dickson (q.v.) and Elizabeth Needham (q.v.), for they had moved to the Silver Court address in March 1728.

CARRICK (JOHN), printer in Dublin, Bedford Row, 1767–78. He was admitted to the guild in 1767, served as Warden in 1771, Master in 1775, and on the Council from 1776 to 1778. He died in 1778 (*Guild Records*).

CARSON (JAMES), bookseller, printer, and publisher in Dublin, (1) Christ Church Yard (1713–14); (2) the King George, Fishamble Street (1715–16); (3) Coghill's Court, Dame Street, opposite to the Castle Market (1718–43); (4) the Bagnio Slip, Temple Bar (1748–65). 1713–65. He was the brother-in-law of Ebenezer and Pressick Rider (qq.v.). He was listed as an intruder in 1718, admitted free of the guild in 1728, paid no fees or quarterage, yet printed for the guild in 1742 (*Guild Records*). In 1720 he acquired the rights to Richard and Elizabeth Dickson's (qq.v.) *Dublin Intelligence*, and printed this through 1724, when the Dicksons again took up the title and apparently squeezed Carson out. In 1725 he started the *Dublin Weekly Journal* and, with James Arbuckle contributing, produced the first literary journal in Ireland and as well the first to illustrate advertisements with woodcuts. In 1747 Carson began publicizing the cause of governmental reform, partially supported Charles Lucas, and developed the *Journal* into Ireland's first non-demagogic political newspaper (Munter, *Irish Newspapers*). He died in 1765 (*Pue's Occurrences*, 19 Feb.).

CARTER (CORNELIUS), printer and publisher in Dublin, the Post Office Coffee House, Fishamble Street, 1696–1729. He also printed from the back of Dick's Coffee House, Skinner Row, on occasion from 1696 to 1703. He was admitted to the guild in 1696, was never sworn but listed through 1715, and paid no quarterage (*Guild Records*). He was a notorious Tory who repeatedly lent his press to party factionalism, most blatantly in support of Edward Lloyd (q.v.), 1710–14. He mostly published poems, pamphlets, and polemics, but he pioneered the newspaper press as well, and in this can be styled the father of yellow journalism in Ireland. He printed and published six original newspapers, experimented with evening editions, reprinted London papers, including the *Examiner*, and at various times printed *Pue's Occurrences*. His most successful newspaper was the *Flying Post or the Postmaster*, 1699–1724, the first to solicit advertisements and to offer long-term subscription rates (Munter, *Handlist* and *Irish Newspapers*). Carter also held the lucrative Irish monopoly for "The Fam'd Royal Eye Water" (see Elizabeth Pue). Dunton was taken in by Carter, finding him a "witty Man" and an "honest Printer" who "charms a thousand ways" (*Dublin Scuffle*): a premature judgment, for Carter's indictments and prosecutions by courts and parliament became legend—1704, 1708, 1712, 1715, 1721, 1725, 1727—resulting in his twice being imprisoned and in self-exile from Ireland in 1715 and 1716. Among the charges were publishing false news, forging imprints of other printers (see Thomas Walsh), and, with Bryan Wilson (q.v.), printing an error-ridden New Testament, 1698 (see Thomas Somervell). He died in 1734 (*St. John's Par. Reg.*, Dublin).

CARTLAND (**ROBERT**), printer in Dublin, 1753. He was apprenticed to Oliver Nelson (q.v.) in 1743, and in 1748 the guild denied his prayer for discharge (*Guild Records*). An obituary notice in 1753 provided the only other reference: "Last Wednesday died at his house in Hoey's Court, Mr. Robert Cartland, printer" (*Dublin Journal*, 2 June).

CASIE (**JOSEPH**), bookbinder in Dublin, 1746–50. He was admitted to the guild as a quarter brother in 1746 and paid quarterage through 1750 (*Guild Records*). He died intestate in 1750 (*Dublin Grant Book*).

CASTELLS or CASTLES (JOHN), bookbinder in Dublin, 1738–57. He was admitted to the guild as a quarter brother in 1738 and paid quarterage through 1757 (*Guild Records*). He died in 1770 (*Dublin Grant Book*).

CECIL or CECILL (GEORGE), printer in Dublin, 1767–69. He was apprenticed to Hugh Boulter Primrose Grierson (q.v.) in 1760, admitted free of the guild by service in 1767, and paid no quarterage. He was marked "Dead" in the 1770 Clerk's list (*Guild Records*). He printed Joseph Sterling's *Bombarino*.

CHAMBERS (THOMAS), engraver in Dublin (1746–50?), and in London (1750?–89?). 1746–89? He apparently studied with Andrew Miller (q.v.); his first known print was "Mary Gore, aged 103," 1746. He found ample employment, including engraving for Harris' *Life of William III*, 1749, a print of *Charles Lucas*, 1749, and plates for Smith's *History of Cork*, 1750. He continued an active career in London, but died an impoverished suicide in either 1789 or 1792 (Strickland, *Irish Artists*).

CHAMBERLAINE or CHAMBERLAIN (DILLON), bookseller, printer, and publisher in Dublin, (1) Smock Alley (1759–61); (2) Faulkner's Head, Dame Street, facing Fownes Street (1761–80). 1759–80. He was recorded as a quarter brother in the guild in 1760 and paid quarterage through 1770 (*Guild Records*). In 1759 the *Shepherd*, a short-lived weekly, was advertised as being sold by Chamberlaine. In 1773 he experimented with his own journal, the *Dublin Register of Politicks, History and Literature*, and in 1774 he published *A complete catalogue of modern books, (printed in Ireland) From the Beginning of the Century*. He was responsible for many other publications, including various plays by Shakespeare. He died in 1790.

CHANDLER (Mrs.), bookseller in Cashel, 1724. Sole reference: an advertisement in 1724 listed Mrs. Chandler as one of the provincial sellers of the "Fam'd Royal Eye Water" supplied by Cornelius Carter (q.v.) (*St. James Evening Post*, 15 and 22 July).

CHANDLER (ELLIS), bookseller in Cork, Fin's Quay, 1774–76. (*Dictionary 1726–75*). He also was referred to as a bookseller in 1776 (*Notes and Queries*, 29 May 1910).

CHANTREY (E.), bookseller in Dublin, Dame Street, 1726. He is referred to as a bookseller in 1726 (Gilbert, *History of Dublin*).

CHANTRY (JOHN), bookseller in Dublin, (1) next door to Ralph Dutton's Arms, Clarendon Street (1719); (2) opposite the Watch House, College Green (1720–26); (3) the corner of Sycamore Alley, Dame Street (1727–42). 1719–42. He was a bookseller and publisher in London, 1693–1708? (*Dictionary 1668–1725*). He was admitted to the guild as a quarter brother, "being a free stationer of London," in 1719 and paid quarterage through 1742 (*Guild Records*). He auctioned and sold many collections and libraries. Among his publications were Clarendon's *History of the Rebellion*, 1719, Keating's *History of Ireland*, 1723, and Thomas Vernon's *Chancery Cases*, 1726. He died in 1742 (*Dublin News Letter*, 26 Oct.).

CHERRY (JOHN), printer in Limerick, Pery Street, 1761–69. He printed *A Schedule of the Toll for the City of Limerick*, 1761, Robert's *Juvenal Poems*, 1763, and he was listed as a printer in the *Limerick Directory* for 1769.

CHURCHILL (JOSEPH), stationer in Dublin, the back of Dick's Coffee House, Skinner Row, 1698–1700. He was a journeyman to John Brent (q.v.). Perhaps he was enrolled with the guild as a result of a decree in 1698 ordering "that all persons of this Guild do enter theire severall respective Journeyman & Bind and Enroll y Apprentices within ten days" (*Guild Records*).

CLARE (B.), bookseller in Dublin, 1749 (*Dictionary 1726–75*).

CLARK (HENRY), stationer in Dublin, 1702–13. He was apprenticed to Matthew Gun (q.v.), fined for intrusion in 1702, admitted free of the guild by service in 1704, and paid quarterage through 1713 (*Guild Records*).

CLARKE or CLARK (JOHN), bookseller in Dublin, 1702–23. He was a journeyman to William Norman (q.v.) in 1702, admitted free of the guild in 1703, and paid quarterage through 1724 (*Guild Records*).

CLAY (WILL), stationer in Dublin, High Street, 1679. He was a journeyman to William Weston (q.v.) in 1679 (*Guild Records*).

CLIFFORD (N.), bookseller in Wexford, 1774 (*Dictionary 1726–75*).

CLOSE (SAMUEL), engraver in Dublin, (1) the Ring and Pearl, upper Blind Quay (1770–84); (2) 134 Capel Street (1785–1807). 1770–1807. He did many illustrations for books and magazines, such as the *Hibernian Magazine*, and many plates as well, including Thomas Hardy, 1794, the "Custom House," 1796, and "View of Merion Square," 1802. He died in 1807 (Strickland, *Irish Artists*).

COBB (EDWARD), bookseller in Dublin, 1681–95. He was a journeyman to John Foster (q.v) in 1681, admitted free of the guild in 1682, and paid quarterage through 1695. Isaac Warriner (q.v.) served him as a journeyman in 1685 and 1686 (*Guild Records*).

COLLES (JOHN), bookseller in Dublin, Dame Street, at the corner of Temple Lane, 1770?–71. He was apprenticed to his uncle William Colles (q.v.) in 1766, was never admitted free of the guild, but practiced (*Guild Records*). In 1771 he went to New York, where he died in 1807 (Glascott and Colles, *Pedigree of the Family of Colles in Ireland*).

COLLES (WILLIAM), bookseller and publisher in Dublin, 17 Dame Street, 1766–89. He was apprenticed to William Smith (q.v.) in 1759, was admitted free of the guild by service in 1767, and paid quarterage through 1788 (*Guild Records*). He joined various stationers to publish Smollett's *Humphrey Clinker*, 1771, some plays of Shakespeare in 1772, and *La Liturgie* [Huguenot], 1777. He died in 1790 (Glascott and Colles, *Pedigree of the Family of Colles in Ireland*).

COLLIER (GILES), stationer in Dublin, (1) the Rose and Crown, Dame Street (1683–84); (2) Castle Street (1685–88). 1683–88. He was a journeyman to William Norman (q.v.) in 1683 and 1684, and to John North (q.v.) from 1685 to 1688 (*Guild Records*).

COLLIER (JOSEPH), stationer in Dublin, 1746. He was admitted to the guild as a quarter brother in 1746, but paid no quarterage (*Guild Records*).

COLLINS (EDWARD), bookseller, printer, and publisher in Clonmel, Barrack Street, 1771–98. He was the first printer in

Clonmel, and published that town's first newspaper, the *Hibernian Gazette; or, Universal Advertiser*, renamed the following year the *Clonmel Gazette; or, Hibernian Advertiser*. He also printed a variety of tracts, pamphlets, and plays. In 1790 he took George Heaslip into partnership and, upon Collins's death, Heaslip continued the newspaper as the *Clonmel Journal*.

COMPANY OF BOOKSELLERS *see under* Booksellers

COMPANY OF STATIONERS *see* Society of Stationers

CONDY (G.), bookseller in Cork, Castle Street, 1751–62. The colophon in Dodsley's *The Oeconomy of Human Life*, 1751, read "sold by G. Condy in Castle-street." Also, advertisements in the *Munster Journal*, from 23 Jan. 1755 through 22 July 1762, listed Condy as taking "Advertisements and subscriptions . . . for this paper."

CONNOR (CHARLES), bookseller and publisher in Dublin, (1) the Pope's Head, on the Blind Quay, near Essex Gate (1737–45); (2) Ormand Quay, near Essex Bridge (1756). 1737–57. (See Charles O'Connor.) He was admitted to the guild as quarter brother in 1737 and paid quarterage through 1757 (*Guild Records*). He joined with various stationers on different occasions in publishing Collier's *Reflections on Ridicule*, 1737, Cullen's *Remarks on the Introduction to a Devout Life*, 1742, Prévost d'Exiles' *Dean of Coleraine*, 1743 (see Thomas Bacon), and George Faulkner's (q.v.) edition of Sale's *Universal History*, 1744. He died in 1757.

CONNOR (PETER), bookbinder in Dublin, 1757–62. He was apprenticed to Philip Bowes (q.v.), admitted to the guild as a quarter brother in 1757, and paid quarterage through 1762 (*Guild Records*).

CONNOR (WILLIAM), bookseller in Clonmel, 1710. Sole reference: advertisements in 1710 listed him as one of the provincial booksellers taking subscriptions for a Dublin edition of the *Tryal of Doctor Henry Sacheverell* (*Dublin Intelligence*, 24 June and 1 July).

COOKE (THOMAS), bookseller in Dublin, 1701. He was apprenticed to Thomas Sisson (q.v.), and admitted free of the city by service in 1701 (Thrift, *Freemen*).

COOPER (JOHN), stationer in Dublin, the Bible and Crown, Castle Street, 1684–98. He was a journeyman to Mathew Gun (q.v.) in 1684 and 1685, listed simply as journeyman (no master's name) in 1687 and 1688, admitted free of the guild in 1692, and paid quarterage through 1698 (*Guild Records*).

COOPER (SAMUEL), stationer in Dublin, 1712–24. He was admitted free of the city as a stationer by special grace in 1712 (Thrift, *Freemen*), was listed as a guild member from 1713 to 1716, served as Clerk in 1724, and was recorded as "dead" in 1725 (*Guild Records*).

COOPER (T.), printer in Dublin, 1755 (*Dictionary 1726–75*).

CORBETT (DANIEL), engraver in Cork, fl. 1750. He is known only for his plates in Smith's *History of Cork*, 1750, which included a Map of County Cork, "Kantruk Castle," "Youghal," and a "View of Kinsale from the old Fort."

CORBETT (THOMAS), bookseller in Dungannon, 1710–13. Advertisements in 1710 listed Corbett as taking subscriptions for a printing of the *Tryal of Doctor Henry Sacheverell* (*Dublin Intelligence*, 24 June and 1 July), and in 1713 as selling Richardson's edition of the *Book of Common Prayer*, "... all in Irish and English, the Elements of the Irish Language being added to every one of them" (*Dublin Gazette*, 11 July). There was a Thomas Corbet, printer (?), in Oxford in 1694, and a Thomas Corbett, auctioneer and bookseller, in London 1715–43 (*Dictionary 1668–1725*).

CORBITT or CORBETT (CHARLES), stationer in Dublin, the Rose and Crown, Dame Street (1684–85). 1684–88. He was a journeyman to William Norman (q.v.) in 1684 and 1685, and to Nathaniel Tarrant (q.v.) from 1686 to 1688 (*Guild Records*).

CORCORAN or CORKORAN (BARTHOLOMEW), bookseller and printer in Dublin, Inns Quay, near the Cloister, 1744–91. He was admitted to the guild on petition, being a "hawker residing on Inn's Key," as a quarter brother in 1744 and paid quarterage through 1770 (*Guild Records*). He printed and published a good deal both for the chapmen trade and for more sophisticated readers. In 1767 he printed a *Survey of the Liberties and Franchises of the City of Dublin*, various Shakespeare plays—*Merchant of Venice*, 1766, *Othello*, 1767, and *Romeo and Juliet*, 1769—and in 1784 he published Brocas' engraving of Father Austin (Gilbert, *History of Dublin*). He died in 1792.

CORCORAN or CORKORAN (DANIEL), bookseller in Dublin, 1744–66. He was admitted to the guild as a quarter brother in 1744 and paid quarterage through 1766 (*Guild Records*). He was probably related to Bartholomew Corcoran (q.v.).

COSGROVE (P.), printer in Dublin, near the Theatre Royal, Smock Alley, 1704. He was probably a journeyman to

Francis Dickson (q.v.). In 1704 his imprint was on three editions of the *Flying Post or the Post Master*, ". . . Re Printed by P. Cosgrove near the Theatre-Royal in Smoak Alley" (28 Aug., 2 and 5 Oct.), the printing establishment of Francis Dickson.

COSTELLO, COSTOLA, or COSTILO (JOHN), stationer in Dublin, 1680–98. He was a journeyman to Edward Powell (q.v.) from 1680 to 1683, admitted to the guild in 1685, and paid quarterage through 1698 (*Guild Records*). Possibly he was the same as John Elo (q.v.), the surname being but another spelling variation. If so, Costello served William Norman (q.v.) as a journeyman in 1683, and was in England in 1684.

COTTER (JOSEPH), bookseller, printer, and publisher in Dublin, under Dick's Coffee House, Skinner Row, 1744–50. He was admitted to the guild as a quarter brother in 1744 and paid quarterage through 1750 (*Guild Records*). In 1748 he printed a periodical, the *Reformer* (Munter, *Handlist*).

COTTER (SARAH), bookseller, printer, and publisher in Dublin, under Dick's Coffee House, Skinner Row, 1751–70. She was the widow of Joseph Cotter (q.v.), was admitted to the guild as a quarter brother in 1755, and paid quarterage through 1770 (*Guild Records*). She married Joseph Stringer (q.v.) in 1768 (*Dublin Grant Book*). In 1751 she printed a *Poem on Mrs. Wiffington's performing . . . in the "Distressed Mother,"* in 1761 she published Shakespeare's *Measure for Measure*, and in 1762 she subscribed to fourteen sets of George Faulkner's (q.v.) edition of Swift's *Works*. She died about 1774.

COTTER (THOMAS), bookseller and publisher in Dublin, beneath Dick's Coffee House, Skinner Row, 1700? He is mentioned by Gilbert as being a bookseller and publisher about 1700 (*History of Dublin*).

COTTON (THOMAS), bookseller, printer, and publisher in Dublin, at the Bowling Green Printing House, on the Strand, near Bachelor's Walk (1714); in Cork, Castle Street, near the Exchange (1715–22?); in Waterford (1722?–29); and possibly in Kendal (1731–33). 1714–33? He was one of the pioneers of the provincial newspaper press. In 1714, in partnership with Andrew Welsh (q.v.), he printed the *Dublin Weekly Journal* (Munter, *Handlist*), and by 1715 they were in Cork, where they printed *The Freeholder's Answer to the Pretender's Declaration*. Possibly they published a newspaper, the *Cork Intelligence*, in 1718 and 1719 (Caulfield, *Cork Council Book*). Around 1722 he moved to Waterford, and in 1729 he published the first newspaper in that city, the *Waterford Flying Post* (Munter, *Handlist*). A Thomas Cotton, the first printer in Kendal who also published that town's first newspaper, the *Kendal Courant*, 1731–33, is probably the same Cotton (Nicholson, *Annals of Kendal*; Timperly, *Dictionary of Printers and Printing*).

COULTER (JAMES), bookseller, printer, and publisher in Londonderry, 1736–48. An advertisement in 1736 listed Coulter as taking subscriptions for a printing of Rollin's *Ancient History* (*Dublin Evening Post*, 3 June). Also, in 1737 he took subscriptions for Virgil's *Works*, in 1744 for Sale's *Universal History*, and in 1748 Abraham Bradley (q.v.) announced that his publications were sold by Coulter (*Dublin Courant*, 8–12 May). In 1741 he printed and published the *Scriptural Doctrine of Original Sin Asserted and Explained*.

COUPLES (THOMAS), bookseller in Dublin, 1754. Sole reference: he was mentioned in the subscribers' list in 1754 as

"Thomas Couple, Bookseller," having taken six copies of an edition of Budgell's *Memoirs of the . . . Family of the Boyles.*

COX (?), printer in Youghal, 1770. Sole reference: he was listed in Cotton's *Typographical Gazeteer* as a printer in 1770.

COX (J.), bookseller in Galway, 1747. Sole reference: advertisements in the *London Magazine*, Jan. 1746/47 and Apr. 1747, listed Cox as one of the provincial sellers of the journal.

CRABB (JOHN), bookseller in Dublin, 1717. Sole reference: he is referred to as a bookseller in 1717 (*Notes and Queries*, 28 May 1910).

CRAFT (JAMES) *see* James Croft

CRAIG, CRAIGE, or CRAGE (JOHN), printer in Dublin, 1730–71. Probably he was a journeyman to William-Shaw Anburey (q.v.) in 1730: "Mr. Phill Brady, the News Boy who was Committed to Bridewell . . . for Selling . . . a Libel," was released on condition that he prosecute Anburey, who "assisted by one Craige, alias Jack the Catch Pole, a fellow who used to get his Livelyhood about Colledge Green," printed the libel (*Dublin Intelligence*, 21 Mar. 1729/30). In 1771 appeared obituary notices for a "Mr. John Craig, Printer" (*Hibernian Journal*, 12 June; *Pue's Occurrences*, 15 June).

CRAMPTON (PHILLIP), bookseller and publisher in Dublin, (1) Addison's Head, opposite the Horse Guard, Dame Street, or, Dame Street, at the Horse Guard, opposite Castle Lane (1726–45); (2) the Angel and Bible, Dame Street (1746–48). 1726–48. He was apprenticed to Joseph Leathly (q.v.), admitted to the guild as a quarter brother in 1726, as a free brother in 1728, and paid quarterage through 1748. He served as Warden in 1735 and as Master in 1742 (*Guild Records*). The Angel and Bible was the shop of George and Alexander Ewing (q.v.), whom Crampton apparently joined in partnership in 1746. He was an Alderman of Dublin from 1755. He was responsible for numerous publications including Homer's *Iliad*, 1734, an edition of the *Spectator*, 1737, and Shakespeare's *Henry IV*, 1756. In 1742 he jointly published one of the rival translations of Prévost d'Exiles' *Dean of Coleraine* (see Thomas Bacon), and in 1747 Shakespeare's *Works*. He died in 1792 at the age of 96 (Gilbert, *History of Dublin*).

CRAWFORD (WILLIAM), bookbinder in Dublin, Werburgh Street, 1768–83. He was admitted free of the guild by special grace in 1768 and paid quarterage through 1780. In 1783 an apprentice, William Leeson, was reassigned from Crawford to Benjamin Keightly (q.v.), and in the Clerk's list for that year Crawford was recorded as having "absconded" (*Guild Records*).

CRAWLEY (ESTHER), printer and publisher in Waterford, the Euclid's Head, Peter Street, 1764–76. She was one of the principal printers in Waterford. In 1764, with her son John Crawley (q.v.), she began publication of the *Waterford Journal* (it was mentioned in the *Dublin Journal*, 1 Sept. 1764, and a 1 Oct. edition was quoted in the *Freeman's Journal*, 6 Nov. 1764). She died in 1776 (*Leinster Journal*, 2 Feb.).

CRAWLEY (JOHN), printer and publisher in Waterford, the Euclid's Head, Peter Street, 1764–77. He was a partner with his mother from 1764 to 1776. They printed and published the *Waterford Journal* from 1764, and John continued this for a year after his mother's death (see Esther Crawley).

CROFT or CRAFT (JAMES), papermaker in Dublin, 1683–93. Parish records list the baptisms and burials of the children of James Croft (or Craft), "paper-maker," between the years 1683 and 1693 (*St. Nicholas Within Par. Reg.*, Dublin; *St. Michan Par. Reg.*, Dublin).

CROFTON (EDMUND or EDWARD), bookseller and printer in Kilkenny, 1757?–67? Little is known of this man. A 1757 Kilkenny headstone inscription read in part: "Dorothy Crofton, wife of Edmund Crofton, Printer and Stationer . . . died . . . Aged 59 years" (Egan's *Illustrated Guide to Kilkenny*). His one certain imprint, *Socrates: A Dramatic Poem*, is undated (possibly 1759) and was by "Edward Crofton & Co." In 1759 he is mentioned in the subscribers' list as having purchased fifty copies of an edition of Kennedy's *Modern Elements of Numeral Arithmetic*. There is some evidence that he secretly printed Burke's *Hibernia dominicana*, 1762, and finally a notice in Finn's *Leinster Journal* read "Edward Crofton, a citizen of Kilkenny almost forty years past . . . greatly reduced in trade . . . would willingly serve any noble or gentleman" (4–7 Feb. 1767).

CROFTON (WILLIAM), bookseller in Dublin, 1729–45. He was sued by the guild for intrusion in 1729, admitted free by service to George Winslow (q.v.) in 1735, and paid one year's quarterage; but Edward Beatty (q.v.), who was admitted free in 1745, had served his apprenticeship to Crofton (*Guild Records*).

CROFTON (WILLIAM), bookbinder in Dublin, 1761–87. He was admitted free of the guild in 1761, paid quarterage through 1767, appeared on the Clerk's lists through 1789 as in arrears, but against his name in 1787 was the note "dead" (*Guild Records*).

CROFTS (?), engraver in Dublin, 1736? Sole reference: his name appears as an engraver jointly with John Brooks (q.v.) of a "View of the Obelisk on the Boyne" (Strickland, *Irish Artists*).

CRONIN or CRONNIN (Timothy), bookseller in Cork, 1748–54. In 1748 Abraham Bradley (q.v.) announced that his publications were sold by Cronin (*Dublin Courant*, 8–12 May), and in 1754 the Cork Corporation paid Cronin for "Law books supplied" (Caulfield, *Cork Council Book*).

CROOKE (Andrew), bookseller, printer, and publisher in Dublin, (1) His Majesty's Printing House, Skinner Row (1680–84); (2) Ormond Quay (1685–98); (3) Cork Hill, near Copper Alley, or, Blind Quay, near Copper Alley, or, the Royal Arms, Copper Alley, sometimes as His, Her, or Their Majesties Printing House (1693–1727); (4) the King's Arms, Copper Alley (1727–32). 1680–1732. He was the son of John and Mary Crooke (q.v.) and the younger brother of John Crooke Jr. (q.v.). His first wife was Catherine, who died about 1701, and his second wife and widow was Anne (q.v.). In 1678 his brother deeded to him one-half of the King's Printer office, and in 1680, having come of age, he joined his mother and brother in partnership at the Skinner Row address. Following his brother's death in 1683, and his mother's retirement in 1684, Andrew moved to the Ormond Quay address, and later opened the second shop near Copper Alley. His first imprint was in 1684. He was admitted free of the guild in 1696, was listed by the Clerk through 1715, but paid no quarterage (*Guild Records*). From the death of John Jr., Benjamin Tooke (q.v.) had exercised the position of King's Printer in Ireland, but in 1685 Andrew, along with Samuel Helsham (q.v.), was made his assignee, and until 1689 they jointly shared the position. The post was lost to James and Richard Malone (q.v.) under James II, but Andrew regained the patent in 1693 and held it until his death in 1732 (*Lib. Munerum*, ii, 95). In 1688 he printed for the City Corporation (*Cal. Anc. Rec. Dublin*), and as King's Printer he published "by authority" the *Dublin Intelligence* from 1690 to 1705? (Munter, *Handlist*). He printed *Whalley's Almanack* in 1691, and by 1705 through 1713 he published his own *Almanack*. The output of his press was considerable, printing Latin classics, and also in German and French. Dunton praised him in 1698, though noting that "his Circumstances are not so great" (*Dublin Scuffle*); still, in later years, he became one of the foremost stationers in Dublin. He died in 1732 (*Dublin Evening Post*, 29 June).

CROOKE (**ANNE**), bookseller and printer in Dublin, the King's Arms, in Pembroke Court, Castle Street, or, in Pembroke Court, Copper Alley, 1732–35. She was the second wife and widow of Andrew Crooke (q.v.). In 1735 she advertised book sales (*Dublin Impartial News Letter*, 14 Sept. and 23 Nov.). In 1758 an Anne Crooke, possibly the widow or a daughter, married Thomas Wilkinson (q.v.) (*Dublin Grant Book*; *St. John's Par. Reg.*, Dublin).

CROOKE (**EDMUND**), bookseller in Dublin, 1638. He is known only from his will, proved in Dublin in 1638. In this he refers to his brother John Crooke (q.v.), and speaks of having a sum of £300 in the hands of his partners John Crooke, Thomas Allott (q.v.), and Richard Sergier (q.v.). Perhaps for a brief period he was in charge of the Dublin branch of John Crooke's business.

CROOKE (**JOHN**), bookseller, printer, and publisher in London (1638–69); and in Dublin, St. Austin's, King's Printing Office, Castle Street, or next the Castle Gate (1638–69). 1638–69. He was the patriarch of a family of Dublin stationers. He operated establishments concurrently in London and Dublin. He was the brother-in-law of Benjamin Tooke (q.v.), and in Dublin for some time was in partnership with Richard Sergier (q.v.), possibly Thomas Allott (q.v.), and briefly with his brother Edmund Crooke (q.v.). In 1640, with Sergier, he printed William Ince's *Lot's Little One*. In 1660 he was granted a patent for life as King's Printer in Ireland, and did homage for the grant with the publication of *A Panegyrick . . . for Return . . . of our Royal Charles*. Besides extensive government work and some private publication, he printed Ireland's second newspaper, Samuel Dancer's *Mercurius Hibernicus*, 1663 (Munter, *Irish Newspapers*). He died in London in 1669, and was succeeded by his wife, Mary Crooke (q.v.).

CROOKE (**JOHN JR.**), printer in Dublin, Ormond Quay, 1669–83. He was the son of John and Mary Crook (qq.v.) and the elder brother of Andrew Crooke (q.v.). On the death of John Sr., Andrew and John Jr. were placed under the guardianship of their uncle Benjamin Tooke (q.v.). Tooke was appointed King's Printer in Ireland in 1669 (an office he considered to hold in trust for the two Crooke boys); in 1671 he surrendered the post and it was regranted jointly to John Jr. and Tooke (with the work actually being carried on by Tooke), and in 1671 John, in turn, deeded half of the position to his brother Andrew. It is possible that John was never really trained as a printer and never became a master printer. His first imprint was in 1679 jointly with Tooke, and through 1683 John's name never appeared alone. Among their publications were Titus Oates's *A True Narrative and Discovery of . . . the Horrid Popish Plot*, 1679, the *Book of Common Prayer*, 1680, and Bourke's *Almanack*, 1683. Crooke died in 1683.

CROOKE (**MARY**), bookseller and printer in Dublin, (1) St. Austin's, King's Printing House, Castle Street (1669–78); (2)

His Majesty's Printing House, Skinner Row (1678–84); and a second establishment, (3) Ormond Quay (1679–84). 1669–84. She was the widow of John Crooke (q.v.), the sister of Benjamin Tooke (q.v.), and the mother of John Jr. and Andrew Crooke (qq.v.). Neither of her sons was of age when her husband died, so, assisted by her brother Tooke, she continued the family business herself. In 1679 she brought John Jr. into partnership and the following year Andrew, also in 1680 executing a deed to divide the profits of the Printing House among all three. In 1681 she turned the Skinner Row establishment over to her sons while she continued to operate that on Ormond Quay. She did little printing outside of an occasional pamphlet, such as *The very Copy of a Paper Delivered to the Sheriffs upon the Scaffold on Tower-Hill . . . by Algernon Sidney*, 1683. She retired from business in late 1684.

CROSS (EDWARD), bookseller in Dublin, Capel Street (1773–76. In 1773 he signed a memorial to the Irish House of Commons against additional duties of foreign paper (BL 1890.e.5. (239)). Also, in 1773 marriage announcements referred to him as "Mr. Cross, Capel street, bookseller" (*Dublin Journal*, 25 Mar.; *Hibernian Journal*, 26 Mar.).

CROSS (RICHARD), bookseller, printer, and publisher in Dublin, 29 Bridge Street, 1757–1809. He was apprenticed to David Gibson (q.v.) in 1750, and admitted to the guild as a quarter brother by service in 1757, "it being inconvenient for him to become free at present." He paid quarterage through 1771, again in 1786 and 1787, and was admitted a free brother by special grace in 1793 (*Guild Records*). He was a leading Catholic stationer; his publications included, with James Fitzsimons (q.v.), O'Conor's *Essay on the Rosary*, 1772, and, alone, a *Life of . . . St. Patrick*, 1782, and Burke's *Works*, 1792. He died in 1809.

CRUMP (Mrs.), bookseller in Dublin, Marlborough Street, opposite the Society House, 1747. Sole reference: in 1747 she was listed as one of the sellers of Samuel Powell Jr.'s (q.v.) edition of Wesley's *Principles of a Methodist*.

CUDMORE (DANIEL), bookbinder in Dublin, Buchanan's Head, Damask Street, near George's Lane, 1718. In 1718 he was listed as a journeyman to John Afleck (q.v.) but also as an intruder (*Guild Records*).

CUDMORE (DANIEL), bookbinder in Dublin, 1744–84. He was apprenticed to William Smith (q.v.), admitted to the guild as a quarter brother in 1744, as a free brother by service in 1756, paid quarterage through 1784, and was marked "dead" on the Clerk's list in 1787 (*Guild Records*). He was possibly the son of Daniel Cudmore (q.v.), the 1718 intruder.

CUFF (THOMAS), bookseller in Roscommon, 1747–48. In 1747 he was listed as a seller of *A New Life of William III* (*Dublin Courant*, 9 Jan.), and advertisements in the *London Magazine*, Jan. 1746/47 through Dec. 1748, listed Cuff as one of the provincial sellers of the journal.

CUMIN (J.), bookseller in Clonmel, 1747–48. Advertisements in the *London Magazine*, Jan. 1747/48 through Dec. 1748, listed Cumin as one of the provincial sellers of the journal.

CUMMING or CUMING (THOMAS), printer in Cork, 1746–47. In 1746 he printed Davies' *A Farewell Sermon*, in 1747 he reprinted two London pamphlets, *The Thistle* and *A Candid and Impartial Account of the Behaviour of Simon Lord Lovat*, and in 1747 he was paid for printing for the Cork Corporation (Caulfield, *Cork Council Book*).

CUNNINGHAM (JOHN), stationer in Dublin, 1677. In 1677 he was listed as a quarter brother (*Guild Records*).

CURRAN (ELINOR), bookseller in Dublin, St. Patrick Street, opposite Bride's Alley, 1735. Sole reference: in 1735 she is referred to as keeping "an Old Book Shop, in St. Patrick Street" (*Dublin Journal*, 15 Apr.).

D

DALTON (CHRISTOPHER), printer in Dublin, 1750s. Sole reference: an obituary notice in 1756 referred to him as a printer (*Dublin Journal*, 13 Nov.).

DALTON (JAMES), bookseller and publisher in Dublin, (1) the corner of Bride's Alley, St. Patrick Street (1731–?); Sir Isaac Newton's Head, on Temple Bar (1750–53). 1731–53. He was admitted to the guild as a quarter brother in 1731 and paid quarterage through 1753 (*Guild Records*). In 1736 he published Aubin's *The Noble Slaves*, and, from that date, numerous Shakespeare plays, including *Hamlet, Othello, Julius Caesar, Henry VIII*, and *The Merry Wives of Windsor*, 1753. He died in 1753 (*Pue's Occurrences*, 6 Nov.).

DALTON (JAMES, Mrs.), bookseller in Dublin, Sir Isaac Newton's Head, on Temple Bar, 1753–57. She was the widow of James Dalton (q.v.), and one of the three women to appear for the first time, 1754, listed among the quarter brothers of the guild. From 1754 to 1757 she continued the same quarterage as her husband, being listed as Mrs. Dalton in 1754 and as "widow Dalton" in 1756 and 1757 (*Guild Records*).

DALTON (SAMUEL), bookseller, printer, and publisher in Dublin, the entrance to Darby Square, Werburgh Street, 1730–63? He was apprenticed to Thomas Hume (q.v.), admitted free of the guild by service in 1735, paid quarterage through 1739, and was summoned in 1743 for failure to continue quarterage payments (*Guild Records*). He printed and published numerous works, many of a dissenting nature. In 1734 he started *Dalton's*

Impartial News Letter, a journal that lasted about one year (Munter, *Handlist*). His last noted activity was a subscription to George Faulkner's (q.v.) edition of Swift's *Works*, 1762. In 1807 the *Hibernian Journal* recorded the death of a Samuel Dalton in North Carolina, "aged 115 years. . . . He was but once married and there are now living upwards of 600 of his offspring" (3 July).

DANCER (SAMUEL), bookseller and publisher in Dublin, the Horse Shoe, or, next door to the Bear and Ragged Staff, Castle Street, 1662–68. He published a variety of religious, legal, political, and literary works, the majority printed by John Crooke (q.v.), and was the recognized publisher for the Irish Church Convocation (*Dictionary 1641–67*). In 1663 he was summoned before the Irish Commons for publishing the Speaker's speech (*Commons' Journ. Ire.*, ii, 293). In 1663 he published Ireland's second newspaper, *Mercurius Hibernicus*, which survived some fifteen issues, and from 1664 he continued various efforts at news publications through broadsheets, such as *The Summe of Intelligence* (Munter, *Irish Newspapers*).

DANIEL (?), papermaker in Dublin, 1773. Sole reference: in 1773 he signed, as Daniel and White (q.v.), a petition to the Irish House of Commons from papermakers objecting to the removal of duties on foreign paper (BL, 1890.e.5. (232)). He is possibly the same as James Daniel (q.v.).

DANIEL (COMBRA), bookbinder and bookseller in Cork, opposite the Main Guard, 1723–34. In 1723 he was paid by the Cork Corporation for binding 230 Bibles (Caulfield, *Cork Council Book*). An advertisement in 1726 listed Daniel as taking subscriptions for George Risk's (q.v.) printing of Pack's *Miscellaneous Works* (*Dublin Weekly Journal*, 2 July), and from that date to 1734 he took subscriptions or subscribed to a variety of Dublin publications, including Defoe's *The Compleat English Tradesman* and the *Plays* of Ben Jonson. He died in 1734, his will being proved in the Cork and Ross Diocesan Court.

DANIEL (**JAMES**), papermaker in Dublin, (1) Jarvis Street (?); (2) Abbey Street (?). 1759–82. He was admitted to the guild as a quarter brother in 1759, as a free brother in 1764, and paid quarterage through 1782 (*Guild Records*). He had a paper mill at Newbridge, County Kildare, and from 1770 to 1773 was associated with Stamper (q.v.), and possibly with White (q.v.) in 1773, for in that year a "Daniel and White" signed a petition to the Irish House of Commons objecting to the removal of duties on foreign paper (BL, 1890.e.5. (232)).

DAVENPORT (**HUMPHREY**), papermaker in Dublin, 1730–40s? In 1730 he leased a paper mill at Newbridge, near Leixlip, from John Randall (q.v.), and operated it until the 1740s (Phillips, unpublished thesis).

DAVIS or DAVYS (**DUDLEY**), stationer in Dublin, 1682–98. He was admitted free of the guild in 1682 and paid quarterage through 1697. In 1697 his name was removed from the list of sworn brothers (*Guild Records*).

DAVIS (**ROBERT**), bookbinder in Dublin, 1760s. In 1764 he was listed as the father of John Davis, an apprentice to William Fleming (q.v.), and in 1767 he petitioned the guild to have his son's apprenticeship transferred to William Smith Jr. (q.v.) (*Guild Records*).

DAVIS (**WILLIAM**), bookseller in Dublin, 1762–65. He was apprenticed to Richard James (q.v.) in 1752, apparently admitted free of the guild by service in 1762, and paid quarterage through 1765 (*Guild Records*).

DAVISON (JOHN), engraver in Dublin, 1731?–44. He was apprenticed to Philip Simms (q.v.) in 1724. He contributed maps and other engravings to Faulkner's (q.v.) edition of Sale's *Universal History*, 1744 (Strickland, *Irish Artists*).

DAVYS (FERNANDO), bookseller in Dublin, (1) Ross Lane, opposite the Toy Shop (1722–26); (2) Essex Street (1727–29); (3) Abbey Street (1729). 1722–29. Strickland erroneously identifies him as a Dublin painter (*Irish Artists*). In 1722 he petitioned the guild to be admitted free under an act to encourage "Protestant strangers," but refusing the fine he was later ordered prosecuted as an intruder. In 1725 he was admitted free and paid quarterage through 1728 (*Guild Records*). He occasionally advertised sales in the *Dublin Weekly Journal*.

DAWSON (JAMES), bookseller in Londonderry, 1710–31? Various newspaper advertisements listed Dawson as taking subscriptions for, or selling, Dublin publications from the *Tryal of Doctor Henry Sacheverell* (*Dublin Intelligence*, 24 June and 1 July 1710) to Whalley's *Almanack* (*Dublin Journal*, 18 Dec. 1731).

DAWSON (JAMES, Mrs.), bookseller in Londonderry, 1735–36? She was probably the widow and successor of James Dawson (q.v.). Advertisements in 1735 listed "Widow Dawson" as taking subscriptions for Faulkner's (q.v.) edition of Swift's *Works* (*Dublin Journal*, 1 Mar. and 12 Apr.). A repeated advertisement in the same journal of 14 Feb. 1735/36 had dropped her name.

DAWSON (JAMES JR.), bookseller in Londonderry, 1762? Possibly a son and successor of Mrs. James Dawson (q.v.). Sole reference: he was mentioned in the subscribers' list as having purchased six sets of Faulkner's (q.v.) 1762 edition of Swift's *Works*.

DEANE (WILLIAM), stationer in Dublin, 1677–79. He was admitted free of the guild in 1677, listed in 1678 and 1679, and his name crossed out in the 1680 Council list (*Guild Records*).

DEBENHAM (JOHN), engraver in Dublin, (1) the Raven, Castle Street (1767–68); (2) Golden Key, High Street, opposite St. Nicholas Church (1768–73); (3) Castle Street (1773–75); (4) College Green (1775); (5) 52 Castle Street (1775–85); (6) 15 Anglesea Street (1785–91); (7) 17 Charlemont Street (1791–92). 1767–92? He came to Ireland from England in 1767 and quickly advertised "his unfeigned thanks for encouragement since his arrival in this kingdom." He petitioned for freedom of the guild by composition and was admitted in 1769, paid quarterage through 1787, served as Warden in 1773, and on the Council from 1776 to 1792, when he was at last removed for not paying quarterage (*Guild Records*). In 1773 he contributed to a subscription for a monument to Dr. Charles Lucas (*Guild Records*), and in 1775 was appointed an inspector of "Dies and Plates" in the Stamp Office (*Commons' Journ. Ire.*, ix, app. ccclxxii–ccclxxvi). He was still living in 1800.

DEEBLE (W.), engraver in Cork, 1750s? His signed work appeared in two eighteenth-century publications, Crownwell's *Excursions through Ireland* and a bookplate of "Patrick Blair, M.D., of Blair's Castle, Cork." He may have worked in Bristol as well (Strickland, *Irish Artists*).

DE HONDT (PETER) *see under* Hondt

DE LAAFA (CHARLES) *see under* Laafa

DEMPSEY (JOHN), stationer in Dublin, 1729–58? Possibly Catholic, he was recorded as paying fees as a quarter brother, from 1729 to 1740. The steep increase in his yearly fee could indicate a prosperous business. In 1758 he was summoned by the guild for arrears in payment (*Guild Records*).

DEMPSEY (L.), engraver in Dublin, 1728–39. In 1728 he engraved a portrait of Matthew Prior for the frontispiece of George Grierson's (q.v.) edition of Prior's *Poems*, and in 1739 he furnished plates for Walter Harris' (q.v.) edition of Ware's *Works* (Strickland, *Irish Artists*).

DE PIENNE (PETER) *see under* Pienne

DICEY (JOHN), bookseller in Dublin, 1762. Sole reference: he was mentioned in the subscribers' list as having purchased twelve sets of Faulkner's (q.v.) 1762 edition of Swift's *Works*.

DICKIE (WILLIAM), bookseller and printer in Armagh, Market Street (1740–71). 1740–71. A staunch Presbyterian stationer, he was sworn free of the city of Armagh in 1740, served on the grand jury yearly from 1742 to 1771, and as High Constable in 1750. An advertisement in 1740 listed Dickie as taking subscriptions for Risk's *Roman History* (*Dublin News Letter*, 10 May). In 1743 he became Armagh's first printer, purchasing a press made by Francis Joy (q.v.). He continued to subscribe to Dublin publications while himself printing various dissenter sermons and pamphlets. From 1760 to 1766 he printed city advertisements, the assizes of bread, petitions for Parliament, etc., and in 1765 became the official printer for Armagh. He died in 1771.

DICKSON (CHRISTOPHER), printer and publisher in Dublin, (1) General Post Office Printing House, next door to the Punch Bowl, Temple Bar (1726–28); (2) Post Office Yard,

Sycamore Alley (1729–49). 1726–49. In 1726 he was mentioned in the subscribers' list of an edition of Defoe's *The Compleat English Tradesman*. By 1727 he was printer to the post office in Dublin, in 1727 he published a newspaper for a few months, and in 1738 he printed the *Dublin Daily Advertiser* for James Hamilton (q.v.) (Munter, *Handlist*). He also printed occasional catalogues for book sales and auctions. In 1735 a benefit performance at the Theatre Royal of *The Merry Wives of Windsor* was given for Dickson "at the Particular Desire of several Persons of Quality" (*Dublin Journal*, 19 Apr.). He died in 1749, "insulted and abused by some Ruffians in Fishamble-street, the week before, and never was able to go abroad afterwards" (*Dublin Courant*, 21 Jan).

DICKSON (ELIZABETH), bookseller, printer, and publisher in Dublin, (1) Union Coffee House (1713–15), or, Hanover Coffee House, Cork Hill (1715–?); (2) next door the Angel and Bible, or Seven Stars, opposite Castle Market, Dame Street (1725–28); (3) Silver Court, next door to the sign of the Golden Hammer and Heart, opposite the Rose Tavern, Castle Street (1728). 1713–28. She was the wife of Francis Dickson (q.v.), whose business enterprises she inherited. In 1714 she married Gwyn Needham (q.v.) and the two, along with Elizabeth's eldest son, Richard Dickson (q.v.), worked in partnership for many years. They jointly continued publication of the *Dublin Intelligence*, introduced new periodicals (Munter, *Handlist*), while printing various pamphlets and polemics largely in the Whig cause. In 1728 she retired from printing to manage the Globe Coffee House on Essex Bridge. In 1730 she sought aid from the city of Dublin, being "by misfortunes much reduced," and was granted £10 (*Cal. Anc. Rec. Dublin*). Nothing more of her is heard until her death in 1755 "of gradual and lingering decay, in the 81st year of her age" (*Dublin Journal*, 22–25 Nov.).

DICKSON (FRANCIS), bookseller, printer, and publisher in Dublin, (1) Cork Hill (1699–1701?); (2) Oxman Town Coffee House (1702–05), or, Dickson's Coffee House, Church Street (1705–06); (3) Union Coffee House, Cork Hill (1707–13); a second press was set up, in partnership with Stephen Powell (q.v.), to print the *Flying Post: or, the Post-Master*, next door to the Post Office, in the Lord Chief Baron's Yard, Cork Hill (1707–13); also, Dickson apparently used the presses of various other stationers on occasion, for he had imprints of Cork Hill in 1704 and 1705; over against the Pelican, or, Four Courts Coffee House, Winetavern Street, in 1701, 1702, 1706, 1707, and 1710; and Smock Alley near Theatre Royal (the press of P. Cosgrove [q.v.]) in 1703, 1704, and 1705. 1699–1713. In 1702 he was summoned before the guild for intrusion, but remained independent of that body all his career (*Guild Records*). Still, he was a prominent printer for fourteen years despite being an intruder, an uncompromising Williamite, and a controversial Whig. He printed handbills, pamphlets, and books, and served as unofficial printer to the Irish House of Commons from 1708, but his chief claim to fame is as one of the pioneers of the Irish newspaper press. He experimented with seven different periodicals (Munter, *Handlist*), two of which were long-lived, and his *Dublin Intelligence* went far in making the newspaper an everyday part of Dublin life. His success involved, as well, combining printing with coffee houses and the marketing of everything from water jugs to patent medicines. He died in November 1713.

DICKSON (RICHARD), bookseller, printer, and publisher in Dublin, (1) Hanover Coffee House, Cork Hill (1714–?); for a time he worked at two different presses, (2) the Cheshire Cheese, opposite the Bear, Crane Lane (1724–27), and (3) next door the Angel and Bible, or Seven Stars, opposite Castle Market, Dame Street (1725–28); (4) Silver Court, next door to the sign of the Golden Hammer and Heart, opposite Rose Tavern, Castle Street (1728–48). 1714–48. He was the eldest son of Francis and Elizabeth Dickson (qq.v.) and, having served an irregular apprenticeship, joined his mother and step-father, Gwyn Needham (q.v.), in partnership. His first imprint was *R. Dickson The Dublin Intelligence*, 10 Oct. 1714. He experimented with other periodicals (Munter, *Handlist*), and published various tracts and pamphlets. Richard became the sole proprietor of his father's business ventures in 1730, indulging in the petty stationers' squabbles and claims, while continuing the patent drug business under the billing of Dickson's "Elixir-Ware-House."

DIGBY (EDWARD), printer in Cork, 1770. Sole reference: in 1770 he printed *Midas; An English Burlesque. As it is performed at the Theatre Royal, in Convent Garden* (RIA, H.P., 356-3).

DILLON (IGNATIUS), bookseller in Dublin, (1) the Bible, High Street (1740); (2) Bridge Street (1759). 1740–59? He was the son of Luke Dillon (q.v.). In 1740 he announced that he was continuing his deceased father's business, but three months later he offered the entire stock and wares at auction (*Dublin News Letter*, 12 Apr. and 19 July). In October 1740, Thomas Brown (q.v.) took over the premises and most of the stock with a declaration that "Widow Dillon and family have entirely quitted the Bookselling" (*Dublin News Letter*, 18 Oct.). There is no further notice of Ignatius until 1759, when he was listed as a stationer in "Bridge Street," and admitted to the guild as a quarter brother (*Guild Records*).

DILLON (LUKE), bookseller and publisher in Dublin, the Bible, High Street, 1711–40. A Catholic, he was admitted to the guild as a quarter brother in 1711 and paid quarterage through

1739. The high fees would suggest a degree of success in business (*Guild Records*). In 1717 he is mentioned in the subscribers' list for Powell's *A Brief Discourse in Vindication of the Antiquity of Ireland*, in 1720, with John Gill (q.v.), he published Pomey's *The Pantheon*, and in 1727, with a coterie of stationers, Rollin's *Method of Teaching and Studying Belles Lettres*. His business was largely in the country trade: books of piety and devotion, and chapbooks. He died in 1740 (*Dublin Daily Post, and General Advertiser*, 5 Jan.).

DINNIS (**GEORGE**), printer in Dublin, 1737. Sole reference: he was recorded as a printer when he married Sarah Young, widow, on 2 Mar. 1737 in St. John's Parish Church (*Dictionary 1726–75*).

DIRICK (**JOHN**), papermaker in Dublin, ?–1692. Sole reference: he was recorded in the parish register as a "Paper Maker" at his burial in 1692 (*St. Michan Par. Reg.*, Dublin).

DIXON (**?**), engraver in Dublin, d. 1695. Sole reference: in 1695 the Parish Register of St. John's recorded the death of "Mr. Dixon the Engraver" (Strickland, *Irish Artists*).

DIXON (**JOHN**), engraver in Dublin, Church Street, 1760?–65. In 1760 he engraved Rocque's map of Dublin county, in 1763 he provided portraits for Exshaw's *Annual Register* and published various landscape designs, and his print of Lord Taaff in 1763 caused him to be praised as

> Dixon, that youth accomplished to impart
> the justest transcript with the finest art

(*Sleator's Public Gazetteer*, 12 Mar.). He left for London in 1765 where he remained, having a distinguished career until his death in 1811 (Gilbert, *History of Dublin*).

DIXON (THOMAS), engraver in Dublin, Cork Hill, 1740–63. He was the brother of John Dixon (q.v.). In 1744 he provided the plate entitled the "Tower of Babel" for Faulkner's (q.v.) edition of Sale's *Universal History*, and in 1760 he etched some landscapes, but after 1758 he carried on his father's hosier business (Strickland, *Irish Artists*).

DOBSON (ELIPHAL), bookseller and publisher in Dublin, (1) Cork Hill (1680–85?); (2) the Stationers' Arms, Castle Street (1689?–1719). 1680–1719. He was admitted free of the guild in 1680 and paid quarterage through 1718. He was an active member, serving as Warden in 1692, 1698, and 1699, on the Council from 1693, and for a brief period as Master in 1703, though he refused to take the "Little Oath" (*Guild Records*). He was styled a "great Dissenter" by Dunton (*Life and Errors*). He fled Ireland during the reign of James II and was attainted by the Patriot Parliament for having done so (King's *State of the Protestants*), but returned sometime in 1689. He published the *Daily Courant* from possibly 1705 to 1719 (Munter, *Handlist*), and a long list of books, often in conjunction with fellow stationers. In 1706 he published an edition of William Barton's *Psalms*, with music, and in 1714, with William Binauld (q.v.), he published a folio Bible, the first printed and published in Dublin (an earlier attempt by James Malone [q.v.] had the sheets seized by the authorities). In 1719 he joined a more permanent partnership with Robert Owen (q.v.) and Richard Gunn (q.v.) in competition with a coterie of George Risk (q.v.), George Ewing (q.v.), and William Smith (q.v.). He died in 1720.

DOBSON (ELIPHAL JR.), bookseller, papermaker?, and publisher in Dublin, the Stationers' Arms, Castle Street, 1710?–32. He was the second son of Eliphal Dobson (q.v.) and carried on his father's business. The imprint of *An Excellent New Song*

. . . by Mr. Durffey, 1710, read "Printed for Eliphal Dobson, junior." He was not admitted free of the guild until 1718, and paid quarterage through 1730. He served on the Council from 1719, as Warden in 1720, and, though elected Master in 1727, he refused the oath and position, a dissenter like his father; still, in 1731 he was elected a Sheriff of the City of Dublin (*Guild Records*). His publication list was long, including Defoe's *Robinson Crusoe*, 1719, an octavo Bible, 1722 (a printing of 10,000 copies), an eight-volume Plutarch's *Lives*, 1730, and several works in partnership with John and Sarah Hyde (qq.v.) from 1728. He might have had an interest in papermaking, for in 1727 he offered for sale a "Fee Farm Lease of a Paper Mill, at the Red-Mills in Chappelizard" (*Dublin Journal*, 8–12 Aug.). He died in 1732 (*Dublin Evening Post*, 7 Nov.).

DOBSON (JANE), bookseller and publisher in Dublin, the Stationers' Arms, Castle Street, 1732–34. She was the wife of Eliphal Dobson Jr. (q.v.), and made a brief effort to continue her husband's business. She published with John Hyde (q.v.) in 1733, but early in 1734 sold her husband's stock at auction (*Pue's Occurrences*, 12 Jan.).

DODD (EGERTON), printer in Dublin, (1) King's Arms, Skinner Row (1681); (2) The Rose and Crown, Dame Street (1683). 1681–99. In 1681 he was listed as a journeyman to George Foster (q.v.), and again in 1683 to William Norman (q.v.). He was admitted free of the guild in 1684 and paid quarterage through 1699; the list in 1689 records "with K. James" (*Guild Records*).

DONNOGHUE (DENIS), printer in Cork, (1) near Dennis's Lane, Main Street (1772–?), (2) Broad Lane (1774?–76). 1772–76. In 1772 he printed a short-lived newspaper, the

Cork Gazette, various poems and primers, and in 1775 Leland's *History of Ireland*.

DORE (WILLIAM), papermaker in Ireland, 1773. Sole reference: in 1773, as a papermaker, he signed a petition to the Irish House of Commons objecting to the removal of duties on foreign paper (BL, 1890.e.5. (232)).

DOUGLAS or DOUGLASS (GEORGE), printer in Dublin, College Green (1770–71); and printer and publisher in Londonderry, in the Diamond (1772–96). 1770–96. The sole reference to Douglas in Dublin was an advertisement listing him, along with William Spotswood (q.v.) and Thomas Stewart (q.v.), as publishers of *Watson's Gentleman's and Citizen's Almanack* (*Dublin Chronicle*, 2 Jan. 1770). Perhaps Douglas was a journeyman to the other two partners. In Londonderry, Douglas founded the *Londonderry Journal and Donegal and Tyrone Advertiser* in 1772. A year later he joined in partnership with James Blyth (q.v.). When this partnership dissolved is not certain, but in 1795 Douglas advertised the journal for sale (*Dublin Evening Post*, 17 Oct.), and in 1796 he was "presented with three silver cups on his leaving for America" (Hempton, *Siege and History of Londonderry*).

DOWDAL (WILLIAM), bookseller in Dublin, (1) next door to the sign of London, Castle Street (1702–?); (2) Skinner Row (?–1716). 1702–16. He was in trade in 1702 but not admitted to the guild until 1703. In 1704 he served as Beadle and paid quarterage through 1716 (*Guild Records*). When he moved to Skinner Row is not certain, but in 1707 an advertisement for "the purging Elixir . . . to be had at . . . Mr. Dowdal's" gives that address (*Flying Post*, 30 Sept.).

DOWLING (BARNABY), bookseller in Dublin, 1740. Sole reference: he was mentioned in the subscribers' list as having taken six copies of Powell's 1740 printing of Whyte's *Poems on Various Subjects.*

DOWLING (LUKE), bookseller and publisher in Dublin, next door to the Wool Sack, High Street, 1679–1742? He was apprenticed to James Malone (q.v.), but was twice denied membership in the guild, "being a Romanist." Late in 1698 he was admitted as a quarter brother and paid quarterage through 1741 (*Guild Records*). His religion proved little handicap, for Dowling dominated the country trade for many years, advertising "all Country Chapmen and others may be furnished with most Sorts of Histories, School Books, Books of Piety and Devotions" (*Dublin Courant*, 3 Sept. 1720). He published several works and held frequent book auctions through the 1720s, becoming a man of considerable wealth and property. It is not known when he retired; his last business notice appeared in 1742, but he died in 1758 "in an advanced age" (*Pue's Occurrences*, 20 May).

DOWNES (BARTHOLOMEW), bookbinder in London (1617?–36), and Dublin (1617?–20?). 1617?–36. In 1617, as a representative of the London Company of Stationers, he was appointed by the privy council one of the King's Stationers in Ireland, along with Felix Kingston (q.v.) and Matthew Lownes (q.v.), and confirmed by patent in 1618 (*Lib. Munerum*, ii, 95). It is not certain whether he ever came to Dublin in person, although the original agreement suggested that he would (Gilbert, *History of Dublin*). His role as King's Stationer was possibly only titular, as his brother, Thomas Downes (q.v.), described Bartholomew "as only a workman employed in binding books and not using any other trade." He died in 1636.

DOWNES (THOMAS), bookseller in London (1609–58), and Dublin, St. Nicholas Street (1617?–38). 1609–58. As a member of the London Company of Stationers, he appears to have played a prominent role in organizing that body's Irish "stock." His brother, Bartholomew Downes (q.v.), was an earlier recipient of the King's Stationer in Ireland patent in 1618, but in 1620 a regrant of this was made to Thomas and Felix Kingston (q.v.). Whether Thomas ever came to Ireland in person is uncertain, but in 1620 there was a notice by "Thoms. Downes, of the Citie of Dublin, Stationer" (*Proclamations*, Council of the Society of Antiquaries). He ended his connection when the Irish privileges were purchased by William Bladen (q.v.).

DOYLE (JAMES), bookbinder in Cork, d. 1768. Sole reference: an obituary notice in 1768 read, "Died in Corke, Mr. James Doyle, bookbinder" (*Dublin Mercury*, 4 Oct.).

DROZ (REV. JEAN PIERRE), bookseller and publisher in Dublin, College Green, 1744–51. He was admitted free of the guild as a quarter brother in 1744 and paid quarterage through 1751 (*Guild Records*). As a bookseller he stocked primarily classics and continental publications. He published a quarterly, the *Literary Journal*, 1744–49, and his last known imprint was Clayton's *Essay on Spirit*, 1750. He also served as the minister to the French congregation of St. Patrick's. He died in 1751.

DUFF (JOHN), engraver in Dublin, (1) 13 Smock Alley (1770–76); (2) 44 Essex Street (1777–82); (3) 17 Exchange Street (1782–87). 1770–87. He was principally employed in periodical and book illustrations, contributing to Exshaw's *London Magazine*, as well as several bookplates in Campbell's *Philosophical Survey of the South of Ireland* and Ledwich's *Irishtown and Kilkenny*. He died in 1787.

DUGAN (**PATRICK**), bookseller and publisher in Dublin, Cork Hill, 1718–26. He was apprenticed to Matthew Gun (q.v.), was admitted free of the guild by service in 1718, and paid quarterage through 1726, although listed in 1724 as "left off business" (*Guild Records*). He published several notable works, including Defoe's *Robinson Crusoe*, 1719, Clarendon's *History of the Rebellion*, 1719, Shadwell's *Works*, 1720, and Keating's *History of Ireland*, 1723. However, his widow petitioned the guild to be admitted to the "Poor List" in 1764.

DUNBAR (**ROBERT**), printer in Dublin, 1758. Sole reference: he was listed as a printer when his will was proved in the Dublin Prerogative Court in 1758 (*Dictionary 1726–75*). The notation "printer" was possibly a mistake for "painter."

DUNN (**LARRY**), printer and publisher in Dublin, Dame Street, 1753–57. He was a member of a coterie of stationers— Peter Wilson (q.v.), John Exshaw (q.v.), Henry Saunders (q.v.), and Matthew Williamson (q.v.)—who introduced the periodical *Universal Advertiser* in 1753. Various members of the group dropped their association with the enterprise until Dunn himself quit in 1757, leaving Williamson the sole proprietor.

DUNTON (**JOHN**), bookseller in Dublin, 1698. He was a bookseller and publisher in London, 1674–1700? (*Dictionary 1668–1725*). He experimented in selling books by auction when he took a cargo of books to Boston, Massachusetts, in 1685. In 1698 he took a similar cargo to Dublin, where he held a series of auctions at various coffee-houses; the resulting competition with Irish stationers led to quarrels, notably with Patrick Campbell (q.v.). The latter events Dunton set forth in his *Dublin Scuffle*, 1699.

DUPIN (**NICHOLAS**), papermaker in Dublin, 1691–97? In 1690, in partnership with Henry Million (q.v.), he was granted a fourteen-year monopoly by letter patent for "makeing all sorts of writeing and printing paper" in Ireland, and the two men formed the Company of White Papermakers. They were previously associated in an English linen company. In 1691 Dupin brought to Ireland five Dutch journeymen papermakers and built a mill at Rathfarnham, County Dublin. Whether Million ever came to Ireland is uncertain; however, by 1694 he had dropped out of the partnership, and by 1697 the Company passed to Col. John Perry (q.v.).

DURNEENE (J.), printer in Dublin, (1) Pembroke Court (1728); (2) next door to Waly's head, St. Patrick Street (1729). 1728–29. He printed *Miss Gall's letter, to a certain c-o-l-l beau*, 1728, and *A new and mournful elegy*, 1729.

DYTON (TIMOTHY), bookseller, printer, and publisher in Dublin, (1) at Newton's Head, Dame Street, or later, 11 Dame Street (1760–?); (2) 21 Great Ship Street (?–1796). 1760–96. In 1761 he married Alice James (q.v.), the widow of Richard James (q.v.), and continued the latter's business. He was admitted free of the guild by special grace in 1761 and paid quarterage through 1788. He was an active guild member, serving as Warden in 1769, as Master in 1773, and on the Council from 1770 (*Guild Records*). He printed the *Dublin Gazette*, 1761–96, and it was during his proprietorship that the periodical became an official government publication, with the appointment of a "compiler" in 1776. Dyton published an occasional work like Shakespeare's *Merchant of Venice*, 1762, but his press output was largely limited to parliamentary work from 1772 to 1780. From 1757 to 1783 he served as Master to St. Patrick's Hospital in Dublin. He died "at his home near Stillorgan, County Dublin" in 1796.

E

EAGAR (GEORGE), papermaker in Ireland, 1692? In 1692, in partnership with Edmund Buckridge (q.v.) and William Sutton (q.v.), he obtained a King's letter granting an Irish monopoly of fourteen years for the making of "all sorts of coloured papers." There is no evidence that the three ever acted on their patent or even came to Ireland from England.

EATON (RICHARD), papermaker in Dublin. 1754–56. In 1754, in partnership with Robert Nixon (q.v.) and Joshua Kinnier (q.v.), he started a paper mill at Kilternan, County Dublin. They went under the name of Papermakers of Kilternan. In 1755 they petitioned Parliament for assistance in papermaking (*Commons' Journ. Ire.*, v, 237), and in 1756 Kinnier became the sole owner of the business; no more is heard of Eaton.

EDMUND (BRICE), bookseller and publisher in Dublin, at Addison's Head, Dame Street, 1753–56. He was admitted to the guild as a quarter brother in 1753 and paid quarterage through 1756. He took into partnership William Whitestone (q.v.) from 1753 to 1754 (*Guild Records*). In 1756 he published Shakespeare's *Richard III*.

EDWARDS (MARY), bookbinder, bookseller, and publisher in Cork, Castle Street, 1773–81. In 1773 she published Secker's *Five Sermons against Popery*, in 1779 she was listed as a stationer and paid by the Cork Corporation the large sum of £30 for unspecified services, and in 1781 they paid her "for binding two sets of acts" (Caulfield, *Cork Council Book*).

EDY (SAMUEL) *see* Samuel Ady

ELO (JOHN), stationer in Dublin, 1683–88. He was listed as a journeyman to Edward Powell (q.v.) in 1683, but Powell's name was scored out and William Norman's (q.v.) entered. In 1684 he was recorded as "In Engld," and from 1685 to 1688 again as a journeyman (*Guild Records*). Possibly he was the same as John Costello (q.v.), the surname being but another spelling variation. If so, Elo first served Edward Powell as a journeyman from 1680 to 1683, and remained active until 1689.

EMERSON (RICHARD), stationer in Dublin, 1680. In 1680 he was listed as a journeyman to Anthony Lawrence (q.v.), paid quarterage for one year, and in 1681 was listed as "dead" (*Guild Records*).

ENNIS (R.), printer in Dublin, Thomas Street, 1775 (*Dictionary 1726–75*).

ERVIN (GEORGE), bookseller in Dublin, 1718 (Thrift, *Freemen*).

ESDALL (ANNE), bookseller, printer, and publisher in Dublin, on the Blind Quay, at the corner of Copper Alley, Cork Hill, 1749–55. In 1749 she printed *Esdall's News Letter* while her husband James Esdall (q.v.) was a fugitive abroad. Upon the death of her husband in March 1755 she advertised her intention of continuing the family business for herself and "four helpless Children." She printed Gibson's *Experimental Philosophy* for Oliver Nelson (q.v.), but in June 1755 she advertised the sale of the printing stock and equipment (*Dublin Journal*, 7 June). In 1768 she petitioned the guild for relief, and again on the death of her son William (q.v.) in 1795, as being "aged 77" and "reduced to very distress'd circumstances" (*Guild Records*).

ESDALL (**JAMES**), bookseller, printer, and publisher in Dublin, (1) over against Smock Alley, Fishamble Street (1743–44); (2) on the Blind Quay, at the corner of Copper Alley, Cork Hill (1745–55). 1743–55. He was apprenticed to George Faulkner (q.v.), was admitted free of the guild by service in 1743, and paid quarterage through 1755 (*Guild Records*). In 1752 he published Fielding's *Amelia*, and in 1754 Budgell's *Memoirs of the . . . Family of the Boyles*. In 1744 he started two newspapers, the *Flying Post* and the *General News Letter* (later *Esdall's News Letter*), the latter continuing to 1755. In 1749 he printed Charles Lucas' *Censor, or Citizen's Journal*, one issue of which led to his being ordered to the bar of the House of Commons for "scandalous, factious, and seditious Libels" (*Commons' Journ. Ireland*, v, 12–13). Esdall fled to London and remained out of Ireland for over a year. He died in 1755.

ESDALL (**WILLIAM**), engraver in Dublin, (1) 11 Mary Lane (1771–77?); (2) Temple Bar Court (?); (3) 3 Gordon's Lane, Ranelagh (1794–95). 1772–95. He was the son of James and Anne Esdall (qq.v.), was apprenticed to Henry Saunders (q.v.), was admitted free of the guild by birth in 1777, and paid quarterage through 1792 (*Guild Records*). He produced many bookplates, notably in Goldsmith's *The beauties of Goldsmith*, 1783, and Preston's *Poetical Works*, 1783. His work also appeared in Exshaw's *London Magazine* and in the *Hibernian Magazine* between 1774 and 1794. He died in 1795 (see Anne Esdall).

EWING (**ALEXANDER**), bookseller, printer, and publisher in Dublin, the Angel and Bible, Dame Street, opposite the Castle Market, 1744–65. He was the son of George Ewing (q.v.), and was taken into partnership by his father in 1744 (*Dublin Courant*, 16 June). He was never a registered apprentice nor sworn free of the guild, and he was recorded as a "foreigner" in 1763 and fined for not "riding the franchise"; other than this, his irregular association with the stationer's trade was never questioned (*Guild Records*). He shared with his father a broad range of printing and publishing, by themselves and, on occasion, with various other stationers. He did much printing for the Irish House of Commons from 1754 to 1758 (*Commons' Journ. Ire.*, vi, app. pp. xxiii, xxv, and clxxxii). Following his father's death, Alexander continued the family business until his own death a year later. His will was proved in 1765 in the Prerogative Court at Dublin.

EWING (GEORGE), bookseller, printer, and publisher in Dublin, at the Angel and Bible, Dame Street, opposite the Castle Market, 1719–64. He was apprenticed to his future brother-in-law George Grierson (q.v.), was admitted free of the guild by service in 1719, and paid quarterage through 1763. He was an active guild member, serving as Warden in 1728, Master in 1733, and on the Council from 1728 (*Guild Records*). He participated in many loose partnerships and cooperative printing and publishing ventures, most notably a highly-developed working arrangement with George Risk (q.v.) and William Smith (q.v.) from 1726 through 1756, and with his son Alexander (q.v.), whom he took into partnership in 1744. His first publication was *Country House, a Farce*, 1719, and from that date he took on a broad variety of projects from serial publication and almanacs to Greek and Latin classics. He was accused of pirating Pope's edition of Shakespeare's *Works* in 1725, and in 1742 he became involved in a factional dispute among Dublin stationers over rival translations of Prévost d'Exiles' *Dean of Coleraine* (see Thomas Bacon). Among his many publications are Fielding's *The Miser*, 1733, and Richardson's *Pamela*, 1741; Rapin's *History of England*, 1725, Moryson's *History of Ireland*, 1735, and Robertson's *History of Scotland*, 1759; Burnet's *History of his Own Time*, 1734, and King's *State of the Protestants*, 1744; and the *Works* of Jonson, 1729, Ware, 1739, Shakespeare, 1747, and Swift, 1758. He also published the *Dublin Almanack* from 1728 to 1738, and in 1737, with his partners Risk and Smith, was instrumental in revitalizing Richard Reilly's (q.v.) floundering *Weekly Oracle* and making it into the successful *Dublin News-Letter* (Munter, *Irish Newspapers*). He died in 1764, "an eminent Bookseller who lived to an advanced Age, with great Credid [sic] and Reputation" (*Freeman's Journal*, 17 Apr.).

EWING (**Thomas**), bookseller, printer, and publisher in Dublin, (1) the Angel and Bible, Dame Street (1766–68); (2) Capel Street (1769–75). 1766–75. He was the son of Rev. George Ewing, was apprenticed to his grandfather George Ewing (q.v.), was allowed as a quarter brother in 1766, was admitted free of the guild by service in 1767, and paid quarterage through 1774 (*Guild Records*). He took over the family business following the death of his uncle Alexander Ewing (q.v.). He printed very little, except for various pamphlets of Charles Lucas, Ewing being active in pro-Lucas political affairs through the 1760s. He published many books, including Smollett's *Humphrey Clinker*, 1771, the collected *Works* of Shakespeare, 1771, "delightfully printed and engraved," Goldsmith's *Life of Dr. Parnell*, 1773, Homer's *Iliad*, 1770, a fourth edition of Johnson's *Dictionary*, 1775, and various Greek and Latin classics. He died in 1776, and his will was proved in the Prerogative Court at Dublin.

EXSHAW (**Mrs. E.**), bookseller in Galway, 1647–48. She is among the provincial booksellers listed as agents for the *London Magazine* for Jan. 1646/47 and Jan. 1647/48.

EXSHAW (EDWARD), bookseller and publisher in Dublin, (1) the Bible, on the Blind Quay, near Cork Hill (1733–37); (2) the Bible, on Cork Hill, over against the old Exchange, or, the Bible, one door above Copper Alley, near Cork Hill (1737–48). 1733–48. He was apprenticed to George Ewing (q.v.), was admitted free of the guild by service in 1733, paid quarterage through 1747, and served as Warden in 1747 (*Guild Records*). He published religious tracts, cook books, and newspapers, and sold "Dr. Anderson's Pills, Dr. Stroughton's Drops, Bateman's Drops and British Oil" (*Dublin Courant*, 3–6 Dec. 1748). With Samuel Powell (q.v.) he reprinted the *Weekly Miscellany*, 1734–35, with Alice Reilly (q.v.) he published the *Dublin News-Letter*, 1741–43, and he started the *English Registry* in 1749. Among his other publications are Exquemelin's *Bucaniers of America*, 1740, Hoyle's *Short Treatise on the Game of Whist*, 1743, Tillotson's *Sermons*, 1740, and Shakespeare's *Works*, 1747. In 1748 he took his son John (q.v.) into partnership and within the year died, his will being proved in the Prerogative Court at Dublin.

EXSHAW (JOHN), bookseller, printer, and publisher in Dublin, the Bible on Cork Hill. 1748–76. He was apprenticed to his father, Edward Exshaw (q.v.), was admitted free of the guild by service in 1749, and paid quarterage through 1776. He was an active guild member, serving as Warden in 1758, as Master in 1766, and on the Council from 1767 (*Guild Records*). He was taken into partnership by his father in 1748, and upon the latter's death continued the family business with his stepmother, Sarah Exshaw (q.v.), until 1753, and then by himself. He published the *London Registry, Exshaw's Magazine*, which included music printing, and, with a coterie of stationers, the *Universal Advertiser*, an anti-government paper (Munter, *Irish Newspapers*). Also, with various combinations of stationers, he printed and published the *Works* of Horace, 1764, and of

Shakespeare, 1766. In 1753 he was party to a long dispute over Richardson's *Sir Charles Grandison*. Through knavery, Exshaw, with Peter Wilson (q.v.) and Henry Saunders (q.v.), obtained sheets of the London edition as they were printed and brought out their own pirated printing, effectively ending an arrangement of George Faulkner (q.v.) with Richardson for the Irish edition. Through the 1760s, Exshaw was one of the leaders in the masters' struggle against journeymen combinations. He died in 1777, his will being proved in the Prerogative Court at Dublin.

EXSHAW (SARAH), bookseller and publisher in Dublin, the Bible, on Cork Hill. 1748–53. She was the second wife of Edward Exshaw (q.v.) (*St. Werburgh Par. Reg.*, Dublin), and the stepmother of John Exshaw (q.v.). On the death of her husband, she became the business partner of her stepson. They jointly published the *London Magazine* and the *English Registry* from 1748 to 1753; then Sarah left the stationer's trade and set up a lace shop: "The Widow Exshaw, at the Lace Hood in Golden-lane, being just arrived from Flanders & hath imported . . . Point and Brussels Lappets, Brussels and Point Ruffles for Gentlemen" (*Dublin Journal*, 13 Oct. 1753).

EYRES (MATHEW), printer in Cork (1752 and 1771?); journeyman in Limerick (1760s). 1752–71? In Cork in 1752 he printed *Oratour Displayed or Calumny Refuted*. He is referred to as the principal journeyman of John Ferrar (q.v.) in Limerick, and as having deserted him in 1771 to return to Cork (Herbert, *Limerick Printers and Printing*). An obituary notice in 1798 read: "Died Last-night in Fishamble-lane, Mr. Mathew Eyres, Printer" (*New Cork Evening Post*, 19 Dec.).

F

FABRI or FABRIJ (JACQUES), bookseller in Dublin, Dame Street, 1699–1714. He was admitted to the guild as a quarter brother in 1699, was summoned in 1700 as an intruder, paid quarterage through 1714, and was not listed in 1715 (*Guild Records*). Possibly a French refugee, he specialized in French publications (Gilbert, *History of Dublin*).

FACKMAN (WILLIAM), printer in Cork, 1766. Sole reference: in 1766 he was paid "£1-4*s*-2*d* . . . for printing work done" for the City Corporation (Caulfield, *Cork Council Book*).

FAIRBROTHER (SAMUEL), bookbinder, bookseller, printer, and publisher in Dublin, the King's Arms, Skinner Row, over against the Thosel, 1713–53. He served an irregular apprenticeship to Joseph, John, and Elizabeth Ray (qq.v.), was admitted free of the guild in 1713, and paid quarterage through 1752. He served as Warden in 1725, was elected Master in 1727 but refused to serve, and served on the Council from 1722 (*Guild Records*). When Elizabeth Ray died in 1713 she willed her "printing presses, and all the Materialls thereunto belonging," along with £2 for mourning, to Fairbrother, and thus began his long and profitable career. He became printer to the city in 1716, to the Irish House of Commons from 1719 to 1749, binding the Journals for that body, and King's Stationer from 1723 to 1749 (see Nicholas King). From 1715 through 1737 he printed the *Vote of the House of Commons*, in 1721 he printed the first Irish edition of Swift's writings, *Miscellanies in Prose and Verse*, undoubtedly pirated, and with various stationers such things as *Geographical Itineraria . . . of the Travellers*

. . . *into Asia, Africa and America,* 1722, Vernon's *Chancery Cases,* 1726, and Ware's *Works,* 1739. In 1731 he was appointed to a guild committee on printing piracy; three years later he aroused the wrath of Sheridan by pirating various George Faulkner (q.v.) editions of Swift's and Sheridan's writings. In their correspondence, Sheridan proposed a satire on "Foulbrother," to which Swift replied, "I like your project, [Fairbrother] is an arrant rascal in every circumstance" (Ball, *Correspondence of Jonathan Swift*). A contemporary poem addressed to Faulkner concluded:

> The Dean's so great a Man of Taste,
> All covet to Read him in haste;
> More from thy Press, than any other:
> Let what will happen to Fairbrother

(*Dublin Journal,* 4 Feb. 1734/35). Fairbrother retired in 1753, and his stock in trade was sold by auction (*Dublin Journal,* 12 May). He died in 1758, "aged 74" (*Magazine of Magazines,* Mar.).

FALLAN (EDWARD), printer in Ireland, 1739? Sole reference: in 1739 a public notice read, "Fugitive for debt and beyond the seas surrendered to keeper of Naas Gaol to take benefit of act for relief of insolvent debtors, Edward Fallan, last of Leixlip, Printer" (*Dublin Gazette,* 8 Dec.).

FARQUHAR (PEYTON), bookseller and printer in Dublin, Castle Street, 1701?–29? He was the brother of the celebrated dramatist George Farquhar. Peyton was apprenticed to Jacob Milner (q.v.); the date of the indentures is not certain, but Milner died in 1701. In 1704 Farquhar is referred to as a bookseller (Gilbert, *History of Dublin*), and in 1704 he printed and published the *Stage Coach,* the first Irish edition of George Farquhar's play. In 1718 he was summoned by the guild as an intruder, paid quarterage in 1719 and 1720, was admitted free of the guild in 1722, and again paid quarterage through 1729 (*Guild Records*). He died in 1760, remembered as an "eminent maker of London Ink Powder for 50 years" (*Dublin Journal*, 23 May).

FARRIER or FERRAR (WILLIAM), bookbinder and bookseller in Limerick, 1729–54. He was an active bookseller, subscribing to many Dublin publications, including Jonson's *Works*, 1729, King's *State of the Protestants*, 1730, Ware's *Works*, 1739, Faulkner's 20-volume edition of Sale's *Universal History*, 1744, and Exshaw's *London Magazine*, 1747 and 1748. He was always referred to as Farrier in the subscribers' lists until 1748, from which date he was listed as Ferrar (*Dublin Journal*, 2 Jan.).

FAULKNER (GEORGE), bookseller, printer, and publisher in Dublin, (1) Pembroke Court, Castle Street (1724–26); (2) Christ Church Yard (1726–28); (3) the Pamphlet Shop, opposite the Thosel, Skinner Row (1729–30); (4) Essex Street, opposite the Bridge, or, the Blind Quay, at the corner of Parliament Street, opposite the Bridge (1730–65); (5) 15 Parliament Street (1765–75). 1724–75. He was apprenticed to Thomas Hume (q.v.), possibly served as a journeyman to William Boyer, printer in London (Nichols, *Literary Anecdotes of the Eighteenth Century*), began trade in Dublin in 1724, was admitted free of the guild in 1728, and paid quarterage through 1774. He served as Warden in 1764 and stood for Master three times and for the Council twice but on all occasions failed to gain majority support (*Guild Records*). He began his career as a pamphlet printer of dubious virtue and practice, but was to become the dominant Irish stationer of the eighteenth century, respected for his public and patriotic spirit, and, although a Protestant, he publically condemned the repression of Ireland's

Catholics. Among his early pamphlets was a collection of Swift's controversial *Drapier's Letters*, which, along with other materials relating to the Wood's half-penny affair, Faulkner published under the title *Fraud Detected: Or, The Hibernian Patriot*, 1725. He entered the fledgling field of newspaper production with the *Dublin Post-Boy* and the *Dublin Journal* in 1725, but neither proved successful until Faulkner took into partnership James Hoey (q.v.) from 1727 to 1730. It was Hoey's organizational abilities that launched the success of these papers and of the partnership in general. In 1730, following the dissolution of his partnership with Hoey, Faulkner became Swift's printer, the prescient forecast being:

> Poor, honest, George, Swift's Works to Print!
> Thy Fortune's made, or Nothing's in't.
> Subscribers, a vast Number shew
> There is no want of Money now

(*Dublin Journal*, 4 Feb. 1734/35). From 1735 he continually published Swift's *Works*, and added to this success with numerous other projects, notably Sale's *Universal History*, a 20-volume edition, 1744–45, and, with a coterie of stationers, the *Works* of Shakespeare, 1747. Faulkner had his problems with government prosecution and with controversies within the trade. In 1731 he was ordered before the bar on account of a newspaper article, absconded, but was taken into custody the following session and severely reprimanded (*Lords' Journ. Ire.*, iii, 192–93, 230, 233–34), and in 1736 he was committed to Newgate over a pamphlet allegedly reflecting adversely on a member of Parliament, but was released within six days upon paying his fine and giving each legal officer a copy of Swift's *Works* (*Commons' Journ. Ire.*, iv, 211–14). In 1741, when Thomas Bacon (q.v.) attempted to enter the printer's trade with the publication, by agreement with Richardson, of an Irish edition of *Pamela*, Faulkner got hold of the text and brought out a pirated copy, the beginning of the end of Bacon's career. In 1753 Richardson granted Faulkner the Irish rights to *Sir Charles Grandison*, and a major dispute developed. John Exshaw (q.v.), Henry Saunders (q.v.), and Peter Wilson (q.v.) obtained sheets of the London edition, proceeded to bring out a pirated version, and Faulkner, after trying to arrange a settlement between these three and Richardson, withdrew altogether from the undertaking. Richardson refused to exonerate Faulkner, and presented his accusations of collusion in an addendum to his own London publication (*Sir Charles Grandison*, 1754). Faulkner weathered his many troubles to become the most successful of Dublin stationers, publishing broadly—for example, Virgil's *Works*, 1755, and Chesterfield's *Letters*, 1774. He was elected Sheriff of Dublin in 1767 but declined to serve, and set a precedent by paying 100 guineas in lieu of the normal £10 fine for such refusal. In 1770 he was named an Alderman of Dublin, and in the same year proclaimed "Sir George, the Prince of Printers, the Emperour of Grub" (*Freeman's Journal*, 23 Nov.). In 1775 he took his third wife, and later in the year died, aged 76, "remarkable for having been the favourite printer of Dean Swift, and the printer of the Dublin Journal; and for several oddities, all innocent and some of them, the most beneficial natured" (*Dodsley's Annual Register*).

FERRAL (**CHARLES**), printer in Dublin, 1726–27. He was apprenticed to Richard Dickson (q.v.), but repeatedly broke his indentures, first in 1726 (*Dublin Post-Man*, 21 Mar.), and finally having "run away for the fourth time" in 1727 (*Dublin Intelligence*, 28 Feb.). He apparently went to work for Cornelius Carter (q.v.), for in 1727 he and Carter "were taken into Custody and Committed to Newgate for publishing a most Scandalous Paper," a forgery of Thomas Walsh's (q.v.) *Castle Courant* (*Dublin Intelligence*, 28 Mar.). No more is heard of Ferral, but Carter soon returned to business.

FERRAR (JOHN), bookseller, printer, and publisher in Limerick, (1) near the Exchange (1765?–67); (2) the New Printing House, Quay Lane (1769–85). 1765?–85. He was the son of William Farrier (q.v.). He authored and published *Poems on several Subjects*, 1765, and first printed in 1767 his own *History of the City of Limerick*. From that date he printed and published numerous works, including a newspaper, the *Limerick Chronicle*, 1768–81, the *Limerick Directory*, 1769, and a second edition of Hayes' *Works*, 1785. He was printer to the City of Limerick in 1778 and 1779. In 1785 he sold his printing business, but continued work as an insurance agent in Cork at Sir Harry's Mall, about 1802 moving to Dublin where he died (Herbert, *Limerick Printers and Printing*).

FERRAR (WILLIAM) *see* William Farrier

FERRARA (ANDREW), printer in Dublin, the sign of Sancho's Head, Bribery Lane, 1772. Sole reference: his imprint was on a pamphlet, *An Epistle . . . to Alderman George Faulkner*, 1772.

FINN (EDMOND), bookseller, printer, and publisher in Cork (1766), and Kilkenny, (1) St. Mary's Churchyard (1767); (2) High Street (1767–77). 1766–77. He was the brother-in-law of Michael Butler (q.v.). He first printed in Cork, a *New Collection of Latin Words*, 1766, and then moved to Kilkenny where he started *Finn's Leinster Journal*, later simply the *Leinster Journal*, 1767. He continued this until his death in 1777, and then his wife and widow, Catherine, carried on the business and newspaper until 1780.

FISHER (JOHN), bookseller in Dublin, (1) the Old Exchange, Cork Hill (1760–63?); (2) Little Ship Street (1763?–74?). 1760–77. He was admitted free of the guild in 1760, paid quarterage through 1774, and was listed as in arrears in 1777 (*Guild Records*).

FISHER (**JONATHAN**), engraver in Dublin, 1775–95? In 1775 he received disbursements from the Commons in connection with the Stamp Act for engraving and for repairing dies, and was listed as "Supervisor of Stampers and printers" (*Commons' Journ. Ire.*, ix, app. pp. ccclxxiii–ccclxxv). In his will, William Esdall (q.v.) left "Two pair of new, and two pair of old, plates for Jonathan Fisher."

FITZGERALD (**CATHERINE**) *see* Catherine Hicks

FITZGERALD (**RICHARD**), printer and publisher in Dublin, (1) Channel Row (1709–20); (2) the Rein Deer, Montrath Street (1721–22). 1709–22. A Catholic, he printed and published various eulogies, speeches, and ballads, particularly for the street hawkers. In 1722 he was "bound over to appear at the Quarter-Sessions of the City the 3d of next Month, for Printing and Selling a Seditious Ballad for which 2 Men for Singing them with Roguish Additions are now in Newgate" (*Whalley's News-Letter*, 14 Mar.). He died in 1722 (*Whalley's News-Letter*, 24 Sept.).

FITZPATRICK (**GODFREY**), bookbinder in Dublin, 1756. Sole reference: in 1756 he was admitted to the guild by petition as a quarter brother (*Guild Records*).

FITZPATRICK (**PATRICK**), engraver in Dublin, (1) Skinner Row (1760–66); (2) upper Blind Quay (1767–?); (3) Fownes Street (?–1788). 1760–88. In 1760 he was awarded a prize by the Dublin Society for "landscapes from copper plates," and again in 1763 for a print. He advertised "Crests for Booksellers" and "cuts for books" (Strickland, *Irish Artists*).

FITZSIMONS (**JAMES**), bookseller in Dublin, 1717–24. He was admitted to the guild as a quarter brother in 1717 and paid quarterage through 1724 (*Guild Records*).

FITZSIMONS (**JAMES**), bookseller and publisher in Dublin, Chapel Alley, Bridge Street, 1772. A Catholic, he published, in partnership with Richard Cross (q.v.), O'Conor's *Essay on the Rosary*, 1772.

FITZSIMONS (**RICHARD**), bookseller in Dublin, High Street, 1750–82. A Catholic, he was fined for intrusion in 1751, admitted as a quarter brother in 1752, and paid quarterage through 1771 (*Guild Records*). In 1773 he signed a petition to the Irish House of Commons objecting to the removal of duties on foreign paper (BL, 1890.e.5. (239)). In 1782 an advertisement announced that "Anthony Fox . . . has purchased the concerns &c. of Mr. Richard Fitzsimons who has retired from business" (*Hibernian Chronicle*, 23 May).

FLEAKE (**JOHN**) *see* John Afleck

FLEASON or FLEESON (**THOMAS**), bookseller in Dublin, 1698–1723. He was apprenticed to Jacob Milner (q.v.), was admitted free of the guild by service in 1698, and paid quarterage through 1723. He was an active member of the guild, serving on the Council from 1712, as Warden in 1712, and as Master in 1716. In 1724 he was listed as "Does not follow business" (*Guild Records*). He died intestate in 1730 (*Dublin Grant Book*).

FLECK (**JOHN**) *see* John Afleck

FLEETWOOD (**CHARLES**), engraver in Dublin, fl. 1764. He was apprenticed to Michael Ford (q.v.); in 1758 and again in 1764 he was awarded a premium by the Dublin Society for "new designs engraved on copper" (Strickland, *Irish Artists*).

FLEMING or FLEMYNGE (JOHN), bookseller and publisher in Dublin, the Angel and Bible, High Street, 1740–50? A Catholic, he was apprenticed to Luke Dillon (q.v.), admitted to the guild as a quarter brother in 1740, and paid quarterage through 1750 (*Guild Records*). He was a grandson of John Fleming, a Drogheda merchant, and the second cousin of John Fleming (q.v.), a Drogheda printer. In 1740 he "opened a shop . . . next door to where Mr. Dillon lived, having sorted himself out of Mr. Dillon's stock" (*Dublin News-Letter*, 18 Oct.). His main trade was with country merchants and dealers in histories and religious books. From 1740 to 1745 he joined with Thomas Browne (q.v.) in publishing Butler's *Almanack*.

FLEMING (JOHN), bookbinder in Dublin, 1754–65. In 1754 he "demanded" his freedom, was admitted to the guild as a free brother, and paid quarterage through 1765. He was fined for not "riding the franchise" in 1761, and in the same year an apprentice was enrolled to him (*Guild Records*). Possibly he was a son of John Fleming (q.v.) of the Angel and Bible address.

FLEMING (JOHN), bookseller and publisher in Dublin, Sycamore Alley (1764–68?); and in Drogheda (1769–83?). 1764–83? He was admitted free of the guild in 1764, paid quarterage through 1769, was listed as "lives in Drogheda" in 1769, '70, and '71, as "in Country" in 1775, and as in arrears of fees in 1783 (*Guild Records*). He probably was related to, and, while in Dublin, in partnership with, William Fleming (q.v.) of the same business years and address. On the death of the editor Walter Harris, Fleming and Robert Bell (q.v.) acquired from the executors the remaining sheets of Harris' (q.v.) edition of

Ware's *Works*. The two partners reprinted the preface, issued a new title-page dated 1764, and published it as their own edition. Bell's business failed, possibly the result of such practices, and within a year Fleming also quit his Dublin trade. Whether or not he moved to Drogheda, worked as a journeyman, or actually set up business in that town is uncertain. Quite likely the guild records reflect confusion over the two John Flemings, the Dublin stationer who left in 1768 or so and John Fleming the Drogheda bookseller (q.v.), who had just completed his apprenticeship and entered business.

FLEMING (JOHN), bookseller, printer, and publisher in Drogheda, West Street, 1770–85. He was apprenticed to George Faulkner (q.v.), admitted free of the guild by service in 1770, and was recorded as in arrears of fees in 1777 and 1779 (*Guild Records*). He was the grandson of John Fleming, a Drogheda merchant, and second cousin to John Fleming (q.v.), a bookseller at the Angel and Bible, Dublin. He was the first printer in Drogheda whose name is known. He printed *Letter of Sir Henry Tichborne to his Lady of the Siege of Drogheda*, 1772, and a play, Garrick's *Irish Widow*, 1773. The *Drogheda Journal* was possibly started by him in 1775 or earlier, but by 1781 this paper was being printed by Charles Evans. He died in 1785 (Bentham, *Abstracts*).

FLEMING (THOMAS), bookseller and engraver in Dublin, the Salmon, High Street, 1725–70? An advertisement in 1725 announced "Thomas Fleming, Copper-Plate Printer and Graver from London, does Shop-keepers Advertisements or Sign-plates, Tobacco Prints, marks for Wiggs and Gloves, Bills of parcels, and all other Printing and Engraving on Copper at London Prices" (*St. James's Evening Post*, Oct.). He was a Catholic whose shop dealt mainly in prints and engravings (Gilbert, *History of Dublin*).

FLEMING (**WILLIAM**), bookbinder in Dublin, Sycamore Alley, 1764–68? He was admitted to the guild as a free brother in 1764, paid quarterage through 1768, was listed as "abroad" in 1769, and as "in England" in 1770 and 1771 (*Guild Records*). He probably was related to, and in partnership with, John Fleming (q.v.), of the same business address and years. When John Fleming's and Robert Bell's (q.v.) business ventures fell on bad times, William appears to have quit Dublin.

FLEMYNGE (**JOHN**) *see* John Fleming

FLETCHER (**JOHN**), printer in Dublin, 1753?–58? He printed James Byrn's (q.v.) *Dublin Spy*, from 1753 to 1754, one of two rival editions of that title. In 1758 he was one of the subscribers to Byrn's edition of *Historical Collections out of several Protestant Historians.*

FLIN or FLINN (**LAURENCE LARKIN**), bookbinder and bookseller in Dublin, the Bible, Temple Court, Castle Street, 1771–87. He was the son of Thomas and Elizabeth Larkin, and the nephew of Lawrence Flin (q.v.)—his mother's brother (Bentham, *Abstracts*). He was apprenticed to Lawrence Flin, was admitted free of the guild by service in 1771, and paid quarterage through 1797. He served on the Council from 1776 and as Warden in 1781 (*Guild Records*). He took over his uncle's business upon the latter's death in 1771 and assumed the surname Flin at that time.

FLIN, FLINN, FLYN, or FLYNN (**LAWRENCE**), bookbinder, bookseller, and publisher in Dublin, (1) Winetavern Street, opposite Cork Street (1754–57); (2) the Bible, Temple Court, Castle Street (1758–71). 1754–71. He was apprenticed to George Goulding (q.v.), was admitted to the guild as a free brother in 1754, and paid quarterage through 1770. He was an active guild member, serving as Warden in 1770 and on the Council from 1770 (*Guild Records*). With James Esdall (q.v.) and John Torbuck (q.v.), he printed and published Budgell's *Memoirs of the . . . Family of the Boyles*, 1754, and, alone, brought out a second edition in 1755. In 1759 he published an edition of the New Testament in Irish (roman letter) for use in Scotland, *A Pocket Plan of the City and Suburbs of Dublin*, 1765, and Harris' *History of Dublin*, 1766. From 1758 he held auctions "at the Golden Ball, the North Side of College Green opposite the statue of King William." He died in 1771, "an eminent Bookseller, of unblemished Character" (*Freeman's Journal*, 12 Oct.).

FLYN or FLYNN (WILLIAM), bookseller, printer, and publisher in Cork, the Shakespeare, near the Exchange, 1767–1801. He was the nephew of Lawrence Flyn (q.v.) (Bentham, *Abstracts*). He was very active and productive in the trade. From 1768 to 1801 he printed and published the *Hibernian Chronicle*, and two editions of collected essays from that paper as the *Modern Monitor, or Flyn's Speculations*, 1771, 1774. He also did much printing for the Cork Council between 1770 and 1798 (Caulfield, *Cork Council Book*).

FORBES (SAMUEL), printer in Dublin, the Lord Mountjoy, Crane Lane, 1744–80? In 1744 he appears as a partner with Augustus Long (q.v.) in publishing the *Dublin Gazette* (Munter, *Handlist*). In 1767 he was admitted free of the guild and paid quarterage through 1780. He was listed as "dead" in the 1781 Clerk's list (*Guild Records*). There is no other notice of Forbes.

FORD (MICHAEL), engraver and publisher in Dublin, (1) Ann Street, near Dawson Street (1745–46); (2) Vandyke's Head, at the corner of the Blind Quay, Cork Hill (1746–63).

1745–63. A portrait painter, print maker, and publisher, he first published the prints of others, such as Andrew Miller's (q.v.) Duke of Cumberland, 1745, and Cromwell and Lambert, 1746. In 1746 he took over the business of John Brooks (q.v.), and changed the name of the shop from Sir Isaac Newton's Head to Vandyke's (Gilbert, *History of Dublin*). He published his own prints after 1748, including Hugh Boulter, 1747, Henry Boyle, 1748, and Countess of Coventry, 1752. He died intestate in 1765.

FORREST (**WILLIAM**), printer in Dublin, Hoey's Alley, 1727–28. He printed *Apollo's advice to all freeholders*, 1727, and Fontenelle's *Conversation with a Lady on the Plurality of Worlds*, which he printed for the partnership of George Risk (q.v.), George Ewing (q.v.), and William Smith (q.v.).

FORSTER or FOSTER (**GEORGE**), bookseller and publisher in Dublin, 1672–82. He was admitted to the guild as a free brother in 1672, served as Warden in 1678, on the Council from 1679, and was listed as "defunct" in 1682 (*Guild Records*). In 1681 he published William Lilly's *Strange and Wonderful Prognostications, being a relation of many universal accidents that will come to pass in this year.*

FORSTER or FOSTER (**HENRY**), printer in Dublin, the King's Arms, Skinner Row, 1683–88. He was listed as a journeyman to John Forster (q.v.) from 1683 to 1688 (*Guild Records*).

FORSTER or FOSTER (**JOHN**), bookseller and publisher in Dublin, the King's Arms, Skinner Row, 1677–1706. He was listed as a journeyman to George Forster (q.v.) in 1677, as a free brother of the guild in 1678, and served as Beadle in 1679,

Warden in 1688 and 1693, as Master in 1694, and on the Council from 1683. In 1706 he was marked as "dead" (*Guild Records*). He published the *Life and Death of . . . Redmond O'Hanlyn*, 1682, *Adminiculum puerile, or a Help to School-boys*, 1694, and in 1704 and 1705 a sermon and a tract by E. Synge.

FRANCE (RICHARD), printer in Dublin, 1764. In 1764 his will was proved in the Diocesan Court at Dublin (*Dictionary 1726–75*).

FRANCTON or FRANKE (JOHN), bookbinder, book-seller, printer, and publisher in Dublin, (1) in Mr. William Ussher's House, at the foot of the Bridge (1600–?); (2) St. Patrick Street (1603); (3) Castle Street (?–1619). 1600–19. Some believe that he arrived in Dublin as early as 1592, and possibly served and then succeeded William Kearney (q.v.); however, Francton's first known imprint was in 1600. In 1604 he received a patent as the first King's Printer in Ireland, which allowed him a monopoly to "imprint, bynde, setforth, offer to sale, or sell . . . within this Kingdome of Ireland, any bookes, volumes, Statutes, proclamations, Almanackes, or other bookes" (*Lib. Munerum*, ii, 95). In 1608 he was made free of the city, and in 1612 was elected Sheriff (*Cal. Anc. Rec. Dublin*). In addition to a great deal of official work—proclamations, acts, etc.— he printed the New Testament, 1602, and the *Book of Common Prayer*, 1608, both in Irish, Farmer's *Prognosticall Almanacke*, 1612, and his last imprint was Dermod O'Meara's *Pathologia haereditaria generalis*, 1619. By 1617 a covetous London Company of Stationers was pressuring to take over the Irish trade, and Francton was growing older; thus the Privy Council in England urged the Lord Deputy of Ireland "to deal with him there for the Surrender of his Patent" (BL, Sloan MS 4756, fol. 153). Francton thus sold his patent rights to three representatives of the London guild, Felix Kingston (q.v.), Matthew Lownes (q.v.), and Bartholomew Downs (q.v.), in 1618 (Munter, *Irish Newspapers*). He died in 1620.

FRANKE (JOHN) *see* John Francton

FRANKLIN (JOHN), bookseller in Dublin, High Street, 1681–83. He was admitted free of the guild in 1681, was recorded as a journeyman to William Weston (q.v.) in that year, paid quarterage through 1683, and was listed in 1684 and after as "In Engd" (*Guild Records*). In 1700 there was a will for a John Franklin, yeoman (*Dublin Grant Book*).

FULLER (MARY), bookseller and printer in Dublin, the Globe and Scales, Meath Street, 1736–37. A Quaker, she was the widow and succesor of Samuel Fuller (q.v.). She died in 1737, and her will was proved in the Prerogative Court at Dublin.

FULLER (SAMUEL), bookseller, printer, and publisher in Dublin, the Globe and Scales, Meath Street, 1719–36. He was a part-time Quaker schoolmaster whose chief publications were schoolbooks and religious tracts. In 1719 he advertised the publication of a *Book of Sermons* (*Dublin Intelligence*, 2 May), and in 1728 he wrote and published a controversial Quaker polemic, *A Serious Reply to . . . Joseph Boyse . . . Preacher among the Presbyterians*. He also published Tacquet's *Euclid*, 1728, Butler's *Almanack*, 1731, and Fuller's *Mathematical Miscellany*, 1735, the last possibly of his own authorship. He died in 1736, and his will was proved in the Prerogative Court at Dublin.

FYNLA (Abraham), bookseller in Cavan, 1710. Sole reference: advertisements in 1710 listed him as one of the provincial booksellers taking subscriptions to a Dublin edition of the *Tryal of Doctor Henry Sacheverell* (*Dublin Intelligence*, 24 June and 1 July).

G

GARDINER (**Edward**), bookseller in Dublin, 1735–70. He was apprenticed to William Smith (q.v.), was admitted free of the guild in 1735, and paid quarterage through 1744. He was entered as a journeyman in 1770, and from 1771 to 1777 was described in the poor list as a "decayed brother" (*Guild Records*).

GARDINER (**Henry**), bookseller in Dublin, 1750s. He was apprenticed to George Goulding (q.v.), but apparently did not complete his apprenticeship. He was listed as a shopkeeper to Peter Wilson (q.v.) in 1758, and died in 1759 (*Guild Records*).

GARDINER (**Robert**), bookseller and printer in Belfast, 1713–34. His known imprints include the *Psalms of David*, 1713, the *Whig's Vindication*, 1715, a controversial tract, *Personal Persuasion no Foundation for Religious Obedience*, 1720, and two more religious pamphlets in 1729.

GARLAND (**Halhed**), printer and publisher in Dublin, (1) opposite the Custom House Gate, Essex Street (1744–47); (2) at (or under) Walsh's Coffee House, Essex Street (1748–49?); and in London (1752?–64). 1744–64. He served his apprenticeship to Samuel Richardson in London, having been apprenticed in 1730, and later he took out his freedom with the London Stationer's guild in 1752 (Sale, *Samuel Richardson: Master-printer*). When he came to Dublin is not known, but in 1744 he subscribed to the Irish "Society for inquiring into . . .

the several Counties of Ireland" (*Dublin Courant*, 8 May). He founded and published the periodical *Universal Journal*, 1745–47, and published the *Dublin Gazette* "by Authority," 1746–48. In the latter year he joined in partnership with Augustus Long (q.v.), and in the service of Castle politicians they published anti–Charles Lucas pamphlets and two newspapers, the *Tickler*, 1748–49, and *Patriot*, 1749 (Munter, *Irish Newspapers*). It is not certain when he left Ireland, probably between 1749 and 1752, but his last known publication was Shakespeare's *Othello*, printed in London in 1764.

GARLAND (**WILLIAM**), printer in Dublin, 1774. Sole reference: he was referred to as a printer in wedding announcements in 1774 (*Freeman's Journal*, 19 Feb.; *Hibernian Journal*, 21 Feb.).

GENT (**THOMAS**), printer in Dublin, London, and York, 1710–78. He had a long and controversial career as a printer in London and York from 1710 to 1778 (*Dictionary 1668–1725*). Prior to this he was enrolled as an apprentice to Stephen Powell (q.v.), but broke his indentures and ran away to England. He returned to Dublin and worked briefly as a journeyman to Thomas Hume (q.v.) in 1715 and again in 1718 (Gent, *Life of Thomas Gent*).

GEORGE (**DENNIS**), printer in Dublin, 1749–69. He was an apprentice to George Grierson (q.v.), was admitted free of the guild in 1749, but paid no quarterage. His name appeared in the Clerk's list in 1769 (*Guild Records*).

GIBALL (**DAVID**), printer in Dublin, Dick's Coffee House, Skinner Row, 1763–76. He was the brother of Sarah Pue (q.v.) (Bentham, *Abstracts*), and joined her in business shortly after her marriage to John Roe (q.v.). He shared in the printing business to 1776, particularly in the publication of *Pue's Occurrences*.

GIBSON (DAVID), bookbinder and publisher in Dublin, Bridge Street, 1748–68. He was admitted free of the guild by service in 1748, paid quarterage through 1758 and again in 1764, had assigned to him five apprentices between 1750 and 1768, and was listed as "dead" in the 1769 Clerk's list (*Guild Records*). In 1752 and 1753 he published *Poor Robin's Almanack or Diversion for the Ladies*.

GILBERT (WILLIAM), bookbinder, bookseller, printer, and publisher in Dublin, (1) Crow Street (1761–68); (2) 26 South Great George's Street (?–1813). 1761–1813. He was admitted free of the guild by composition in 1761, paid quarterage through 1792 at least, and served on the Council from 1786 (*Guild Records*). He married Ann Stephenson (q.v.), the widow of James Stephenson (q.v.), about 1764. Through a very long career he was best known as a bookbinder. However, in 1780 he published Young's *Tour of Ireland*, and in 1790 he printed and published *Browne's Arguements in the Court of the King's Bench* and a *Speech of George Ponsonby*.

GILES (?), bookseller at Leap, County Offaly, 1720. Sole reference: in an advertisement in 1720 he was listed as one of the provincial booksellers taking subscriptions for a Dublin edition of Increase Mather's *Sermons* (*Dublin Courant*, 4 July).

GILL (JOHN), bookseller and publisher in Dublin, the corner of Christ Church Lane, High Street, 1696–1721. He was apprenticed to William Norman (q.v.), went into trade in 1696, was admitted free of the guild by service in 1697, and paid quarterage through 1721. He was an active member of the guild, serving as Warden in 1704, Master in 1706, and on the Council from 1702 (*Guild Records*). In 1710 he published, with a large coterie of stationers, the *Tryal of Doctor Henry Sacheverell*, and, in 1719, Defoe's *Robinson Crusoe*, Prideaux's *Old and New Testament . . . in the History of the Jews*, and Hooker's *Works*, all three with various combinations of stationers. He died in 1721.

GILLAM (JOHN or JOHANNES), bookbinder in Dublin, 1724–25. Sole reference: he was apprenticed to William Wight (q.v.), and admitted free of the city by service in 1724 (*Cal. Anc. Rec. Dublin*; Thrift, *Freemen*).

GILLESPY (JOHN), bookseller in Dublin, 1770s? He was apprenticed to William Whitestone (q.v.) in 1763, never took out his freedom of city or guild, but apparently went into business (*Guild Records*). He died in 1773, his will being proved in the Prerogative Court at Dublin.

GLADWELL (THOMAS), bookseller in Dublin, 1750–83. He was apprenticed to George Risk (q.v.), was admitted to the guild by petition as a quarter brother in 1750, admitted free by service in 1764, and paid quarterage through 1782. He last appeared on the Clerk's list in 1783 (*Guild Records*).

GLASCOCK (THOMAS), printer in Dublin, 1681. Sole reference: he is referred to as having appeared in the guild records as a printer in 1681 (*Trans. Biblio. Soc. London*, vii, 84 [1904]).

GLINN (HUGH), printer in Waterford, 1742. Sole reference: a notice in 1742 read "Hugh Glinn, printer of the *Waterford-News-Letter*, was committed to St. Patrick's gaol by order of the Mayor and Recorder of said city for printing a paragraph reflecting on a certain Bishop" (*Dublin News Letter*, 9 Jan.).

GOLDEN (CHRISTOPHER) *see* Christopher Goulding

GOLDEN (GEORGE) *see* George Goulding

GOLDING (ANNE) *see* Anne Goulding

GOLDING (ELIZABETH) *see* Elizabeth Goulding

GOLDING (GEORGE) *see* George Goulding

GOODWIN (WILKINS), printer in Dublin (1774–77), and Kildare (1819–26). 1774–1826. He was apprenticed to Henry Saunders (q.v.), was admitted free of the guild by service in 1774, and paid quarterage through 1777. He was listed as in Kildare, 1819–21, as in the "Country," 1822–25, and as "Dead" in 1826 (*Guild Records*).

GORDON (ALEXANDER), printer in Dublin, 1700–16? He was summoned by the guild for intrusion in 1700 and 1701, admitted free on petition in 1704, and paid quarterage through 1716 (*Guild Records*). In 1766 a will for an Alexander Gordon, printer, was proved in the Prerogative Court at Dublin.

GORDON (JOSEPH), bookseller, printer, and publisher in Newry, Market Street, 1775–1801. His first imprint, with Daniel Carpenter (q.v.), was *A Mysterious Doctrine Unriddled*, 1775, and from then to 1801 he was responsible for many pamphlets and tracts. He also printed and published the *Newry Chronicle and Universal Advertiser*, 1777–1801. He died in 1801 (*Belfast News Letter*, 25 Dec.).

GORDON (PATRICK), papermaker in Dublin, 1692–? Sole reference: he was listed as a papermaker in 1692 (*Library*, 5th ser., xiii).

GORMAN (BARTHOLOMEW), printer and publisher in Dublin, the Bible, Bridge Street, 1760–71. He was admitted to the guild as a quarter brother in 1760, paid quarterage through 1762, and a franchise fine in 1764 (*Guild Records*). He was referred to as a publisher by Gilbert (*History of Dublin*).

GOULDEN (GEORGE) *see* George Goulding

GOULDING or GOLDING (ANNE), bookseller and publisher in Dublin, the King's Head, High Street, near Old Cornmarket, 1757–59. She was the daughter of Elizabeth and George Goulding (qq.v.), and carried on the family business following her mother's death. She published Anson's *Voyage Round the World*, 1758, and died in 1759, having been "possess'd of every female virtue that can adorn the fair sex; her capacity and diligence in business was never exceeded" (*Sleater's Public Gazetteer*, 22 Feb.).

GOULDING (CATHERINE) *see* Catherine Hicks

GOULDING or GOLDEN (CHRISTOPHER), bookseller, printer, and publisher in Dublin, the Rein Deer, Montrath Street, 1727–46. A Catholic, he married Catherine Fitzgerald (née Hicks [q.v.]), and together they continued her former husband's (see Richard Fitzgerald) business. He was fined for intrusion in 1727 and 1734, was admitted to the guild as a quarter brother in 1735, and paid quarterage through 1746 (*Guild Records*). With his wife they kept Dublin littered with ballads, poems, and occasional libels and false news accounts, the latter involving them in constant wrangles with other Dublin stationers. He died in 1746, his will being proved in the Prerogative Court at Dublin.

GOULDING or GOLDING (ELIZABETH), bookbinder, bookseller, printer, and publisher in Dublin, the King's Head,

High Street, near Cornmarket, 1749?–57. She was the wife of George Goulding (q.v.), and carried on the business following his death in 1749. She printed various works, including Temple's *History of the Irish Rebellion*, 1751. In 1753 she was listed as a bookbinder with an apprentice enrolled to her (*Guild Records*). She died in 1757, her will being proved in the Prerogative Court at Dublin.

GOULDING, GOLDEN, GOLDING, or GOULDEN (GEORGE), bookseller, printer, and publisher in Dublin, the King's Head, High Street, near Cornmarket, 1719–49. He was apprenticed to John Clarke (q.v.), was fined for intrusion in 1719 and 1720, admitted free of the guild by service in 1722, and paid quarterage through 1748. He was an active guild member, serving as Warden in 1741 (*Guild Records*). He printed and published extensively, often in partnership with Isaac Jackson (q.v.), including various histories of Ireland and America, a life of Oliver Cromwell, and an edition of Defoe's *Robinson Crusoe*. He died in 1749, aged 54 (*Donnybrook Par. Reg.*, Dublin).

GOULDING (GEORGE JR.), bookseller in Dublin, at Shakespeare's Monument, next to the corner of Arran Street, on Ormond Quay, 1764–71. He was the son of Elizabeth and George Goulding (qq.v.), was apprenticed to his sister Anne Goulding (q.v.), was admitted free of the guild by birth in 1764, and was listed as "In England" in 1771 (*Guild Records*).

GOULDING (SIMON), printer in Dublin, the Rein Deer, Montrath Street, 1746–52. A Catholic, he was the son of Catherine and Christopher Goulding (qq.v.), and upon the death of his father continued the family business. He was admitted to the guild as a quarter brother in 1747 and paid quarterage through 1751 (*Guild Records*). He died in 1752 (*Dublin Grant Book*).

GOWAN (**George**), bookseller, printer, and publisher in Dublin, the Spinning Wheel, Back Lane, over against Maculla's Court, 1734–42. He was the second son of Jonathan Gowan (q.v.) (*St. Nicholas Within Par. Reg.*, Dublin), and joined in the family business, first advertising stationery ware, etc. under his own name in 1734 (*Dublin Gazette*, 16 Nov.). He printed and published a *Defense of the Protestant Religion*, 1737, was listed as the printer in one issue of the *Dublin Gazette* (29 Dec. 1739), and last advertised in 1742 (*Dublin Gazette*, 1 May).

GOWAN (**John**), bookseller? and printer in Dublin, the Spinning Wheel, Back Lane, over against Maculla's Court, 1727–33. He was the eldest son of Jonathan Gowan (q.v.) (*St. Nicholas Within Par. Reg.*, Dublin), and was licensed to print the *Dublin Gazette* when not yet eighteen years of age (a reprint of his authority, dated 10 June 1727, appeared in the *Dublin Gazette*, 21 Sept. 1729). His father apparently managed the paper until John came of age, their names both being on the imprint until 1729 (Munter, *Handlist*). From 1729 to 1733 John printed Watson's *Almanack*.

GOWAN (**Jonathan**), bookseller, printer, and publisher in Dublin, the Spinning Wheel, Back lane, over against, or, opposite, Maculla's Court, 1726?–56. In 1726 he printed and published a 5th edition of Defoe's *Every-Body's Business, is No-Body's Business*. From 1727 to 1729 he shared authority with his son John Gowan (q.v.) in printing the *Dublin Gazette*, and continued the newspaper on his own until 1743. In 1743 he printed one issue of a *Supplement to the Dublin News-Letter*, apparently trying unsuccessfully to acquire the title when Alice Reilly (q.v.) retitled her own version the *Dublin Courant* (Munter, *Handlist*). He also printed and published various poems and broadsides, and died "very advanced in years" in 1756 (*Pue's Occurrences*, 25 May).

GRACE (JOHN), stationer in Dublin, Skinner Row, opposite the Thosel, 1698. Sole reference: he apparently was a journeyman to Joseph Ray (q.v.), and in 1698 was ordered into custody for his involvement in the publication of *An Injured Protestant Vindicated* (*Commons' Journ. Ire.*, ii, 250).

GRAISBERRY (DANIEL), printer in Dublin, Back Lane, 1775–85. He was apprenticed to Hugh Boulter Primrose Grierson (q.v.), was admitted free of the guild by service in 1775, and paid quarterage through 1785 (*Guild Records*). He died in 1785 (*Dublin Journal*, 17 Dec.).

GRANT (JOHN), bookseller and printer in Dublin, Strafford Street, 1745; 1761–80. He was apprenticed to James Kelburn (q.v.), and was admitted free of the city of Dublin in 1745 (Thrift, *Freemen*). He took out his freedom of the guild by service in 1761, paid quarterage through 1777, served as Warden in 1768, and on the Council from 1769 to 1780, when an election was held to fill his vacant seat. He was recorded as "abroad" in 1783 (*Guild Records*). Perhaps he was in England from 1745 to 1761.

GREEN (CUSACK), printer in Dublin, Coal Quay, 1754–62? He was admitted to the guild by petition as a quarter brother in 1754, but apparently paid no quarterage (*Guild Records*). In 1762 he printed Shakespeare's *Julius Caesar*.

GREEN (THOMAS), bookseller in Dublin, Fishamble Street, 1731–32? He was admitted to the guild as a quarter brother in 1731 and paid quarterage through 1732 (*Guild Records*).

GRIERSON (GEORGE), bookseller, printer, and publisher in Dublin, (1) the Two Bibles, Essex Street, near the Customs House (1705–32); (2) King's Arms and the Two Bibles, Essex

Street (1732–53). 1705–53. He was admitted free of the guild in 1705, paid quarterage through 1753, served as Warden in 1717, as Master in 1725, and on the Council from 1719 (*Guild Records*). He was twice married, first in 1726 to Constantia Pilkington, who died in 1733, and two years following her death to Jane Cromie, the widowed daughter of James Blow (q.v.). Constantia became renowned as a scholar and press editor and a favorite of Lord Lieutenant Carteret, his patent allowing her to share the title of King's Printer from 1730. Descendants from the two marriages continued in the printing business for several generations. Grierson was, as well, famous in his day, and his printing and publishing undertakings were considerable. Besides serving as King's Printer from 1732 to 1753, he printed, with James Blow, the Bible, 1714, 1739, 1741, and 1755, Pope's *Works*, 1718, the *Book of Common Prayer*, several editions, various plays by Shakespeare, 1721 and 1723, the first Irish edition of Shakespeare's *Works*, eight volumes, 1726, and many classics, including Horace and Virgil. His press output ranged also to Knapp's *Almanack*, 1717–19 (printed at Elizabeth Sadlier's [q.v.] address, School House Lane, near High Street), Petty's *Map of Ireland*, 1725, and reprints of London newspapers, the *Free-Holder* and *Spectator*. He died in 1753, his will being proved in the Prerogative Court at Dublin.

GRIERSON (GEORGE ABRAHAM), bookseller and printer in Dublin, King's Arms and Two Bibles, Essex Street, 1753–55. He was the son of Constantia and George Grierson (q.v.), and succeeded to his father's business on the latter's death. He was also King's Printer for these two years, but in 1753 died in Düsseldorf, Germany, a young man already "esteemed for his vivacity, wit and learning" (*Dublin Journal*, 27 Sept.).

GRIERSON (HUGH BOULTER PRIMROSE), bookbinder, bookseller, printer, and publisher in Dublin, (1) King's Arms and Two Bibles, Essex Street (1758–59); (2) King's Arms, Castle Lane (1759–63); (3) King's Arms, Dame Street (1763–64); (4) King's Arms, Parliament Street (1764–71). 1758–71. He was the son of Jane and George Grierson (qq.v.). His first wife died in 1760, and he married Mary Wilkinson in 1761. He was apprenticed to his father, and was admitted free of the guild by service in 1760 (although he was in business in 1758), paid quarterage through 1767, served as Warden in 1766, as Master in 1770, and on the Council from 1768 (*Guild Records*). He became the King's Printer in 1758, his mother having held the right in trust from the death of his elder step-brother, George Abraham Grierson (q.v.), in 1753, until Boulter came of age. His press work ranged broadly, including editions of the *Book of Common Prayer*, 1765 and 1770, the first edition of the *Irish Statutes*, nine volumes, published between 1765 and 1769, and some music printing, including Trydell's *Two Essays on the Theory and Practice of Music*, 1768. He died in 1771, his will being proved in the Prerogative Court at Dublin.

GRIERSON (JANE), bookseller and printer in Dublin, (1) King's Arms and Two Bibles, Essex Street (1755–59); (2) corner of Castle Lane, Dame Street (1759–64). 1755–64. She was the widowed daughter of James Blow (q.v.), and in 1735 married George Grierson (q.v.). When her stepson George Abraham Grierson (q.v.) died in 1753, she continued the family business in trust for her son Hugh Boulter Primose Grierson (q.v.), along with two executors, James Blow (q.v.) and George Ewing (q.v.), until he came of age in 1758. During this period she occasionally referred to the arrangement as Jane Grierson and Company. For some years after Boulter took over in 1758, she continued to work with him.

GRIERSON (MARY), bookseller, printer, and publisher in Dublin, King's Arms, Parliament Street, 1771–78. Mary, née

Wilkinson, was the second wife of Hugh Boulter Primrose Grierson (q.v.). Upon the latter's death she continued the family business, and kept in trust for their son, George, the right as King's Printer. In 1772 she married John Hay (q.v.), who died a year later. In 1778 she published Lewis' *Candid Philosopher.*

GUN or GUNN (JOHN), bookseller in Dublin, 1690–1712. He was listed as a hawker in 1687 and 1688, was admitted free of the guild in 1690, and paid quarterage through 1712 (*Guild Records*). He was made free of the city of Dublin in 1690 (Thrift, *Freemen*).

GUN, GUNN, or GUNNE (MATHEW), bookbinder, bookseller, and publisher in Dublin, (1) the Bible and Crown, Castle Street (1677–84?); (2) the Bible and Crown, next door to the Crown Tavern, facing the Blind Quay, near Essex Street Gate (1698?–1722). 1677–1722. He was admitted free of the guild in 1677, paid quarterage through 1694 at least, and served as Warden in 1696, as Master in 1710, and on the Council from 1696. He was listed as "dead" in 1723 (*Guild Records*). He was a prominent and successful stationer for long years, who has been frequently referred to as a printer despite there being no evidence that he ever printed. He published broadly, alone and in various partnerships, including a tract, the *Rector's Case*, 1695, a *Full Account of . . . Captain Kidd*, 1701, Ware's *Antiquities*, 1705, and a reprint of the *Medley*, 1711.

GUN (NATHANIEL), bookbinder and bookseller in Dublin, at the Bible, Essex Street, near Essex Gate, 1698. There are three references to a Nathaniel or Nat Gun. Although no specific occupation within the stationer's trade is given, the address, certainly that of Mathew Gun (q.v.), is from Gilbert (*History of Dublin*). E. R. McC. Dix makes a brief reference to a Nathaniel Gun, bookbinder, and Dunton claimed an acquaintance with a Nat Gun, stating "He understands Stenography as well as Bookbinding . . . a constant shop-keeper," and that "This Gun was a constant and generous bidder at my Auctions" (*Dublin Scuffle*). Nathaniel could have been a relative of Mathew Gun, or possibly the references, all derived from Dunton, could be to Mathew Gun—"Nat" being an error for "Mat" in the *Dublin Scuffle*.

GUNN (BENJAMIN), bookseller in Dublin, Capel Street, 1749–81. He was the son of Richard Gunn (q.v.), was admitted free of the city of Dublin in 1749 (Thrift, *Freemen*), and joined his father in business in that year. He was admitted free of the guild in 1755 and paid quarterage through 1779 (*Guild Records.*)

GUNN or GUNNE (RICHARD), bookseller and publisher in Dublin, (1) Capel Street (1710–19); (2) Essex Street (1719–25); (3) Capel Street (1725–58). 1710–58. He was the son of Mathew Gun (q.v.), was admitted free of the guild by service in 1710, paid quarterage through 1757, served as Warden in 1715, was elected Master in 1722 but refused to serve, was on the Council from 1716, and was Treasurer from 1729 to 1753 (*Guild Records*). He was active in publishing, on his own and with various combinations of stationers. In 1709 he published the fifth edition of John Speed's *Batt upon Batt. A Poem*, he shared in the publication of Fiddes' *Theologia speculativa*, 1719, Hooker's *Works*, 1719, the Bible, 1722—an edition of 10,000 (*Cal. Anc. Rec. Dublin*)—the *Book of Common Prayer*, 1724, Ware's *Works*, 1739, and he was involved in the controversy over rival editions of Prévost d'Exiles' *Dean of Coleraine* in 1742 (see Thomas Bacon). Following his death in 1758 his stock was sold at auction (*Book Sale Catalogue*).

GUNN (THOMAS), bookseller in Dublin, Pembroke Court, 1718–30? He was the son of Mathew Gun (q.v.), was listed as an intruder in 1718, petitioned for his freedom of the guild in 1722, was admitted free in 1725, and paid quarterage through 1730 (*Guild Records*). He was made free of the city of Dublin in 1722 (Thrift, *Freemen*).

GUNSON (**GEORGE**), bookseller in Dublin, 1715–16. Elizabeth Sadlier (q.v.) printed for him the 4th and 5th editions of Puffendorf's *Whole Duty of Man* (*Dictionary 1668–1725*).

GWIN (**JAMES**), engraver in Dublin, Cork Hill, 1720?–55? He was employed by George Grierson (q.v.), producing the frontispiece for Grierson's editions of Du Pin's *History of Ecclesiastical Writers*, 1723, a portrait of Milton, 1724, and the frontispiece for the *Book of Common Prayer*, 1750. He engraved the map of the world, the frontispiece for Williamson's *Modern History*, 1755. About 1755 he moved to London (Strickland, *Irish Artists*). Gilbert records a Mr. Gwinn, engraver, Cork Street, "native of Kildare," in 1746 (*History of Dublin*); James Gwin was born in Kildare.

H

HALL (**JOHN**), papermaker in Ireland, 1773. Sole reference: in 1773, as a papermaker, he signed a petition to the Irish House of Commons objecting to the removal of duties on foreign paper (BL, 1890.e.5. (232)).

HALLHEAD (**WILLIAM**), bookbinder, bookseller, printer, and publisher in Dublin, 63 Dame Street, 1773–81. He was admitted free of the guild by special grace in 1773, paid quarterage through 1781, served as Warden in 1780, was elected Master for 1782 but died before he could serve out the term, and was on the Council from 1779 (*Guild Records*). He advertised as being the successor of Anne Leathley (q.v.). In 1778 he printed the Trinity College *Statutes*, and he printed and published Leland's *Demosthenes*, 1777, Hales's *Sonorum doctrina*, 1778, and the first Irish edition of Gibbon's *Decline and Fall of the Roman Empire*, 1781.

HALPEN (**PATRICK**), engraver and publisher in Dublin, (1) Blackmoor's Yard, Anglesey Street (1755–75); (2) 35 Temple Bar (1775–87). 1755–87. He was very active in the trade. In 1760 he received a prize from the Dublin Society for his engraving of a "Head of Mossop." Among his many productions were a *Pocket Plan for the City and Suburbs of Dublin* for Lawrence Flin (q.v.), 1765, a portrait of Robert Burns for James Magee's (q.v.) first Irish edition of Burns's *Poems*, 1767, "Garrick's Statue" as a frontispiece for Ewing's edition of Shakespeare's *Works*, 1771, and he published a portrait of Charles Lucas, 1771 (*Dublin Magazine*, July–Sept. 1929).

HAMILTON (EDWARD), bookseller in Dublin, at the corner of Christ Church Lane, High Street, 1710–43. He was apprenticed to Thomas Servant (q.v.), was admitted to the guild by service in 1710, paid quarterage through 1724 at least, served as Warden in 1724, was elected Master in 1727 but refused to serve, and served on the Council from 1714 (*Guild Records*). He was an active bookseller, frequently subscribing to Dublin publications. He died in 1743, his will being proved in the Prerogative Court at Dublin.

HAMILTON (JAMES), bookseller and publisher in Newry (1727?–36), and Dublin (1736–38). 1727–38. In 1727 he married Ann, the daughter of Richard Pue (q.v.) (*St. Nicholas Within Par. Rec.*, Dublin), and in 1736 he moved from Newry and set up business in Dublin (*Dublin Daily Advertiser*, 28 Oct.). He published Dublin's first daily newspaper, the *Dublin Daily Advertiser*, from 1736 to 1738; however, the venture proved a failure (Munter, *Handlist* and *Irish Newspapers*).

HAMILTON (JOSEPH), bookbinder and bookseller in Dublin, Kennedy's Lane, 1749–97. He was the son of Edward Hamilton (q.v.). His guild activity is unclear, but he was apprenticed to John Bardin (q.v.), admitted free of the guild by service in 1749, paid a Beadle fine in 1751, and served as Clerk from 1771 to 1797 (*Guild Records*). He died in 1797, his will being proved in the Prerogative Court at Dublin.

HAMOND (JAMES), bookseller in Dublin, 1670–77. In 1670 he was admitted free of the city of Dublin (Thrift, *Freemen*). He was admitted free of the guild in 1671, paid quarterage through 1677, and his name was scored out from the 1678 Clerk's list (*Guild Records*). He was listed as a contributor, between 1669 and 1673, to the fund for a hospital and free school, Oxmantown Green, Dublin (Gilbert MS 69).

HANDBURY (MICHAEL), engraver and publisher in Dublin, (1) the Bear, George's Lane (1748–50?); (2) Skinner Row, next door to Dick's Coffee House (1750?–63). 1748–63. He advertised prints in 1748, 1756, and 1763. He engraved maps and a plate of medals for Harris' *Life of William III*, 1749, and the frontispiece for Peter Wilson's (q.v.) *Modern Elements of Numeral Arithmatic*, 1759. The Dublin Society gave him grants to encourage work in "designs on copper plate" in 1758, 1759, and 1763 (Strickland, *Irish Artists*).

HARBIN (THOMAS), printer and publisher in Dublin, the General Post Office Printing House, in the Exchange, Cork Hill, or, Cork House, or, opposite Crane Lane, 1724–26. Harbin joined in partnership with Pressick Rider in 1724 to print "by Authority" the *Dublin Gazette*. They also printed and published Molyneux's *Case of Ireland*, 1725, Browne's *English Expositor Improved*, 1726, and a periodical, the *Dictator*, 1725. The business venture, and the right to publish the *Gazette*, collapsed when Rider fled the country in 1726, a £1,000 reward having been offered for his apprehension concerning the publication of a pamphlet against the government (*Sequin's Hibernian Magazine*, Jan. 1773). In 1726 Harbin printed alone *An Excellent New Ballad*, and then he too left for London. A Thomas Harbin and a Pressick Rider are listed as members of a Masonic Lodge in London in 1731 (*Minutes of the Grand Lodge of Freemasons* [London, 1723–1739], vol. x). Pressick's brother, Joshua, is also listed as a member, and another brother, Ebenezer Rider (q.v.), printed a *Pocket Companion for Freemasons*, 1735. Harbin died in London in 1765, a "Tobacconist, and formerly a printer of this city, of facetious Memory, and well known amongst the Choice Spirits" (*Pue's Occurrences*, 6 Aug.).

HARDING (JOHN), printer and publisher in Dublin, (1) the New Post Office Printing House, corner of Sycamore Alley, Essex Street (1716–20); (2) the middle of Dirty Lane (1720–21); (3) Molesworth Court, Fishamble Street (1721–25). 1716–25. From 1716 to 1720 he operated out of the shop of Edward Waters (q.v.). A high Tory champion, his press output was yet relatively negligible. In addition to various broadsheets and pamphlets, he printed and published the *History of the Kings of Scotland*, 1721, and two newspapers, the *Dublin Impartial News-letter*, 1716–25, and the *Post Boy*, 1718–24. The dishonesty of his reports and their viciousness made Harding quite unpopular among his fellow stationers, a "Common Rap of the Press," and as well with the government. He was tried and acquitted as a pickpocket in 1720, and twice ordered into custody by the Irish House of Commons for his unauthorized reporting. His main difficulties came when he became Swift's printer and publisher of the *Drapier's Letters* in 1723. Harding was imprisoned and, though later released, his health was broken and he soon died—1725 (Munter, *Irish Newspapers*). His last defiant act was to have a son baptized John Draper Harding.

HARDING (SARAH), printer and publisher in Dublin, (1) Molesworth Court, Fishamble Street (1721–25); (2) opposite the Hand and Pen, on the Blind Quay, near Fishamble Street (1725–27); (3) next door to the Crown, Copper Alley (1727–29). 1721–29. She was the widow of John Harding (q.v.), and upon the latter's death continued to print for Swift. She printed the *Present Miserable State of Ireland*, 1721, a pamphlet, *Wisdom's Defeat*, 1725, for which she was taken into custody by the Irish House of Commons, a newspaper, the *Intelligence*, 1728, and a satirical poem in 1728 for which she suffered a brief imprisonment (Munter, *Irish Newspapers*). Her last imprint was Swift's *Modest Proposal*, 1729.

HARRIS (ROBERT), bookbinder in Dublin, 1763–1819? He was apprenticed to William Whitestone (q.v.), admitted free of the guild by service in 1763, paid quarterage through 1790, was listed as "in arrears" in 1819, and reported as dead in the 1822 Clerk's list (*Guild Records*).

HARRISON (C.), bookseller in Limerick, 1763. Sole reference: Herbert refers to him as a bookseller in 1763 (*Limerick Printers and Printing*).

HARRISON (G.), printer in Dublin, (1) Fleet Street (?); (2) Temple Bar (?). 1754–55 (*Dictionary 1726–75*).

HARRISON (GEORGE), bookseller, printer, and publisher in Cork, 37 Meeting House Lane, or, corner of Meeting House Lane, 1731–54. He was an active printer and bookseller. Among his work was *A Letter to . . . the Freeholders . . . of Corke*, 1731, K'eogh's *Botanalogia universalis Hibernica*, 1735, and *An Account of the Life . . . of the Rt. Honourable Henry Boyle*, 1754. In 1738 he published a literary newspaper, the *Medley*, and from 1747 to 1753 he did considerable printing for the Cork Corporation (Caulfield, *Cork Council Book*).

HARRISON (MARY), bookseller and printer in Cork, corner of Meeting House Lane, 1756?–61. She was the wife of George Harrison (q.v.), and carried on the family business from at least 1756. She printed for the Cork Corporation from 1756 to 1761 (Caulfield, *Cork Council Book*).

HARTON (GEORGE), bookseller in Coleraine, 1710. Sole reference: advertisements in 1710 listed him as one of the provincial booksellers taking subscriptions to a Dublin edition of the *Tryal of Doctor Henry Sacheverell* (*Dublin Intelligence*, 24 June and 1 July).

HATTON (RICHARD), printer in Dublin, 1687?–89? Sole reference: the will of William Hatton (q.v.) left his entire estate to his son "Richard Hatton, printer." The will was witnessed by George Brent (q.v.) (Tenison Groves Collection, St. Lawrence file, PROI).

HATTON (WILLIAM), printer in Dublin, 1687?–89? Sole reference: his will, in which he refers to himself as a printer, was dated 1687 and proved 1689. The will was witnessed by George Brent (q.v.) (Tenison Groves Collection, St. Lawrence file, PROI).

HAWKER (HENRY), bookseller, printer, and publisher in Dublin, Homer's Head, Dame Street, 1745–51. He was apprenticed to John Hyde (q.v.), was admitted free of the guild by service in 1745, and paid quarterage through 1749 (*Guild Records*). In 1749 he joined with Augustus Long (q.v.) to publish *The Life and Entertaining Adventures of Mr. Cleveland, Natural Son of Oliver Cromwell* and Molyneux's *Case of Ireland*. He died in 1751.

HAY (DAVID), printer and publisher in Dublin, King's Arms, Parliament Street, 1767–73. He was admitted free of the guild by petition in 1767 and paid quarterage through 1772 (*Guild Records*). He was the brother of John Hay (q.v.), was brought into business with Hugh Boulter Primrose Grierson (q.v.) in 1767, and became his assignee as King's Printer, under which auspices he published two editions of the *Book of Common Prayer*, 1772 and 1773. In 1771 he published, along with several others, Smollett's *Humphrey Clinker*. In 1772 he married Mary Grierson (q.v.), the widow of Boulter, and in 1773 he died in Aix-en-Provence, France (*Hibernian Journal*, 4 Jan.).

HAY (JOHN), bookseller, printer, and publisher in Belfast, (1) the Two Bibles, Bridge Street (1735–59); (2) the Two Bibles, High Street (1759–78). 1735–78. He was the brother of David Hay (q.v.), and a prominent Belfast figure who frequently subscribed to Dublin publications, from Heatly's (q.v.) edition of the *Life and Entertaining Adventures of Mr. Cleveland, Natural Son of Oliver Cromwell*, 1735, to Faulkner's (q.v.) edition of Swift's *Works*, 1762. He worked in various publishing arrangements with other Belfast booksellers and printers, James Blow (q.v.), James Magee (q.v.), and last with Henry and Robert Joy (qq.v.) in 1778. Among his works he printed Fielding's *Journal of a Voyage to Lisbon*, 1755, an *Introduction to English Grammar*, 1765, and Warner's *History of Ireland*, 1770.

HAY (MARY) *see* Mary Grierson

HAYDON (J.), engraver in Dublin, 1739. He engraved two large plates and the ornamental headings for chapters in Harris' edition of Ware's *Works*, 1739 (Strickland, *Irish Artists*).

HEATLY (WILLIAM), bookseller and publisher in Dublin, the Bible and Dove, College Green, 1730–42. He was apprenticed to George Grierson (q.v.), admitted free of the guild by service in 1730, and paid quarterage through 1741 (*Guild Records*). He published the *Life and Entertaining Adventures of Mr. Cleveland, Natural Son of Oliver Cromwell*, 1735, the

Universal Traveller, No. VI, 1735, and Puckle's *The Club. In a Dialogue between Father and Son*, 1737. Richard Pue (q.v.) advertised the continuation of Heatly's auctioneering activities following the latter's death (*Dublin News-Letter*, 11 Jan. 1742/43). Heatly died in 1742, his will being proved in the Prerogative Court at Dublin.

HELME (W.), printer and publisher in Dublin, (1) Blackmoor's Head, Anglesey Street (1721); (2) the Printing Press, Turnstile Alley, College Green (1721–24). 1721–24. He printed and published the short-lived *New Dublin Mercury: or Irish Gazetteer*, 1721, printed Warren's *Abridgement of all the Irish Statutes*, 1723, and Downe's *Lives of the Compilers of the Liturgy*, 1724.

HELSHAM (Samuel), bookseller, printer, and publisher in Dublin, the College Arms, next door to the Bear and Ragged Staff, Castle Street, 1675–89. He was admitted free of the guild in 1675, served as Warden in 1676 and 1677, as Master in 1780, and on the Council from 1678 (*Guild Records*). He printed and published a variety of pamphlets and Archbishop Marsh's *Institutiones logicae*, 1681. In 1684 Helsham and Andrew Crooke (q.v.) were made joint assigns of Benjamin Tooke (q.v.) as King's Printers. They published many government documents and proclamations, as well as continuing such work as the *Quaker's Elegy*, 1685, and Allen's *Operation for the Teeth*, 1686. Helsham died in 1689 (*Diary of William King D.D. while in prison in 1689*).

HENLEY (John), bookseller and publisher in Dublin, Castle Street, 1709–14. He was apprenticed to Jacob Milner (q.v.), later transferred to Eliphal Dobson (q.v.), admitted free of the guild by service in 1709, and paid quarterage through 1714 (*Guild Records*). He has one extant publication, *Seventh Epistle* *of the first Book of Horace, Imitated*, n.d., and after his death in 1714 was accused by John Whalley (q.v.) of having been a Jacobite and responsible for the publication of a controversial polemic, *A Long History of a Short Session of a Certain Parliament* (*Whalley's News-Letter*, 1 Feb. 1715/16).

HEWETSON (**WALTER**) *see* Walter Houston

HICKEY (**BENJAMIN**), bookseller and publisher in Dublin, Essex Street, near Essex Gate (1728), and in Bristol? (1742–54). 1728–54? In 1728 he published, with James Thompson (q.v.), Jevon's *The Devil of a Wife*, and he advertised an edition of Locke's *Thoughts on Education* (*Dublin Intelligence*, 4 May). In 1729 it was alleged that Hickey "pretending to be the Servant of Fernando Davys [q.v.] hath taken up Books and Stationary Ware in the Name of the said Davys from several Persons in this City, and hath given out Counterfeit Notes in the said Davys Name" (*Dublin Weekly Journal*, 8 Feb.). No more is heard of Hickey in Ireland. A Benjamin Hickey was in business as a bookseller in Bristol in 1742 (*Dictionary 1726–75*), and in 1754 he subscribed to 25 copies of a Dublin edition of Budgell's *Memoirs of the . . . family of the Boyles*.

HICKS (**CATHERINE**), bookseller, printer, and publisher in Dublin, the Rein Deer, Montrath Street, 1722–45. A Catholic, she was the daughter of John Hicks (q.v.) and the wife of Richard Fitzgerald (q.v.). Upon the latter's death she married Christopher Goulding (q.v.), and together they continued her former husband's business. She printed and published a wide variety of material, primarily for the country trade and ballad hawkers. Typical of her work was *The Whole Life Actions, Birth, Parentage and Education of Doctor John Andouin, who was Drawn, Hang'd and Quartered*, 1728, for which she was prosecuted for libel. She died intestate in 1745 (*Dublin Grant Book*).

HICKS (JOHN), bookseller in Dublin, (1) Globe Alley (1697–?); (2) Smock Alley (1708?–12). 1697–1712. A Catholic, he was summoned in 1697 by the guild for intrusion (*Guild Records*). In 1708 he advertised "all sorts of the Newest Song Books and Ballads, where Country Chapmen and others, may be furnish'd with the aforesaid Goods," and in 1712 he died, being listed as a "ballad Singer" (*Dublin Grant Book*).

HIGGINS (BRYAN), bookbinder in Dublin, 1715. Sole reference: An Irish manuscript (RIA, MS 23, fol. 16) bears the internal inscription that "This Book was bound by Bryan Higgins of the City of Dublin Gent in the Month of October 1715" (Craig, *Bookbindings*).

HILL (JOSEPH), printer in Dublin, (1) 8 Mary Street (1780?–90); (2) Abbey Street (1799?). 1774–99? He was admitted free of the guild by special grace in 1774, paid one year's quarterage in 1780, had an apprentice enrolled to him in 1784, and was listed in the Clerk's list in 1787 (*Guild Records*). He was admitted free of the city by birth in 1780. He printed sheet songs and half-sheet songs, and a collection of Masonic Songs "between the years 1780 and 1790" (*Proc. Biblio. Soc. Ire.*, 2, no. 5). In 1799 a "Mr. Hill, of Abbey-street, Printer" was "taken into custody, on a charge of Seditious practices" (*New Cork Evening Post*, 15 Mar.).

HIND (ANDREW), printer in Ireland, 1714? Sole reference: "On the 13th of December, Mr. Andrew Hind and Archibald Ashburn (the former a broken master printer, the other a journeyman,) came from their journey from Ireland to York" (Gent, *Life of Thomas Gent*).

HINDE (TIMOTHY), bookseller in Dublin, on Essex Bridge, near Capel Street, 1734–42. He was admitted as a quarter brother in 1734 and paid quarterage through 1742 (*Guild Records*). In 1740, as a bookseller, he advertised the sale of "Nash's blacking" (*Dublin News-Letter*, 5 Aug.).

HODGE (PETER), engraver in Dublin, d. 1756. Sole reference: he was stated to have been an engraver who died in Copper Alley in 1756 (Strickland, *Irish Artists*).

HODGSON (PHILIP), bookseller and publisher in Dublin, (1) on the Blind Quay, near Smock Alley (1717–19); (2) at the lower end of Cork Hill (1719–21?). 1717–21? He was admitted free of the city of Dublin in 1717 (Thrift, *Freemen*), admitted free of the guild in 1718, paid quarterage through 1720, and was carried on the Clerk's list in 1721 (*Guild Records*). He advertised an *Ode to the Right Honourable the Earl Cadogan*, 1719, published, with Patrick Campbell (q.v.) and George Risk (q.v.), Fiddes' *Theologia practica*, 1720, and, with Campbell, *Sermons of Jonathan Smedley*, 1719. His address from 1719 to 1721 is the same as Campbell's, perhaps reflecting a short-lived partnership.

HOEY (JAMES), bookseller, printer, and publisher in Dublin, (1) Christ Church Yard (1726–28); (2) the Pamphlet Shop, opposite the Thosel, Skinner Row (1729–32); (3) the Mercury, next door the Thosel, Skinner Row (1732–65?); (4) the Mercury, 19 Parliament Street (1765?–74). 1726–74. He was a Catholic with no formal training in the stationer's trade— "This Hoey, you may know, was bred to the mean employ of selling old iron by retail" (*Peter La Boissier's Starry Interpreter*, 1740)—and in 1726 started business with an "old worn out Printing Press" (*Advice from Fairy-Land*, 1726). A year later he joined in partnership with George Faulkner (q.v.). He was admitted to the guild as a quarter brother in 1728, paid quarter-age through 1766, had his quarterage raised on three occasions "on account of his following a considerable trade," and paid a franchise fine in 1770 (*Guild Records*). He quickly became known as a "Compiler, Writer, Corrector, and Author," and was chiefly responsible for the success of the partnership's two newspapers, the *Dublin Journal*, 1727–30, and the *Dublin Post-Boy*, 1727–30. A quarrel led to the break-up of the partnership, and for some time both partners continued to publish identical titles. Hoey was to publish several other successful newspapers, among them the *General Advertiser*, 1737, the first in Ireland designed to appeal primarily to the advertiser. Hoey lived down his early reputation as a pamphlet printer, "a Sponger, or Retailer of small jests . . . affirm'd of a Mollying, Beastly Temper," becoming both respectable and successful. Among his many publications were a series of almanacs, beginning with the pirated title *Whalley's Almanack*, 1720, O'Conor's *Dissertations on the antient history of Ireland*, 1753, and Shakespeare's *King Lear*, 1768. He did some music printing, including Handel's *Messiah*, 1749, and in 1737 inaugurated the first lending library in Ireland (*General Advertiser*, 13 Jan.). He died in 1775 (*Dublin Journal*, 27 May), leaving two sons in the trade, James Hoey Jr. (q.v.) and Peter Hoey (q.v.).

HOEY (JAMES JR.), bookseller, printer, and publisher in Dublin, (1) the sign of the Mercury, next door the Thosel, Skinner Row (1753–65?); (2) Parliament Street, four doors to Essex Street, or, the Mercury, 19 Parliament Street (1765?–81?). 1753–81? A Catholic, he was the son of James Hoey (q.v.) by his first wife, Elizabeth. When James Jr. joined his father in business is not clear. He had an apprentice enrolled to him in 1753, and paid franchise fines as a quarter brother in 1764 and 1770, but never paid quarterage (*Guild Records*). Still, in 1766 he joined with other Dublin stationers in a published complaint against irregulars and intruders in the trade! (*Freeman's Journal*, 26 Apr.). He printed and published extensively: a newspaper, the *Dublin Mercury*, 1766–73—which drew the Protestant protest:

> Ready with quips and wanton wile
> Each new-fledged patriot to revile
> At uncorrupted worth to smile
> Or thrice a week to thunder.

—Walpole's *Castle of Otranto*, 1765, Smollett's *Humphrey Clinker*, 1771, Shakespeare's *Twelfth Night*, 1769, and *Timon of Athens*, 1772, as well as printing for the Irish House of Commons (*Commons' Journ. Ire.*, Reprint ix, app. ccccx). He died in 1787 (Bentham, *Abstracts*).

HOEY (PETER), bookseller, printer, and publisher in Dublin, (1) Milton's Head, Skinner Row (1770–86?); (2) the Flying Mercury, 33 Ormond Quay (1788?–1801). 1770–1801. He was the son of James Hoey (q.v.) by his second wife, Jane. His mother was a Protestant, but Peter was raised a Catholic. He was admitted free of the guild by petition in 1793 but paid no quarterage (*Guild Records*). He appears to have worked first for Oliver Nelson (q.v.), and perhaps to have succeeded him in business. In 1773 he signed a memorial to the Irish House of Commons against additional duties on foreign paper (BL, 1890.e.5. (239)). From 1770 to 1773 he printed and published the *Public Journal*, and in 1791 he printed *A general catalogue of books . . . published in Dublin from the year 1700*. He died in 1801 and was succeeded by his wife and widow, Margaret Hoey.

HOLLAND (THOMAS), papermaker in Dublin, 1723. Sole reference: in 1723 he leased a paper mill at Milltown Bridge, County Dublin, from Edward Waters (q.v.).

HOLMES (PHILIP), engraver in Dublin, d. 1702. Sole reference: the *St. Nicholas Within Par. Reg.*, Dublin, records the burial, 1702, of "Philip Holmes, an engraver, a poore Englishman."

HOMES (J.), bookseller in Belfast, 1726. Sole reference: an advertisement in 1726 listed Homes as taking subscriptions for an edition of Pack's *Miscellaneous Works* (*Dublin Weekly Journal*, 2 July).

HONDT (PETER DE), bookseller in Dublin, 1741–42? He was a bookseller at The Hague, and by 1741 was in partnership with T. Becket (q.v.) in Dublin (Phillips, unpublished thesis). He was admitted free of the guild in 1742 (*Guild Records*).

HOOD (DANIEL), bookseller in Cork, (1) opposite the Main Guard (1734–37); (2) Tuckey's Quay (1760); (3) Daunt's Bridge, near the Grand Parade (1782–84?). 1734–84? He was possibly the nephew or stepson of Combra Daniel (q.v.). The latter married Sarah Hood in 1713, and when Combra died, Daniel Hood succeeded him in business, becoming the Cork agent to 1737 for Risk, Ewing, and Smith (qq.v.) and later for George and Alexander Smith. In 1736 Hood took subscriptions for Rollin's *History of the Egyptians* (*Dublin Evening Post*, 3 June), but in 1737 he seems to have failed in business. He reappeared in 1760 with the advertisement for Hawke's *The Adventurer* (*Cork Evening Post*, 16 June), and from 1782 to 1784 he advertised books and lottery tickets for sale (*Cork Evening Post*, 26 Sept. 1782, 18 Sept. 1783, 26 Apr. 1784). He died in 1789 (*Dublin Evening Post*, 23 May).

HOOD (GEORGE), stationer in Dublin, 1638. Sole reference: he was admitted free of the city of Dublin in 1638 (Thrift, *Freemen*).

HOPKINS (**Jo.**), bookseller in Dublin, 1762. Sole reference: he was mentioned in the 1762 subscribers' list as having taken 25 sets of Faulkner's (q.v.) edition of Swift's *Works*.

HORAN (**James**), bookseller in Dublin, 1762. Sole reference: he was mentioned in the 1762 subscribers' list as having taken 7 sets of Faulkner's (q.v.) edition of Swift's *Works*.

HOSPITAL (**Christopher**), bookbinder in Dublin (1748–49?), and Cork (1776?). 1748–76. He was admitted free of the guild in 1748 and paid quarterage through 1749 (*Guild Records*). He died in Cork in 1776 (*Dublin Journal*, 21 Nov.).

HOUSDEL, HOUSDELL, or HOUSDEN (**William**), bookseller in Dublin, 1718–34. He was apprenticed to Peter Laurence (q.v.), listed as an intruder in 1718, admitted free of the guild by service in 1720, and paid quarterage through 1734 (*Guild Records*). He was admitted free of the city of Dublin in 1719 (Thrift, *Freemen*).

HOUSTON or HEWETSON (**Walter**), printer in Dublin, (1) the Blue Bible, Skinner Row (1701–?); (2) the sign of the Bible, on the Blind Quay, near Cork Hill (1705–15). 1701–15. He was a journeyman to Patrick Campbell (q.v.), was listed as an intruder in 1701 and 1702, admitted free of the guild in 1703, and paid quarterage through 1715 (*Guild Records*). He was admitted free of the city of Dublin in 1703 (Thrift, *Freemen*).

HOWES (**Joseph**), bookseller and publisher in Dublin, the King's Arms, Castle Street, 1670–93. He was admitted free of the guild in 1670, served as Warden in 1672 and 1673, was elected Master in 1678 but refused to serve, was on the Council from 1677, and in 1693 was recorded as "dead" (*Guild Rec-*

ords). He was admitted free of the city of Dublin in 1670 (Thrift, *Freemen*). He published Ware's *Reformation of the Church in Ireland*, 1681, in the same year several tracts and pamphlets on the popish plot—e.g., *Several Informations . . . Concerning the Horrid Popish Plot*—and *An Account of the Persecutions and Oppressions of the Protestants in France*, 1686.

HOWES (ROBERT) *see* Robert Hughes

HUBERTI (GASPAR), engraver in Kilkenny, 1645. In 1645 he engraved "A Prospect of the late Seidge [sic] of the Forte of Duncannon" (Strickland, *Irish Artists*).

HUDDLESTON (THOMAS), engraver in Dublin, (1) the Black Lion, the corner of Temple Lane (1770); (2) 52 South Great George's Street (1777). 1770–77. In an advertisement in 1770 he described himself as "a young beginner" (Strickland, *Irish Artists*).

HUGHES or HOWES (ROBERT), bookseller and publisher in Dublin, 1637–71. He was admitted free of the guild in 1637 (*Guild Records*), free of the city of Dublin in 1648 (*Cal. Anc. Rec. Dublin*), and in 1650 was appointed to collect the "Keyadge" of Dublin. He published a pamphlet in 1644, *Catalogus librorum MSS in Biblioteca Jac. Waraei*, 1648, and Ambrose White's *An Almanack and Prognostications*, 1665. In 1669 he was listed as a contributor to the fund for a hospital and free school on Oxmantown Green, Dublin (Gilbert MS 69). He died in 1671 (Library of the Society of Genealogists, London).

HUME or HUMES (THOMAS), bookseller, printer, and publisher in Dublin, (1) the White Hart, Copper Alley (1714–16); (2) over against the sign of the Bible or, the Time, on the lower end of Cork Hill (1716–18); (3) next to Walsh's

Head, Smock Alley (1718–19?); (4) Customs House Printing House, Smock Alley (1724–25); (5) Customs House Printing House, next door to the Merchant's Coffee House, Essex Street (1725–29); (6) Walsh's Head, Smock Alley (1730). 1715–30. He was admitted free of the city of Dublin in 1718 (Thrift, *Freemen*), admitted free of the guild by petition in 1718, paid quarterage through 1726, became a pensioner in 1735, and his widow was granted 10*s* 10*d* for his burial expenses in 1738 (*Guild Records*). He first joined in a brief partnership with A. Meres (q.v.), publishing tracts and pamphlets, but within a year took over the business and alone launched a career as a journalist. He first published reprints of London newspapers, the *Englishman*, 1715, and the *Free-Holder*, 1715–16, and then his own *Postman: an Historical Account*, 1716–26 (see Edwin Sandys Jr.), *Dublin Courant*, 1716–29, and *London Post-Man*, 1727 (Munter, *Handlist*). He also printed and published the *Cobler of Preston* [*Taming of the Shrew*], 1716, the first Shakespearean alteration printed in Ireland, and the *True Interest of the Irish Nation*, 1716, in Irish. In 1725 he moved into the shop of Edwin Sandys Jr. Hume was twice called before the bar of the Irish House of Lords and reprimanded for unauthorized printing (*Lords' Journ. Ire.*, ii, 686, 689–91, 817). His business ventures finally failed through an unsuccessful newspaper circulation war with George Faulkner (q.v.). Hume's printing stock was sold at auction in 1730 (*Dublin Weekly Journal*, 14 Mar.), and he last advertised a pamphlet sale from the shop of a fellow stationer. He was a prisoner for debt in the Four Courts Marshalsea in 1736 (*Dublin Gazette*, 8 May 1737) and died a pauper in 1737 (*St. John the Evangelist Par. Rec.*, Dublin).

HUNTER, (JAMES), bookseller, printer, and publisher in Dublin, (1) the Bible and Mitre, on the Blind Quay (1759–60); Sycamore Alley (1760–88). 1759–88. He was admitted free of the guild in 1759 and paid quarterage through 1788 (*Guild Records*). In 1759 he joined in partnership with Michael North (q.v.), and they published the periodical the *Public Magazine.* By 1760 he was in business for himself, and published the *Dublin Chronicle and Universal Advertiser*, 1760–62?, and the *Independent Irish*, 1770. He died in 1789, his will was proved in the Prerogative Court at Dublin, and he left two sons, James and William, who continued in the stationer's trade.

HURLEY (J.), bookbinder in Limerick, 1769. Sole reference: Herbert refers to him as a bookbinder in 1769 (*Limerick Printers and Printing*).

HUSBAND (JOHN ABBOTT), bookseller, printer, and publisher in Dublin, (1) Coghill's Court, Dame Street (1768); (2) 28 Abbey Street (1776?–94). 1768–94. He was apprenticed to his aunt Alice Reilly (q.v.) and possibly succeeded her in business, was admitted free of the guild by service in 1768, and paid quarterage through 1787 (*Guild Records*). He printed and published a wide variety of works, including Phillip's *Life of Reginald Pole*, 1765, Smollett's *Humphrey Clinker*, 1771, Shakespeare's *Timon of Athens*, 1772, and Hooker's *Ecclesiastical Polity*, 1773. He died in 1795, and his will was proved in the Diocesan Court at Dublin.

HUSSEY (NICHOLAS), printer and publisher in Dublin, opposite the Hand and Pen, on the Blind Quay, 1727–29. He apparently took over the shop of Sarah Harding (q.v.), and printed and published tracts and pamphlets—e.g., *A New Poem on the Procession of Journeymen Taylors*, 1727. He tried, unsuccessfully, to enter periodical journalism with a series of newspapers, the *Dublin Post Boy*, 1728–29, the *Weekly Post, or the Dublin Impartial News Letter*, 1729, and the *Flying Post, or, the Dublin Post-Man*, 1729 (Munter, *Handlist*).

HUTCHINSON (JAMES), bookseller in Dromore, 1751. Sole reference: he was listed in the colophon in 1751 as one of the sellers of Clark's *A Brief Survey of some Principles maintained by the General Synod of Ulster*.

HUTCHINSON (THOMAS), printer and publisher in Dublin, at the Rein Deer, Charles Street, opposite Montrath Street, 1753. He apparently took over the business of Simon Goulding (q.v.), and his only known work was two issues of the *Dublin Spy*, 1753, and a pamphlet, *A Morsel from a Wolf in Bloudy Sheep's Clothing*, 1753. Possibly he was the same as the Galway printer of the same name.

HUTCHINSON (THOMAS), printer and publisher in Galway, 1754–59. Possibly he was the same as the Dublin Thomas Hutchinson. He was the first printer in Galway, and printed and published that town's first newspaper, the *Connaght Journal*. In 1756 he had an apprentice assigned to him by the Dublin guild who, upon Thomas' death in 1759, was transferred by his widow to Samuel Powell (q.v.) (*Guild Records*).

HYDE (JOHN), bookseller, printer, and publisher in Dublin, Dame Street, 1707–28. He was apprenticed to William Norman (q.v.), admitted free of the guild by service in 1707, paid quarterage through 1728, served as Warden in 1711, as Master in 1719, and on the Council from 1709 (*Guild Records*). He was the son-in-law of Joseph Ray (q.v.), a staunch Tory, and a prominent bookseller and publisher who did little printing until late in his career. With various combinations of stationers, his publications included the *Book of Common Prayer*, 1713, the Bible, 1722, Hooker's *Works*, 1724, Fiddes' *Theologia speculativa*, 1719, and Clarendon's *History of the Rebellion*, 1719. He printed and published Swift's *Gulliver's Travels*, 1726. He died in 1728, and his will was proved in the Prerogative Court at Dublin.

HYDE (SARAH), bookseller, printer, and publisher in Dublin, Dame Street, 1728–46. She was the daughter of Joseph Ray (q.v.), the widow of John Hyde (q.v.), and upon the latter's death continued the family business. She printed an edition of the *Book of Common Prayer*, 1730, and, with various other stationers, her joint publications included Plutarch's *Lives*, 1730, Cervantes' *Don Quixote*, 1733, Ware's *Works*, 1739, and one of the rival translations of Prévost d'Exiles' *Dean of Coleraine*, 1742 (see Thomas Bacon). She retired from business in 1746, her stock being sold at auction, and she died in 1750, her will being proved in the Prerogative Court at Dublin.

I

INGHAM (CHARLES), bookseller in Dublin, 1769–73. Sole reference: in 1773 he signed a memorial to the Irish House of Commons from "Printers, Booksellers, Stationers and Card-Makers" against additional duties on foreign paper (BL, 1890. e.5. (239)).

J

JACKSON (Isaac), bookseller, printer, publisher, and type-founder in Dublin, the Globe and Bible, later the Globe, Meath Street, 1737–72. A Quaker, he succeeded to the business of Mary Fuller (q.v.). He was admitted to the guild as a quarter brother on petition in 1754 and paid quarterage through 1770 (*Guild Records*). He printed school books, Quaker tracts, and Butler's *Almanack*, 1745–56. When Isaac Butler (q.v.) died, the *Almanack* was continued as "Jackson's." Among Jackson's other publications are Burton's *History of Oliver Cromwell*, 1743, Gough's *Treatise on Arithmatick*, 1759, and Fuller's *Mathematical Miscellany*, 1770. He was also a typefounder, leaving "all his Letter Puncheons and materials belonging to a letter foundry" to his son Robert Jackson (q.v.). He died in 1772 (*Hibernian Magazine*, June).

JACKSON (Joseph), bookbinder in Dublin, 1718?–51? He was apprenticed to Peter Laurence (q.v.), listed as an intruder in 1718, and again recorded as a bookbinder when his son James was apprenticed to Elizabeth Goulding (q.v.) in 1751 (*Guild Records*).

JACKSON (Robert), bookseller, printer, and publisher in Dublin, the Globe, Meath Street, later as 20 Meath Street, 1770?–93. A Quaker, he was the son and successor of Isaac Jackson (q.v.). He was brought into the business at least by 1770, when they jointly published a second edition of Gough's *Treatise of Arithmatick*. Robert continued to publish school books and Quaker literature, as well as continuing *Jackson's Almanack* to 1793, the rights to which were sold after his death to Patrick Wogan (q.v.) (*Cork Courier*, 20 Dec. 1794). Robert died in 1793, his will being proved in the Diocesan Court at Dublin.

JACKSON (**SERLES**), bookbinder in Dublin, 1769–83? He was apprenticed from the Blue Coat School to Samuel Price (q.v.), admitted free of the guild by service in 1769, and paid quarterage through 1783 (*Guild Records*). He was admitted free of the city of Dublin in 1770 (Thrift, *Freemen*).

JAMES (**ALICE**), bookseller and printer in Dublin, at Newton's Head, Dame Street, 1757–61? She was the wife of Richard James (q.v.), and after the latter's death carried on the business "for the benefit of herself and children" (*Dublin Gazette*, 5 Mar. 1757). She printed and published the *Dublin Gazette*, 1757–61, and occasionally joined with others to publish small works like *The Way to Keep Him: a Comedy*, 1760. She may have printed for the government, for in 1757 she was paid by the Irish House of Commons the large sum of £250 "for losses sustained" (*Commons' Journ. Ire.*, v, 148). She married Timothy Dyton (q.v.) in 1761, who continued the business under his own name.

JAMES (**RICHARD**), bookseller, printer, and publisher in Dublin, Dame Street, opposite Sycamore Alley, or, at Newton's Head, Dame Street, 1746–57. He was apprenticed to George Faulkner (q.v.), went into business in 1746, "it not being convenient for him to become free," was finally admitted free of the guild by service in 1749, and paid quarterage through 1756 (*Guild Records*). He printed and published the *Dublin Gazette*, in partnership with John Butler (q.v.), from 1750 to 1753, and by himself from 1753 to 1757. He published Milton's *Paradise Lost*, 1748, and also several plays, including Shakespeare's *Romeo and Juliet*, 1747. He died in 1757 (*Pue's Oc-currences*, 5 Mar.).

JANS or J'ANS (**CHRISTOPHER**), bookbinder in Dublin, Christ Church Lane, 1683–99. He was admitted free of the guild in 1683 and paid quarterage through 1699 (*Guild Records*). He was admitted free of the city in 1687 (Thrift, *Freemen*). Gilbert refers to him as a Roman Catholic, and states that during the revolution "his books and machinery were seized and confiscated by the Williamites" (Gilbert, *History of Dublin*).

JENKIN (**CALEB**), bookbinder, bookseller, and publisher in Dublin, 58 Dame Street, 1772?–92. He was in business by 1772, admitted free of the guild by special grace in 1780, paid quarterage through 1787, served as Warden in 1784, and was elected to the Council in 1784, but resigned, having been appointed Sheriff of the city (*Guild Records*). He was admitted free of the city in 1784 (Thrift, *Freemen*), and made an Alderman by 1790. Among his publications, jointly with others, are Shakespeare's *Timon of Athens*, 1772, *La Liturgie* [Huguenot], 1777, and Young's *Tour of Ireland*, 1780. In 1785 he tendered for the binding of the Parliamentary *Journals* (Craig, *Bookbindings*), and he died in 1792 (*Gentleman's and London Magazine*, Mar.).

JESUITS *see* Brother Nicholas Sarrazin

JOHNSON (**ARTHUR**), bookseller in London (1602–21), and Dublin (1621–30). 1602–30. He is stated to have moved from London to Dublin about 1621 and to have set up as a stationer (*Dictionary 1557–1640*). He died in 1631, his will being proved in the Prerogative Court at Dublin.

JOHNSON (RICHARD), bookseller in Dublin, 1698–1715. He was apprenticed to William Norman (q.v.), in trade by 1698, admitted free of the guild by service in 1701, and was carried on the Clerk's list to 1715 but paid no quarterage (*Guild Records*). He was admitted free of the city in 1701 (Thrift, *Freemen*).

JOHNSTON (RICHARD), bookseller and publisher in Belfast, 1753–60? He published Blair's *Doctrine of Persuasion*, 1753, several pamphlets in 1758 and 1759, and Foote's *The Minor: a Comedy*, 1760. He was listed as a printer (*Dictionary 1726–75*), but there is no evidence that he ever was. He died by 1764, being referred to in that year as "the late Richard Johnston" (*Freeman's Journal*, 14 Feb.).

JOHNSTON (WILLIAM), bookseller in Dublin, in Crooked Staff, 1749 (*Dictionary 1726–75*).

JOLY (J.), printer in Dublin, 1756. Sole reference: in 1756 he printed the *Dublin Intelligence* (24 Feb.–22 June).

JONES (DAVID), bookseller and publisher in Cork, 1691–1711. He published a *Pastoral Admonition directed by the Bishop of Cork*, 1691, Bishop Burnet's *Sermon Preached at Whitehall*, 1691, and was listed as selling William Norman's (q.v.) publication *The London-Master: or, the Jew Detected*, 1694. In 1705, 1710, and 1711, in regard to various land transactions, he is listed as a stationer (Registry of Deeds, 4-477-1177, 4-333-1009, and 6-232-2034).

JONES (EDWARD), printer in London (1688–1706), Londonderry (1689?), and Dublin, the King's Hospital, Oxmantown (1690). 1688–1706. He was appointed King's Printer in

England upon the accession of William and Mary, and came to Ireland with William in 1689, along with a press, to print government proclamations. In Londonderry he possibly printed *An Abstract of the King and Queen's Declaration*, 1689, and in Dublin he printed *A Form of Prayer to be Used on Friday, the 15th of August*, 1690. By 1691 he was back in London, where he died in 1706.

JONES (EDWARD), printer in Dublin, Dirty Lane, 1740. Sole reference: he printed *The Last and True Speech of Mr. Sewell*, 1740.

JONES (ELIZABETH), bookseller, printer, and publisher in Dublin, Clarendon Street, 1739–41. She was the daughter of Theophilus and Jane Jones (qq.v.), and continued the *Dublin Evening Post* to 1741. She published, with others, Ware's *Works*, 1739, and, alone, a *Letter of . . . Advice to a Young Lady*, 1740. In 1756 she married Thomas Dixon (q.v.) (Strickland, *Irish Artists*).

JONES (JANE), bookseller, printer, and publisher in Dublin, Clarendon Street, 1736–39. She was the widow of Theophilus Jones (q.v.), "a Lady of Birth and Family; but who . . . by Misfortunes, were under the Necessity of printing a News-Paper by Subscription, for their support and to maintain a numerous Family" (*Dublin Journal*, 2 Sept. 1750). She continued the *Dublin Evening Post* to 1741. She began the printing of Ware's *Works*, 1739, but died "of Vomiting Blood" before its completion (*Dublin Gazette*, 2 June 1739), and was succeeded by her daughter Elizabeth Jones (q.v.).

JONES (RICHARD), printer in Dublin, King's Arms, Skinner Row, 1694–1702. He was listed as a journeyman in 1694 (no master's name), a journeyman to John Forster (q.v.) in 1696, and fined for intrusion in 1699, 1700, and 1702 (*Guild Records*).

JONES (THEOPHILUS), bookseller, printer, and publisher in Dublin, opposite to Coppinger's Lane, Clarendon Street, 1732–36. He was a surveyor when he began his stationer's career as a publisher in 1732, acquired a printing press in 1734, and enjoyed considerable success in a short two years. He was admitted free of the city in 1734 (Thrift, *Freemen*), was admitted free of the guild in 1734, and paid quarterage through 1735 (*Guild Records*). He published the first successful evening newspaper in Dublin, the *Dublin Evening Post*, 1732–34, then became a printer and took over its printing as well, 1734–36. His press output included Templemain's *History of England*, 1734, a *Pocket Companion for Free-Masons*, 1735, and Dodley's *Toy Shop*, 1735. When James Hoey (q.v.) announced his own publication of the *Toy Shop*, Jones denounced this as "Pyratical . . . a method not at all uncommon to said Gentleman" (*Dublin Evening Post*, 15 Mar. 1734/35). He died in 1736 (*Dublin Evening Post*, 7 Apr.), and was succeeded by his widow, Jane Jones (q.v.).

JONES (THOMAS), papermaker in Dublin, 1701. Sole reference: in 1701 he leased a paper mill at Rathfarnham, County Dublin, from Lord Wharton (Phillips, unpublished thesis).

JONES (WOOD GIBSON), printer and publisher in Dublin, Suffolk Street (1767–70) and later (1777–82), and in Newry (1770–77). 1767–82. He was apprenticed to George Faulkner (q.v.), but quit his apprenticeship early and joined in his family's oil, pickle, and grocer business in Dame Street. In 1767 he was admitted to the guild by special grace, and paid quarterage through 1770. On his return to Dublin in 1777 he again paid quarterage through 1779, served on the Council from 1779, and was carried on the Clerk's list until 1782 (*Guild Records*). He printed a *List of Absentees of Ireland*, 1767, and printed and published Foster's *An Essay on Hospitals*, 1768. In 1770 he moved to Newry, and joined in partnership with Christopher Wynne (q.v.). They published the *Newry Journal*, 1770–74. From 1774 to 1777 Jones worked alone in Newry. There is no evidence of his work following his return to Dublin, and he died in 1782 as the result of an accident in the Music Hall, Fishamble Street.

JOY (**FRANCIS**), bookseller, papermaker, printer, and publisher in Belfast, the Peacock, Bridge Street, 1737–48? He began trade as a tailor, but became a self-made master stationer, making type, ink, paper, printing press, and all, by dint of his own genius. He frequently subscribed to Dublin publications, and in 1737 started the first Belfast newspaper, the *Belfast News-Letter, and General Advertiser*, 1737–47. He constructed and sold printing presses (Munter, *Irish Newspapers*), claiming in 1748 that two of these were operating in Newry and Armagh. He built two paper mills in Randalstown, the first in 1743, and a third in Ballymena in 1747 (*World's Paper Trade Review*). He twice petitioned the Irish House of Commons for assistance in his papermaker ventures (*Commons' Journ. Ire.*, v, 17). He turned his business in Belfast over to his two sons, Henry and Robert Joy (qq.v.), in 1748 while he continued to operate the paper mills.

JOY (**HENRY**), bookseller, printer, and publisher in Belfast, (1) Bridge Street (1747–?); (2) High Street (1765). 1747–89. He was the son of Francis Joy (q.v.), and in partnership with his brother Robert Joy (q.v.) continued the family business and the *Belfast News-Letter* to 1785, then with his son Henry Joy Jr. from 1785 to 1789. Over the imprint H & R Joy the two brothers printed and published extensively: various plays, histories, sermons, tracts, etc., including the *Belfast and Poor Robin's Almanack*, 1753, the *Young Clerk's Vade-Mecum*, 1754, Cocker's *Arithmatic*, 1756, and *Hiram, or the Grand Master-key to the Door of both Ancient and Modern Free-Masonry*, 1765. Henry died in 1789, his will being proved in the Prerogative Court at Dublin.

JOY (**ROBERT**), bookseller, printer, and publisher in Belfast, (1) Bridge Street (1747–?); (2) High Street (1765). 1747–85. He was the son of Francis Joy (q.v.), and in partnership with his brother Henry Joy (q.v.) continued the family business and the *Belfast News-Letter* to 1785. The partners carried on an active trade to 1785 (see Henry Joy). Robert died in 1785, his will being proved in the Prerogative Court at Dublin.

KEARNEY or O'KEARNEY (JOHN), printer in Dublin, 1571. He was the treasurer of St. Patrick's Cathedral, and apparently not a printer by trade, but in 1571 he likely printed *Alphabetum et ratio legendi Hibernicum et Catechismus*, the first book printed in Irish, and possibly he printed as well a religious poem and a broadside in the same year. He was the uncle of William Kearny (q.v.), and he died about 1581.

KEARNEY (WILLIAM), printer in London (1573?–92?), and Dublin, (1) the Cathedral Church of the Blessed Trinity (1592–95); (2) Trinity College (1596). 1573?–98. He was the nephew of John Kearney (q.v.). In 1587 the Privy Council in England informed the Lord Deputy of Ireland that Kearney, a man who "had by the space of fourteene yeares, as well here in England as in some forraine parts, applyed him self to the art and mystery of printing," had been appointed to come to Ireland and to print the New Testament in Irish. He moved to Dublin about 1592 under this warrant. By 1595 he was referred to as the Queen's Printer, and in that year printed a proclamation against Hugh O'Neill, in both English and Irish. Working at Trinity College, he printed part of the New Testament but never completed the work. He died about 1599.

KEATING (JAMES), bookseller and publisher in Dublin, 1738–44. He was admitted to the guild as a quarter brother in 1738 and paid quarterage through 1744 (*Guild Records*). In 1742 he jointly published one of the rival translations of Prévost d'Exiles' *Dean of Coleraine* (see Thomas Bacon).

KEHOE (D.), printer and publisher in Dublin, ca. 1740s. Sole reference: he was stated to have printed and sold in 1740 Purcell's mezzotint print "William III" (Strickland, *Irish Artists*).

KEIGHTLY (BENJAMIN), bookbinder in Dublin, 1770–89. He was apprenticed to George Burnett (q.v.), admitted free of the guild by service in 1770, paid quarterage through 1787, and was listed on the Clerk's list in 1789 (*Guild Records*).

KELBURN or KILBURN (ALEXANDER), bookbinder in Dublin, 1768–89? He was the son of James Kelburn (q.v.), was admitted free of the guild by birth in 1758, paid quarterage through 1788, was listed as "dead" in 1787, but was again listed in the Clerk's list in 1789 (*Guild Records*).

KELBURN or KILBOURNE (JAMES), bookbinder, bookseller, and publisher in Dublin, 1734–66. He was apprenticed to George Ewing (q.v.), admitted free of the guild by service in 1734, and paid quarterage through 1766 (*Guild Records*). He was admitted free of the city in 1734 (Thrift, *Freemen*). In 1748 and 1749 he published several of Charles Lucas' political polemics, for which he was taken into custody by the Irish House of Commons in 1749 (*Commons' Journ. Ire.*, v, 12).

KELLINGTON (JOB) *see* Job Killington

KELLY (IGNATIUS), bookseller and publisher in Dublin, Mary Lane, 1738–53. He was a Catholic, admitted to the guild as a quarter brother in 1738, and paid quarterage through 1752 (*Guild Records*). He had a prosperous business, printing mostly devotional books like de Sales's *Introduction to a Devout Life*, 1742, largely for the country trade. In 1742 he jointly published one of the rival translations of Prévost d'Exiles' *Dean of Coleraine* (see Thomas Bacon). He died in 1753, his will being proved in the Prerogative Court at Dublin.

KELLY (Mrs.), bookseller in Dublin, Mary Lane, 1753?–60? She was a Catholic and the widow of Ignatius Kelly (q.v.). In 1755 she was served a warrant for intrusion, in 1757 admitted to the guild as a quarter brother, and appears to have paid quarterage through 1763 (*Guild Records*). However, in 1760 there was published *A Short Introduction of Grammar*, "Printed for the Executors of the late Widow Kelly, for the benefit of her Children."

KENDALL (THOMAS), printer in Dublin, 1733?–49? He was apprenticed to John Hyde (q.v.), admitted to the guild as a quarter brother in 1733, admitted free in 1749, but paid no quarterage (*Guild Records*). He was admitted free of the city in 1749 (Thrift, *Freemen*). Possibly he worked as a journeyman for Sarah Hyde (q.v.) until she retired from business.

KENNAN (BENJAMIN), printer in Dublin, d. 1758. Sole reference: an obituary notice in 1758 read "Died in Ballsbridge, Benjamin Kennan, printer" (*Dublin Journal*, 7 Jan.).

KENNY (JOHN), stationer in Dublin, 1765–71. He was apprenticed to Oliver Nelson (q.v.), admitted free of the guild in 1765, listed in the Clerk's list as a journeyman in 1770 and 1771, and as "in England" from 1772 to 1777 (*Guild Records*). He was admitted free of the city in 1765 (Thrift, *Freemen*).

KIDD (SAMUEL), bookseller in Coleraine, 1737. He is referred to in the subscribers' list as a bookseller and as having taken six sets of Rollin's *Method of Teaching and Studying Belles Lettres*.

KIERNAN (FARRELL), printer in Dublin, Christ Church Lane, 1770–71 (*Dictionary 1726–75*).

KIERNAN (JOHN), bookseller and printer in Dublin, 1772–73. He was apprenticed to Matthew Williamson (q.v.), did not take out his freedom of the guild, but went into practice (*Guild Records*). He advertised the opening of his shop in 1772 (*Dublin Mercury*, 3 Mar.), and signed an appeal on behalf of reduced tradesmen in 1773 (*Public Journal*, 27 Aug.).

KIERNAN (MARY), bookseller and printer in Dublin, Christ Church Yard, 1772 (*Dictionary 1726–75*).

KILBOURNE (JAMES) *see* James Kelburn

KILBURN (ALEXANDER) *see* Alexander Kelburn

KILLINGTON or KELLINGTON (JOB), bookseller in London (1681?–83), and Dublin, the College Arms, next door to the Bear and Ragged Staff, Castle Street (1685?–88). 1681?–88. He was a bookseller in London from 1681? to 1683 (*Dictionary 1668–1725*), and was listed as a journeyman to Samuel Helsham (q.v.) in Dublin from 1685 to 1688 (*Guild Records*).

KILTERNAN (PAPERMAKERS OF) *see* Richard Eaton, Joshua Kinnier, *and* Robert Nixon

KINEER (JOSHUA) *see* Joshua Kinnier

KING (C.), stationer in Dublin, 1773. Sole reference: in 1773 he signed a memorial to the Irish House of Commons from "Printers, Booksellers, Stationers and Card-Makers"

against additional duties on foreign paper (BL, 1890.e.5. (239)).

KING (GILES), engraver in London (1732–44?), and Dublin (1744?–46). 1732–46. Among his engravings were a series of Irish landscapes, 1744 and 1745, and plates for Smith's *History of Waterford*, 1746 (Strickland, *Irish Artists*).

KING (NICHOLAS), stationer in Dublin, 1718–23. He petitioned the guild in 1715, was refused freedom after "confessing himself no artist," but nevertheless was appointed King's Stationer in Ireland in 1718, acting through a deputy, Samuel Fairbrother (q.v.). The guild petitioned against his appointment—"the said Nicholas King being no brother of this Guild or Person skilled in the Art & Mystery of a Stationer"—to no avail (*Guild Records*). King resigned as King's Stationer in 1723 (Hist. MSS Comm. 2nd rep. 178).

KINGSTON or KYNGSTON (FELIX), printer in London (1597–1651), and Dublin, St. Nicholas Street (1617?–38). 1597–1651. In 1617, as a representative of the London Company of Stationers, he was appointed by the Privy Council in England the King's Stationer of Ireland, along with Bartholomew Downes (q.v.) and Matthew Lownes (q.v.), confirmed by patent in 1618 (*Lib. Munerum*, ii, 95). In 1620 a regrant of this patent to Kingston and Thomas Downes (q.v.) allowed them a monopoly of all printing, bookbinding, and bookselling in Ireland. Under this authority, and as the London company's representative in Dublin, Kingston printed several works with the Stationers' imprint, but also under his own he printed Dermod O'Meara's *Pathologia haereditaria generalis*, 1619, the earliest book printed in Ireland in Latin type. Kingston's Irish connection ended in 1638 when the privileges were sold to William Bladen (q.v.).

KINNIER, KINEER, or KINNEAR (JOSHUA), paper-maker, printer, and publisher in Dublin, (1) the Green Man, on the lower Blind Quay, Fishamble Street (1743–45); (2) the corner of Fishamble Street, near the Blind Quay (1745–67?). 1743–77. He was recorded in business in 1743, possibly in partnership with Zachariah Martineau (q.v.), was admitted free of the guild in 1744, paid quarterage through 1766, and was carried on the Clerk's list until 1777. He was an active guild member, serving as Warden in 1761 (*Guild Records*). In 1744 he was embroiled in a controversy over rival editions of Sale's *Universal History*, Kinnier supporting Margaret Rhames (q.v.) against George Faulkner (q.v.). Kinnier was in a loose partnership with Augustus Long (q.v.), first at the Blind Quay where they published number 5 of the *Harleian Miscellany*, 1744 (*Dublin Courant*, 17 July), and continuing through 1749, although Long had established his own shop in 1745. In 1754, in partnership with Richard Eaton (q.v.) and Robert Nixon (q.v.), he started a paper mill at Kilternan, County Dublin. They went under the name of Papermakers of Kilternan. In 1755 they petitioned Parliament for assistance in papermaking (*Commons' Journ. Ire.*, v, 237), and in 1756 Kinnier became the sole owner of the business and had his own watermark. He appears to have sold his printing and publishing business to Michael North (q.v.) in 1767, while continuing his papermaking. In 1773 he signed a petition to the Irish House of Commons from papermakers objecting to the removal of duties on foreign paper (BL, 1890.e.5 (232)). He died in 1777.

KINNIER (WILLIAM), printer and publisher in Carlow, Dublin Street, 1771–86? He was the first printer in Carlow, and was known almost solely for his newspapers. In 1771 he started the *Carlow Journal*, changing the name in 1774 to the *Carlow Journal; or, Leinster Chronicle*, and continuing to 1785. In 1778 he printed a *Treatise upon . . . Linen Manufacture*. Kinnier died in 1786 (*Dublin Journal*, 16 Sept.), and was succeeded by his widow, Mary Kinnier.

KNIGHT (GEORGE), printer and publisher in Cork, Castle Street, 1754–82. He was in partnership with James Knight (q.v.), their relationship being unknown. In 1771 they joined Phineas Bagnell (q.v.) in publishing the *Cork Evening Post*, in 1777 Bagnell purchased their interest in the paper, and in 1781 the Knights repurchased the right to its title. George Knight apparently died in 1782.

KNIGHT (JAMES), papermaker, printer, and publisher in Cork, Castle Street, 1754–1810. He was in partnership with George Knight (q.v.), their relationship being unknown. From 1771 to 1777 they joined Phineas Bagnell (q.v.) in publishing the *Cork Evening Post*, in 1781 they purchased the paper outright from Bagnell, and the following year they leased his premises on Castle Street as well. About 1784 James built a paper mill, or possibly acquired that of Phineas Bagnell. The Knight mill was known as Glintown, County Cork, which was in fact adjacent to Ballyosheen (and thus, perhaps, the same premises as Bagnell's). From 1782 to 1791 James was joined by John Knight, and then from 1791 to 1810 by Henry Knight; the various partnerships continued the publication of the *Cork Evening Post*, and also did a great deal of printing for the Cork Corporation (Caulfield, *Cork Council Book*).

KNOWLES (THOMAS), printer and publisher in Dublin, Essex Street, 1749–51. His only press work was on behalf of the court and aldermanic party in the Charles Lucas controversy of these years (Munter, *Irish Newspapers*). Knowles printed and published a series of anti-Lucas broadsides and polemics, such as *Mr. De Lat—che's GALLANTT-SHEW*, 1749, and several ephemeral periodicals, the *Censor Extraordinary*, 1749,

Political Monitor, 1749, *Church Monitor*, 1749, and *The Nettle*, 1751.

KYNGSTON (FELIX) *see* Felix Kingston

L

LAAFA (Charles de), bookseller in Cork, 1704–23? He was paid by the Cork Corporation for supplying newspapers in 1704 and again in 1714. Possibly payments recorded from 1715 to 1723—at which time Phineas Bagnell (q.v.) began supplying the Corporation—were made as well to de Laffa (Caulfield, *Cork Council Book*).

LAKE (William), papermaker in Dublin, 1719–22? From 1719 he operated a paper mill in Templeogue, County Dublin, and in 1719 he petitioned the Irish House of Commons for financial assistance in papermaking (*World's Paper Trade Review*).

LAMB (John), bookseller and publisher in Dublin, Winetavern Street, near Christ Church, 1731–52. He was fined for intrusion in 1731, admitted to the guild as a quarter brother in 1736, and paid quarterage through 1752 (*Guild Records*). He published Blyth's *Devout Paraphrase on the Seven Penitential Psalms*, 1749, and subscribed to six copies of Manning's *Account of the Catholic Faith*, 1750. A John Lamb died in 1765, his will being proved in the Prerogative Court at Dublin.

LAMB (William), bookseller in Dublin, 1743–47. He was admitted to the guild as a quarter brother in 1743 and paid quarterage through 1747 (*Guild Records*). A William Lamb died in 1764, his will being proved in the Prerogative Court at Dublin.

LARKING (**BARTHOLOMEW**), bookbinder in Youghal, 1639. Sole reference: he was admitted free of the city of Youghal and listed as a bookbinder in 1639 (Caulfield, *Council Book of the Corporation of Youghal*).

LAURENCE (**ANTHONY**) *see* Anthony Lawrence

LAUTIL or LAUTELL (**PIERRE**), bookseller in Dublin, Dame Street, 1742–49? A French Huguenot, he was admitted free of the guild by petition in 1742, and paid quarterage through 1743 (*Guild Records*).

LAW (**ANN**), printer in Dublin, the Reindeer, Montrath Street, 1763. She was possibly the wife or daughter of Samuel Law (q.v.) (*Dictionary 1726–75*).

LAW (**ROBERT**), printer in Dublin, Castle Street (1774–?), and in Limerick, (1) Mill Lane, near the Main Guard (1788–89); (2) at the corner shop of the Exchange (1789). 1774–89. An announcement of his marriage in 1774 referred to him as a printer in Castle Street (*Freeman's Journal*, 9 July). In Limerick he printed and published the *Limerick Herald, and Munster Advertiser*, 1788–89.

LAW (**SAMUEL**), bookseller and printer in Dublin, Montrath Street, 1755–78. He possibly started work as early as 1752 at the Reindeer, the former premises of Simon Goulding (q.v.). He was admitted to the guild as a quarter brother in 1755, as a free brother in 1761, paid quarterage through 1765, and in 1774 paid quarterage owing. A complaint was registered against him in 1761 by an apprentice for back wages due, which the guild ordered paid, and a petition was made against him in 1775 by another apprentice (*Guild Records*). In 1773 he signed a memorial to the Irish House of Commons against additional duties on foreign paper (BL, 1890.e.5. (239)). In 1774 he advertised: "In a few days will be published (or rather revived) by Samuel Law ... *The Dublin News-Letter*" (*Hibernian Journal*, 19 Jan.). It had but a short existence, and by 1778 Law was a prisoner for debt in Four Courts Marshalsea.

LAWLER (THOMAS), printer in Dublin, the Golden Key, Dame Street, 1731–37. He was apprenticed to Aaron Rhames (q.v.), admitted free of the guild by service in 1731, and paid quarterage through 1737 (*Guild Records*). He was admitted free of the city in 1733 (Thrift, *Freemen*).

LAWRENCE or LAURENCE (ANTHONY), bookseller in Dublin, (1) Rose and Crown, Dame Street (1678); (2) the Bible and Crown, Castle Street (1678–?). 1678–1709? A Catholic, he was a journeyman to William Norman (q.v.) in 1678, but later in the year transferred to Matthew Gun (q.v.). He was in business for himself by 1680 when he was admitted free of the guild, but he was never sworn and paid no quarterage. There is a reference to a Thomas Wilton "journeyman to Mr. Lawrence" in 1718 (*Guild Records*). In 1708 Lawrence was "taken into custory of her Majesty's messingers, on suspicion of Printing and Vending Popish Prayer Books contrary to Law" (*Dublin Intelligence*, 20 Nov.), but he turned state's evidence and was released (*London Gazette*, 18–21 Feb. 1708/9).

LAWRENCE (MARY), bookseller and publisher in Dublin, the Bible and Crown, on the Merchant's Quay, near the Old Bridge, 1709–27. She was the widow of Peter Lawrence (q.v.), and in 1722 took into partnership her son-in-law John Watson (q.v.). They made two attempts at publishing almanacs, the *Irish–English Almanack*, 1724, and the *Citizen's Almanack*, 1727.

LAWRENCE (PETER), bookseller and publisher in Dublin, Merchant's Quay, 1697–1709. He was apprenticed to his brother-in-law Thomas Servant (q.v.), admitted free of the guild by service in 1697, served in the Council from 1705, and as Warden in 1707 (*Guild Records*). He was admitted free of the city in 1697 (Thrift, *Freemen*). In 1706, with other stationers, he published William Barton's *Psalms*. He died in 1709, and was succeeded by his widow, Mary Lawrence (q.v.).

LAWRY (ARCHIBALD) *see* Archibald Lowry

LEACH (JOHN), bookseller and publisher in Dublin, Castle Street, 1666. Sole reference: he published Thomas Bladen's *Praxis Francisci Clarke*, 1666 (*Dictionary 1641–67*).

LEATH (WILLIAM), bookseller in Dublin, 1566. He was associated with Humphrey Powell (q.v.) in selling English prayer books, 1566, and may have succeeded Powell in business (*Irish Book Lover*, Apr.–May 1941).

LEATHLEY (ANNE), bookseller, printer, and publisher in Dublin, at the corner of Sycamore Alley, Dame Street, later, 63 Dame Street, 1758–74. She was the widow of Joseph Leathley (q.v.), and continued the family business, her first advertisement appearing in 1759 (*Sleater's Public Gazetteer*, 6 Mar.). She was listed by the guild as an intruder in 1763 (*Guild Records*). Her publications, jointly with other stationers, included Ossian's *Works*, 1763, Shakespeare's *Works*, 1766, Smollett's *Humphrey Clinker*, 1771, and, alone, the *Letters of Lady Rachel Russell*, 1774. She died in 1775 (*Hibernian Magazine*, Dec.).

LEATHLEY (JOSEPH), bookseller, printer, and publisher in Dublin, at the corner of Sycamore Alley, Dame Street, 1718–

57. He was apprenticed to John Hyde (q.v.), listed as an intruder in 1718, admitted free of the guild by service in 1719, paid quarterage through 1757, served as Warden in 1732, as Master in 1746, and on the Council from 1735 (*Guild Records*). His sister Elizabeth married Thomas Whitehouse (q.v.) in 1725. Leathley was a successful stationer, publishing a variety of pamphlets, song-books, and, with various combinations of stationers, such undertakings as Smith's *Sermons*, 1719, Shadwell's *Works*, 1720, Keating's *History of Ireland*, 1723, Ware's *Works*, 1739, and Shakespeare's *Works*, 1747. He died in 1757 (*Pue's Occurrences*, 18 Oct.), and in 1758 his bound stock, "consisting of near 3000 Volumes of Books in most Faculties and Languages," was sold at auction (*Sleater's Public Gazetteer*, 21 Nov.). He was succeeded by his widow, Anne Leathley (q.v.).

LEATHLEY (SAMUEL), printer in Dublin, (1) St. Audeon's Arch (1772?–74); (2) Ormond Quay (1782–89). 1772–89. He was apprenticed to Augustus Long (q.v.), was admitted free of the guild by service in 1773, and paid quarterage through 1774. He was recorded as "dead" in the 1789 Clerk's list (*Guild Records*). He was admitted free of the city in 1764. He printed the *Freeman's Journal*, 1776–82.

LEE (JOHN), bookbinder in Dublin, 1735. Sole reference: "John Lee, a Bookbinder and another person were committed to Newgate for robbing the printer hereof [George Faulkner (q.v.)] of several Setts of the Writings of JS. [Swift] DDDSP" (*Dublin Journal*, 15 Apr. 1735).

LEE (JOHN), bookseller and publisher in Dublin, in the Musical Way, 1773–89? He was admitted free of the guild by petition and paid quarterage through 1789 (*Guild Records*). He was admitted free of the city in 1783. He was primarily a music seller. He joined in partnership with Edmund Lee, relationship unknown, in publishing music engravings from 1788 to 1789.

LEE (SAMUEL), bookseller and publisher in London (1677–93), and Dublin, Skinner Row, near the Thosel (1693–94). 1677–94. He began a long and troubled career in London, which Dunton summarized as "Such a Pirate, such a Cormorant was never before. Copies, Books, Men, Shops, all was one, he held no propriety, right or wrong, good or bad, till at last he began to be known, and the booksellers, not enduring so ill a man among them to disgrace them spewed him out, and off he marched for Ireland where he acted as *felonious-Lee* as he did in London" (*Dictionary 1668–1725*). In Dublin he published Thomas Munley's *Present State of Europe*, 1693, *Last Speech and Confession of Mr. James Geoghegan, Priest*, 1694, and, posthumously, Syrus' *A Clear . . . Explication of the History of . . . Jesus Christ*, 1695. He died in October 1694, his will being proved in the Prerogative Court at Dublin.

LEE (WILLIAM), stationer in Dublin, College Arms, next door to the Bear and Ragged Staff, Castle Street, 1682–87. He was listed as an intruder in 1682, as a journeyman to Samuel Helsham (q.v.) from 1683 to 1687, and as "gon" in 1688 (*Guild Records*).

LEONARD (PETER), printer in Dublin, 1773. Sole reference: in 1773 he was referred to as a printer and "one of Alderman Faulkner's [George Faulkner (q.v.)] men" (*Hibernian Journal*, 24 Jan.).

LESLIE (CHARLES), bookseller and publisher in Dublin, the Cock, Castle Street, 1745–46. In 1745 he published *An Allusion to the third ode of the first book of Horace*, and in 1746 he advertised the publication of the twelfth and later the sixteenth volumes of Sale's *Universal History* (*Dublin Gazette*, 3 June). George Faulkner (q.v.), the publisher of the history to that date, accused Leslie of interloping, and a war of rival claims followed (*Dublin Journal*, Sept. and Oct. 1746; *Dublin Courant*, Oct. 1746). Leslie finally withdrew from the project.

LETCHER (Mr.), bookseller in Tralee, 1694. Sole reference: he was listed in the colophon as being one of the provincial sellers of the *London Master: or, the Jew Detected*, 1694.

LILBURN or LILLBURN (WILLIAM), bookbinder in Dublin, 1767–77? He was apprenticed to James Stephenson (q.v.), later transferred to William Gilbert (q.v.), was admitted free of the guild by service in 1767, paid quarterage through 1769, had an apprentice enrolled in 1772, was listed in 1777 as in arrears of quarterage, and in 1783 as being "abroad" (*Guild Records*). He was admitted free of the city in 1768 (Thrift, *Freemen*).

LINEAL (GEORGE) *see* George Lyneall

LINN (HENRY), bookbinder in Belfast, d. 1786. Sole reference: an obituary notice read, "Died in the Poor-House of Belfast, aged 90, Mr. Henry Linn, the oldest bookbinder probably in Ireland" (*Dublin Journal*, 14 Nov. 1786).

LISSE or LISLE (M.), engraver in Limerick, d. 1774. He was an engraver and drawing master from Paris. His death notice in the *Freeman's Journal* listed him as Monsieur Lisse and in the *Dublin Journal* as M. Lisle.

LITTLE (GEORGE), stationer in Dublin, 1714–21? He was apprenticed to Patrick Campbell (q.v.), was admitted free of the guild by service in 1714, in the same year was recorded as a journeyman to Campbell, and was listed in the Clerk's list in 1715, 1716, and 1721 (*Guild Records*).

LLOYD (EDWARD), printer and publisher in Dublin, (1) Oxman Town and Printing Coffee House, Church Street (1703–5); (2) the publishing house, the New Post Office Printing House, Essex Street, at the corner of Sycamore Alley (1707–13), and in London (1732–36). 1703–36. He was a notorious Jacobite coffee-house proprietor and publisher. He was twice referred to as a printer (*Report of the Committee, in relation to Edward Lloyd*, 1713; *Commons' Journ. Ire.*, iii, 486–88), but there is no real evidence that he ever printed; indeed, his Dublin addresses were the shops of other stationers: that of 1703–5, Francis Dickson's (q.v.), and that of 1707–13, Edward Waters' (q.v.). He was in partnership with Richard Pue (q.v.), publishing the periodical *Impartial Occurrences*, 1703–6. In 1707 he was ordered into custody for publishing a *Postscript to Mr. Higgins's Sermon*, and absconded (*Lords' Journ. Ire.*, ii, 172–73). In the politically troubled years of Anne, under the Viceroyalty of Ormond and Lord Chancellorship of Phipps, Lloyd's Tory sympathies were allowed free reign. In 1712 he was again ordered to trial for publishing the *Memoirs of Chevalier de St. George* (*Lords' Journ. Ire.*, ii, 447–48), but Ormond ordered the charges dropped. The same year Lloyd began publication of *Lloyd's News-Letter*, a vehemently anti-Whig periodical. When Ormond was replaced by Shaftsbury in 1713, the House of Lords renewed their inquiry into Lloyd's case and he was forced to flee to London (Munter, *Irish Newspapers*). Years later in London he published a *Description of the City of Dublin*, 1732, and *Thoughts on Trade*, 1736.

LONG (AUGUSTUS), bookseller, printer, and publisher in Dublin, (1) the Lord Mountjoy, Crane Lane (1743–44); (2) the Green Man, on the lower Blind Quay (1744); (3) the

Bible and Dove, one door above Parliament House, College Green (1745); (4) at Essex Bridge (1746–47); (5) under Walsh's Coffee House, Essex Street (1748); (6) on the Back Quay (1749–74?). 1743–74? Until 1749 he worked out of the shops of others: Samuel Forbes (q.v.), 1743–44, Joshua Kinnier (q.v.), 1744, William Heatly (q.v.), 1745, and Halhed Garland (q.v.), 1746–48. Long first set up on his own on the Back Quay. In 1743 he was appointed printer of the *Dublin Gazette*, and from 1744 to 1745 jointly printed this with Forbes. In 1744, with Kinnier, he printed the *Harleian Miscellany*. In 1747 Long advertised an auction of books at Merchant's Coffee House, Essex Street (*Dublin Journal*, 14 Mar.). From 1748 through 1749 Long and Halhed Garland, in the service of the Castle clique—Cox, Cooke, and Burton—published anti–Charles Lucas pamphlets and two newspapers, the *Tickler*, 1748–49, and the *Patriot*, 1749. In 1749 Long became printer to the post office and apparently adopted a more respectable persona. He was admitted to the guild as a quarter brother in 1752, admitted free in 1764, and paid quarterage through 1772 (*Guild Records*). In 1750 he attempted a new periodical, the *Play-House Journal*, a theater review, "to treat the merit and demerit of dramatic writers and performers." He died in 1774 (*Freeman's Journal*, 10 Feb.).

LONG (Catherine), bookseller in Limerick, 1769–74. She was listed as a bookseller from 1769 to 1771 (Herbert, *Limerick Printers and Printing*), in 1773 she was listed in the subscribers' list for James Williams' (q.v.) printing of the *Merchant Directory*, and in 1774 an advertisement referred to her as a bookseller (*Hibernian Journal*, 28 Sept.).

LONG (Henry), printer in Limerick, ? Sole reference: he was listed as a printer whose daughter married Joseph Sexton (q.v.). Sexton's dates were 1747–82, but no dates were given for Long (Herbert, *Limerick Printers and Printing*).

LORD (HENRY), printer in Dublin, the Angel and Bible, Cook Street, 1750–55. He is reported as a Catholic printer for these years (*Dictionary 1726–75*). This is based upon Collins' *Life in Old Dublin* and is undoubtedly an error for Patrick Lord (q.v.). No evidence exists for a Henry Lord of Dublin.

LORD (PATRICK), bookseller, printer, and publisher in Dublin, (1) the Angel and Bible, Cook Street (1743–61); (2) Bridge Street (1761–62). 1743–62. A Catholic, he was admitted to the guild as a quarter brother in 1743 and paid quarterage through 1761 (*Guild Records*). He printed Catholic devotional books and pamphlets—e.g., the *Farmer's Letters* of the 1750s—and was constantly harassed for these pro-Catholic tracts. His press output included *State Letters of the Right Honourable Richard Earl of Cork*, 1743, Manning's *Account of the Catholic Faith*, 1750, and, most noteworthy, O'Connor's *Case of the Roman Catholics*, 1755, although in the production of the last, Lord was reported "so timid that he stopped the press on account of being informed . . . that the strokes against the Court of Rome . . . would disgust the Popish Clergy and damn the work" (O'Conor, *Memoirs of Charles O'Conor, Belanagare*). A Cork edition of the work was banned in the same year (*A Letter from a Gentleman in Dublin to his Friend in Cork*, 1755). It appears that Lord's troubles mounted, for in 1762 he left off business and under some duress was "in a hurry of removing his things when he quitted the house in Bridge Street" (Hist. MSS Comm., 8th rep., app. pt. 1). He died in Cork in 1785 (*Hibernian Chronicle*, 7 Apr.).

LORD (THOMAS), bookseller, printer, and publisher in Cork, (1) Exchange Coffee House, Castle Street (1767–70?); (2) Lord's New Printing House (1783?, 1790); also in Cashel

(1770–80, 1788), Youghal (1780–84), Clonmel (1786), Carlow, Dublin Street (1788), Waterford (1792–93), and Roscrea (1798). 1767–98. A Catholic, he was the son of Patrick Lord (q.v.). His long, itinerant career began in Cork where he married the daughter of Cornelius Sullivan (q.v.) (*Freeman's Journal*, 3 Nov. 1767), and apparently succeeded to his father-in-law's business at what had been Sullivan's first address. Within a few years he began moving about like a traveling show, becoming, in turn, the first printer in Cashel and Roscrea. He printed ballads, pamphlets, and controversial works like Brook's *Trial of Catholics*. His other work included a *Prospect of Poetry*, Cork 1770, he wrote and published a *History of the City of Youghal*, Youghal, 1780, he started *Lord's Munster Herald or, General Advertiser*, Cashel, 1788, and in the same year, with a printer named Eustace, founded the *Carlow Mercury, or Leinster Advertiser*, Carlow. Back in Cork he printed *The Relieving of Gibraltar*, 1783?, and the *Cork Weekly Magazine, or, Universal Repository*, 1790. His professional life appears to have ended in Roscrea in 1798, "where the press was burnt in that year by the yeomanry in suspicion of printing seditious ballads" (Burke, *History of Clonmel*).

LOWIS (JOHN), bookseller and printer in Londonderry, 1735–48. A *Sermon*, 1735, bears his imprint as does a *Seasonable Warning*, 1745, and he took subscriptions for Dublin editions of Rollin's *Ancient History*, 1736, Virgil's *Works*, 1737, and Tillotson's *Sermons*, 1738. He was one of the undertakers of Faulkner's (q.v.) edition of Sale's *Universal History*, 1745, and in 1748 Abraham Bradley (q.v.) announced that his publications were sold by Lowis (*Dublin Courant*, 8–12 May). In 1738 Lowis advertised for the apprehension of a runaway apprentice, Richard Stocks, "about eighteen Years Age, Ill grown, Black-brow'd, Pock-freckled, Shambling-legg'd and Flat-sol'd" (*Dublin News-Letter*, 28 Jan.).

LOWIS (ROBERT), printer in Londonderry, 1771. Possibly a successor of John Lowis (q.v.); their relationship is unknown. He printed a pamphlet in 1771 (*Dictionary 1726–75*).

LOWNES (MATTHEW), bookseller in London (1591–1625), and Dublin (1617?–20?). 1591–1625. In 1617, as representative of the London Company of Stationers, he was appointed by the Privy Council, along with Bartholomew Downes (q.v.) and Felix Kingston (q.v.), one of the King's Stationers in Ireland (*Lib. Munerum*, ii, 95). It is doubtful whether he ever went to Ireland, and two years later, 1620, the patent was reissued in the names of Kingston and Thomas Downs (q.v.). Lownes died in 1625.

LOWRY, LAWRY, or LOWRIE (ARCHIBALD), bookseller in Dublin, (1) the Bible and Crown, Castle Street (1700–?); (2) Bride's Alley (1711?–29). 1700–29. He was a journeyman to Matthew Gun (q.v.) in 1700, listed as an intruder in 1711, admitted free of the guild in 1712, and paid quarterage through 1729 (*Guild Records*). He was admitted free of the city in 1713 (Thrift, *Freemen*).

LOWRY (ISAAC), printer in Londonderry, 1764. Sole reference: in 1764 he printed a *Sermon Preached from Rom. 5c. 7v.* (*Biblio. Soc. Ire.*, viii, no. 2).

LOWRY (JOSEPH), bookbinder in Dublin, Essex Street (1684). 1683–84. He was listed as an intruder in 1683, and as a journeyman to Jacob Milner (q.v.) in 1684 (*Guild Records*).

LUCAS (JOHN), printer and publisher in Dublin, 1772–73. He was the nephew of Dr. Charles Lucas, and, with Amyas Griffith, he printed and published the *Public Monitor, or New Freeman's Journal*, 1772–73.

LYNCH (ELIZABETH), bookseller, printer, and publisher in Dublin, Skinner Row, with a law bookshop in the Four Courts, 1769–91. She published Howard's *Almeyda*, 1769, *Siege of Namur*, 1773, and printed and published Jacob's *Law Grammar*, 1772. In 1773 she signed a memorial to the Irish House of Commons against additional duties on foreign paper (BL, 1890. e.5. (239)). On her death her stock was sold at auction (Phillips, unpublished thesis).

LYNCH (MARTIN), bookseller in Galway, 1710. Sole reference: advertisements in 1710 listed him as one of the provincial booksellers taking subscriptions to a Dublin edition of the *Tryal of Doctor Henry Sacheverell* (*Dublin Intelligence*, 24 June and 1 July).

LYNEALL or LINEAL (GEORGE), printer in Dublin, Chequer Lane (1767–77?, 1787–89), and in Wexford (1778?–87). 1767–89. He was apprenticed to Samuel Powell (q.v.), was admitted free of the guild by service in 1767, paid quarterage through 1777 and again in 1787, and was listed in the Clerk's list to 1789 (*Guild Records*). He was admitted free of the city in 1767 (Thrift, *Freemen*). It is likely that he was in Wexford during the years when he paid no quarterage to the Dublin guild, and in 1779 he printed *A Constitutional Sermon*, Wexford.

LYNOTT (ALICK), bookseller in Galway, 1762–74. He was listed in the subscribers' list as taking seven sets of Faulkner's (q.v.) edition of Swift's *Works*, 1762, and an advertisement in 1774 lists him as a seller of patent drugs (*Hibernian Journal*, 28 Sept.).

LYONS (EDWARD), engraver in Dublin, (1) over the cloth shop, near Essex Bridge, opposite Brooke's glass shop (1752–

53?); (2) at the Three Sugar Loaves, next door to Mr. Saul's, Grocer, Fishamble Street (1760?–63); (3) the Parrot, next door to the Globe Coffee House, Essex Street (1763?); (4) 24 Essex Street, next door to the Ballast Office (?–1789). 1752?–89? He was a herald painter and an engraver, producing many bookplates, among them James La Touche's, Charles Lucas', and Leonard McNally's, and among his publications were Tom Echlin, 1752, Rev. John Murphy, 1753, and "Crazy Crow," 1764. He retired about 1789 and died in 1801.

Mc

McALLISTER, McALISTER, or McALLESTER
(THOMAS), bookbinder and publisher in Dublin, 1768–90. He
was apprenticed to William Gilbert (q.v.), admitted free of the
guild by service in 1768, paid quarterage through 1781, was
listed as in arrears in 1787, and on the Clerk's list to 1789 (*Guild
Records*). He was admitted free of the city in 1768 (Thrift,
Freemen). He published, with other stationers, Steele's *Town
Talk*, 1790.

McCLELLAND (JOSHUA), bookseller in Dublin, the Sycamore Tree, Sycamore Alley, 1731–34. He was admitted to the
guild as a quarter brother on petition in 1731 and paid quarterage through 1734 (*Guild Records*).

McCONNEL (R.), printer in Belfast, 1768. Sole reference:
his imprint was on a 1768 chapbook (*Catalogue of the Chap
Books and Broadsides*, Harvard University).

McCULLOH, McCULLOCH, or McCULLOUGH
(ALEXANDER), bookseller, printer, and publisher in Dublin,
(1) Skinner Row (1754–62); (2) Henry Street (1763–71?,
1786?–89), and Birr (1772?–85?). 1754–89. He was admitted
free of the guild in 1754, paid quarterage through 1771 and
again in 1786, was recorded as "in country" in 1775 and 1783,
and listed in the Clerk's list to 1789 (*Guild Records*). His publications were primarily newspapers. In Dublin he printed and
published the *General Advertiser*, 1754, the *Dublin Evening
Post*, 1756–57, the *Public Register: or, Freeman's Journal*,
1763–66, and the *Dublin Evening Packet*, 1770–71. In 1758

he was listed as a bookseller and seller of "Walker's Patent Genuine Jesuit Drops" (*Sleater's Public Gazetteer*, 23 Sept.). About 1772 he went to Birr where he was the first printer in that town and started its first newspaper, the *Birr Weekly Journal*, 1774, and also printed an arithmetic book, 1775. It appears that he returned to Dublin about 1785 or 1786.

McCULLOUGH (WILLIAM), printer in Dublin, d. 1755. Sole reference: an obituary notice in 1755 read "Died suddenly, Mr. William McCullough, printer" (*Dublin Journal*, 24–28 June).

McDANIEL (MICHAEL) *see* Michael McDonnell

McDANIEL (THOMAS) *see* Thomas McDonnell

McDONALD (DARBY) *see* Darby McDonnell

McDONALD (JOHN) *see* John McDonnell

McDONNELL or McDONALD (DARBY), papermaker in Dublin, 20 Cook Street, 1773–99. In 1773 he signed a petition to the Irish House of Commons objecting to the removal of duties on foreign paper (BL, 1890.e.5. (232)). He was probably a successor to Michael McDonnell (q.v.).

McDONNELL or McDONALD (JOHN), papermaker in Dublin, (1) 2 Bridge Street; (2) 2 Dirty Lane; (3) 31 Cook Street. 1773?–1800. In 1773 he signed a petition to the Irish House of Commons objecting to the removal of duties on foreign paper (BL, 1890.e.5. (232)). He was probably a successor to Michael McDonnell (q.v.).

McDONNELL or McDANIEL (MICHAEL), papermaker in Dublin, 1749–58. He built two paper mills at Tallaght, County Dublin in 1749. He was served with a warrant for intrusion in 1755 (Guild Records). In 1755 he petitioned Parliament for assistance in paper manufacturing and in 1757 received £200 (*Commons' Journ. Ire.*, vi, 30–32). From 1750 he received annual premiums from the Dublin Society for the encouragement of papermaking. He established a long line of family papermakers under various names—Daniel, McDaniel, McDonald, and McDonnell—sources indicating religious bias being partly responsible for the variation in spelling.

McDONNEL or McDANIEL (THOMAS), bookseller and printer in Dublin, (1) Meath Street (1770–76?); (2) 50 Essex Street (1788?–99). 1770–99. A Catholic, he was admitted free of the guild in 1793 (*Guild Records*). In partnership with Michael Mills (q.v.) he printed and published the *Hibernian Journal or Chronicle of Liberty*, 1770–99, and he printed and published the *Dublin Weekly Journal*, 1785–97. In 1793 he was taken into custody over the printing in the *Hibernian Journal* of an "Address of United Irishmen to the Volunteers of Ireland," but was freed upon giving evidence (*A Full Report of the Trial at the Bar ... of William Drennan*, 1794). He died in 1809, his will being proved in the Prerogative Court at Dublin.

McENROY (MATHIAS) *see* Mathias Muckleroy

McMAHON (JOHN), papermaker in Dublin, Parliament Street, 1764–73. He was an apprentice to Henry Saunders (q.v.), but did not complete his apprenticeship (*Guild Records*). He had a paper mill in Donnybrook, County Dublin, from 1764 to 1773.

M

MACKY (S.), printer in Cork, on the Flags, near North Gate, 1773 (*Dictionary 1726–75*).

MACLANE (EDWARD), printer in Dublin, 1729 (*Dictionary 1726–75*).

MADOCKS (HANAH), bookseller in Dublin, New Row, 1718–29. He was listed by the guild as an intruder in 1718 (*Guild Records*), and in 1729 he advertised Brooking's Map of Dublin (*Dublin Weekly Journal*, 15 Feb.).

MAGEE (JAMES), bookseller, printer, and publisher in Belfast, (1) near the Four-corners, Bridge Street (1736–44); (2) the Crown and Bible, Bridge Street (1744–89). 1736–89. He was in partnership with Samuel Wilson (q.v.) from 1736 to 1744. They did some printing and publishing and took subscriptions to many Dublin publications. After 1744 Magee occasionally joined in printing projects with John Hay (q.v.) and James Blow (q.v.). On his own, Magee was a prolific printer of plays, music, political tracts, and chapbooks, including the *Belfast Courant*, 1745–46, Burns's *Poems*, 1767, the first edition printed out of Scotland, the Belfast *Almanack*, 1772, and *Magee's Belfast Almanack*, 1786. His last imprint was a *Sermon*, 1789. He was succeeded by his son William Magee.

MAHON (D.), bookseller in Strokestown, 1747. Sole reference: an advertisement in 1747 listed him as one of the provincial sellers of Exshaw's *London Magazine* (*London Magazine*, Jan.).

MAHON (PATRICK) *see* Patrick Meighan

MAIN (ROBERT), bookseller and publisher in Dublin, (1) Dame Street, opposite Fownes Street (1750–51); (2) at Homer's Head, Dame Street (1751–54). 1750–54. He was admitted to the guild as a quarter brother in 1750, admitted free in 1751, and paid quarterage through 1753 (*Guild Records*). In 1751 he moved into the shop of the deceased Henry Hawker (q.v.). In 1753 he published Smollett's *Ferdinand Count Fathom* and a *History of Jemmy and Jenny Jassamy*; then Main got involved in the affair of Richardson's *Sir Charles Grandison* (see George Faulkner). Faced with a pirated Irish edition of *Grandison* by John Exshaw (q.v.), Henry Saunders (q.v.), and Peter Wilson (q.v.), Richardson entered into negotiations with Main to sell his English edition at a lower rate than asked in London, hoping that "Mr. Main will disappoint the worst robbers." Main was supplied as well with Richardson's broadside attacking Faulkner, to be distributed in Dublin gratis. The Irish stationers saw this as an "execrable design" against their printing business (*Dublin Spy*, 5 Nov. 1753), and the pirates persevered to publication. Main eventually received 750 copies of the London edition from Richardson but realized little profit and lost all support from his fellow stationers. In 1754 he went bankrupt and his stock was sold at auction.

MAINWARING (BARTHOLOMEW), bookseller in Dublin, at Corelli's Head, College Green, opposite Anglesey Street, 1737. He was listed as a bookseller and music publisher in 1737 (Gilbert, *History of Dublin*). He was the brother of William Mainwaring (q.v.), who succeeded Bartholomew in business. Bartholomew died in 1758 (*Dublin Grant Book*).

MAINWARING (WILLIAM), printer and publisher in Dublin, at Corelli's Head, College Green, 1738–63. He was primarily a music printer and seller and succeeded his brother Bartholomew Mainwaring (q.v.) in business. He was in partnership with William Neal (q.v.) from 1740 to 1741. He published a variety of oratorios, country dances, Irish airs, etc., including Geminiani's *Harmonical Guide*, 1740, and the *Formation of Harlequin*, 1758, and he published as well the *Monthly Masque*, 1749–54. He died in 1763 and was succeeded by his widow, Mrs. William Mainwaring (q.v.).

MAINWARING (WILLIAM, Mrs.), printer and publisher in Dublin, at Corelli's Head, College Green, 1763–65. She was the widow of and successor to William Mainwaring (q.v.). She revived the *Monthly Masque*, and printed this from 1763 to 1765.

MAKRUEL (JAMES), bookseller in Waterford, 1713. Sole reference: an advertisement in 1713 listed him as one of the provincial sellers of the *Book of Common Prayer* (*Dublin Gazette*, 11 July).

MALONE (DANIEL), engraver and typefounder in Dublin, Crampton Quay (1750–52?). 1746–70. His engraving work included frontispieces for Melmoth's *Letters of Pliny*, two editions, 1748 and 1751, the *Preceptor*, 1761, Miller's *Gardiner's Dictionary*, 1764, and Gough's *Arithmatic*, 1770. In 1748 he joined in partnership with Robert Perry (q.v.) to design and produce type. In 1749 they advertised "all manners of printing types in use" (*Dublin Journal*, 7 Feb.), and in 1750 they opened a new foundry. The Dublin Society awarded them £10 for the encouragement of type manufacture, and they petitioned Parliament for further assistance, but nothing came of the request (*Commons' Journ. Ire.*, v, 229). Advertisements for publications in 1753, 1756, and 1761 announced the use of "Malone and Perry" type, but it appears that after 1752, or so, Malone was not active in the typefounding partnership.

MALONE (JAMES), bookseller, printer, and publisher in Dublin, Skinner Row, 1672–1718. A Catholic, he was admitted free of the city as a stationer in 1672 (Thrift, *Freemen*), admitted free of the guild in 1676, paid quarterage through 1693, and was listed in the Clerk's list to 1718 (*Guild Records*). He printed and published "all sorts of Prayer-Books, Books of Piety, Devotion and school books," as well as chapbooks for the country trade. During the Glorious Revolution he became a captain in the army of James II and the semi-official government printer. Later it was claimed that during this period he had seized the press of Joseph Ray (q.v.) (*Commons' Journ. Ire.*, ii, 250–64). He was made an Alderman in 1689 and, jointly with his son Richard Malone (q.v.), King's Printer in 1690 (*Lib. Munerum*, ii, 95). During these years he printed tracts and pamphlets in James's cause—e.g., *A Relation of . . . the last Campaign, betwixt His Majesty's Royal Army and the Forces of the Prince of Orange sent to joyn the Rebels*, 1689—and also the *Dublin Gazette*, 1689–90, the official Jacobite organ (Munter, *Handlist*). The moment of glory brought its retribution: with James's defeat Malone lost his position as King's Printer, in 1696 he was disfranchised by the Dublin Assembly (*Cal. Anc. Rec. Dublin*), and the guild followed by rescinding his freedom. In 1698 he was taken into custody by the Lord Lieutenant for publishing the New Testament (see Thomas Somervell), and the guild subsequently condemned the work for having "many Errors, etc, throughout the Impression." In 1703 he was sentenced to nine years' imprisonment for publishing the *Memoirs of King James*, but apologized and was released (*Commons' Journ. Ire.*, ii, 366–71, 380, 389–90), and in 1708 he was fined and imprisoned for publishing a *Manual of Devout Prayers*, but, again denying any "evil intent or meaning," his prison sentence was dropped (*Dublin Intelligence*, 20 and 28 Nov.). During Anne's reign passions died down and Malone could be remembered for his attendance at music halls,

> There you might see old Alderman Malone,
> Who cou'd relate the Feats of forty one.

His long, turbulent career ended with an advertisement that he was leaving business and would sell his stock at auction (*Pue's Occurrences*, 16 Dec. 1718), the stock being purchased by Luke Dowling (q.v.). Malone died in 1721, his will being proved in the Prerogative Court at Dublin.

MALONE (RICHARD), printer in Dublin, Skinner Row, 1690. In 1690, jointly with his father, James Malone (q.v.), he was appointed King's Printer in Ireland (*Lib. Munerum*, ii, 95). It is doubtful that he took any part in the bookselling or printing business, the appointment notwithstanding.

MANKLIN (RICHARD), bookseller in Dublin, the White Hart, Ship Street, 1683. In 1683 he was listed as an intruder and a journeyman to William Norman (q.v.)—although the address listed, the White Hart, Ship Street, was not Norman's— and in 1684 recorded as "In Engl" (*Guild Records*). A Richard Manklin or Mancklin was a bookseller in York, 1697–1725 (*Dictionary 1668–1725*).

MANNING (WILLIAM), printer and publisher in Dublin, High Street, near Corn Market, 1726. He printed and published the *Dublin Postman*, 1726 (Munter, *Handlist*).

MANSARGH or MANSERGH (RICHARD), paper-maker in Dublin, Cook Street, 1769–77. In 1773 he signed a petition to the Irish House of Commons objecting to the removal of duties on foreign paper (BL, 1890.e.5 (232)).

MARCHBANK (**ROBERT**), bookseller and printer in Dublin, (1) at Cole's Alley, Castle Street (1769–73?); (2) 18 Chancery Lane; (3) 11 New Buildings, Dame Street (1786). 1746?–1801? He was printer for the University from 1746 to 1773. He was admitted free of the guild by petition in 1773, paid quarterage at least through 1788, and was listed on the Clerk's list in 1789 (*Guild Records*). He was admitted free of the city in 1773 (Thrift, *Freemen*). He was well known for his excellent work, which included *A Specimen of Printing Types*, 1769, Shakespeare's *As You Like It*, two editions, 1783 and 1786, *Macbeth* and *Othello*, 1786, and *Unconnected Hints and Hints and Loose Ideas upon an Union*, 1800. He died in 1803, and was succeeded by his son Robert Marchbank Jr.

MARTIN (**RICHARD**), printer and publisher in Wexford, 1769?–74. He was the first printer in Wexford, and printed and published that town's first newspaper, the *Wexford Journal*, from 1769? to 1774.

MARTINEAU (**ZACHARIAH**), printer in Dublin, lower Blind Quay, Fishamble Street, 1743–49. Perhaps he was a journeyman to, or in partnership with, Joshua Kinnier (q.v.), and was recorded as in practice in 1743. He was admitted to the guild as a quarter brother by petition in 1744 and paid quarterage through 1749 (*Guild Records*).

MASON (**J.**), printer in Dublin, Dame Street, 1727. Sole reference: in 1727 he printed *The Little Beau's Lamentation*.

MASON (**Mrs. URSULA**), bookseller in Maryborough, County Laoighis, 1747–48. She was listed as one of the provincial sellers of Exshaw's *London Magazine* (*London Magazine*, Jan. 1746/47 to Jan. 1747/48).

MATURIN (WILLIAM), bookseller in Cork, 1775–99. He supplied the Cork Mayor and Council with Irish and English newspapers from 1775 to 1785 and again from 1794 to 1799 (Caulfield, *Cork Council Book*).

MAXWELL (Rev. JOHN), bookseller and publisher in Dublin, Winetavern Street, 1710–23? He was admitted to the guild as a quarter brother in 1718 and paid quarterage from 1720 to 1723 (*Guild Records*). In 1718 he advertised an edition of Hooker's *Works*, but a coterie of Dublin stationers quickly brought out a rival edition and offered it at an absurdly low price (evidently their revenge for his refusing to pay quarterage) (*Dublin Courant*, 25 May 1719); he duly paid quarterage the following year. He died intestate in 1744 (*Dublin Grant Book*).

MEARS (JOHN), bookseller in Dublin, 1711–18. He was listed as an intruder in 1711 and 1718 (*Guild Records*).

MEIGHAN or MAHON (PATRICK), bookseller in Drogheda, 1690–1729. He is listed as a bookseller from 1690 to 1700 (D'Alton, *History of Drogheda*), and he took subscriptions to various Dublin publications from 1710 to 1729 (*Dublin Intelligence*, 24 June 1710, 2 Sept. 1728, and 22 Feb. 1728/29).

MENDY or MENDEY (WILLIAM), bookseller in Dublin, 1670?–73. He was admitted free of the guild in 1670 and paid quarterage through 1672 (*Guild Records*). He was admitted free of the city in 1671 (Thrift, *Freemen*). He died intestate in 1673, with John North (q.v.) being named administrator of the property until William Mendy Jr. (q.v.) came of age (*Dublin Grant Book*).

MENDY or MENDEY (WILLIAM JR.), bookseller and publisher in Dublin, in the Exchange, Cork Hill, 1679–1716. He was apprenticed to his father, William Mendy (q.v.), admitted free of the guild by service in 1679, paid quarterage through 1715, and was listed in the Clerk's list in 1716 (*Guild Records*). He was admitted free of the city in 1679 (Thrift, *Freemen*). He was one of the first to advertise in the newspapers, listing for sale *English Military Discipline* in 1685 (*News-Letter*, 26 Dec.), and in 1692 he published a *Speech made to His Grace the Duke of Ormond*.

MERES (A.), bookseller and printer in Dublin, the White Hart, Copper Alley, 1714–15. He printed a catalogue of plays in 1714 (Baker, *Biographia dramatica*), and joined in a brief partnership with Thomas Hume (q.v.) in 1715. They printed tracts and pamphlets—e.g., *The Right of the Sovereign in the Choice of his Servants*, 1715—and late in 1715 Hume apparently bought out Meres's share of the business.

MILLER (ANDREW), engraver, printseller, and publisher in London, 1737–41, and Dublin, (1) Sir Isaac Newton's Head, at the corner of the Blind Quay, Cork Hill, opposite Lucas's Coffee House (1741–43); (2) the Golden Head, the upper end of Fleet Street, near Lazar's Hill (1743); (3) Hog Hill, near the Round Church (1744–56?). 1737–56? He practiced in London from 1737 to 1741, came to Dublin in 1741, and soon established himself as the foremost engraver there in the eighteenth century. He first worked with John Brooks (q.v.), setting up for business himself in 1743. Among his many prints were Dean Swift, 1743, Archbishop Ussher, 1744, Cromwell and Lambert, 1746, and his last known work "The Farmer," 1756. In 1749, during the Charles Lucas controversy, Anne Esdall (q.v.) was summoned for printing a pro-Lucas article deemed offensive, but upon the authorities' finding that she had received the manuscript from Miller, he was ordered to Newgate (*Commons' Journ. Ire.*, v, 27). It was Miller the authorities really wanted, for he had published a portrait of Lucas bearing the inscription "An Exile for his Country, who, for seeking LIBERTY, lost it" (Briton, *History of the Dublin Election*, 1753). He was back at work within the year, and died in 1763.

MILLER (**JACOB**) *see* Jacob Milner

MILLIKIN (**JOHN**), bookseller and publisher in Dublin, (1) Skinner Row (1768–71); (2) College Green (1771–73); (3) Grafton Street (1784–90); (4) 10 Grafton Street (1790–1811). 1768–73 and 1784–1811. He was admitted free of the guild in 1767, paid quarterage through 1774, was listed as "abroad" [England] for 1773–83, and again paid quarterage from 1784 to 1811; in 1797 he served as Master (*Guild Records*). He published many works, including Harris' *Hibernica*, 1770, Shakespeare's *Timon of Athens*, 1772, and Molyneux's *Case of Ireland*, 1773. He died in 1811.

MILLION (**HENRY**), papermaker in Dublin, 1690?–94? In 1690, in partnership with Nicholas Dupin (q.v.), he was granted a fourteen-year monopoly by letter patent for "makeing all sorts of writing and printing paper" in Ireland, and the two men formed the Company of White Papermakers. They were previously associated in an English linen company. In 1691 Dupin brought to Ireland five Dutch journeyman papermakers, and built a paper mill at Rathfarnham, County Dublin. How long Million continued as a partner, or whether he ever came to Ireland, is uncertain. However, in 1694 he had turned to other Irish ventures, having received a patent for the cultivation of "saffeflower" (*World's Paper Trade Review*, 52, no. 4).

MILLS (**MICHAEL**), bookbinder, bookseller, printer, and publisher in Dublin, (1) St. Audeon's Arch (1770–?); (2) Capel Street, later 135 Capel Street (1785?–86); (3) 36 Dorset Street (1786–1808). 1770–1808. He was apprenticed to Joshua Kinnier (q.v.), admitted free of the guild by service in 1770, and paid quarterage at least through 1788. He was an active guild member, serving on the Council from 1776, as Warden in 1778, and as Master in 1785 (*Guild Records*). He was admitted free of the city in 1771 (Thrift, *Freemen*). In partnership with Thomas McDonnell (q.v.) he published the *Hibernian Journal or Chronicle of Liberty*, 1770–79, with other stationers, Lewis' *Candid Philosopher*, 1778, and he printed and published *Anacharsis*, 1795. In 1785 he tendered for the binding of the Parliamentary journals (Craig, *Bookbindings*). He died in 1808.

MILNER or MILLER (**JACOB**), bookseller and publisher in Dublin, (1) The Rose and Crown, Dame Street (1683); (2) Essex Street, over against Essex Bridge (1684–1701). 1682–1701. He was listed as an intruder in 1682, as a journeyman to William Norman (q.v.) in 1683, admitted free of the guild in 1684, paid quarterage through 1699, served as Warden in 1697 and 1700, and as Master in 1701 (*Guild Records*). He was admitted free of the city in 1684 (Thrift, *Freemen*). Among his publications were *Some Fruits of Solitude*, 1693, Congreve's *The Mourning Muse of Alexis*, 1695, one of the few Irish printings of Congreve's poems, and Bishop Stearne's *Tractatus de visitatione infirmorum*, 1697. In 1698, along with Patrick Campbell (q.v.), he affixed the title-page and preface of Cocker's popular text to Hodder's *Arithmatick*, obviously to move some unsold stock. The guild intervened, and forced the destruction of the edition (*Guild Records*). Milner was one of the booksellers felt by Dunton to "feed upon Books without being much the wiser for what they contain" (Young's *Tour of Ireland*). He died in 1701, his will being proved in the Prerogative Court at Dublin, and was succeeded by his wife, Mary Milner (q.v.).

MILNER (**Mary**), bookseller in Dublin, Essex Street, over against Essex Bridge, 1701–2. She was the widow of Jacob Milner (q.v.), and succeeded her husband in business. In 1702 she married John Rathbone (q.v.), who carried on the business until 1716.

MITCHELL (**John**), printer and publisher in Dublin, (1) Sycamore Alley (1763–68?); (2) Skinner Row (1771?–73). 1763–73. He was admitted free of the guild in 1763 and paid quarterage through 1772 (*Guild Records*). With various other stationers he published Shakespeare's *Works*, 1766, and *Timon of Athens*, 1772, and Smollett's *Humphrey Clinker*, 1771. He died in 1773.

MOIDY (**William**), bookseller in Dublin, Dame Street, 1718. He was apprenticed to William Norman (q.v.), but never took out his freedom, and in 1718 was listed as an intruder (*Guild Records*).

MONCRIEFF or MONCRIEFFE (**Richard**), bookseller and publisher in Dublin, Capel Street, 1762–90. He was in business in 1762 when he subscribed to Faulkner's (q.v.) edition of Swift's *Works*, and he was admitted free of the city in 1770. He was admitted free of the guild by petition in 1773, paid quarterage through 1785, had an apprentice enrolled to him in 1787, and was listed in the Clerk's list in 1789 (*Guild Records*). He was appointed an Alderman in 1784. With various other stationers, his publications included Smollett's *Humphrey Clinker*, 1771, Shakespeare's *Timon of Athens*, 1772, *La Liturgie* [Huguenot], 1777, and Sheffield's *Irish Commerce*, 1785. He died in 1798, his will being proved in the Prerogative Court at Dublin.

MONDETT (WILLIAM), papermaker in Dublin, 1758–68. He had a paper mill at Whitechurch, County Dublin, in partnership with Moses Verney (q.v.).

MONTGOMERY (HUGH), bookseller in Dublin, the Bible and Crown, next door to the Crown Tavern, facing the Blind Quay, near Essex Street Gate, 1700. He was listed as a journeyman to Mathew Gun (q.v.) in 1700 (*Guild Records*). A Hugh Montgomery was a bookseller in London in 1703 (*Dictionary 1668–1725*).

MOOR (JOHN) *see* John Moore

MOORE (ANNE), bookseller and publisher in Dublin, at Erasmus' Head, Dame Street, 1752–54. She was the widow of Thomas Moore (q.v.), and continued the family business, publishing Lodge's *Peerage*, 1754. She died in 1754, her will being proved in the Prerogative Court at Dublin.

MOORE (CHARLES), bookseller in Dublin, 1769–83. He was the son of Thomas Moore (q.v.), was admitted free of the guild by birth in 1769, paid quarterage through 1780, and was listed in the Clerk's list until 1783 (*Guild Records*). He was admitted free of the city in 1770 (Thrift, *Freemen*).

MOORE (EDWARD), bookbinder in Dublin, High Street, 1687–1706. A Catholic, he was admitted free of the city in 1687 (Thrift, *Freemen*), admitted to the guild as a quarter brother in 1694, paid quarterage through 1706, in which year he had his fees reduced "in regard to his poverty," and was listed as "dead" in 1706 (*Guild Records*).

MOORE (JOHN), stationer in Dublin, 1639–40. He possibly served as a journeyman to Edmund Crooke (q.v.) (*Dictionary 1557–1640*), and was admitted free of the city in 1639 (Thrift, *Freemen*).

MOORE or MOOR (JOHN), bookseller in Dublin, the Rose and Crown, Dame Street, 1684–86. He was listed as a journeyman to William Norman (q.v.) and as an intruder in 1684, was admitted to the guild as a quarter brother in 1685, paid quarterage in 1686, and was listed as "gon" in 1687 (*Guild Records*).

MOORE (JOHN), bookseller in Enniskillen, 1710. Sole reference: advertisements in 1710 listed him as one of the provincial booksellers taking subscriptions to a Dublin edition of the *Tryal of Doctor Henry Sacheverell* (*Dublin Intelligence*, 24 June and 1 July).

MOORE (JOHN), bookseller in Waterford, 1719. Sole reference: advertisements in 1719 listed him as taking subscriptions for Prideaux's *Old and New Testaments connected in the History of the Jews* (*Dublin Courant*, 31 Jan.) and for Fiddes' *Theologia speculativa* (*Dublin Intelligence*, 14 Nov.).

MOORE (THOMAS), bookseller and publisher in Dublin, at Erasmus' Head, Dame Street, 1730–52. He was apprenticed to Aaron Rhames (q.v.), admitted free of the guild by service in 1730, paid quarterage through 1750, and served as Warden in 1751 (*Guild Records*). He was admitted free of the city in 1730 (Thrift, *Freemen*). He was an active publisher and became a man of some wealth and property. Among his publications were

Shakespeare's *Hamlet* and *Henry IV*, 1731, and *Henry VIII*, 1758, and, in conjunction with other stationers, Ware's *Works*, 1739, Shakespeare's *Works*, 1747, and the *English Registry*, 1748 and 1749. He died intestate in 1752 and was succeeded by his widow, Anne Moore (q.v.).

MORRIS (JOHN), printer in Dublin, the Green Man, Fishamble Street (1763), and in Philadelphia, Pennsylvania (1764–73). 1763–73. He was apprenticed to Thomas Hutchinson (q.v.) of Galway and, upon the latter's death in 1759, Morris was reassigned to Samuel Powell Jr. (q.v.) in Dublin for his remaining four years (*Guild Records*). He never took out his freedom of the guild, but in 1763 he printed *Methodism Anatomize'd* in Dublin, and in 1764 he was printing in Philadelphia (Evans, *American Bibliography*).

MOXON (JOHN), bookseller in Dublin, King's Arms, Skinner Row, 1683–86. He was listed as a journeyman to John Forster (q.v.) from 1683 to 1686 and as "gon" in 1687 (*Guild Records*).

MUCKELRATH (ANT.), papermaker in Dublin, 1773. Sole reference: in 1773 he signed a petition from papermakers to the Irish House of Commons objecting to the removal of duties on foreign paper (BL, 1890.e.5. (232)).

MUCKELROY or McENROY (MATHIAS or MATHEW), papermaker in Dublin, 1772–83. He had a paper mill at Rathfarnham, County Dublin. In 1773 he signed a petition from papermakers to the Irish House of Commons objecting to the removal of duties on foreign paper (BL, 1890.e.5. (232)).

MURPHEY (GEORGE), printer in Dublin, 1768–78. He was apprenticed to Samuel Powell Jr. (q.v.), was admitted free of the guild in 1768, and paid quarterage through 1778 (*Guild Records*). He was admitted free of the city in 1768 (Thrift, *Freemen*).

MURPHEY (JAMES), printer in Dublin, 1771. Sole reference: in 1771 he is recorded as printing Parnell's *Poems* (*Biblio. Soc. Ire. Pub.*, iii, 101); however, "James Murphey" is probably an error for John Murphey (q.v.).

MURPHEY (JOHN), bookseller and printer in Dublin, Skinner Row, 1753–89. He was admitted free of the city by service in 1753, free of the guild in 1754, paid quarterage through 1781, one of his apprentices, John Pasley, took out his freedom in 1789, and Murphey was listed in the Clerk's list to 1789 (*Guild Records*). In 1766 he joined with other Dublin stationers in a published complaint against irregulars and intruders in the trade (*Freeman's Journal*, 26 Apr.). In 1773 he signed a memorial to the Irish House of Commons against additional duties on foreign paper (BL, 1890.e.5. (239)), and in the same year he contributed to a subscription for a monument to Dr. Charles Lucas (*Guild Records*). He died in 1795 (*Dublin Grant Book*).

MURRAY (NATHANIEL), engraver in Dublin, Fishamble Street, 1744?–67. He is recorded as working as an engraver from 1744 and as exhibiting in 1767 (Strickland, *Irish Artists*), and he is referred to as an engraver in 1748 (*Dublin Courant*, 8 Nov.).

MURTAGH (Mrs.), bookseller in Dublin, Christ Church Yard, 1722. Sole reference: an advertisement in 1722 listed "Mrs. Murtagh, Bookseller" as taking subscriptions for a *Compleat New History of Scotland* (*Harding's News-Letter*, 14 July).

MUSGROVE (**THEOPHILUS**), printer and publisher in Dublin, 1729. Sole reference: the imprint on a *Poem on the procession of journeymen smiths*, 1729, read "printed by and for Theophilus Musgrove" (*see under* Theophilus Musgrave in *Dictionary 1726–75*).

MYERS (**JOHN**), bookseller and bookbinder in Dublin, 1720–45. He was admitted free of the guild in 1720, paid quarterage through 1745, and served as Warden in 1741 (*Guild Records*). He was admitted free of the city in 1736 (Thrift, *Freemen*). He died in 1745.

MYERS (**JOHN JR.**), bookbinder in Dublin, 1745–49? He was apprenticed to his father, John Myers (q.v.), admitted free of the guild by petition in 1745, paid quarterage through 1749, and petitioned to be admitted to the poor list in 1770, which request was granted (*Guild Records*). He was admitted free of the city in 1745 (Thrift, *Freemen*).

N

NEAL or NEALE (JOHN), bookseller and printer in Dublin, Christ Church Yard, 1721–37. He was a musical instrument maker and primarily a music printer and publisher. He was the president of the Charitable Musical Society. His printing and publishing included the *Book of Irish Tunes*, 1724, Gay's *Beggar's Opera*, 1729, and *Collection of Country Dances*, 1734. He died in 1737 and was succeeded by his son William Neal (q.v.).

NEAL or NEALE (WILLIAM), bookseller and printer in Dublin, Christ Church Yard, 1734–41. In 1730 he advertised as a musical instrument maker (*Dublin Journal*, 17 Mar.). In 1734 he joined his father, John Neal (q.v.), in business as a bookseller and music printer and publisher, and in 1740 he printed and published a *Collection of Favorite Songs*. From 1740 to 1741 he was in partnership with William Mainwaring (q.v.). He was primarily responsible for the construction of the Music Hall, Fishamble Street, and left off business to become its first manager–director in 1741. He died in 1769.

NEAL (WILLIAM) *see* William Neill

NEALE (SAMUEL), papermaker in Cork, 1769. He was in partnership with Caleb Beale (q.v.). They had a paper mill in Spring-hill [adjoining Riverstown], County Cork (*Irish Book Lover*, 1, no. 3).

NEEDHAM (ELIZABETH) *see* Elizabeth Dickson

NEEDHAM (Gwyn), bookseller and printer in Dublin, who worked at two different presses, the first (1) Union Coffee House (1714–15), or, Hanover Coffee House, Cork Hill (1715–19?); (2) next door the Angel and Bible, or, Seven Stars, opposite Castle Market, Dame Street (1725–28); (3) Silver Court, next door to the sign of the Golden Hammer and Heart, opposite Rose Tavern, Castle Street (1728–30); the second (1) Blind Quay, near Essex Bridge (1718?–19); (2) Golden Phoenix, Sycamore Alley, near the Post Office (1719–24?); (3) Cheshire Cheese, opposite the Bear, Crane Lane (1724–28?). 1714–30. He married Elizabeth Dickson (q.v.), the widow of Francis Dickson (q.v.), in October 1714, and joined in a printing partnership with her and her son Richard Dickson (q.v.). Francis had willed two presses to Elizabeth, and apparently she and Richard supervised one while Gwyn worked at the second. In 1718 he was listed as an intruder by the guild, he petitioned for entry in 1719, was admitted free, and was carried in the Clerk's list until 1724 (*Guild Records*). He shared in the printing of the Dickson family newspapers (Munter, *Handlist*), and in various pamphlet projects as well, occasionally getting involved in minor trouble with the Irish Parliament. His imprint no longer appeared after 1730, and in 1755 he is referred to as being an officer in his Majesty's customs at the port of London (*Dublin Journal*, 22/25 Nov.).

NEIL (Charles), printer in Dublin, ca. 1720s. Sole reference: an announcement in 1732 of persons "being fugitive for debt" and seeking "to take the benefit of the act for the relief of insolvent debtors," listed among the petitioners "Charles Neil, late of the city of Dublin, printer" (*Dublin Gazette*, 19 Feb.).

NEIL (J.), printer in Dublin, near the Old Bridge, 1730. Sole reference: his only imprint was on the *Last Speech, Confessions and Dying Words of Catherine McCanna*, 1730.

NEILL or O'NEILL (PATRICK), bookseller, printer, and publisher in Belfast, 1694–1705. He was one of Belfast's pioneer printers, certainly in trade by 1694, although no imprint of his exists before 1697. Throughout his business years he was associated with his brother-in-law, James Blow (q.v.). Together they printed various works including the New Testament sometime between 1694 and 1705 (no copy is known to survive); Neill also worked alone under the imprint "Patrick Neill and Company," the bulk of his publications being religious tracts and sermons. He died in 1705.

NEILL or NEAL (WILLIAM), bookbinder in Dublin, 1774. He was apprenticed to John Bardin (q.v.) and admitted free of the guild by service in 1774. There are no further references (*Guild Records*).

NELSON (OLIVER), printer and publisher in Dublin, (1) the Printing Office, Cork Hill (1736–37); (2) at Milton's Head, Skinner Row (1737–75). 1736–75. He was apprenticed to George Grierson (q.v.), admitted free of the guild by service in 1737, paid quarterage through 1774, served as Warden in 1750, as Master in 1755, as Treasurer from 1755 to 1766, and on the Council from 1756 (*Guild Records*). He was admitted free of the city in 1736 (Thrift, *Freemen*). For a year he worked out of the shop of Richard Reilly (q.v.), and then set up his own business. In 1745 he purchased the *Dublin Courant* from Alice Reilly (q.v.), and published a wide variety of works, usually in conjunction with other stationers. These included Collier's *Reflections upon Ridicule*, 1737, Richardson's *Pamela*, 1741, Harris' *Life of William III*, 1749, and Gibson's *Experimental Philosophy*, 1753. During the Charles Lucas affair, Nelson led the guild in fighting for press freedom, lent his own press to Lucas' support, and printed some pro-Lucas pamphlets by Edmund Burke (Samuels, *Early Life of . . . Edmund Burke*). In 1758 he was admitted by special grace free of the Holy Trinity Guild of Merchants, only the second stationer in Dublin to be so honored. In 1759, upon the death of Mary Pepyat (q.v.), Nelson became printer to the city of Dublin (*Cal. Anc. Rec. Dublin*). He died in 1775 (*Hibernian Magazine*, July).

NICHOLLS (REBECCA), bookseller in Limerick, 1719. Advertisements in 1719 list her as one of the provincial booksellers taking subscriptions, or selling, Prideaux's *Old and New Testaments connected in the History of the Jews* (*Dublin Courant*, 31 Jan.) and Fiddes' *Theologia speculativa* (*Dublin Intelligence*, 14 Nov.).

NIHIL (IGNATIUS), bookseller in Londonderry, 1731. Sole reference: he was listed as one of the provincial sellers of *Whalley's Almanack for the Year of Christ 1732* (*Dublin Journal*, 18 Dec.).

NIXON (ROBERT), papermaker in Dublin, 1754–56. He was apprenticed to Oliver Nelson (q.v.) in 1750 but did not complete his apprenticeship (*Guild Records*). In 1754, in partnership with Richard Eaton (q.v.) and Joshua Kinnier (q.v.), he started a paper mill at Kilternan, County Dublin. They went under the name of Papermakers of Kilternan. In 1755 they petitioned Parliament for assistance in papermaking (*Commons' Journ. Ire.*, v, 237), and in 1756 Kinnier became the sole owner of the business. Nixon does not appear to have continued in the stationer's trade. He died in 1786.

NOBLE (JAMES), printer in Dublin, 1771–81. He was apprenticed to Richard James (q.v.), admitted free of the guild by service in 1771, paid quarterage through 1777, and was listed on the Clerk's list until 1781 (*Guild Records*). He was admitted free of the city in 1771 (Thrift, *Freemen*). He died in 1781 (*Dublin Grant Book*).

NORMAN (WILLIAM), bookbinder, bookseller, printer, and publisher in Dublin, the Rose and Crown, Dame Street, 1676–1705. He was admitted free of the guild in 1676, paid quarterage through 1705, served on the Council from 1680, as Master in 1684, 1688, 1698, and in 1701 completed the Master's term of Jacob Milner (q.v.) (*Guild Records*). He was admitted free of the city in 1676 (Thrift, *Freemen*). He was a prominent Dublin stationer, employing several apprentices and journeymen, and establishing one of the few strong printing houses before the lapse of the licensing act. He was an early book auctioneer (Gilbert, *History of Dublin*), and in 1683 described himself as "Bookbinder to his Grace the Duke of Ormond" (*Salt Water Sweetned*, 1683). He published, often with other stationers, a variety of works—e.g., *A Judgement of the Comet*, 1682, *London Master: or, the Jew Detected*, 1694, and Congreve's *The Mourning Muse of Alexis*, 1695. When Dunton came to Dublin in 1689 he tells us that Norman, "a little squat Man, who loves to live well," offered to purchase his entire stock of London books (*Dublin Scuffle*). In 1692 Norman acted as semi-official printer to the Irish Commons, publishing the *Votes of the House of Commons*. He died in 1705.

NORRIS (RICHARD), bookseller and publisher in Dublin, (1) the Indian, Dame Street (1726); (2) at the corner of Crane Lane, Essex Street (1729). 1719–48. He was admitted free of the city in 1719 (Thrift, *Freemen*). He was admitted free of the guild by petition in 1719, paid quarterage through 1748, and served as Warden in 1733 (*Guild Records*). In 1723 he published, with other stationers, Keating's *History of Ireland*, and in 1727 he published alone Thomson's *Summer. A Poem*.

He was also a book auctioneer, publishing in 1723 a *Catalogue of Books . . . to be sold by Auction* (*Dublin Weekly Journal*, 12 Jan.).

NORTH (JOHN), bookseller in London (?), and Dublin, (1) Castle Street (1659); (2) Skinner Row (1696). 1659?–1697. It is possible that he worked in London prior to 1659, for he was a member of the London guild of stationers. He is one of the early successful booksellers in Dublin, and is first referred to in a 1659 imprint: "London, Printed by E. Cotes, and are to be sold by John North, Bookseller, in Castle Street at Dublin" (Harison's *Threni Hybernica; or, Ireland sympathizing with England and Scotland*, 1659). He, with Benjamin Tooke (q.v.), was one of the charter members of the Dublin guild of stationers in 1670, he paid quarterage through 1697, served as the guild's first Warden in 1671, on the Council from 1677, and as Master in 1675 and 1692 (*Guild Records*). His name occasionally appeared as the seller of Dublin publications: e.g., *Tryal of William, Viscount Stafford*, 1681, and *A Judgement of the Comet*, 1682. He was listed as a contributor, between 1669 and 1677, to the fund for a hospital and free school, Oxmantown Green Dublin (Gilbert MS 69, pp. 377–88). He died in 1697 (*Dublin Grant Book*).

NORTH (MICHAEL), bookseller, printer, and publisher in Dublin, (1) the Bible and Mitre, on the Blind Quay (1755–60?); (2) Great Ship Street (?–1767); (3) the corner of Fishamble Street, near the Blind Quay (1767–90). 1755–90. He was apprenticed to Oliver Nelson (q.v.), was admitted free of the guild by service in 1755, paid quarterage through 1769, and was carried on the Clerk's list until 1789 (*Guild Records*). In 1759, he took James Hunter (q.v.) into a partnership of one year, and started the *Public Magazine*. In 1767 North purchased the printing business of Joshua Kinnier (q.v.), and several years later, from the 1780s to 1790, he apparently joined in partnership with Joshua Kinnier Jr., for during this period various apprentices are recorded as gaining freedom of the guild by service to "Messrs. North and Kinnier, printers." In 1790 Joshua Kinnier Jr.'s son, Phillip Kinnier, gained freedom of the guild by birth and took over the partners' business.

NUN (BENJAMIN), papermaker in Dublin, (1) Bridge Street (1751–71); (2) 46 Bridge Street (1771–76). 1751–76. He joined his son-in-law Thomas Watson (q.v.) in partnership in papermaking, advertising a "New Paper-Mill lately erecting in Company, beholden Ben Nun and Thomas Watson, now finished and at work" (*Sleater's Public Gazetteer*, 19 Dec. 1758), and they continued working together until 1771. The mill was Millmount, near Rathfarnham, County Dublin. In the latter year Nun took his son Richard Nun (q.v.) into partnership as "Ben Nun and Son." They had their own watermark. In 1773 they signed a petition to the Irish House of Commons objecting to the removal of duties on foreign paper (BL, 1890.e.5. (232)).

NUN (RICHARD), papermaker in Dublin, (1) 46 Bridge Street (1771–93); (2) 21 Bridge Street (1794–1800). 1771–1800. He was taken into partnership by his father, Benjamin Nun (q.v.), in 1771, and they worked together until 1776, and then Richard worked alone until 1793. The mill was Millmount, near Rathfarnham, County Dublin, and they had their own watermark. In 1794 Richard joined Clement Taylor and Nicholas Graham as "Nun and Company," which continued in business until 1800.

O'CONNOR (?), printer and publisher in Galway, 1775–1809. He printed and published the *Galway Chronicle*, 1775–1809.

O'CONNOR (CHARLES), bookseller in Dublin, 1737. Sole reference: he was mentioned in the subscribers' list as a bookseller and as having taken twelve sets of Rollin's *Methods of Teaching and Studying Belles Lettres*, 1737. He is probably the same as Charles Connor (q.v.).

O'CONNOR (JAMES), bookseller and publisher in Drogheda, 1728 (*Dictionary 1726–75*).

O'KEARNEY (JOHN) *see* John Kearney

O'NEILL (PATRICK) *see* Patrick Neill

OSBORNE (HENRY), bookseller in Dublin, Skinner Row, 1728–62? He was apprenticed to Robert Owen (q.v.), admitted free of the guild by service in 1728, and paid quarterage through 1729 (*Guild Records*). In 1729 he advertised the sale of Leslie's *Theological Works* and Wood's *Institutes* (*Dublin Journal*, 15 Mar.), in 1744 he subscribed to Faulkner's (q.v.) edition of Sale's *Universal History*, and in 1762 was listed in the subscribers' list as having taken ten sets of Faulkner's edition of Swift's *Works*.

OSBORNE or OSBOURN (WILLIAM), printer in Dublin, (1) the Blue Ball, Arundel Court, near St. Nicholas Gate

(1723); (2) at the Bible, Cork Hill (1768). 1723?–68. In 1723 John Whalley (q.v.) advertised "Whereas William Osbourn, a Printer, and my Servant, hath, for some time past without my Leave or Lycense, Deserted my Service . . . These are to require that no one Entertain, Imploy or Abbet him" (*Whalley's News-Letter*, 12 Mar.). Years later, in 1768, John Exshaw (q.v.) notified the guild that his employee William Osborne, "journeyman printer (an infirm old man, sixty-eight years of age) . . . now respected as the eldest tradesman of his profession in Dublin," was set upon by members of a fledgling journeymen's combination who "did cut and maim the said William Osborne and his wife." The guild offered a £50 reward for the apprehension of his assailants (*Dublin Mercury*, 29 Sept.; *Guild Records*).

OVERTON (**JOHN**), printer in Dublin, 1728. Sole reference: in 1728 he printed the *Whole Sentence of Death Pronounced . . . against Doctor John Andouin* (Thorpe MS, pp. 12, 113, National Library of Ireland, Dublin).

OWEN (**MARY**), bookseller in Dublin, the Dolphin, Skinner Row, 1747–53. She was the widow of Robert Owen (q.v.), and continued the family business to 1753. She was listed in advertisements between the years 1747 and 1753 as taking subscriptions for various publications, and in 1753 she advertised the auction of "All the household furniture, etc. belonging to Mrs. Mary Owen" (*Dublin Journal*, 24 Apr.). There are no more trade references to her, and she died in 1765 (Library of the Society of Genealogists, London).

OWEN (**ROBERT**), bookseller, printer, and publisher in Dublin, the Dolphin, Skinner Row, 1713–47. He was apprenticed to John Forster (q.v.), admitted free of the guild by service in 1713, paid quarterage through 1747, served on the Council from 1719, as Warden in 1720, and as Master in 1722 (*Guild Records*). He was admitted free of the city in 1713 (Thrift, *Freemen*). He was one of the leading stationers in Dublin in the first half of the eighteenth century, publishing extensively, usually in conjunction with other stationers. Among his publications were Clarendon's *History of the Rebellion*, 1719, the Bible, 1722, an edition of more than 10,000, Plutarch's *Lives*, 1729, Cervantes' *Don Quixote*, 1733, and Shakespeare's *Works*, 1747. Owen died in 1747, his will being proved in the Prerogative Court at Dublin, and was succeeded by his wife, Mary Owen (q.v.).

P

PALLISERS (**WALTER**), bookseller in Cork, 1750–60. He supplied the city council of Cork with English and Irish newspapers from 1750 to 1760 (Caulfield, *Cork Council Book*).

PANNELL (**JOHN**) *see* John Pennell

PAPERMAKERS OF KILTERNAN *see* Richard Eaton, Joshua Kinnier, *and* Robert Nixon

PARKER (**JAMES**), printer and publisher in Dublin, 28 Temple Bar, 1773–78. He was admitted free of the guild in 1773 and paid quarterage through 1777 (*Guild Records*). He was admitted free of the city in 1773 (Thrift, *Freemen*). In 1774 he printed and published the *Public Advertiser: or the Universal Chronicle* and the *Public Avenger, or The Theatrical Chronicle*. He died in 1778, his will being proved in the Prerogative Court at Dublin.

PARKER (**MICHAEL**), bookseller, printer, and publisher in Sligo, Castle Street, 1771–91. He was the brother of Stephen Parker (q.v.) and a nephew of Robert Perry (q.v.). He was apprenticed to Henry Saunders (q.v.), admitted free of the guild by service in 1771, but paid no quarterage (*Guild Records*). He was the first printer in Sligo and started that town's first newspaper, the *Sligo Journal and Weekly Advertiser*, 1771, continued as the *Sligo Journal* to 1791. He died in 1791, his will being proved in the Prerogative Court at Dublin.

PARKER (**STEPHEN**), typefounder in Dublin, (1) Crampton Quay (1765–?); (2) Lazar's Hill (1769); (3) Grafton Street, near Stephen's Green (1770–95). 1765–95. He was apprenticed to his uncle Robert Perry (q.v.), admitted free of the guild by service in 1767, and paid quarterage at least through 1786 (*Guild Records*). He was admitted free of the city in 1768 (Thrift, *Freemen*). He was the brother of Michael Parker (q.v.), and started a long line of Parker family typefounders, which continued well into the nineteenth century. Upon his uncle's death, Parker advertised: "The Business is carried on by his Nephew, Mr. Stephen Parker, who . . . conducted the business during his Uncle's Indisposition" (*Dublin Gazette*, 9 Nov. 1765). Marchbank's *A Specimen of Printing Types*, 1769, used Parker's types. Parker died in 1795.

PARRANT (**?**), stationer in Dublin, the Rose and Crown, Dame Street, 1686–88. He is listed as a journeyman to William Norman (q.v.) from 1686 to 1688 (*Guild Records*).

PARRY (**JOHN**) *see* John Perry

PATERSON (**JAMES**), bookseller in Maghera, 1751. Sole reference: he was listed in the colophon as one of the provincial sellers of Clark's *A Brief Survey of some Principles maintained by the General Synod of Ulster*, 1751.

PAYNE (**THOMAS**), papermaker in Dublin, Charlemont Street, 1773–83? He was apprenticed to Thomas Slator (q.v.), and upon the latter's death assigned to Edward Burroughs (q.v.), admitted free of the guild by service in 1773, paid quarterage through 1775, and was listed on the Clerk's list until 1783 (*Guild Records*). He was admitted free of the city in 1773 (Thrift, *Freemen*).

PEMBROCK (Thomas), printer in Cork, 1734. Sole reference: in 1734 he was paid for printing by the city of Cork with the added note "and for the future Alderman George Bennett [q.v.] shall print what shall be wanted for the Corporation" (Caulfield, *Cork Council Book*).

PENNELL, PENNEL, or PANNELL (John), bookseller and publisher in Dublin, (1) the Three Blue Bonnets, St. Patrick Street (1723–30?); (2) the Hercules, St. Patrick Street (1735?–39). 1723–39. He was admitted to the guild as a quarter brother in 1723, as a free brother in 1737, and paid quarterage through 1739 (*Guild Records*). In 1726 he subscribed to Defoe's *The Compleat English Tradesman*, in 1730 he published the *Constitution of the Free Masons*, and in 1735, with Theopilus Jones (q.v.), a *Pocket Companion for Free-Masons*. He advertised the sale of "Whalley's famous Golden Pills and Elixir Cardiacs" from 1735 to 1738 (*Dublin Journal*, 11 Jan. 1734/35, 5 Aug. 1738).

PEPYAT (Henry), bookseller and printer in Dublin, Silver Court, Castle Street (1759–64 and 1768–71?), and the Isle of Man (1765?–68?). 1759–71? His relationship to the other Pepyat stationers of Dublin is unknown; possibly he was a son of Mary Pepyat (q.v.), but certainly not of Jeremiah or Sylvanus (qq.v.). He was admitted free of the guild by special grace in 1759, paid quarterage through 1764, and again from 1768 to 1771 (*Guild Records*). He took over the family business from Mary Pepyat (q.v.) upon the latter's death. He printed a circular "Proposals for establishing a Printing House in the Isle of Man," n.d., in which prospectus he sought financial assistance of between £50 and £100 to set up for a minimum of three years in the Isle of Man, take a Manx apprentice, and publish a newspaper to be called the *Manx Journal*. What became of the project is not known, but perhaps this accounts for his absence from Dublin and the lack of mention in the guild records between the years 1765 and 1768.

PEPYAT (JEREMIAH), bookseller and publisher in Dublin, Skinner Row, 1702–24. He was apprenticed to John North (q.v.), and upon the latter's death assigned to Joseph Ray (q.v.), admitted free of the guild by service in 1702, paid quarterage through 1723, served on the Council from 1708, as Warden in 1709, and was recorded as "out of the Kingdom" in 1724 (*Guild Records*). He was admitted free of the city in 1702 (Thrift, *Freemen*). He was the brother of Mary and Sylvanus Pepyat (qq.v.). He published a variety of works, and engaged in a minor pamphlet war with Thomas Servant (q.v.) from 1709, culminating with Synge's *Defense of Himself*, 1711. He also published the *Tryal of Doctor Henry Sacheverell*, 1710, a *Metrical Psalter*, 1718, and *Geographia itineraria . . . of the Travellers . . . into Asia, Africa and America*, 1722. In 1718 he took his brother Sylvanus Pepyat into partnership and then, having gotten into debt, left for England in 1724, his brother continuing the business in Dublin. In London, Samuel Palmer, a printer, had long contemplated composing a history of printing, but George Psalmanazar says that Palmer, "knowing himself unequal to the task," turned the project over to Pepyat, "a broken Irish bookseller" who amused "him with fair promises for near three quarters of a year," getting nothing ready for the press "but a few loose and imperfect extracts"; thus the work was turned over to Psalmanazar, who saw it through to completion (Psalmanazar, *Memoirs of . . . George Psalmanazar*). Nothing more is heard of Jeremiah Pepyat.

PEPYAT (MARY), bookseller, printer, and publisher in Dublin, (1) Skinner Row (1739–43?); (2) Silver Court, Castle Street (1743?–59). 1739–59. She was the sister of Jeremiah Pepyat (q.v.), and continued the family business to 1759. She was the printer to the city of Dublin from 1740 to 1759, having petitioned in 1740 that she had actually transacted all the city printing business for the past year because Sylvanus "was for long in weak condition" (*Cal. Anc. Rec. Dublin*). In 1743 she printed and published a poem, *Mendico-Hymen: or, the Beggar's Match.* She died in 1759 (*Sleator's Dublin Gazetteer*, 23 Oct.).

PEPYAT (SYLVANUS), bookseller and publisher in Dublin, Skinner Row, 1718–39. He was apprenticed to his brother Jeremiah Pepyat (q.v.), admitted free of the guild by service in 1718, paid quarterage through 1739, and served as Warden in 1735 (*Guild Records*). He was admitted free of the city in 1718 (Thrift, *Freemen*). He was taken into partnership by his brother in 1718, and from 1724 conducted the business by himself. He was printer to the city of Dublin from 1726 to 1739, having petitioned in 1726 that his brother Jeremiah had "affairs obliging him to continue in England" (*Cal. Anc. Rec. Dublin*). In 1738 he published, with other stationers, Horace's *Art of Poetry*, Harrison's *Catechism*, and Aeschylus' *Agamemnon*. He died in 1739 (*Dublin Journal*, 6 Oct.) and was succeeded in business by his sister Mary Pepyat (q.v.).

PERRY or PARRY (JOHN), typefounder in Dublin, (1) Crampton Quay (1749–50); (2) Meath Street (1755). 1719?– 55. He was probably a relative of Robert Perry (q.v.). In 1719 he advertised as a cutler (*Whalley's News-Letter*, 20 Sept.), and appears to have been employed by Robert Perry and Daniel Malone (q.v.) in 1749 and 1750. In 1755 a John Parry advertised: "Letter Founder from London, furnishes ... Types with proper Ink for marking Red and Black. He is to be spoken with ... at Mr. Jackson's [Isaac Jackson (q.v.)] Letter Foundry in Meath Street" (*Pue's Occurrences*, 1 Nov.).

PERRY or PERY (JOHN), papermaker in Dublin, 1697. In 1697 he took over the direction of a paper mill in Rathfarnham, County Dublin (see Nicholas Dupin), and in the same year petitioned Parliament "that a clause may be inserted in some act to restrain the destruction of white rags and for the confirmation of their letters patent for the white paper manufacture in this Kingdom." A House committee receiving the petition was instructed to "prevent stock jobbing," and the petition was not acted upon (*Commons' Journ. Ire.*, ii, 931).

PERRY (ROBERT), printer and typefounder in Dublin, Crampton Quay, 1747–65. He was possibly a Quaker, was admitted free of the guild in 1751, paid quarterage through 1758 when he was allowed exemption from fees as "not practicing the trade of printer," but paid a franchise fine in 1764 (*Guild Records*). In 1748 he joined in partnership with Daniel Malone (q.v.) to design and produce type, and by 1749 they advertised a variety of good Irish type for sale (*Dublin Journal*, 7 Feb.). A new foundry was opened in 1750, in which year the Dublin Society awarded them £10 for their project. A petition to Parliament in 1755, for encouragement in type manufacture, was never acted upon (*Commons' Journ. Ire.*, v, 229). Although the name "Malone and Perry" was continued, Perry appears to have been managing the business alone from about 1752 (colophon in Evans' *A Letter to the Rev. Moore Booker*, 1752). Perry died in 1765, praised for bringing "Letter-founding to an equal Degree of Perfection here, as in England" (*Dublin Gazette*, 9 Nov.).

PERY (JOHN) *see* John Perry

PETERS (JOSEPH), stationer in Dublin, 1700. He was listed as a journeyman to Joseph Ray (q.v.) in 1700 (*Guild Records*).

PIENNE (**Peter de**), printer in Waterford (1647, 1651–52), and Cork (1648–49). 1647–52. He was the first printer in Waterford, printing the *Lives of the Glorious Saint David . . . And . . . Saint Kieran*, 1647. In 1648 and 1649 he was in Cork, printing in the Royalist cause the *Eikon Basilike. The Pourtraicture of His Sacred Majesty in His Solitudes and Sufferings*, 1649. When the latter city was taken by the Cromwellians, he appears to have moved back to Waterford where he then used his press for the Commonwealth, printing Cook's *Monarchy: No Creature of God's Making*, 1651, and *An Act for the Settling of Ireland*, 1652. In the latter year the Council for the Affairs of Ireland seized his press and "forbeare paying of Peter de Pienne any Sallary as Printer" (*Commonwealth Council Book*). No more is heard of de Pienne.

PILKINGTON (**Martha**), bookseller, printer, and publisher in Cork, Castle Street, 1729–57. She was the widow of Thomas Pilkington (q.v.). She printed and published many pamphlets from 1743 to 1749—e.g., the *Bishop of Cork's Pastoral Letter*, 1743, *An Answer to a Letter*, 1748, and *A Letter from a Clergyman of the Diocese of Cork*, 1749. She also took subscriptions for various Dublin publications. Abraham Bradley (q.v.) announced that she sold all of his (*Dublin Courant*, 8–12 Mar. 1748/49). From 1755 to 1757 she occasionally printed for the Cork Corporation (Caulfield, *Cork Council Book*).

PILKINGTON (**Thomas**), bookseller and publisher in Cork, Castle Street, 1729–45. He took subscriptions for a variety of Dublin publications, from Jonson's *Plays*, 1729, to Harris' *Life of William III*, 1745. In 1741 he published the *Memoirs of Alexander Ramkins*. He was succeeded by his widow, Martha Pilkington (q.v.).

PILLSWORTH (**Benjamin**), bookbinder in Dublin, Exchequer Street, d. 1779. He was enrolled as an apprentice bookbinder to Joshua Sheppard (q.v.) in 1762, but there are no other guild references (*Guild Records*). He died in 1779, his will being proved in the Prerogative Court at Dublin.

PIM (**John**), bookseller in Dublin, 1744. Sole reference: in 1744 he was listed in the subscribers' list as having taken seven sets of Faulkner's (q.v.) edition of Sale's *Universal History*.

PLUMMER (**Richard**), bookseller and publisher in Cork, 1657. Sole reference: the colophon in 1657 for *The Agreement and Resolution of Severall Associated Ministers in the County of Corke* read "Printed by William Smith [q.v.] for Richard Plummer and are to be sold at his house in Corke."

POLLACKE (**David**), stationer in Dublin, the Rose and Crown, Dame Street, 1677–78 and 1680–81. 1677–1709. He was recorded as a journeyman to William Norman (q.v.) from 1677 to 1678 and from 1680 to 1681, as a journeyman to John Blakesley (q.v.) from 1678 to 1680, as in Scotland from 1681 to 1682, was admitted free of the guild in 1682, and paid quarterage through 1709 (*Guild Records*).

POLLARD (**Isaac**), bookseller in Dublin, d. 1713. Sole reference: he was recorded as a bookseller when he died intestate in 1713 (*Dublin Grant Book*).

POMAREDE (**Daniel**), engraver in Dublin (1742–52?), and Belfast, at John Templeton's, North Street, next door to the sign of the Still (1753?–65). 1742–65. He was a silversmith as well as an engraver, and was listed as a quarter brother in the Goldsmith's guild in 1744. In 1742 he engraved "Spectacle de la Nature, or Nature Displayed," but chiefly he engraved maps for, e.g., Faulkner's (q.v.) edition of Sale's *Universal History*, 1744, Smith's *History of Waterford*, 1746, and Harris' *Life of William III*, 1749. About 1753 he moved to Belfast and there engraved the frontispiece for *Hiram, or the Grand Master-Key to the Door of both Ancient and Modern Free-Masonry*, 1765.

PORTER (**JAMES**), bookseller and printer in Dublin, Skinner Row, 1760–91. He was admitted free of the guild in 1760, paid quarterage through 1778, and was listed in the Clerk's list in 1789 (*Guild Records*). He was admitted free of the city in 1760 (Thrift, *Freemen*). In 1771 he was listed as a bookseller and a seller of a patent medicine, the "Pure Inspissated Juice of Liquorice" (*Dublin Chronicle*, 10 Sept.), in 1773 he signed a memorial to the Irish House of Commons against additional duties on foreign paper (BL, 1890.e.5. (239)), and in 1775 he advertised in an open letter as a candidate for city printer (*Freeman's Journal*, 18 July). He died in 1791 and was succeeded by his son William Porter.

POTTER (**JOHN**), stationer in Dublin, 1742–56. He was admitted to the guild as a quarter brother in 1742, paid quarterage through 1748, was served with a warrant for non-payment of fees in 1755, and had his quarterage raised in 1756 (*Guild Records*).

POTTS (**JAMES**), bookbinder, bookseller, printer, and publisher in Dublin, (1) Swift's Head, Dame Street (1761–75); (2) 7 Dame Street (1775–?); (3) 62 Dame Street (?–1796). 1761–96. There was only one James Potts, Dublin stationer (see *Dictionary 1726–75*), as the wills of John Potts, Athlone merchant, 1738, and James Potts, Dublin, 1796, verify (Bentham,

Abstracts). He was apprenticed to George Faulkner (q.v.), in business by 1761, listed as an intruder in 1763, as a quarter brother in 1769, paid franchise fines in 1764 and 1770, was admitted free of the guild in 1782, stood for election to the Council in 1786, and paid quarterage from 1782 through 1787 (*Guild Records*). In 1766 he joined with other Dublin stationers in a published complaint against irregulars and intruders in the trade (*Freeman's Journal*, 26 Apr.). He published the *Dublin Courier*, 1760–66, started the *Hibernian Magazine*, 1771, printed *Saunder's News-Letter, and Daily Advertiser* from 1755, and in 1772, along with John Giffard, purchased the latter periodical, continuing its publication until 1796. Among his other publications, all with other stationers, were Shakespeare's *Midsummer Night's Dream*, 1764, *Works*, 1766, and *Timon of Athens*, 1772, and Smollett's *Humphrey Clinker*, 1771. In 1785 he tendered for the binding of the Parliamentary *Journals* (Craig, *Bookbinding*). In 1794 Potts was horsewhipped by his erstwhile partner John Giffard who, "indicted for assaulting Mr. J. Potts was rebound to take his trial at the next commission" (*Dublin Evening Post*, 20 Dec.). Giffard was convicted, but had his sentence reduced to a nominal fine through governmental influence (*Dublin Evening Post*, 11 July 1795). Potts never recovered from the beating and he died in 1796, his will being proved in the Prerogative Court at Dublin. He was succeeded by his son John Potts.

POTTS (**JOHN**), bookseller, printer, and publisher in Belfast, the Angel and Bible, Bridge Street (1739). 1731–40. He was admitted free of the city in 1731 as a bookseller (Young, *Belfast Town Book*). With Samuel Wilson (q.v.) and James Magee (q.v.) he printed and published Duchal's *Sermon Occasioned by the Death of the Reverend Mr. Hugh Scot*, 1736, and Dodsley's *Sir John Cockle, A Dramatic Tale*, 1738, and he took subscriptions to many Dublin publications, including Ware's *Works*,

1739, Virgil's *Works*, 1737, Tillotson's *Sermons*, 1738, and Rollin's *Roman History*, 1740. He died in 1760.

POWELL (Edward), stationer in Dublin, 1678–83. He was listed as a journeyman to Joseph Wild (q.v.) in 1678, admitted free of the guild in 1680, had a journeyman, John Costello (q.v.), registered to him from 1680 to 1683, and was listed as "In Engl" in 1683 (*Guild Records*). He was admitted free of the city in 1683 (Thrift, *Freemen*). An Edward Powell was a bookbinder in London in 1698 (*Dictionary 1668–1725*).

POWELL (Humphrey), bookseller, bookbinder, printer, and publisher in London (1548–?49), and Dublin, (1) in the Great Tower by the Crane [Merchant's Quay] (1551); (2) St. Nicholas Street (1566). 1548?–67. He printed some eight books in London (Duff, *A Century of the English Book Trade*), and in 1550 was provided with £20 by the Privy Council in England to set up trade in Ireland (*Acts of the Privy Council*, iii, 84). He thus became the first known printer in Dublin, and in 1551 published the first known book printed in Ireland, the *Book of Common Prayer*. Three other imprints of Powell are known, a *Proclamacyon set fourth . . . against Shane O'Neil*, 1561, a proclamation "against the rebels of the O'Conors," 1564, and *A Brefe Declaration of Certein Principall Articles of Religion*, 1567. In 1567 he received a pension from the government and apparently retired from business.

POWELL (Samuel), printer and publisher in Dublin, (1) Crane Lane, near Essex Street (1728–62); (2) Dame Street, later, 42 Dame Street, opposite Fownes Street (1762–75). 1728–75. He was apprenticed to his father Stephen Powell (q.v.) and apparently completed his apprenticeship with his brother Sylvester Powell (q.v.), admitted free of the guild in

1731, paid quarterage through 1775, served as Warden in 1745, on the Council from 1751, and as Master in 1752 (*Guild Records*). He was admitted free of the city in 1731 (Thrift, *Freemen*). He was working with his brother in 1728, and in 1729 he received £100 and possibly bought his brother's share of the business (see Edward Bate). He became one of the leading Dublin stationers, his printing and type falling little short of the productions of Baskerville's famous Birmingham press. He was a music printer: e.g., a Huguenot psalter, *Les Psaumes de David*, 1731, and *A Collection of Hymns and Sacred Poems*, 1749. He printed for the stationers' guild, 1734–50, the *Gentleman's and Citizen's Almanack*, 1734–70, and was printer to the "Incorporated Society for promoting English Protestant Schools," 1750–71. Among his many other works were Shakespeare's *Hamlet* and *Henry IV*, 1731, Farquhar's *Stage Coach*, 1732, Moryson's *History of Ireland*, 1735, Ware's *Works*, 1739, Wesley's *Principles of a Methodist*, 1747, and he printed and published Vallencey's *Essay on the Antiquity of the Irish Language*, 1771. In 1763 he took his son Samuel Powell Jr. (q.v.) into partnership, the colophons to 1766 often reading "Powell and Son." He died in 1775, his will being proved in the Prerogative Court at Dublin. He left his printing equipment and stock to his daughter Sarah Allen, who apparently sold it to George Bonham (q.v.).

POWELL (SAMUEL JR.), printer in Dublin, Dame Street, opposite Fownes Street, 1763–66. He was apprenticed to his father, Samuel Powell (q.v.), admitted free of the guild by birth in 1763, and paid quarterage through 1766 (*Guild Records*). He was admitted free of the city in 1765 (Thrift, *Freemen*). He was taken into partnership with his father in 1763, married in 1765 (*Pue's Occurrences*, 23 Mar.), and died in 1766 "in the 23d year of his age" (*Freeman's Journal*, 16 Aug.).

POWELL (STEPHEN), printer and publisher in Dublin, (1) the Post Office, or, the Old Post Office, Printing House, Fishamble Street (1697–98); (2) the back of Dick's Coffee House, Skinner Row (1698–1700); (3) the Printing Press, or, the Printing House, over against the Crown Tavern, or, formerly the Crown Tavern, or, the Crown, Fishamble Street (1703–11); (4) the Printing Press, Copper Alley (1714–22); a second press was set up, in partnership with Francis Dickson (q.v.), to print the *Flying Post: or, the Post-Master*, next door to the Post Office, in the Lord Chief Baron's Yard, Cork Hill (1707–13). 1697–1722. He served an apprenticeship in London, was admitted free of the Dublin guild in 1700, paid quarterage at least through 1717, served as Warden in 1718, and on the Council from 1719 (*Guild Records*). He was admitted free of the city in 1704 (Thrift, *Freemen*). He became one of the foremost Dublin printers of the time, and the founder of a line of printers—his daughter married Edward Bates (q.v.), while Stephen was the father of Sylvester and Samuel Powell (qq.v.) and the grandfather of Samuel Powell Jr. (q.v.). From 1697 to 1698 he was in a loose partnership with John Brent (q.v.) and John Brocas (q.v.). Dunton called Powell "the very Life and Spirit of the Company" (*Dublin Scuffle*). They printed and published *Articles of Peace* and Boyse's *Sermons Preached on Various Subjects*, 1697 (a reprint of the latter by Powell in 1711 was deemed "false and scandalous" by the Irish House of Lords and "ordered burnt by the Common Hangman" [*Lords' Journ. Ire.*, ii, 414]), and they published some of the first music printing in Ireland, William Barton's *Psalms*, "with music," 1698. Powell experimented in newspaper publications both in partnership with Francis Dickson and alone: e.g., the *Flying Post: or, the Post-Master*, 1704–13, the *Dublin Mercury*, 1705–7, and the *Postman and The Historical Account*, 1712 (Munter, *Hand-list*). Other Powell publications included Howell's *Discourse* *on the Woollen Manufactury*, 1698, *History of Caledonia: or the Scots Colony in Darien*, 1699, McCurtin's *Brief Discourse in vindication of the Antiquity of the Irish Language*, 1717, and an almanac, *Tom Tatler's Astral Gazar*, 1722. The later well-known Thomas Gent (q.v.) was apprenticed to Powell but found him a drunkard and fiend—"Three years I with a tyrant strove to live"—and fled in 1706. When Gent returned to Dublin in 1715 he was seized by Powell and had to purchase his discharge (Gent, *Life of Thomas Gent*). In 1722 Powell "Dy'd of a Dropsy" (*Whalley's News-Letter*, 24 May), leaving his worldly goods to his wife, Deborah, his son Sylvester succeeding him in business.

POWELL (SYLVESTER), printer and publisher in Dublin, (1) the Printing Press, Copper Alley, near Cork Hill (1722–27); (2) Crane Lane, near Essex Street (1728–29). 1722–29. He was the son of Stephen Powell (q.v.), and upon the latter's death succeeded him in business. He printed and published a few plays and poems—e.g., Shadwell's *Libertine, A Tragedy*, 1724, *Love for Money: or, the Boarding House, A Comedy*, 1726, and Thomson's *Summer. A Poem*, 1726—as well as two editions of Swift's *Gulliver's Travels*, 1726 and 1727. He attempted a new form of periodical, the *Temple-Oge Intelligence*, 1726–28, a breezy broadsheet concerned with the doings, dances, and scandals of the "Spas," and in 1729, with James Arbuckle, an adherent of the Shaftsbury school of philosophy, contributing copy, the *Tribune*, a controversial and unsuccessful running critique of Ireland's economic and political problems.

> To what dull and dismal Pass
> A-B--kle's Labours, come, alas!

He apparently was not a good business man, for in 1723 his mother, Deborah, had to petition the city council for relief, which was granted (*Cal. Anc. Rec. Dublin*), and in 1729 Sylvester ceased work when his mother deeded the printing equipment to Edward Bate (q.v.).

POWELL (WILLIAM), bookseller and publisher in Dublin, at the corner of Christ Church Lane, over against the Thosel, 1743–52. He was apprenticed to Samuel Fairbrother (q.v.), admitted free of the guild by service in 1743, paid quarterage through 1748, and served as Warden in 1747 (*Guild Records*). He was admitted free of the city in 1743 (Thrift, *Freemen*). In 1743 he announced the opening of his shop, stating that he had "furnish'd himself with a choice and curious collection of Books," and hoped for "the custom and recommendation of all his friends and acquaintances" (*Dublin Gazette*, 15 Nov.). In the same year he published *Levee, A Farce*, and he took subscriptions to various publications, Sale's *Universal History*, 1744 and 1746, and the *Dublin Courant*, 1746–50. In 1745 he listed himself as a bookseller and brewer (*Dublin Courant*, 14 Aug.). He died in 1752, his will referring to him as a merchant (Bentham, *Abstracts*).

PRICE (SAMUEL), bookseller and publisher in Dublin, (1) Dame Street, over against Crane Lane (1751–64); (2) 55 Henry Street (1783–88?). 1751–88? He was apprenticed to Abraham Bradley (q.v.), was admitted free of the guild by service in 1751, paid quarterage through 1781, served as Warden in 1760, and on the Council from 1762 (*Guild Records*). He was admitted free of the city in 1752 (Thrift, *Freemen*). His publications included, with other stationers, Fielding's *Amelia*, 1752, Shakespeare's *Midsummer Night's Dream*, 1764, and, alone, Goldsmith's *The beauties of Goldsmith*, 1783. He died in 1793, his will being proved in the Prerogative Court at Dublin.

PROCTOR or PROCTER (EPHRAIM), printer and publisher in Athlone, 1770–93. He was apprenticed to Samuel Powell (q.v.), but did not complete his apprenticeship (*Guild Records*). He became the first printer in Athlone, and started that town's first newspaper, the *Athlone Chronicle*, 1770–93.

PUE (ELIZABETH), bookseller and publisher in Dublin, the back of Dick's Coffee House, Skinner Row, 1722–30? She was the widow of Richard Pue (q.v.), and continued the family business—Coffee House and newspaper. For a time, under her management, *Pue's Occurrences* became an unofficial government organ, utilized to attack figures like John Harding (q.v.). Four times Elizabeth was secretly paid by the government to include anti-Harding copy in her paper (Munter, *Irish Newspapers*). In 1722 she published the *Life and Surprising Adventures of Don Jullani de Trezz*. From 1723 to 1725 she was in an advertisement war with Cornelius Carter (q.v.) over the sale of a patent drug. Carter apparently was miffed at Elizabeth's turning over the printing of the *Occurrences* to Thomas Walsh (q.v.) and not to himself, and attacked her for selling the "Fam'd Royal Eye Water" that he considered his Dublin monopoly. He protested that "she has had none come out of England these many years past and that our's is fresh," adding to this charge that "her Husband ow'd me near 200 l. when he dy'd" and that she "never gave one farthing" (*St. James Evening Post*, 6 Oct. 1723). Five years later Elizabeth still persisted: "Just arrived from London, a fresh quantity" of the eye water and "sold no where else"! (*Dublin Intelligence*, 13 July 1728). Sometime between 1728 and 1730 Elizabeth retired, and turned the business over to her son Richard Pue Jr. (q.v.).

PUE (JAMES), printer and publisher in Dublin, the back of Dick's Coffee House, Skinner Row, 1758–62. He was the nephew of Richard Pue Jr. (q.v.), and took over his uncle's business upon the latter's death in 1758 (*Universal Advertiser*, 23 Dec.). He died in 1762, his will being proved in the Prerogative Court at Dublin, and was succeeded in business by his widow, Sarah Pue (q.v.).

PUE (RICHARD), bookseller, printer, and publisher in Dublin, the back of Dick's Coffee House, Skinner Row, 1698–1722. There were two Richard Pues, father and son. Richard Pue senior was first renowned for his Coffee House, which became the chief center for book auctions from at least 1698. It was also an early gathering spot for Tory sympathizers:

> Ye quidnuncs! who frequently come into Pue's,
> To live upon politicks, coffee, and news.

It was also the central stage for the 1698 "scuffle," for Dunton, who came to Dublin to sell a large quantity of London-printed books in that year, came to believe that an original promise for him and Richard Wilde (q.v.) to use Dick's to auction off his books was broken and the Coffee House instead let to a rival auctioneer, Patrick Campbell (q.v.) (Dunton, *Dublin Scuffle*). A printing press was set up in the back of the Coffee House and was used by Stephen Powell (q.v.), John Brocas (q.v.), and John Brent (q.v.) in their partnership years, 1689 to 1700, and perhaps by Brent and Brocas to 1701. Pue was admitted free of the city as a dyer in 1701 (Thrift, *Freemen*), and in 1703 began his stationer's career, one of the few successful printers and publishers to remain outside the guild. In partnership with Edward Lloyd (q.v.) he started the *Impartial Occurrences*, 1703; by 1707 Pue was the sole proprietor, and he restyled the newspaper *Pue's Occurrences*. It became, along with Dickson's *Dublin Intelligence*, one of the leading papers of the time. Pue also published a few pamphlets: e.g., the *Votes of the House of Commons*, "by authority," 1707, and *The Happiness of the Present Establishment and the Unhappiness of Absolute Monarchy*,

1708. During the later years of Anne's reign he used his paper in blatant support of Tory dominance, and was made to pay following her death. In 1715 he was ordered arrested over a paragraph "highly reflecting on the late House of Commons," which had been printed eight months before! Pue fled, returning only after Parliament was prorogued, but in 1717 he was again ordered into custody for the offense. Nothing more appears regarding the case, and Pue began publishing immediately after the Parliamentary session ended (*Commons' Journ. Ire.*, iii, 18, 141). Pue died in 1722 (*Whalley's News-Letter*, 24 May), and was succeeded by his wife, Elizabeth Pue (q.v.).

PUE (RICHARD JR.), bookseller, printer, and publisher in Dublin, the back of Dick's Coffee House, Skinner Row, 1730?–58. He was the son of Elizabeth and Richard Pue (qq.v.), and between 1728 and 1730 took over the family business. His first imprint appeared on the newspaper *Pue's Occurrences* in 1730. He completely altered and revitalized the *Occurrences*, converting it from its Tory inclination to a staunch Whig advocacy, soliciting a broad country circulation, and coming to monopolize the advertisements for rural land and property sales. During his proprietorship the journal was one of the three dominant newspapers of the time, along with George Faulkner's (q.v.) and James Hoey's (q.v.). In 1735 Pue began music printing with the publication of *Ariets or Ballads*. He announced in 1743 that he had "undertaken the business of Auctioning Books" himself (*Dublin News-Letter*, 11 Jan.), which he continued until 1746, and in 1744 he was one of the undertakers of Faulkner's (q.v.) edition of Sale's *Universal Advertiser*. He died in 1758 (*Sleater's Public Gazetteer*, 16 Dec.), and was succeeded by his nephew James Pue (q.v.).

PUE (SARAH), printer and publisher in Dublin, the back of Dick's Coffee House, Skinner Row, 1762–76. She was the widow and successor of James Pue (q.v.), whom she had married in 1761 (*Dublin Grant Book*). In 1763 she married John Roe (q.v.) (*Dublin Grant Book*), and in the same year took into partnership her brother David Giball (q.v.). The three continued the Coffee House business and the publication of *Pue's Occurrences* until John's death in 1774, and then for two more years by Sarah and David (Gilbert, *History of Dublin*).

PUNSTER (THOMAS), printer in Dublin, 1652. Sole reference: a petition by Thomas Punster, printer, was referred to Daniel Hutchinson, Mayor of Dublin, who found the petitioner "to bee debauched and given to drinking, and Idle Company," and "That caused him to be punished according to Law" (*Commonwealth Council Book*, Orders 1651–53).

PURCELL (RICHARD), engraver in Dublin (1746–55?), and London (1755?–66). 1755–66. He was a pupil of John Brooks (q.v.), and possibly worked for some time in Dublin with Andrew Miller (q.v.). His Dublin work was sold primarily by William Wilkinson (q.v.) and Thomas Silcock (q.v.). Among his Dublin prints were "William at the Siege of Namur," 1748, and portraits of Samuel Madden, n.d., Oliver Cromwell, n.d., and Rev. John Cennick, 1754. About 1755 he went to London and there produced a large body of distinguished work, many of the prints signed Chas. Corbutt or C. Corbutt, an alias adopted to avoid creditors (Strickland, *Irish Artists*).

PURFIELD (MICHAEL), stationer in Dublin, 1755–66. He was admitted to the guild as a quarter brother in 1755 and paid quarterage through 1763 (*Guild Records*). He was probably a journeyman.

QUINTENE (WILLIAM), bookbinder in Dublin, 1576. Sole reference: he was a Scottish bookbinder who was granted denization in 1576 (*Twelfth Rep. D. K. PROI*, fiant no. 2837).

R

RAMSAY (Mr.), bookseller in Belfast, 1729. Advertisements in 1729 list him as taking subscriptions for Jonson's *Plays* (*Dublin Intelligence*, 22 Feb.), and Kings's *State of the Protestants* (*Dublin Intelligence*, 2 Sept.).

RAMSAY (HUGH), bookseller, printer, and publisher in Waterford, the Quay, 1740–85? He was a prominent Waterford stationer, and from 1740 took subscriptions for many Dublin publications: e.g., Rollin's *Roman History*, 1740, and Harris' *Life of William III*, 1749. He was one of the provincial undertakers of Faulkner's (q.v.) edition of Sale's *Universal History*, 1744, and in 1748 Alexander and George Ewing (qq.v.) and Abraham Bradley (q.v.) advertised that he sold their publications. In 1765 he took his son James Ramsay (q.v.) into partnership, and in the same year they began the *Waterford Chronicle*, long the leading Waterford newspaper. Hugh died in 1795, aged 93.

RAMSAY (JAMES), bookseller, printer, and publisher in Waterford, the Quay, 1765–96? In 1765 he was taken into partnership by his father, Hugh Ramsay (q.v.), and they jointly published the *Waterford Chronicle* from that year. They printed many books—e.g., Carter's *Select Poems*, 1772. James became prominent in Waterford civic affairs, serving as Sheriff from 1781 to 1783 and as Mayor in 1790.

RANDALL or RANDAL (JOHN), papermaker in Newbridge, 1729–54. In 1729 he built a paper mill at Newbridge, near Leixlip, County Kildare, and for some years appears to have leased this to Humphrey Davenport (q.v.). In 1737 Randall petitioned Parliament for assistance in building another paper mill "in the best Dutch Manner," and was granted £500 (*Commons' Journ. Ire.*, iv, 107, 241–43). A publication in 1749 advertised that it was printed on paper made by "Mr. Randall at New-bridge" (*Dublin Journal*, 18 Nov.), as did both Harris' *Life of William III*, 1749, and a *Letter to the Rev. Moore Booker*, 1752. These had Randall's watermark. He died at New-bridge in 1754, having "the misfortune to be thrown from his Horse . . . by which he fractured his Skull and expired in three Hours" (*Pue's Occurrences*, 26 Oct.).

RANDALL or RANDAL (ROBERT), papermaker in Dublin, Dirty Lane, at Thomas Street, 1748?–78. He was admitted free of the city by service in 1748 (Thrift, *Freemen*). He was apprenticed to Edward Waters (q.v.), admitted free of the guild by special grace (his indentures had not been properly registered) in 1749, paid quarterage through 1772, and was carried in the Clerk's list to 1778 (*Guild Records*). What relation he was to John Randall is not known. By 1757 Robert had a paper mill at Rathfarnham, for in that year he petitioned Parliament for assistance, detailing the production of his Rathfarnham mill and seeking money to continue the construction of a new paper mill at Little Newton, near Rathfarnham, and was granted £300 (*Commons' Journ. Ire.*, vi, 29, 32). He had his own watermark. Some confusion attends the dates and the name Robert Randall. In 1757 the petitioner claimed to have been involved in papermaking for some thirty years, and when a Robert Randall died in 1781 a notice read "aged 92, formerly an eminent Paper-maker" (*Dublin Journal*, 26 Apr.). Quite likely there were two Robert Randalls, an elder and younger, for he would appear unlikely to have completed an apprenticeship at near sixty years of age!

RANSOM (WILLIAM), bookseller in Dublin, 1746–83. He was apprenticed to George Ewing (q.v.), admitted free of the guild by service in 1748, and paid quarterage through 1782 (*Guild Records*). He was admitted free of the city in 1746 (Thrift, *Freemen*). He died in 1783, his will being proved in the Prerogative Court at Dublin.

RATHBONE (JOHN), bookseller in Dublin, Essex Street, over against Essex Bridge, 1702–16. He was a glover and skinner to 1702, when he petitioned the guild that, "whereas he hath married Mrs. Mary Milner [q.v.] Widow and Relict of Jacob Milner [q.v.] stat. deceased and hath bought his stock and designed to keep the shop and follow the trade of stationer and bookseller," he begged his freedom. He was admitted free of the guild in 1702 and paid quarterage through 1716 (*Guild Records*). He died in 1734, his will being proved in the Prerogative Court at Dublin.

RAY (ELIZABETH), bookseller, printer, and publisher in Dublin, Skinner Row, opposite the Thosel, 1703–13. She was the widow of Joseph Ray (q.v.), and upon the latter's death took over the family business. In 1709 she took her son John Ray (q.v.) into partnership, and in the same year they petitioned the city council to be allowed to continue as City Printers, which was granted (*Cal. Anc. Rec. Dublin*). In 1713 she printed and published the *Church Catechism Explained*. She died in 1713, her will being proved in the Prerogative Court at Dublin, and was succeeded in business by Samuel Fairbrother (q.v.).

RAY (JOHN), bookseller and printer in Dublin, Skinner Row, opposite the Thosel, 1709–12. He was apprenticed to his father, Joseph Ray (q.v.), was admitted free of the guild in 1709, paid quarterage through 1712, and served on the Council from 1711 (*Guild Records*). He was admitted free of the city in 1709

(Thrift, *Freemen*). He joined his mother, Elizabeth Ray (q.v.), in partnership in 1709, and printed for the city in 1710 and 1711 (*Cal. Anc. Rec. Dublin*). He died in 1712 (*Guild Records*).

RAY (JOSEPH), bookbinder, bookseller, printer, and publisher in Dublin, (1) College Green (1681?–94); (2) the Three Naggs Heads, Essex Street (1695–97); (3) Skinner Row, opposite the Thosel (1698–1708). 1676–1708. He was admitted free of the guild in 1678, paid quarterage through 1708, served on the Council from 1683, as Warden in 1686 and 1694, and served out the term of Eliphal Dobson (q.v.) as Master in 1704 (*Guild Records*). He was admitted free of the city in 1680 (Thrift, *Freemen*). He established one of the largest and most successful printing houses of the period, printing and publishing a variety of poems, trials, sermons, and letters: e.g., *Tryal and Condemnation of Dr. Oliver Plunket*, 1681, the first printing of Molyneux's *Case of Ireland*, 1698, and Walker's *Epictetus*, 1702. He also printed Dublin's first modern newspaper, the *News-Letter*, 1685–88?, and the semi-official government paper the *Dublin Intelligence*, 1690. He was printer to the city from 1681 to 1708 (*Cal. Anc. Rec. Dublin*), and bound Parliamentary journals between 1705 and 1708. In 1685 he led an unsuccessful guild struggle against the appointment of a King's Printer for Ireland, "which privileges were destructive to the whole faculty of stationer members" (*Guild Records*). In 1689, during the period of Jacobite control, Ray's stalwart Church of England defense led to his having his press seized by the authorities (see James Malone), and in 1698 he was imprisoned for printing the *Injured Protestant Vindicated*, but upon petition was ordered to be fined "and on his knees receive the reprimand of this House" (*Commons' Journ. Ire.*, ii, 248–64). Via a series of marriages the Ray family created an interlocking relationship of Irish stationers: Ray's sister to William Winter (q.v.), his wife's sister to William Norman (q.v.), a daughter to John Hyde (q.v.), another to Thomas Fleming (q.v.), a granddaughter to George Esdall (q.v.), and another to James Magee (q.v.). Ray died in 1708, his will being proved in the Prerogative Court at Dublin. He was succeeded in business by his wife, Elizabeth Ray (q.v.).

REA (**John**), printer in Dublin, Exchequer Street (1792?–1802?). 1775–1802? He was apprenticed to John Exshaw (q.v.) from the Blue Coat School, admitted free of the guild by service in 1775, paid quarterage through 1787, was listed in the Clerk's list to 1789, and had an apprentice, James Clement, enrolled to him in 1792, who was admitted free by service to Rea in 1802 (*Guild Records*). He was admitted free of the city in 1775. Only one Rea imprint is known, Goldsmith's *The beauties of Goldsmith*, 1783.

REDWOOD (**John**), bookseller, printer, and publisher in Cork, (1) near the Exchange (1715–21); (2) Castle Street (1723). 1715–23. In 1715 he was listed in the colophon as the seller of the *Freeholder's Answer to the Pretender's Declaration*; in 1721, among other imprints, trials, sermons, etc., he published Puckle's *The Club. In a Dialogue between Father and Son* and the *Beauty of Holiness in the Common Prayer*; and in 1723 he printed and published *The Spiritual Week* and Steele's *Conscious Lovers*.

REILLY (**Alice**), printer and publisher in Dublin, the Stationer's Hall, Cork Hill, 1741–68? She was the widow of Richard Reilly (q.v.), and upon the latter's death took over the family business. In 1748 the guild ordered her to pay quarterage, and she is listed as having paid in 1755 and 1756. She had three apprentices enrolled to her and the last, her nephew John Abbott Husband (q.v.), was admitted free by service in 1768. She was also a tenant of the guild, working out of the upper level of their hall (*Guild Records*). She continued the *Dublin News-Letter*, and joined with Edward Exshaw in its publication from 1741 to 1743. In 1744 she started the *Dublin Courant*, which she sold to Oliver Nelson (q.v.) in 1745. Among her other imprints were Shakespeare's *As You Like It*, 1741, Burton's *Lectures in Natural Philosophy*, 1751, Richardson's *Sir Charles Grandison*, 1753, and book catalogues in 1755 and 1760. In 1766 she joined with other Dublin stationers in a published complaint against irregulars and intruders in the trade, pledging that they would "not be received or employed in any of our Printing Houses" (*Freeman's Journal*, 26 Apr.). She died in 1778 "in the 76th year of her age, who for many years carried on extensively the printing business" (*Freeman's Journal*, 25 Apr.) and possibly was succeeded in business by John Abbott Husband.

REILLY (C.), printer and publisher in Dublin, 1728–29. Sole reference: he is stated to have printed and sold various prints by Thomas Beard (q.v.) in 1728 and 1729 (Strickland, *Irish Artists*).

REILLY or REILY (JAMES), bookseller, printer, and publisher in Armagh, English Street, 1771–99. He was admitted free of the city in 1771. He printed for the city corporation in 1774 and 1778 (*Municipal Records of the City of Armagh*). He printed and published *A Mysterious Doctrine*, 1775, and an edition of the Bible, 1794.

REILLY (RICHARD), printer and publisher in Dublin, the Stationer's Hall, or, the Printing Office, Cork Hill, 1735–41. A Reily or Reilly (R.) printed in London in 1730 and was "believed to have gone over to Ireland" (*Dictionary 1726–75*). In 1735 Reilly printed Parnell's *Poems* and a reprint edition of the *Guardian*. He was admitted free of the guild in 1736, paid quarterage through 1740, and was a tenant of the guild, working out of the upper part of the hall (*Guild Records*). He was admitted free of the city in 1736 (Thrift, *Freemen*). He started a newspaper, the *Weekly Oracle; or, Universal Library* in 1735, and in 1736, with assistance from the partnership of George Risk (q.v.), George Ewing (q.v.), and William Smith (q.v.), the floundering *Oracle* was revitalized, renamed the *Dublin News-Letter*, and quickly became a formidable rival of the long-established journalistic giants (Munter, *Irish Newspapers*). It became, as well, the official organ of the Dublin Society, in which they published their transactions and at the same time guaranteed the sale of 500 copies per issue (*Dublin News-Letter*, 22 Jan. 1736/37). Reilly also published the Society's *Weekly Observations*, 1738–40. He printed a variety of other works, including the first edition of Bacon's *Compleat System of Revenue of Ireland*, 1727, Carthy's *Translation of Longinus*, 1738, and Shakespeare's *Henry IV*, *Henry VIII*, and *King Lear*, 1739. He died in 1741, administration granted by the Prerogative Court at Dublin, and was succeeded by his wife, Alice Reilly (q.v.).

REILY (JAMES) *see* James Reilly

REYLEY (GARRETT), bookseller in Dublin, Cook Street (1711). 1697–1711. He was ordered fined as an intruder in 1697 and again in 1711 (*Guild Records*).

REYNOLDS (JOHN), printer and publisher in Loughrea, 1766?–73? He was the first printer in Loughrea and printed and published that town's first newspaper, the *Connaght Mercury, or Universal Advertiser*, from 1766. In the same year he printed *Proposals for Printing by Subscription . . . Dissertation on the origins of the . . . Races of Ireland*. In 1773 an advertisement read, "Five Guineas Reward. Ran away, on Saturday night . . . from the service of John Reynolds, Printer, in Loughrea, Arthur Neal . . . and James Farrell" (*Hibernian Chronicle*, 22 Nov.).

RHAMES (AARON), printer and publisher in Dublin, (1) the Three Keys, St. Nicholas Street (1703–9); (2) the back of Dick's Coffee House, Skinner Row (1709–16?); (3) opposite the Pyed Horse, or, Tillotson's Head, Capel Street (1719?–34). 1703–34. He was apprenticed to John Ray (q.v.), petitioned for freedom in 1703 (the decision being deferred for lack of quorum!), summoned as an intruder in 1711, admitted free of the guild in 1714, paid quarterage at least through 1729, served on the Council from 1721, as Warden in 1723, and as Master in 1728 (*Guild Records*). He was admitted free of the city in 1714. A man of mild Tory sympathies, he established one of the leading printing houses of the day, with descendants carrying on the trade through three generations to 1809. He was, however, persistently unsuccessful as a journalist, attempting three times to publish newspapers: the *Dublin Courant, or The Diverting Post*, 1705, the *Diverting Post*, 1709, and again the *Diverting Post*, 1725—each survived but a few issues. He printed the first extant Irish edition of the Bible, 1714 (folio), and an octavo edition in 1722, the *Book of Common Prayer*, 1716 and 1724, and a metrical *Psalter*, 1718. He printed some of the earliest heraldic work in Ireland and printed sheet music from 1729 to 1732. He was printer to the Dublin Society from 1732 to 1736, first printing for them Tull's *Horse Hoeing Husbandry*, 1732. Among his other works were Berkeley's *Essay Towards a New Theory of Vision*, 1709, Burnet's *History of His Own Time*, 1724, and Dobbs's *Essay on the Trade . . . of Ireland*, 1734. He died in 1734 (*Dublin Evening Post*, 10 Dec.), and was succeeded by his widow, Margaret Rhames (q.v.).

RHAMES (**Benjamin**), bookseller, printer, and publisher in Dublin, the Sun, 16 Upper Blind Quay, 1753–75. He was the son of Aaron and Margaret Rhames (qq.v.), and opened a bookselling, haberdashery, and music shop in 1753. He began music printing about 1760, his publications including *La Casina*, 1761, *Haste to the Wedding*, 1763, and Gibson's *Collection of Catches, Glees, &c.*, 1765. He died in 1775 and was succeeded by his widow, Elizabeth Rhames (q.v.).

RHAMES (**Elizabeth**), bookseller, printer, and publisher in Dublin, (1) the Sun, 16 Upper Blind Quay (1775–76); (2) the Sun, 16 Exchange Street (1776–78). 1775–78. She was the widow of Benjamin Rhames (q.v.), and carried on the family business until her death in 1778. She was succeeded by her son Frederick Rhames, who continued the business until 1809, when it was sold to Paul Alday.

RHAMES (**Joseph**), printer in Dublin, Tillotson's Head, Capel Street, 1741–45? He was the son of Aaron and Margaret Rhames (qq.v.), and in 1741 was taken into partnership by his mother, Margaret. He was admitted to the guild as a quarter brother in 1741 and paid quarterage through 1743 (*Guild Records*). He died by 1746, for he is referred to as "deceased" in his mother's will dated 23 Oct. 1746 (Prerogative Court, Dublin).

RHAMES (**Margaret**), printer in Dublin, Tillotson's Head, Capel Street, 1735–56? She was the widow of Aaron Rhames (q.v.), and continued the family business upon the latter's death. She printed a variety of works, including Rollin's *Method of Teaching and Studying the Belles Lettres*, 1737, *Vocal Miscellany*, 1738, and Shakespeare's *Macbeth*, 1739. In 1741 she took her son Joseph Rhames (q.v.) into partnership, and in 1744 she took subscriptions for Faulkner's (q.v.) edition of Sale's *Universal History*. She died in 1756 (*Dublin Journal*, 26 June).

RICHARDSON (THOMAS), bookbinder in Dublin, Bride Street, 1670–94. He was admitted free of the guild in 1670 and paid quarterage through 1694 (*Guild Records*). He was admitted free of the city in 1670 (Thrift, *Freemen*). He died in 1694 (*Dublin Grant Book*).

RICHEY (THOMAS), bookseller in Dublin, at Euclid's Head, Dame Street, opposite Crow Street, 1762–73. He had an apprentice enrolled to him in 1762, was admitted free of the guild in 1767, and paid quarterage through 1773 (*Guild Records*). He was admitted free of the city in 1766 (Thrift, *Freemen*).

RICHEY (THOMAS), printer in Waterford, Peter Street, 1764–65. Only one item of his press survives (*Dictionary 1726–75*).

RIDER or RYDER (EBENEZER), bookseller, printer, and publisher in Dublin, George's Lane, 1734–50? He was the brother of Pressick Rider (q.v.) and the brother-in-law of James Carson (q.v.). He began business in 1734, was admitted free of the guild in 1736, and paid quarterage through 1748 (*Guild Records*). He printed and published a great deal, including a *Pocket Companion for Freemasons*, 1735, a *History of Irish Writers*, 1736, Rapin's *History of England*, 1738, and Chetwood's *History of the Stage*, 1749. He also was active in pioneering the periodical press, publishing the *Country Journal*, 1735–36, reprinting the *Scribler*, 1736, and the *Craftsman*, 1739, and printing the *Dublin Daily Advertiser* for James Hamilton (q.v.), 1736–38. When a quarrel led to a split with Hamilton, Rider began publication of the second Dublin daily newspaper, the *Dublin Daily Post, and General Advertiser*, 1739–40 (Munter, *Irish Newspapers*). He died in 1760 (*Pue's Occurrences*, 19 Jan.).

RIDER (JOSEPH), printer in Dublin, 1772. Sole reference: an obituary notice in 1772 read "Death, Last week, Mr. Joseph Rider, printer" (*Freeman's Journal*, 7 May).

RIDER or RYDER (PRESSICK), printer and publisher in Dublin, the General Post Office Printing House, or, the Cork House, in the Exchange, Cork Hill (1724–26), London (1727?–37), and Halifax, Yorkshire (?–1763). 1724–63. He was the brother of Ebenezer Rider (q.v.) and the brother-in-law of James Carson (q.v.). He joined in partnership with Thomas Harbin (q.v.) in 1724 to print "by Authority" the *Dublin Gazette* to 1726. They also printed and published Molyneux's *Case of Ireland*, 1725, Browne's *English Expositor Improved*, 1726, and a periodical, the *Dictator*, 1725. They lost their right to publish the *Gazette* and the partnership broke up. Rider had run afoul of the Dublin authorities by publishing a pamphlet against the government, which in turn offered a £1,000 reward for his apprehension, and Rider fled the country. He next appeared in London—he is listed as a member of a Masonic Lodge in that city in 1731 (*Minutes of the Grand Lodge of Freemasons* [London, 1723–1739], vol. x)—where, it appears, he worked with Henry Haines on the controversial *Craftsman* (*Dictionary 1726–75*). In 1737 a general warrant against the *Craftsman*'s staff led to Rider's house being ransacked, and he fled that city, assuming his mother's maiden name of Darby. For some years he went on the stage as an itinerant comedian, and later, following a general act of grace in 1742, he took up printing in Halifax, Yorkshire as P. Darby (*Dictionary 1726–75*; *Sequin's Hibernian Magazine*, Jan. 1773; see also Thomas Ryder).

RIDGE (J.), engraver in Dublin, 1773. Sole reference: in a 1773 edition of Burke's *Bishop of Ossory*, a map of Ireland is recorded as engraved by "J. Ridge, Dublin."

RISK (GEORGE), bookseller and publisher in Dublin, (1) the London, opposite the Horse Guard, Dame Street (1712–19); (2) the Exchange, Cork Hill (1720–?); (3) corner of Castle Lane, Dame Street, near the Horse Guard (1725–27); (4) at Shakespeare's Head, Dame Street (1728–58). 1712–58. In 1712 he was summoned by the guild as an intruder but, "being newly set to work for himself—therefore desired to be favourably dealt with," was granted freedom of the guild on appeal, and paid quarterage through 1756. He was an active guild member, serving on the Council from 1724, as Warden in 1726, and as Master in 1730 (*Guild Records*). He participated in various joint ventures and in a highly developed association with George Ewing (q.v.) and William Smith (q.v.) from 1726 to 1756. He published many plays, histories, and worked in music publication, notably with the *Poems* of Ramsay in 1724. He was accused of pirating Pope's edition of Shakespeare's *Works* in 1724, and in 1742 he became involved in a factional dispute among Dublin stationers over rival translations of Prévost d'Exiles' *Dean of Coleraine*. Among his many other publications were Fiddes' *Theologia speculativa*, 1719, Swift's *Gulliver's Travels*, 1726, Rollin's *History of the Egyptians*, and Congreve's *Works*, 1736. He also published the *Dublin Almanack* from 1728 to 1738, and in 1737, with his partners Ewing and Smith, was instrumental in revitalizing Richard Reilly's (q.v.) floundering *Weekly Oracle* and making it into the successful *Dublin News-Letter* (Munter, *Irish Newspapers*). He retired from business in 1758, and sold his "entire shop-stock" at auction (*Universal Advertiser*, 2 Dec.). He died in 1762 "aged about 80 . . . a man of fair character" (*Pue's Occurrences*, 20 Feb.).

ROACH (DOMMICK) *see* Dommick Roche

ROBERTSON (J.), bookseller and publisher in Cork, the Naked-man with a Bunch of Keys in his Pocket, near the Bridge,

1754. Sole reference: the colophon lists him as the publisher of Gueulette's *Chinese Tales; or, The wonderful adventures of . . . Fun-Hoam*, 1754.

ROCH (GEORGE), bookseller in Limerick, 1710. Sole reference: advertisements in 1730 listed him as one of the provincial booksellers taking advertisements to a Dublin edition of the *Tryal of Doctor Henry Sacheverell* (*Dublin Intelligence*, 24 June and 1 July).

ROCHE, ROCH, or ROACH (DOMMICK), bookseller in Dublin, Skinner Row, 1723–26. He was admitted to the guild as a quarter brother in 1723, paid quarterage through 1725, and was listed in the Clerk's list in 1726 (*Guild Records*). In 1725 his name appeared as the seller in the colophon of Lewis' *Origines Hebraeae: The antiquities of the Hebrew Republick*.

ROE (Mr.), bookseller in Mountmellick, County Laoighis, 1747–48. An advertisement in 1747 listed him as one of the sellers of *A New Life of William III* (*Dublin Courant*, 9 Jan.), and he was listed in the colophons as one of the sellers of Exshaw's *London Magazine* for 1747 and 1748.

ROE (JOHN), printer and publisher in Dublin, the back of Dick's Coffee House, Skinner Row, 1761–74. He was admitted free of the city in 1761 (Thrift, *Freemen*), paid a guild franchise fine in 1764 but never took his freedom of the guild, and was listed in the records as a "foreigner" (*Guild Records*). Nevertheless, in 1766 he joined with other Dublin stationers in a published complaint against irregulars and intruders in the trade! (*Freeman's Journal*, 26 Apr.). He joined James Pue (q.v.) in some sort of association in 1762, and after the latter's death he married Pue's widow, Sarah (q.v.). In 1763 they brought Sarah's brother, David Giball (q.v.), into the business. John died in 1774, and Sarah and David continued the business.

ROE (SARAH) *see* Sarah Pue

ROGERS (JOHN), bookseller in Dublin, Castle Street, 1699–1711. He was listed as an intruder from 1699 to 1701, had an apprentice, George Winsley (q.v.), go into trade in 1711, and was again listed as an intruder in 1711, with a note that he had another apprentice working for him (*Guild Records*).

ROSS (FORBES), printer and publisher in Dublin, (1) 4 Crane Lane (1773–83?); (2) 16 Trinity Street (1789?–1802). 1773–1802. In 1773 he signed an appeal for assistance on behalf of reduced tradesmen (*Public Journal*, 27 Aug.). He printed the *Freeman's Journal* from 1782 to 1783 and again from 1789 to 1802. In 1782 he started publication of the *Evening Chronicle*.

ROSS (THOMAS), bookseller in Limerick, 1729. In 1729 advertisements listed him as taking subscriptions to Jonson's *Plays* (*Dublin Intelligence*, 22 Feb.), and to King's *State of the Protestants* (*Dublin Intelligence*, 2 Sept.).

ROSS (WILLIAM), bookseller in Dublin, Grafton Street, 1755–65. He became the book auctioneer for Richard Pue Jr. (q.v.) in 1746 (*Pue's Occurrences*, 20 May), and about 1755 opened his own bookshop. He was admitted free of the guild by petition in 1755, paid quarterage through 1765, served on the Council from 1762, and as Warden in 1763 (*Guild Records*). He was admitted free of the city in 1755 (Thrift, *Freemen*). He held book auctions at the back of Dick's Coffee House and at the Lord's Coffee Room in Parliament House. He died intestate in 1765 (*Dublin Grant Book*), his shop-stock being sold at auction in 1766.

ROWLAND (GEORGE), printer in Limerick, ? Sole reference: in 1792 an obituary notice read "On Wednesday se'nnight, at Limerick, of a few days illness, Mr. George Rowland, printer —he was considered, among the professors of that art, as the oldest in Great Britain or Ireland, being capable of discharging the duties assigned to him in that branch, at the age of 85 years" (*Waterford Herald*, 5 Jan.).

RUDD (JAMES), bookseller and publisher in Dublin, the Apollo, Dame Street, 1756–58. He was apprenticed to George Ewing (q.v.), admitted free of the guild by service in 1756, and paid quarterage through 1758 (*Guild Records*). He was admitted free of the city (although listed as a carpenter, his father, Benjamin Rudd's trade) in 1756 (Thrift, *Freemen*). In 1758 he published Shakespeare's *Romeo and Juliet*.

RUSH (JOHN), printer in Dublin, d. 1772. In 1772 his will was proved in the Diocesan Court at Dublin (*Dictionary 1726–75*).

RUSSELL (HUGH), bookseller in Dublin, 1768–? He was apprenticed to Philip Crampton (q.v.), admitted free of the guild by service in 1768, and paid quarterage through 1770 (*Guild Records*). He died in 1790 (*Dublin Grant Book*).

RUSSELL (JAMES), bookseller in Dublin, 1719–20. He was admitted free of the city in 1719 (Thrift, *Freemen*), free of the guild in 1719, and was listed as "dead" in 1720 (*Guild Records*).

RYDER (EBENEZER) *see* Ebenezer Rider

RYDER (PRESSICK) *see* Pressick Rider

RYDER (THOMAS), printer and publisher in Dublin, Cope Street, 1766–74? He was the son of Pressick Rider (q.v.), and was in a brief partnership with Orion Adams (q.v.), jointly publishing plays and operas and Foreman's *Defense of Courage, Honour and Loyalty of the Irish Nation*. In 1774 Ryder petitioned the guild for admission by special grace, but refused to pay the composition fine, and was thus not made free (*Guild Records*). Adams, before he fled Dublin, had involved the partnership in a series of shady deals and considerable debt, "neare six hundred pounds, all of which" Ryder "laboured to discharge . . . as to fix his reputation and firmly establish his credit" (*Sequin's Hibernian Magazine*, Jan. 1773). He later was to garner some little fame as the manager of Dublin's Smock Alley Theatre.

RYLEY (CHARLES), bookseller and publisher in Dublin, against the Castle Gate, Castle Street, 1647. Sole reference: in the colophon he is listed as the publisher and seller of *A Mighty Victory over the Irish Rebels*, 1647.

S

SADLIER (**ELIZABETH**), printer and typefounder in Dublin, (1) School House Lane, near High Street (1715?–22); (2) Blind Quay (1726). 1715?–26. She succeeded Sarah Sadlier (q.v.) in business, and was obviously related to both Sarah and Ralph Sadlier (qq.v.). She printed Puffendorf's *Whole Duty of Man*, two editions, 1715 and 1716, *The Masquerade. A Comedy*, 1719, Burnet's *Exposition of the Thirty-nine Articles*, 1721, and Hooker's *Works*, 1724. In 1717 she printed Knapp's *Almanack* and from 1720 to 1722 LaBoissiere's *Almanack*. In 1719 she advertised types: "several sorts of Letters . . . in as good Mettle as ever mixt in England or Ireland" (*Dublin Impartial News Letter*, 20 Jan.).

SADLIER (**RALPH**), typefounder in Dublin, d. 1703. Sole reference: he was recorded as "Ralph Sadlier, late of Dublin, Letter Founder," and died intestate in 1703 (*Pub. Biblio. Soc. Ire.*, 2, no. 2).

SADLIER (**SARAH**), printer in Dublin, School House Lane, near High Street, 1712?–13? She was probably the widow of Ralph Sadlier (q.v.). She printed a *Sermon*, 1712, and Cocker's *Arithmatic*, 1713. She was succeeded by Elizabeth Sadlier (q.v.), undoubtedly a relative, but the specific relationship is unknown.

SAFTLOW (**WILLIAM**), bookseller in Cork, 1713. Sole reference: an advertisement in 1713 listed him as one of the provincial sellers of a Dublin edition of the *Book of Common Prayer* (*Dublin Gazette*, 11 July).

SANDYS (ANN, ANNE, or ANNA), printer and publisher in Dublin, Customs-House Printing-House, Crane Lane, next door to the Wooden Man, 1705?–24? She was the widow of Edwin Sandys (q.v.), and with her son Edwin Sandys Jr. (q.v.) was taken into partnership with her husband about 1705, then continuing the family business following her husband's death. With her son she published the *Dublin Gazette*, a revived official government paper, 1705–24?, and apparently Ann did other printing for the government. She died in 1749, "formerly Printer to the Revenue of Ireland, and Publisher of the Gazette" (*Dublin Journal*, 21 Jan.).

SANDYS (EDWIN), engraver in Dublin, Crane Lane, 1685?–1708. He was the earliest engraver of any importance in Ireland. He engraved for the government, and was engraver to the Dublin Philosophical Society, 1685–96. For the Society he engraved the portrait of Sir William Petty, the frontispiece for Petty's *Hiberniae delineatio*, 1685. He also engraved a New Map of the City of Londonderry, 1693, and the "Giant's Causeway," 1696. By 1705 he had taken into partnership his wife, Ann Sandys (q.v.), and son Edwin Sandys Jr. (q.v.). He died in 1708 (*56th Rep. D. K. Rec.*, PROI), and was succeeded by his wife and son.

SANDYS (EDWIN JR.), printer and publisher in Dublin, (1) Customs-House Printing-House, Crane Lane, next door to the Wooden Man (1705?–9); (2) Customs-House Printing-House, Essex Street (1709–24). 1705?–24. He was the son of Ann and Edwin Sandys (qq.v.), and joined them in partnership about 1705. In that year he gained the right to publish the *Dublin Gazette* "by Authority." He also published other newspapers, the *Post-Man and The Historical Account*, 1707–13? (the rights to this title apparently acquired by Thomas Hume [q.v.] in 1716), and the *Flying-Post: or, The Post-Master*,

1707–24? Sandys printed as well Higgins' *Sermon*, 1705, Servant's *Remarks upon . . . Partiality Detected*, 1709, Eugene's *Memorial, in the name of the Emperor*, 1712, and Phillip's *Cyder* and Pope's *Temple of Fame*, 1715. In 1724 he was accused of publishing a "seditious libel" in the *Flying Post*, and thus apparently lost his right to publish the *Gazette* to Pressick Rider (q.v.) and Thomas Harbin (q.v.). Perhaps as a consequence he left the stationer's trade, his shop being taken by Thomas Hume. Sandys was admitted free of the city by special grace in 1731 (Thrift, *Freemen*), and in 1733 was appointed "Second Examiner to his Majesty's High Court of Chancery" (*Dublin Evening Post*, 19 June). He died in 1734 (*Dublin Evening Post*, 15 Jan.).

SARGENT (W.), printer and publisher in Cork, 1773–78. In partnership with John Busteed (q.v.) he published the *Hibernian Morning Post or Literary Chronicle*, 1773–76 (the *Hibernian Journal*, 19 Apr. 1773, quoted the *Hibernian Morning Post*, "printed for Busteed and Sargent"). Sargent printed *A Letter from Mr. John Busteed to P. B. Esq., M.D.*, n.d. (probably printed in 1775, for this was obviously a continuation of a petty feud that had opened with Busteed's publication of *Some Structures of the Scotch Doctor's . . . Apology*, 1775). Sargent died in 1778, his will being proved in the Diocesan Court at Cork.

SARRAZIN (Brother NICHOLAS), printer in Kilkenny, 1647–48. He was the printer for the Society of Jesus: "he had charge of our printing press in Kilkenny in 1647" (Hogan, *Chronological Catalogue of the Irish Province, S.J.*), and when in 1648 a dispute arose over the publication of an offensive reflection on Lord O'Neill, the Jesuit answer revealed Sarrazin as their printer.

SAUNDERS (**Henry**), bookseller, printer, and publisher in Dublin, (1) on the Blind Quay, at the corner of Copper Alley, Cork Hill (1749–51); (2) the corner of Christ Church Lane and Skinner Row, opposite the Thosel (1752–56?); (3) at the Salmon, Castle Street, later, 38 Castle Street (1761–73); (4) 20 Great Ship Street (1773–88). 1749–88. He was listed as a journeyman to James Esdall (q.v.) in 1749 (*Commons' Journ. Ire.*, viii, 19), and when the latter fled to London, Saunders apparently took charge of the business. In 1752 he set up on his own in the former shop of William Powell (q.v.). Saunders was admitted free of the guild in 1752, and paid quarterage through 1786. He was an active guild member, serving as Warden in 1775, as Treasurer from 1776 to 1785, on the Council from 1776, and as Master in 1779 (*Guild Records*). He was admitted free of the city in 1752 and appointed Sheriff in 1778 (Thrift, *Freemen*). In 1754 he took over *Esdall's News-Letter*, restyling it *Saunders's News-Letter*, which he published to 1774 when it was in turn purchased by James Potts (q.v.). With John Exshaw (q.v.) and Matthew Williamson (q.v.) he published the *Universal Advertiser*, 1753–58. Among his many other publications were Fielding's *Amelia*, 1752, Sterne's *Tristram Shandy*, 1765, and Shakespeare's *Romeo and Juliet* and *Coriolanus*, 1763, *Works*, 1766, and *Timon of Athens*, 1772. In 1749, during the Charles Lucas controversy, Saunders was among several stationers ordered before the Commons in what was in effect a general summons, but no action was taken against him (*Commons' Journ. Ire.*, v, 12–13). In 1753, along with John Exshaw (q.v.) and Peter Wilson (q.v.), he brought out a pirated edition of Richardson's *Sir Charles Grandison* (see George Faulkner). He died in 1788, his will being proved in the Prerogative Court at Dublin.

SAVAGE (**Mr.**), bookseller in Cork, 1713. Sole reference: in 1713 he was paid by the Cork Council for supplying newspapers, and they ordered "that he forbear sending any more for the future" (Caulfield, *Cork Council Book*).

SCOTT (**JAMES**), bookseller in Kilkenny, 1747–54. He was listed as one of the provincial sellers of Exshaw's *London Magazine* for 1747 and 1748, and in 1747 he took subscriptions for *A New Life of William III* (*Dublin Courant*, 9 Jan.).

SERGIER (**RICHARD**), bookseller and printer in Dublin, St. Austin's, King's Printing House, Castle Street, or, next the Castle Gate, 1638–41. He was in partnership with Edmund and John Crook (q.v.) and possibly with Thomas Allott (q.v.) by 1638. In 1640, with John Crook, he printed William Ince's *Lot's Little One*.

SERVANT (**THOMAS**), bookbinder, bookseller, and publisher in Dublin, (1) St. Patrick's Close (1682–83); (2) Golden Lane (1698); (3) the Bible, Castle Street (1701–10). 1682–1710. He was listed as an intruder in 1682, admitted free of the guild in 1683, paid quarterage through 1710, served on the Council from 1701, and as Warden in 1703 (*Guild Records*). He was admitted free of the city in 1692 (Thrift, *Freemen*). He was the brother-in-law of Peter Lawrence (q.v.). He published, with others, William Barton's *Psalms*, with music, 1706, and, alone, two pamphlets concerning a minor controversy between Bishop Synge, a proctor at St. Patrick's, and the lower house of convocation: *Remarks upon a Letter*, 1709, and *A Reply to a Vindication*, 1710. Dunton, who held few Dublin stationers in high repute, felt that he had "never met with a more scrupulous, or conscientious Man" than Servant (*Dublin Scuffle*). Servant died in 1711 (*Dublin Grant Book*).

SEXTON (**JOSEPH**), papermaker in Limerick, 1747–82. In 1747 he built a paper mill in Limerick, and another by 1749 when he advertised how he had "at great expense built two Paper-Mills within the Liberties" (*Munster Journal*, 15 May). In 1750 and 1753 he received premiums from the Dublin Society "for the best and most Printing Paper" (*Dublin Journal*, 16 June 1753). In 1751 he petitioned Parliament for assistance, claiming to have manufactured paper "for four years past," and he received £200. He petitioned again in 1753, and was voted £500; a further petition in 1755, although favourably reported upon, was never acted upon (*Commons' Journ. Ire.*, v, 96, 174, 185, 237). The mills were described as "flourishing" in 1764 and 1766, and were still in operation at Sexton's death in 1782 (Lenihan, *Limerick: Its History and Antiquities*).

SHACKELTON (ABRAHAM), bookseller in Ballytore, 1738. Sole reference: an advertisement in 1738 listed him as one of the provincial booksellers taking subscriptions to Fenelon's *Dissertation on Pure Love* (*Dublin Journal*, 3 Oct.).

SHARP (Mr.), printer in Dublin, 1722. Sole reference: a notice in 1722 read that "Mr. Sharp the Printer" was "taken into Custody of a Messenger for affirming in Print that the Archbishop of Dublin had refused to Consecrate the Lord Bishop of Leighlin and Ferns" (*Whalley's News-Letter*, 20 Mar.).

SHAW (HENRY), bookseller and publisher in Dublin, Darby Square, Werburgh Street, 1711–24. He was apprenticed to Josias Shaw (q.v.), no relation, admitted free of the guild by service in 1711, and paid quarterage through 1724 (*Guild Records*). He was admitted free of the city in 1711 (Thrift, *Freemen*). In 1720 he published Increase Mather's *Sermons* (*Dublin Courant*, 4 July).

SHAW (JOSIAS), printer in Dublin, Russel's Coffee House, Cork Hill, 1689–1704. He was apprenticed to William Norman (q.v.), admitted free of the guild by service in 1698, listed in the Clerk's list to 1704, and recorded as "dead" in 1704 (*Guild Records*). He was admitted free of the city in 1698 (Thrift, *Freemen*). In 1695 he printed Francis Quarles's *Enchiridion miscellaneum* and in 1699 Wilkins' *The Chase of the Stagg. A Descriptionary Poem*.

SHAW (LEWIS), stationer in Dublin, the Bible and Crown, next door to the Crown Tavern, facing the Blind Quay, near Essex Gate, 1698–1700? He was listed as a journeyman to Mathew Gun (q.v.) from 1698 to 1700, there was no journeyman's list for 1701, and he does not appear on the 1702 list (*Guild Records*).

SHEE or SHEA (JAMES), bookbinder in Armagh, d. 1775. A James Shee was apprenticed to Josiah Sheppard (q.v.) in 1760 but never took out his freedom of the guild (*Guild Records*). An obituary notice in 1775 read "Died in Armagh, Mr. Shea, bookbinder" (*Freeman's Journal*, 8 Aug.).

SHEPPARD or SHEPPERD (HENRY), bookbinder in Dublin, Werburgh Street, 1764–80. He was apprenticed to his father, Josiah Sheppard (q.v.), had an apprentice enrolled to him in 1764, was admitted free of the guild by service in 1768, and paid quarterage through 1780 (*Guild Records*). He was admitted free of the city in 1768 (Thrift, *Freemen*).

SHEPPARD (JOSEPH), bookseller in Dublin, Ann Street, 1754–77. He was admitted free of the guild in 1754 (*Guild Records*), and in 1777 was recorded as being in partnership with G. Nugent.

SHEPPARD (JOSIAH), bookseller and publisher in Limerick, opposite the Exchange, 1740. Sole reference: he was listed in the colophon as the publisher of Rowe's *Devout Exercises of the Heart*, 1740.

SHEPPARD or SHEPPERD (JOSIAH), bookbinder, bookseller, and publisher in Dublin, Skinner Row, 1755–91. He was admitted free of the guild in 1755 and paid quarterage through 1787 (*Guild Records*). He was admitted free of the city in 1755 (Thrift, *Freemen*). He was bookseller and stationer to the "Magdalen Asylum." In 1773 he signed a memorial to the Irish House of Commons against additional duties on foreign paper (BL, 1890.e.5. (239)). He published, with others, *Arabian Nights*, 1776, and Young's *Tour of Ireland*, 1780.

SHEPPARD (THOMAS), bookseller in Dublin, near the Horse Guard, Dame Street, 1704–19? He was admitted free of the city and free of the guild by service in 1704, paid quarterage through 1719, served on the Council from 1708, and as Warden in 1714. In 1719 he asked to be replaced on the Council, "having for some time left off his business" (*Guild Records*).

SHERRARD (RICHARD), stationer in Dublin, 1734–37. He was apprenticed to George Risk (q.v.), admitted to the guild as a quarter brother in 1734, and paid quarterage through 1737 (*Guild Records*).

SHERRY (PATRICK), stationer in Dublin, 1752–59. He was admitted to the guild as a quarter brother in 1752, "to follow the business of a Stationer," and paid quarterage through 1759 (*Guild Records*). He died intestate in 1779 (*Dublin Grant Book*).

SHIRVINTON (ROBERT), bookseller in Kilkenny, 1710. Sole reference: advertisements in 1710 listed him as one of the provincial booksellers taking subscriptions to a Dublin edition of the *Tryal of Doctor Henry Sacheverell* (*Dublin Intelligence*, 24 June and 1 July).

SHORT (**DARBY**), bookbinder in Dublin, 1768. He was apprenticed to John Bradley (q.v.), admitted free of the guild by service in 1768, but there are no other references to him (*Guild Records*).

SILCOCK (**THOMAS**), bookseller, printer, and publisher in Dublin, (1) the Fan and Crown, St. Nicholas Street, opposite the Thosel (1741?–59); (2) the Print Shop, Skinner Row (1760–63?). 1741?–63? He was primarily a printmaker and seller. In 1741 he had an apprentice enrolled to him (Strickland, *Irish Artists*). He published the prints of Andrew Miller (q.v.) and Richard Purcell (q.v.) and, with Paul Smith (q.v.), served as the Dublin agent for the famous London engraver James McArdell (*Freeman's Journal*, 12 Sept. 1751). In 1753 he advertised that he had "set up a Compleat Rolling Press for the Printing off his own Plates, taking in all Manner of Copper Plate Printing at the lowest Rates" (*Dublin Journal*, 16 Jan.). As a mark of the bookseller, he also sold patent drugs—"Walker's Patent Genuine Jesuit's Drops" (*Sleater's Public Gazetteer*, 23 Oct. 1758). His last notice was his marriage in 1763 (*St. Werburgh Par. Reg.*, Dublin).

SIMMS (**PHILIP**), engraver and printer in Dublin, (1) Dame Street (1730?); (2) Crown Alley (1733–49). 1725–49. He was the busiest engraver of his day. Among his many engravings were a portrait of the author for Molyneux's *Case of Ireland*, 1725, the frontispiece for the *Constitution of the Free Masons*, 1730, plates for Faulkner's (q.v.) edition of Sale's *Universal History* and Swift's *Works*, 1744, and illustrations for Cervantes' *Don Quixote*, 1747. In 1735 he advertised as "Engraver and Rolling-press Printer" (*Dublin Evening Post*, 1 Nov.). He was admitted free of the Dublin guild of Goldsmiths in 1736, and probably died in 1749.

SIMSON (**ROBERT**), stationer in Dublin, 1676–86. He was admitted to the guild as a quarter brother in 1676, paid quarterage through 1686, and was listed as "gon" in 1687 (*Guild Records*).

SISSON (**THOMAS**), bookseller in Dublin, 1670–1715. He was admitted free of the guild in 1670, paid quarterage through 1715, and was recorded as "dead" in 1716 (*Guild Records*). He was admitted free of the city in 1670 (Thrift, *Freemen*).

SKY (**JONATHAN**), bookbinder in Dublin, 1754. Sole reference: a 1754 Dublin pamphlet, purporting to be the disposition of a William Fleury, described the events leading to a murder. Among those Fleury listed as being in his company "drinking in the Blue Bell in Capel Street" prior to the incident, was "Jonathan Sky, bookbinder" (*A Full and True Narrative of . . . Murder Committed on the Body of James Eyre Weeks*).

SLATOR (**JOSEPH**), papermaker in Dublin, 1725–43. In 1726 he acquired a mill in Templeogue, County Dublin (*Library*, 5th ser., xiii). At the end of 1742 he transferred the lease to his two sons William Sleater (q.v.) and Thomas Slator (q.v.).

SLATOR or SLEATER (**THOMAS**), papermaker in Dublin, Vicar Street, 1730–65. In 1730 he joined in business with his father, Joseph Slator (q.v.), and in 1742 his father leased his paper mill at Templeogue, County Dublin, to Thomas and his brother William Sleater (q.v.). Thomas took over the actual operation of the mill, and in 1733 petitioned Parliament for assistance and received £500 (Hancock, *History and Antiquities of Tallaght*). He had his own watermark from 1739 to 1765.

He built a second mill at Chapleizod, County Dublin, about 1753. His paper was used for Abraham Bradley's (q.v.) printing of the Commons' *Journals*. He was admitted free of the guild in 1755, "as a mark of esteem as the first great promotor of the Art of Paper Making in the Kingdom of Ireland," and paid quarterage for one year (*Guild Records*). Thomas died in 1767, and was succeeded by his son Thomas Slator Jr. (q.v.).

SLATOR (THOMAS JR.), papermaker in Dublin, (1) Cook Street (1753–76?), with a second place of business (2) Vicar Street and Engine Alley (1755–85?). 1753–85? In 1753 he joined his father, Thomas Slator (q.v.), in running the family's two paper mills at Templeogue and Chapleizod, County Dublin. He had his own watermark by 1769, and in 1773 he signed a petition to the Irish House of Commons objecting to the removal of duties on foreign paper (BL, 1890.e.5. (232)). He died in 1787 and was succeeded by his son, another Thomas Slator.

SLEATER (THOMAS) *see* Thomas Slator

SLEATER or SLATOR (WILLIAM), bookseller, papermaker, printer, and publisher in Dublin, (1) the Pope's Head, Cork Hill (1756–64?); (2) 51 Castle Street (1768?–84?); (3) 28, New Buildings, Dame Street (1787?–89). 1749–89. He was the son of Joseph Slator (q.v.), was apprenticed to Samuel Powell Jr. (q.v.), admitted free of the guild by service in 1756, paid quarterage through 1787, served on the Council from 1766, as Warden in 1777, and as Master in 1782 (*Guild Records*). In 1742 his father transferred his paper mill to his sons, William and his older brother Thomas Slator (q.v.), the latter apparently working it until William completed his apprenticeship, although William appears to have been an active partner by 1749. They built a second mill and in 1753 petitioned Parliament for assistance, receiving £300 (*Commons' Journ. Ire.*, v,

182, 185). They also received premiums from the Dublin Society in 1750 and 1753 for the encouragement of papermaking. William had his own watermark in 1749 and 1751, and a joint watermark with Thomas in 1755. By 1758 William was printer to the University Press, and in the same year the partnership with his brother came to an end, William concentrating on bookselling and publishing. His press work and publications included *Sleater's Public Gazetteer*, 1758–83, Shakespeare's *Winter's Tale*, 1756, *Henry IV*, 1765, and *Catherine and Petrachio* [*Taming of the Shrew*], 1755, and, with other stationers, Smollett's *Humphrey Clinker*, 1771, and Young's *Tour of Ireland*, 1780. He obviously came to identify more with the print trade than with papermaking, for in 1773 he signed a memorial to the Irish House of Commons against additional duties on foreign paper (BL, 1890.e.5. (239)). He died in 1789, his will being proved in the Prerogative Court at Dublin, and was succeeded by his son William Sleater, another son, Joseph Sleater, following the papermaking line.

SLYE (**JOSEPH**), printer in Dublin, 1713?–18? He was an apprentice to John Brocas (q.v.), who died in 1713, did not take out his freedom of the guild nor pay quarterage, but apparently practiced, for in 1718 he was listed as a journeyman and an intruder (*Guild Records*).

SMITH (**FRANCES**), bookseller in Dublin, (1) Dame Street (1773–74), later, 12 Dame Street (1775–82); (2) 5 Palace Street (1783–90). 1773–90. She was the widow of William Smith Jr. (q.v.). She continued the training of an apprentice, Thomas Kinder, placed with her husband in 1772, until assigning the indentures to William Hallhead (q.v.) in 1777 (*Guild Records*). In 1773, as a bookseller, she signed a petition to the Irish House of Commons objecting to the removal of duties on foreign paper (BL, 1890.e.5. (232)), and from 1773 to 1775 she continued her husband's role of supplying the Irish House of Commons with paper and stationery (*Commons' Journ. Ire.*, Rept. ix, ccclxxiii).

SMITH (JOHN), bookseller and publisher in Dublin, (1) the Duchess's Head, Dame Street, opposite the Castle Market (1719–25); (2) the Philosopher's Head, on the Blind Quay (1726–58). 1719–58. In 1719 he and his uncle William Smith (q.v.) arrived from Belfast and set up in partnership (Lepper and Crosslé, *History of the Grand Lodge of Free and Accepted Masons in Ireland*). In 1724 he was summoned before the guild as an intruder, and in 1725 was finally forced to take out his freedom as a "Protestant stranger," paying quarterage through 1756. Still, he served the guild as Warden in 1737, as Master in 1739, and on the Council from 1739 (*Guild Records*). His partnership with William ended in 1725 (*Dublin Weekly Journal*, 1 May), and John took into partnership until 1737 his cousin William Bruce (q.v.). They specialized in Dutch and French books as well as maps and mezzotints, and they published Dobb's *Essay on the Trade . . . of Ireland*, 1729, Burnet's *History of His Own Time*, 1730, and *Debates of the British Parliament*, 1737. Among Smith's other publications were, with Abraham Bradley (q.v.), the second Irish edition of Shakespeare's *Works*, 1739, and, working alone, Sallust's *Works*, 1744, Fielding's *Tom Jones*, 1749, and *Amelia*, 1752. He retired from business in 1758, and his stock was sold at auction (*Universal Advertiser*, 2 Dec.).

SMITH (JONATHAN), stationer in Dublin, 1748–50. He was apprenticed to William Smith (q.v.), relationship unknown, was admitted free of the guild by service in 1748, and paid quarterage through 1750. There is no other notice (*Guild Records*).

SMITH (PAUL), bookseller in Dublin, Crane Lane, 1743–51? He specialized in print selling and publishing. In partnership with John Orpin (q.v.) he published Miller's engravings of Dean Swift and Archbishop King, 1743, and in 1751, with Thomas Silcock (q.v.), he served as Dublin agent for the famous London engraver James McArdell (*Freeman's Journal*, 12 Sept.). He died in 1774 (Strickland, *Irish Artists*).

SMITH (RICHARD), bookseller in Dublin, Dame Street, 1760–65? He was the son of the Dublin bookseller William Smith (q.v.), was admitted free of the guild by birth in 1760, fined for not riding the franchise in 1761, and was listed as "dead" in 1765 (*Guild Records*).

SMITH (ROBERT), bookseller, printer, and publisher in Belfast, 1775–79? He printed and published a pamphlet, *Truth Restored*, 1775, a *Dictionary of Love*, 1777, and another pamphlet, a *Defense of the Rev. John Wesley's Principles*, 1779.

SMITH (SAMUEL), bookseller, printer, and publisher in Dublin, Essex Street, 1758–67. He was apprenticed to his uncle George Faulkner (q.v.) in 1747, never took out his freedom of the guild, and there are no other guild references (*Guild Records*; Bentham, *Abstracts*). He worked out of Faulkner's establishment, and is listed as one of the publishers of *The Way to Keep Him, a Comedy*, 1769, and, with Dillon Chamberlain (q.v.), as printer and publisher of Sterne's *Tristram Shandy*, 1761 (*Dublin Journal*, 14 Feb.).

SMITH (WILLIAM), printer in Kilkenny (1649), and in Cork (1656?–90). 1649–90. In 1649, as printer to the Duke of Ormonde, he printed two proclamations at Kilkenny. In Cork, his imprints included two ballads, 1656, John Davies' *History* *of Charles II*, 1660, a sermon, 1662, *Poems for Church Festivals*, 1681, and McCarthy's *A Chronological Table*, 1690.

SMITH (**WILLIAM**), bookseller and publisher in Dublin, (1) the Duchess's Head, opposite the Castle Market, Dame Street (1719–25); (2) on the Blind Quay (1727–32); and a second shop (3) the Hercules, near Castle Market, Dame Street (1727–71). 1719–71. In 1719 he and his nephew John Smith (q.v.) arrived from Belfast and set up in partnership (Lepper and Crosslé, *History of the Grand Lodge of Free and Accepted Masons in Ireland*). He was admitted free of the guild by petition in 1719, paid quarterage through 1767, served as Warden in 1729, as Master in 1736, and on the Council from 1732 (*Guild Records*). His first partnership ended in 1725, and for a year William traveled on the continent, buying book stock for John Smith (q.v.) and William Bruce (q.v.). In 1727 he was back in Dublin, joining in a long association with George Ewing (q.v.) and George Risk (q.v.), from 1727 to 1756. In 1759 he took his son William Smith Jr. (q.v.) into partnership. Throughout his career William was involved in a variety of undertakings, including publishing the *Life of the Duke of Marlborough*, 1723, Keating's *History of Ireland*, 1723, Townsend's *History of the Conquest of Mexico*, 1726, and the *Dublin Almanack*, 1728–38. In 1766 he published, with his son, the first Dublin edition of Goldsmith's *Vicar of Wakefield*. In 1771 he died "in the 76th year of his age . . . an eminent Bookseller" (*Hibernian Journal*, 31 July).

SMITH (**WILLIAM JR.**), bookseller and publisher in Dublin, the Hercules, near Castle Market, Dame Street, 1759–73. He was apprenticed to his father, William Smith (q.v.), was admitted free of the guild by service in 1760, and paid quarterage through 1772 (*Guild Records*). He joined in partnership with his father and actually began work in 1759, jointly publishing

Dodsley's *Cleone, A Tragedy* (*Sleater's Public Gazetteer*, 23 Dec.). From then until his father's death in 1771 his imprint appears, sometimes alone, sometimes with his father's or various other stationers', on such publications as the first Dublin edition of Goldsmith's *Vicar of Wakefield*, 1766, and Homer's *Iliad*, 1770. From 1771 through 1773 he supplied paper, books, and stationery to the Irish House of Commons at considerable profit (*Commons' Journ. Ire.* Rept. ix, app., cxxviii). At the end of 1772 he was accosted in a petty quarrel and beaten so as to "have lost his life, being confined a long time to his bed with little hopes of recovery" (*Sequin's Hibernian Magazine*, Nov.). He died a few months later (*New Freeman's Journal*, 26 Aug. 1773).

SMITH (WILLIAM), printer in Dublin, Queen's Street, 1774–91. He was the son of Thomas Smith, cloth maker, apprenticed to Henry Saunders (q.v.), admitted free of the guild by service in 1774, and paid quarterage through 1791 (*Guild Records*). Possibly he was the William Smith appointed a stamper in connection with the Stamp Act of 1775 (*Commons' Journ. Ire.*, ix, app. p. ccclxxv).

SOCIETY OF JESUS *see* Brother Nicholas Sarrazin

SOCIETY OF STATIONERS or COMPANY OF STATIONERS, printers and publishers in Dublin, 1618?–38. Three members of the London stationers' guild, Felix Kingston (q.v.), Matthew Lownes (q.v.), and Bartholomew Downes (q.v.), were appointed King's Stationers in Ireland by the Privy Council in England in 1617, and confirmed by patent in 1618 (*Lib. Munerum*, ii, 95). They exercised these rights personally and through factors to 1638 (see Robert Young). During these years many publications bear the imprint of the Society, beginning with Bolton's *Statutes of Ireland*, 1621. They also published Christopher Sibthorpe's *A friendly advertisement to the pretended Catholickes of Ireland*, 1622, which included pages in Greek type, and Ussher's *Answer to a Challenge made by a Jesuite in Ireland*, 1624, which included Hebrew type. Although this partnership operated under some control of the London guild, but a small fraction of their work was registered with that body, indicating a degree of independence of operation. In 1638 William Bladen (q.v.) purchased these Irish privileges from the London company but continued to employ the colophon "Printed by the Society of Stationers" on his 1641 publication, a *Sentence of the Councell of Warre pronounced against Lord Mountnorris*, after which he used his own names in his imprints.

SOMERVELL (THOMAS), bookseller and publisher in Dublin, 1696?–98. He imported English school books for sale in Dublin, and in 1696 he joined in partnership with James Malone (q.v.) and a merchant, Thomas Simpson, to print cheaper school books in Dublin. In 1698, to retrieve losses from an overstock of paper, they determined to use it to publish an edition of the New Testament. Cornelius Carter (q.v.) and Bryan Wilson (q.v.) printed 400 copies for the partners, but before they could be sold, the sheets were taken into custody by the Lords Justices and Council for "errors and defects" in the copy, the stationer's guild having supplied the evidence. Somervell's petition to remedy the errors was rejected, and he failed in business (*State of the Case of Thomas Somervell, Merchant,* King MS Z 3.1.1, no. 1, xxxiii; *Guild Records*).

SPENCER (BOYLE), bookseller in Dublin, 1722–? He was admitted free of the city in 1722 (Thrift, *Freemen*), admitted free of the guild by special grace in 1722, but paid no quarterage, and was recorded as dead by 1767 (*Guild Records*).

SPENCER (JOHN), bookseller in Dublin, 1764?–? He was the son of Boyle Spencer (q.v.), was admitted free of the city in 1764 (Thrift, *Freemen*), admitted free of the guild by birth in 1768, but paid no quarterage, and there are no further references (*Guild Records*).

SPIRE (FRANCIS), printer in Dublin, d. 1754. Sole reference: an obituary in 1754 read "Died on Sunday, Mr. Francis Spire, printer" (*Dublin Journal*, 24 Sept.).

SPOONER (CHARLES), engraver in Dublin (1746?–52), and London (1752–67). 1746?–67. He was a student of John Brooks (q.v.) and became a distinguished artist. His Dublin prints included William Hogarth, 1749, "Lough Lene," 1751, Samuel Madden, 1751, and Thomas Prior, 1752. His subsequent output in London was large. He died in 1767 (Strickland, *Irish Artists*).

SPOTSWOOD (WILLIAM), bookseller, printer, and publisher in Dublin, (1) College Green, opposite Anglesey Street (1770–77); (2) 40 College Green (1777–83), and in Philadelphia, Pennsylvania (1784–93), and Boston, Massachusetts (1793–96). 1770–96. He was apprenticed to Alexander McCullogh (q.v.), was admitted free of the guild by service in 1770, and paid quarterage through 1782 (*Guild Records*). In partnership with Thomas Stewart (q.v.) he published a short-lived newspaper, the *Dublin Chronicle*, 1770, and Moffett's *Sallust*, 1772, and, with Stewart and George Douglas (q.v.), *Watson's Gentleman's and Citizen's Almanack*, 1770. He left Ireland for the United States in 1783, and from 1784 to 1793 was at work as a bookseller and printer in Philadelphia, and then moved his business to Boston from 1783 to 1796 (Evans, *American Bibliography*).

STAMPER (?), papermaker in Dublin, 1770–73. Sole reference: from 1770 to 1773 he is recorded as being in association with James Daniel (q.v.)—"Daniel and Stamper"—in papermaking. Their mill was at Newbridge, County Dublin.

STANLEY (CHRISTOPHER), engraver in Dublin, 1737?–48. He is referred to as "the first seal-engraver of whom there is any record in Dublin" (Warburton, Whitlaw, and Walsh, *History of the City of Dublin*). He died in 1748, and an obituary notice in the *Dublin Courant* called him "one of the best engravers in this city" (Strickland, *Irish Artists*).

STAPLETON (WILLIAM), printer in Dublin, Cork Street, 1730. Sole reference: a notice in 1730 stated that "William Stapleton of Cork Street, printer . . . prisoner for debt in the Meath street Marshalsea . . . design to take advantage of act for relief of insolvent debtors" (*Dublin Gazette*, 5 May).

STARKEY (ROBERT), stationer in Dublin, 1670–75? He was admitted free of the city by fine in 1670 (Thrift, *Freemen*), served the guild as Beadle in 1671, and on the Council in 1675. There are no other guild references (*Guild Records*).

STATIONERS (COMPANY OF or SOCIETY OF) *see* Society of Stationers

STEPHENSON (ALEXANDER) *see* Alexander Stevenson

STEPHENSON (ANN) *see* Ann Stevenson

STEPHENSON (GEORGE) *see* George Stevenson

STEPHENSON (JAMES) *see* James Stevenson

STEPNEY (JOHN), stationer in Dublin, 1632. Sole reference: he was admitted free of the city as a stationer in 1632 (Thrift, *Freemen*).

STERLING (EDWARD), bookbinder and printer in Dublin, 1753–60. In 1753 he was paid the large sum of £5,450 "for printing and binding 400 Copies" of the Commons' *Journals*; in 1756 was appointed to continue such printing; in 1757 was advanced £200 for speeding their completion, and later in the same year received £2,780 as a further payment; and in 1760 he was ordered to complete his printing and binding (*Commons' Journ. Ire.*, v, 177, 393; vi, 27, 32, 231).

STEVENSON or STEPHENSON (ALEXANDER), bookbinder in Dublin, 1774–75? He was admitted free of the guild by special grace in 1774, but there are no other guild references (*Guild Records*). He was employed as a paper stamper in connection with the Stamp Act in 1775 (*Commons' Journ. Ire.*, ix, app. p. ccclxxv).

STEVENSON or STEPHENSON (ANN), bookbinder in Dublin, 1760–64? She was the widow of James Stevenson (q.v.), and succeeded him in business by 1760. She had an apprentice, Charles Lettelier, enrolled to her whose indentures were transferred to William Gilbert (q.v.) in 1764. In the latter transaction Gilbert was described as the "husband of the said Ann Stephenson" (*Guild Records*).

STEVENSON (CATHERINE), printer in Londonderry, 1772. Sole reference: her imprint appeared on one pamphlet in 1772, *Homesius: a Letter addressed to Mr. John Holmes* (*Biblio. Soc. Ire.*, vii, no. 1).

STEVENSON or STEPHENSON (GEORGE), bookseller, printer, and publisher in Newry, 1738–74. For the first thirty years of his career he was a prominent provincial book-seller, taking subscriptions and selling many Dublin publications, including Clark's *Sermons*, 1738, Rollin's *Ancient History*, 1740, Faulkner's (q.v.) edition of Sale's *Universal Advertiser*, 1744, and Exshaw's *London Magazine*, 1747 and 1748. In 1748 Abraham Bradley (q.v.) advertised that all his publications were sold by Stevenson (*Dublin Courant*, 12 Mar.). About 1770 Stevenson began printing and publishing on his own, his works including the *Death of Abel*, 1770, *Regulations formed by the last General Synod*, 1771, and *Some Hints on Planting*, 1773. He died in 1774, his will being proved in the Prerogative Court at Dublin, and was succeeded by his son Robert Stevenson (q.v.).

STEVENSON or STEPHENSON (JAMES), bookbinder in Dublin, 1754–60? He paid the guild a Beadle fine in 1754, had an apprentice enrolled to him, William Lilburn (q.v.), who was later transferred to William Gilbert (q.v.), and paid quarterage from 1754 to 1758, although there is no record of his taking his freedom of the guild. He was listed as "decd" in 1760 when his widow and successor, Ann Stevenson (q.v.), had an apprentice enrolled to her (*Guild Records*).

STEVENSON (ROBERT), printer and publisher in Newry, 1774?–88. He was the son of George Stevenson (q.v.), and upon the latter's death succeeded him in business. In 1775 he acquired the rights to the *Newry Journal, and General Advertiser* from Wood Gibson Jones (q.v.), which he continued to 1798. He also printed and published several works, including *A Sure Guide to Hell*, 1775, a second edition of *Some Hints on Planting*, 1783, and two plays, Home's *Douglas: A Tragedy* and *The Upholsterer; or, What News?*, 1787. He died in 1788, his will being proved in the Prerogative Court at Dublin.

STEWART or STUART (Alexander), bookseller, printer, and publisher in Dublin, (1) the Circulating Library, Dame Street, opposite George's Lane (1774–?); (2) St. Audeon's Arch (?); (3) 18 North King Street, near the Linen Hall (1787); (4) 86 Bridge Street (1791?–1824?). 1774–1824? He was apprenticed to Samuel Law (q.v.), admitted free of the guild by service in 1774, paid quarterage through 1792, and served on the Council from 1789 (*Guild Records*). He was admitted free of the city in 1774 (Thrift, *Freemen*). In 1774 he printed and published *St. Patrick's Anti-Stamp Chronicle*, on which he paid a pamphlet tax, trying, unsuccessfully, to avoid the new stamp tax on newspapers. He compiled, printed, and published almanacs under various titles—the *Irish Merlin; or, Universal Almanack*, 1787, the *Irish Merlin; or City and Country Almanack*, 1792, and the *Telegraphic Almanack*, 1800—as well as registries, the *Universal Registry*, 1787, and the *English Registry*, 1791 and 1798. In 1820 he took into partnership his son Alexander Stewart Jr., who later succeeded him in business.

STEWART (R.), bookseller and printer in Dublin, 200 Abbey Street, 1774–76. In 1774 he printed the *Dublin Weekly Journal*, and he is referred to as a bookseller from 1775 to 1776 (*Dictionary 1726–75*).

STEWART (Thomas), bookseller, printer, and publisher in Newry (1755–69); and in Dublin, (1) the Bible and Crown, on Merchant's Quay, near the Old Bridge (1769–1778); (2) 1 King's Inn Quay (1779–1802). 1755–1802. He served his apprenticeship to George Stevenson (q.v.), and set up in business in Newry in 1755 (*Dublin Journal*, 25 Jan.). In 1760 he advertised for sale "Holman's ink powder" and described himself as the "son of Catherine Stewart, alias Farquhar" (*Dublin*

Journal, 10 June). His mother, Katherine Stewart, had died in Newry the previous month, her obituary notice reading: "in advanced age . . . wife of Mr. Peyton Farquhar [q.v.] of Dublin, bookseller, she was eminent for making Holman's London Ink Powder for 50 years" (*Dublin Journal*, 10 May). Thomas Stewart was the brother-in-law of John Watson Jr. (q.v.), and upon the latter's death moved to Dublin and took over his shop. Stewart was admitted free of the guild by service in 1769, but paid no quarterage (*Guild Records*). In partnership with another brother-in-law, Samuel Watson (q.v.), and as well, for a brief period, with George Douglas (q.v.) and William Spotswood (q.v.)—the partnership sometimes referred to as "Stewart and Co."—he continued the publication of the *Gentleman's and Citizen's Almanack*. With William Spotswood he also published a short-lived newspaper, the *Dublin Chronicle*, 1770, and later Moffett's *Sallust*, 1772. By 1801 he took into partnership his son John Watson Stewart, and they jointly printed the *English Register* in that year. He died in 1802, his will being proved in the Prerogative Court at Dublin, and was succeeded by his son John Watson Stewart.

STOCKDALE (JOHN), printer in Dublin, 63 Abbey Street, 1772–1813. He was apprenticed to Henry Saunders (q.v.), admitted free of the guild by service in 1772, paid quarterage at least through 1792, served on the Council from 1787, and as Warden in 1793 (*Guild Records*). He was admitted free of the city in 1772 (Thrift, *Freemen*). His imprints included Goldsmith's *Vicar of Wakefield* and *Essays, Moral and Literary*, 1793, and the *Press, The Organ of the United Irishmen*, 1797-98, which in the later year was suppressed by the government. In 1802 he took his son John Stockdale Jr. into partnership. He died in 1813 (Madden, *Lives and Times of the United Irishmen*), and was succeeded in business by his son.

STOKES (JAMES), printer in Kilkenny, 1762. He is stated to have printed Burke's *Hibernia Dominicana*, 1762 (*Dictionary 1726–75*), but the imprint was possibly fictitious (*Biblio. Soc. Ire. Proc.*, 3, no. 4; *Irish Book Lover*, 16, no. 1).

STRINGER (JOSEPH), stationer in Dublin, 1768–83? He was admitted free of the guild as a painter–stainer in 1754, married Sarah Cotter (q.v.), the widow of Joseph Cotter (q.v.), in 1768, paid quarterage irregularly, being in arrears in 1777 and 1779, and was last listed as a free brother in 1783 (*Guild Records*). He apparently joined in business with Sarah, though for how long they continued the stationer's trade is uncertain.

STRINGER (SARAH) *see* Sarah Cotter

STUART (ALEXANDER) *see* Alexander Stewart

STUBS or STUBBS (ROBERT), papermaker in Dublin, Cook Street, 1771?–86. He was apprenticed to Thomas Watson (q.v.), admitted free of the guild by service in 1776, and paid quarterage in 1777 and again in 1785 and 1786 (*Guild Records*). He was admitted free of the city in 1777 (Thrift, *Freemen*). In 1773 he signed a petition to the Irish House of Commons objecting to the removal of duties on foreign paper (BL, 1890.e.5. (232)).

SUDWORTH (WILLIAM), printer in Ireland. 1715. Sole reference: he was referred to as a printer from Ireland, "another of the Fraternity," who came to London in 1715 and was befriended by Thomas Gent (q.v.) (Gent, *Life of Thomas Gent*).

SULLIVAN (CORNELIUS), bookseller and publisher in Cork, (1) Exchange Coffee House, Castle Street (1736); (2)

opposite the Main Guard (1737–67). 1736?–67. He was in business by 1736, for he advertised a change of address as "heretofore at the Exchange Coffee-House . . . just open'd Shop where Combra Daniel [q.v.] formerly lived, opposite the Main Guard (and more recently occupied by Daniel Hood [q.v.])" (*Dublin News-Letter*, 4 Jan.). He succeeded Hood as well in becoming the Cork agent for the partnership of George Risk (q.v.), George Ewing (q.v.), and William Smith (q.v.). He was one of the undertakers of, or subscribers to, many Dublin publications, including Virgil's *Works*, 1737, Faulkner's (q.v.) edition of Sale's *Universal History*, 1744, Harris' *Life of William III*, 1749, and Swift's *Works*, 1762. In 1766 he was paid by the Cork Council for a copy of Bolingbroke's *Abridgement of the Statutes* (Caulfield, *Cork Council Book*). He died in 1767 (*Freeman's Journal*, 11 Apr.), and possibly was succeeded in business by his son-in-law Thomas Lord (q.v.).

SUTTON (WILLIAM), papermaker in Ireland, 1692? In 1692, in partnership with Edmund Buckridge (q.v.) and George Eagar (q.v.), he obtained a King's letter granting an Irish monopoly of fourteen years for the making of "all sorts of coloured papers" (*World's Paper Trade Review*, 3, no. 4). There is no evidence that the three ever acted on their patent or even came to Ireland from England.

SWINEY or SWEENEY (BRYAN), printer in Dublin, Montrath Street (1728–30). 1718–30. In 1718 he was indicted for "printing and writing a scandalous Libel Call'd the Execution of Ferdinando Prisaro" for which he was "whipt from Newgate to Lazy Hill" (*The Whole Tryal and Examination of . . . Bryan Swiney*, 1718). Possibly by 1728 Sweeney was a journeyman to Christopher Goulding (q.v.), for in that year it was claimed that "One Goulding in Montrath street, and one Sweeney, a Person formerly Whip'd thro' this City for a like offense

. . . impos'd on the Town, a most horrible and barbarous Libel" (*Dublin Intelligence*, 8 June). Eighteen months later similar charges were made that "The Speeches Printed by one Hussy [Nicholas Hussey (q.v.)] on the Blind Key and by one Sweeney for Golding in Montrath Street . . . were false and scandalous" (*Dublin Intelligence*, 20 Jan. 1729/30).

SWINEY or SWEENEY (EUGENE), bookseller, printer, and publisher in Cork, (1) Paul Street (1753); (2) near the Exchange (1754); (3) at the Peacock, Cross Street, near Broad Lane (1754–?); (4) Fishamble Lane (1770–72?). 1753–72? He was apprenticed to Andrew Welsh Jr. (q.v.), who advertised in 1748: "Run Away . . . from the service of his master, Owen Sweeney, otherwise Eugene Swiney, son of Miles Sweeney late of the City of Limerick" (*Dublin Journal*, 5 Jan.). He must have returned, for he had a long career printing and publishing broadly, including *Swiney's Corke Journal*, 1753–69, and Charles Dwyer's *Anglo-Gallic Grammar*, 1761, Shakespeare's *Coriolanus* and *Macbeth*, 1761, the latter being the first provincial Irish printing of this play, Goldsmith's *Vicar of Wakefield*, 1766, and *Contraction of Lily's Syntaxis*, 1772. From 1755 to 1765 he printed for the Cork Council (Caulfield, *Cork Council Books*). He died in 1781 and was succeeded by his son John M. Swiney.

T

TABB (L.) *see* L. Bixou

TARRANT (NATHANIEL), bookseller in Dublin, 1672–89. He was admitted to the guild in 1672, sworn a free brother in 1680, paid quarterage through 1788, and was recorded as "defunct" in 1689 (*Guild Records*). He was admitted free of the city in 1680 (Thrift, *Freemen*).

TAYLOR (T.), bookseller and publisher in Cork, 1653 or 1654. Sole reference: the colophon in *Scripture Evidence for Baptizing the Infants of the Covenanters*, 1653 or 1654, read "Printed for T. Taylor, Widow, and are to be sold at her Shop in Cork."

TAYLOR (THOMAS), printer in Dublin, the Boot and Three Pigeons, Bridge Street, 1740–47. He was stated to have been in business in 1740 (*Dictionary 1726–75*), was admitted to the guild as a quarter brother in 1741, and paid quarterage through 1744 (*Guild Records*). He died in 1747, his will being proved in the Prerogative Court at Dublin.

TEMPLETON (HUMPHREY), printer in Dublin, Mary Street, 1770?–89? He was apprenticed to John Murphey (q.v.) in 1763, but never took out his freedom of the guild (*Guild Records*); nevertheless he practiced the trade.

TERRY (SAMUEL), bookseller, printer, and publisher in Liverpool (1712–20); Cork, (1) Cock Pit Lane (1721); (2) Dale Street (1722?); and Limerick, on Ball's Bridge (1722–

27). 1712–27. In Liverpool he printed Owen's *Hymns*, 1712, and published the *Liverpoole Courant*. In 1715 Thomas Gent (q.v.) sought employment with Terry but, "the man seeming to have no more business than he thought he could manage," refused to take him on (Gent, *Life of Thomas Gent*). In 1721 Terry moved to Cork, where in 1721 he printed *Pietas Corcagiensis, or, a View of the Green-Coat Hospital*, Puckle's *The Club. In a Dialogue between Father and Son*, and Bisse's *Beauty of Holiness in the Common Prayer*. In 1722 he moved to Limerick, and in a loose partnership with L. Bixou (q.v.) published the second book printed in that city, *The Libertine School'd*, 1722, and *A Sacramental Cathechism*, 1723. Alone, Terry printed and published *An Abstract of the several Publick Charities*, 1722, a *Sermon*, 1725, and *The Wonder of Ireland, Or, A Strange Account of the Moving Bog*, 1727.

THIBOUST (ABRAHAM), printer and publisher in Dublin, next door to the sign of the Bull's Head, Big Ship Street (1722–24). 1722–32? He was of French Huguenot descent, but in 1732 was married in St. Michan's Church, Dublin (*St. Michan's Par. Reg.*). From 1722 to 1724 he was in partnership with James Watts (q.v.), and they jointly published the *Dublin Mercury* in these years. They were involved in a petty circulation war with John Harding (q.v.), whose vicious accusation of their printing "false and old News" they answered in kind: "take no heed of anything that shall proceed from the Caprico's of a Fellow of so mean Reputation" and one who was "Try'd at the King's Bench for picking the Pocket of a Certain Person of the Town" (*Dublin Mercury*, 15 Jan. 1722/23). Nothing more is heard of Thiboust after 1724 except for his marriage in 1732.

THOMAS (EDWARD), printer in Dublin, 1774–79? He was apprenticed to Henry Saunders (q.v.), admitted free of the guild by service in 1774, and paid quarterage through 1779. He was dead by 1784, for in that year "Sophia Thomas, Widow of the late Edward Thomas" petitioned the guild to be put on the Poor List. She was so admitted in 1792! (*Guild Records*).

THOMAS (WILLIAM), papermaker in Ireland, 1731. Sole reference: in 1731 a public announcement read: "Deserted the 10th of March 1730–1, from the Hon. Col. Robert Murray's Regiment . . . William Thomas, 5 feet 10 inches high, by trade a papermaker, black hair, swarthy complexion, down looken, and well limbed" (*Dublin Gazette*, 20 Mar.).

THOMSON (DANIEL) *see* Daniel Thompson

THOMSON (JAMES) *see* James Thompson

THOMPSON, THOMSON, or TOMPSON (DANIEL), bookseller, printer, and publisher in Dublin, (1) Essex Street, over against Essex Bridge (1702); (2) near Cork Hill (1707); (3) Cole's Alley, Castle Street (1714–15). 1702–18. He was a journeyman to John Rathbone (q.v.) in 1702, listed as a journeyman with no master in 1703, petitioned the guild for his freedom in 1707, but was never sworn, and paid quarter-age through 1708, from 1710 through 1713, and again from 1716 through 1718 (*Guild Records*). An advertisement in 1707 listed him as a bookseller and a seller of "The purging Elixir" (*Flying Post: or, the Post-Master*, 30 Sept.). In 1710 he published a reprint of the *Examiner*. His Tory support of Edward Lloyd (q.v.) got him into trouble in 1714. A reward was offered for information concerning the printer and publisher of *A Long History of a Certain Session of a Certain Parliament*, 1714—an exposé of official policies which Thompson had printed—and a year later John Whalley (q.v.) informed, but "Thompson, a Jacobite, who long since hearing there was a warrant . . . against him for that Pamphlet fled for England" (*Whalley's News-*

Letter, 1 Feb. 1715/16). Political tension lessened, and Thompson apparently returned to Dublin a short time later.

THOMPSON (EDWARD), stationer in Dublin, 1768. He was apprenticed to Oliver Nelson (q.v.), admitted free of the guild by service in 1768, but there are no other guild references (*Guild Records*).

THOMPSON or THOMSON (JAMES), bookbinder, bookseller, printer, and publisher in Dublin, (1) High Street (1722–26); (2) Cork Hill, next door to Lucas's Coffee House (1726–33). 1721–33? He was admitted to the guild as a quarter brother in 1722, and paid quarterage through 1733 (*Guild Records*). In 1721 he was listed as a bookbinder in his marriage record (*St. Michan's Par. Reg.*, Dublin). In 1726 he printed Phipp's *A New Poem*; he published O'Conner's *Poems, Pastorals and Dialogues*, 1726, and, with Benjamin Hickey (q.v.), Jevon's *The Devil of a Wife*, 1728. He took subscriptions for and sold James Delacourt's *Art of Beauing*, 1730, and *A Reply to Dr. Robinson's Answer . . . in a Letter to a Friend*, 1733. He died intestate in 1742 (*Dublin Grant Book*).

THOMPSON (NATHANIEL), printer and publisher in Dublin (1665–66?), and London (1673?–88). 1665–88. Three Dublin prints bear his name: for Robert Hughes (q.v.) he printed *An Almanack and Prognostications for the Year of our Lord 1665*, and, on his own, *A Discourse Grounded on Prov. 12. 5.*, 1666, and Thomas Bladen's *Praxis Francisci Clarke*, 1666. About the latter year he moved to London, where he had a long, controversial career, printing for Nonconformists and Roman Catholics, which brought him into repeated troubles with the stationers' guild in London and the government (*Dictionary 1668–1725*).

THOMPSON (PRICE), bookbinder in Dublin, 1768–79. He was apprenticed to Edward Beatty (q.v.), admitted free of the guild by service in 1768, and paid quarterage through 1779 (*Guild Records*). He was admitted free of the city in 1770 (Thrift, *Freemen*). He died intestate in 1783 (*Dublin Grant Book*).

THOMPSON (WISDOM), printer in Dublin, 1767. He was apprenticed to Henry Saunders (q.v.), admitted free of the guild by service in 1767, but there are no other guild references (*Guild Records*).

THORNTON (CHARLES), bookseller in Dublin, 1726–28. He was the son of Robert Thornton (q.v.), and possibly was employed by, or in a brief partnership with, his brothers Thomas and Robert Thornton Jr. (qq.v.). He was admitted to the guild as a quarter brother in 1726, and paid quarterage through 1728 (*Guild Records*). He was admitted free of the city in 1727 (Thrift, *Freemen*).

THORNTON (ROBERT), bookbinder, bookseller, printer, and publisher in Dublin, (1) the Unicorn, Skinner Row (1682); (2) the Leather Bottle, Skinner Row (1687); (3) Capel Street (1691); (4) Essex Street (1701–18). 1681–1718. He was listed in the Clerk's list in 1681, admitted free of the guild in 1682, paid quarterage through 1718, served on the Council from 1696, as Warden in 1702, and as Master in 1713 (*Guild Records*). He was admitted free of the city in 1782 (Thrift, *Freemen*). He was an active stationer, establishing many "firsts" in the trade. He published the first modern Irish newspaper, the *News-Letter*, 1685–88?, which was also the first to take advertisements, and later, with Benjamin Tooke (q.v.), the *Dublin Intelligence*, 1690–93, which was the official Williamite journal for these years (Munter, *Handlist*). He was the first music printer in

Ireland, advertising "the choicest New Songs with Musical Notes," 1686; and he was one of the first Dublin book auctioneers, 1688 (Dunton, *Dublin Scuffle*). He printed and published a variety of works—e.g., Dryden's *The Medall*, 1682, and *Civil Articles of Lymerick*, 1692. He was King's Printer from 1692 to 1718, during the early period of which, 1692–1705, he bound the Irish Parliamentary *Journals*. He was sometimes referred to as Major in respect to his commission in the Dublin militia, the "Grenadeers." In 1713 he was found "guilty of a breech of the privileges of this House, in disturbing the election of citizens of the City of Dublin," was ordered to "be taken into custody" (*Commons' Journ. Ire.*, iii, 383), and appears to have been incarcerated until Queen Anne's death. He died in 1718, and was succeeded by his three sons, Robert Jr., Thomas, and Charles Thornton (qq.v.). Still, his widow, Anne, had to petition the city for relief in 1724, due to being by "misfortunes much reduced" (*Cal. Anc. Rec. Dublin*).

THORNTON (ROBERT JR.), bookseller and publisher in Dublin, (1) the St. Luke's Head, Dame Street (1722); (2) the Fan, Dame Street, opposite Eustace Street (1724–25); (3) College Green (1729–36). 1718–36. He was the son of Robert Thornton (q.v.), admitted free of the guild by birth in 1718, but there are no other guild references to him (*Guild Records*). By 1722 he took his brother Thomas Thornton (q.v.) into partnership, and in 1726 brought in a third brother, Charles Thornton (q.v.). He took subscriptions for *Geographia itineraria . . . of the Travellers into Asia, Africa and America*, 1722, for Faulkner's (q.v.) edition of the *Drapier's Letters*, 1725, and, with other stationers, published Ware's *Works*, 1739. He advertised as a book auctioneer from 1722 to 1724.

THORNTON (THOMAS), bookseller and publisher in Dublin, (1) the St. Luke's Head, Dame Street (1722); (2) the

Fan, Dame Street, opposite Eustace Street (1724–25); (3) College Green (1729–41). 1722–41. He was the son of Robert Thornton (q.v.) and by 1722 joined in partnership with his brother Robert Thornton Jr. (q.v.). In 1726 a third brother, Charles Thornton (q.v.), also joined them. He paid quarterage to the guild from 1725 to 1738, served as Warden in 1739, but there is no record of his taking out his freedom (*Guild Records*). He was admitted free of the city in 1727 (Thrift, *Freemen*). He published a *Life of the Duke of Marlborough*, 1722, Shadwell's *Libertine, A Tragedy*, 1724, and Defoe's *Life of Jonathan Wild*, 1725. From 1729 to 1740 he was Dublin's most active book auctioneer, publishing numerous catalogues of books to be sold by auction. He died in 1741 (*Dublin Journal*, 3 Nov.).

TIBBO (?), stationer in Dublin, the back of Dick's Coffee House, Skinner Row, 1698–1701? He was listed as a journeyman to John Brent (q.v.) from 1698 to 1700, and was carried on the Clerk's list in 1701. There are no other guild references (*Guild Records*).

TODD (Thomas), stationer in Dublin, 1773. He was the nephew of George Faulkner (q.v.), and apparently operated out of the latter's shop in 1773. Throughout 1773 he advertised, in the *Dublin Journal*, patent medicines "to be had of T. Todd, at the Printers," and in the same year he signed a memorial to the Irish House of Commons from "Printers, Booksellers, Stationers and Card-Makers" against additional duties on foreign paper (BL, 1890.e.5. (239)).

TOMLIN (Mr.), bookbinder in Ireland, 1773. Sole reference: an obituary notice in 1773 read, "Died at Portarlington, the wife of Mr. Tomlin, bookbinder" (*Hibernian Journal*, 2 July).

TOMPSON (**DANIEL**) *see* Daniel Thompson

TOOKE (**BENJAMIN**), bookseller, printer, and publisher in London (1666–1716), and Dublin, (1) his Majesty's Printing House, Skinner Row (1669–84); (2) Ormond Quay (1684–93?). 1666–1716. He was apprenticed to his brother-in-law John Crooke (q.v.), admitted free of the London guild in 1666, elected as Warden in 1688, and, as a prominent member of the stationers' fraternity, was involved in many stock deals of that Stationers' Company. In Ireland, with John North (q.v.), he was one of two charter members of the Dublin guild of stationers, but there is no record of his paying quarterage, and he held no offices (*Guild Records*). Upon the death of John Crooke, Tooke became guardian of Crooke's children, John Jr. and Andrew Crooke (qq.v.), and developed a Dublin business both to assist the fortunes of the two young Crookes and Tooke's sister, Mary Crooke (q.v.), and as a profitable branch of his London operation, consequently operating establishments concurrently in London and Dublin (*Dictionary 1668–1725*). In 1669 Tooke was appointed King's Printer in Ireland, the patent being reissued in 1671 in the names of Tooke and John Crooke Jr. (*Lib. Munerum*, ii, 95). John Jr. remained but a titular partner, never being trained as a stationer or printer, though he shared billing in the colophons of many works. From 1684 to 1689 Samuel Helsham (q.v.) and Andrew Crooke acted as Tooke's assigns as King's Printer. The output of Tooke's Irish press was prodigious; from 1669 to the 1680s he printed numerous government acts, statutes, and proclamations as well as speeches and sermons. Other publications included *An English Introduction to the Latine Tongue*, 1670, one of many school books, Bramhall's *Works*, 1677, an edition of the *Book of Common Prayer*, 1680, Bourke's *Almanack*, 1683–84, and Plunkett's *New Almanack*, 1679 and 1684. With Robert Thornton (q.v.)

he published the *Dublin Intelligence*, 1690–93, a semi-official government organ for these years. Tooke resigned his King's Printer patent in 1693, and Andrew Crooke was appointed to the position for life; from this date Tooke appears to have withdrawn from his Dublin business. He died in London in 1716, and was succeeded there by his son Benjamin Tooke Jr.

TORBUCK (**JOHN**), bookseller, printer, and publisher in London (1737–41?), and Dublin, (1) the Bear, Skinner Row (1743); (2) Kevin Street, near the Court House (1749); (3) the Bristol, Sycamore Alley (1754). 1737–54. In London he published *Church of England's Complaints against Careless Non-residents*, 1737 (*Dictionary* 1726–75), a book catalogue, 1739, and *A Compleat Collection of the Debates of the Parliament of England, 1668–1731*, 9 vols., "London reprinted, with considerable improvements and sold by John Torbuck in Clare Court, Drury-lane," 1741. Between 1741 and 1743 he moved to Dublin, and in the latter year he published Andrew Miller's (q.v.) print of James Annesley (*Dublin Journal*, 12 Mar.). In 1746 he offered to auction the library of Dean Swift, was apparently involved in supervising the cataloguing of the library, and in 1749, with George Faulkner (q.v.), signed a "Bookseller Certificate" verifying the charges for the said cataloguing (Williams, *Dean Swift's Library*). In 1754 he published, with others, Budgell's *Memoirs of the . . . Family of the Boyles*. He died or retired by late 1754, for a second edition of Budgell's book was printed for Lawrence Flin (q.v.), 1755, and consisted of the same sheets as the first with a new title-page.

TOULMIN (**THOMAS**), bookseller, printer, and publisher in Dublin, the Mitre, College Green, 1717–19. He printed and published an early experiment in evening newspapers, the *Dublin Evening Post*, which proved unsuccessful and was soon re-titled the *Dublin Post*, 1719. In the same year he falsely reported a British naval defeat and was quickly dubbed a printer of the "Jackish Party" by the incorrigible Whig John Whalley (q.v.), who reported that for the offense "Thom Toulmin . . . was by order of the Government . . . taken into Custody and Committed to New-Gate" (*Whalley's News-Letter*, 15 Apr.). Toulmin was soon released, and continued publishing through 1719.

TURNER (THOMAS), papermaker in Dublin, 1723–30. In 1723 or 1724 he apparently purchased Daniel Ashworth's (q.v.) paper mill at Templeogue, County Dublin. In 1727 was advertised *A Plain and Easy Method . . . to Get Longitude at Sea*, "discovered by Thomas Turner . . . the Great Improver of the Linnen and Paper Manufactures in the Kingdom of Ireland" (*Dublin Weekly Journal*, 18 Nov.).

TWEEDY (THOMAS), printer in Dublin, d. 1747. Sole reference: he died in 1747, his will being proved in the Prerogative Court at Dublin.

TYLER (JOHN), bookseller in Dublin, d. 1757. Sole reference: an obituary notice in 1757 read, "Died yesterday in Georges-Lane, Mr. John Tyler, formerly a Bookseller in Dublin" (*Dublin Journal*, 19 Mar.).

TYPOGRAPHIA ACADEMIAE, Printing House in Dublin, Grafton Street, 1738. This was the printing press of Trinity College, Dublin. John Stern, Bishop of Clogher, was instrumental in its founding. "In 1733 he made a present of a 1000 l. to the College of Dublin to build a Printing House, and in 1735, 200 l. more towards buying Types for the Use of the said House" (*Exshaw's Magazine*, July 1745). The press was furnished with fonts of Greek and Latin type, and in 1738 produced its first book, *Platonis . . . Dialogi,* followed by the publication of Helsham's "Philosophy Lectures" (*Dublin News-*

Letter, 3 Nov.). From that date it printed numerous classics, including the famous John Hawkey's editions of Juvenal, 1744, Horace, 1745, Sallust, 1747, and Virgil, 1753. Various printers worked at the press, including Richard Reilly (q.v.), 1739, Robert Marchbank (q.v.), 1746–73, William Sleater (q.v.), 1758, and William Watson (q.v.), 1761 and 1773.

U

UNIACK (JAMES), stationer in Dublin, 1671–81. He was admitted free of the guild in 1671 but there is no record of his paying quarterage, served on the Council from 1677, and was listed as "defunct" in 1681 (*Guild Records*). He was admitted free of the city in 1671 (Thrift, *Freemen*). He died in 1681, his will being proved in the Prerogative Court at Dublin.

UNIVERSITY PRINTING HOUSE *see* Typographia Academiae

USHER (JOHN), printer? in Dublin, above the Bridge, 1571. In 1571 he was listed in the colophons of two works, both in Irish, a broadside and an *Alphabetum et Ratio Legendi Hibernicum et Catechismus* (*Dictionary 1557–1640*). Disagreement as to the correct translation of the Irish—i.e., "printed by" or "printed at the cost of"—make uncertain whether he actually was connected with the stationer's trade. A convincing case against was given by E. R. McC. Dix (*Proc. RIA*, 28, sec. c, no. 8).

V

VALANCE or VALLANS (THOMAS), stationer in Dublin, 1692–98. He was admitted free of the guild in 1692 and paid quarterage through 1698, but there are no other guild references to him (*Guild Records*).

VALLANCE or VALANCE (JAMES), bookseller and publisher in Dublin, (1) Suffolk Street, near Grafton Street (1764–69?); (2) 6 Eustace Street (1792?–1808). 1764–1808. He was admitted to the guild as a quarter brother in 1764, but there are no other guild references to him (*Guild Records*). He was very active as a book auctioneer: there are sale catalogues by him, from that for the shop-stock of William Ross (q.v.), 1766, to that for the *Library of an Antiquarian*, 1800. In 1773 he signed a memorial to the Irish House of Commons against additional duties on foreign paper (BL, 1890.e.5. (239)), and in 1780, with others, he published Young's *Tour of Ireland*. He died in 1808, his will being proved in the Prerogative Court at Dublin, and was succeeded by his son James Vallance Jr.

VERDON or VERDYN (ANDREW), printer in Dublin, 1613–18. He was admitted free of the city in 1713 (*Cal. Anc. Rec. Dublin*). With mounting discontent over the work of John Francton (q.v.) as King's Printer in Ireland, in 1718 Verdon, with William Wight (q.v.), was granted a reversion of Francton's patent by James I. However, the Privy Council in England took exception, having found "both, men of meane Sorte, and insufficient," and urged the Lord Deputy of Ireland "to make a stay of the Reversion" and instead to work to get Francton to surrender the patent to representatives of the English Company of Stationers (BL, Sloan MS 4756, fol. 153). Nothing more was heard of Verdon.

VERLING (Mr.), bookseller in Cork, 1731. Sole reference: he was listed in 1731 as one of the provincial sellers of *Whalley's Almanack for the Year of Christ, 1732* (*Dublin Journal*, 18 Dec.).

VERNEY (Mr.), bookseller in Dublin, Little Ship Street, 1747. Sole reference: in 1747 he was listed in the colophon as one of the sellers of Powell's edition of Wesley's *Principles of a Methodist*.

VERNEY (Moses), papermaker in Dublin, Church Street, 1769–85. 1758–85. He had a paper mill at Whitechurch, County Dublin, in partnership with William Mondett (q.v.) from 1758 to 1768. He had his own watermark in 1760. In 1773 he signed a petition to the Irish House of Commons objecting to the removal of duties on foreign paper (BL, 1890.e.5. (232)).

WALKER (THOMAS), bookbinder, bookseller, and publisher in Dublin, Cicero's Head, Dame Street, or later, 79 Dame Street, 1770–88? He was apprenticed to John Exshaw (q.v.), admitted free of the guild by service in 1783, although he had been in business since 1770, and paid quarterage through 1788 (*Guild Records*). He was admitted free of the city in 1783 (Thrift, *Freemen*). Among his publications, with other stationers, were Smollett's *Humphrey Clinker*, 1771, Shakespeare's *Timon of Athens*, 1772, and, alone, Shakespeare's *Tempest*, 1775. He also published *Walker's Magazine* from 1772, which included much music printing, and the *Hibernian Magazine*, which he acquired from James Potts (q.v.). In 1785 he tendered for the binding of the Parliamentary *Journals* (Craig, *Bookbinding*). About 1788 he was succeeded in business by his son Joseph Walker.

WALLACE (JOHN), bookbinder in Dublin, 1771–88. He was the son of William Wallace (q.v.), was admitted free of the guild by birth in 1771, and paid quarterage through 1788 (*Guild Records*). He was admitted free of the city in 1771 (Thrift, *Freemen*).

WALLACE (WILLIAM), bookbinder in Dublin, Meeting House Lane, 1728–66. He was admitted free of the guild by service in 1728, and paid quarterage through 1764 (*Guild Records*). He was admitted free of the city in 1728 (Thrift, *Freemen*). He died in 1766 (*Freeman's Journal*, 9 Sept.).

WALSH (EDWARD), bookseller in Dublin, d. 1773. Sole reference: an obituary notice in 1773 read, "Died in Bridge street, Mr. Edward Walsh, bookseller" (*Hibernian Journal*, 16 Apr.).

WALSH (THOMAS), printer and publisher in Dublin, at the back of Dick's Coffee House, Skinner Row, 1722–28, 1734. 1722–34. He was admitted free of the city in 1728 (Thrift, *Freemen*), free of the guild by petition in 1728, and paid quarterage through 1734 (*Guild Records*). He was associated with Elizabeth Pue (q.v.) in some capacity, as a journeyman or partner, and printed *Pue's Occurrences* for her from 1722 to 1730. He also printed an occasional pamphlet—e.g., *His Majesty's Speech to both Houses of Parliament*, 1727, and a *Full Account of the Tryal of John Andouin*, 1728—and he published his own newspapers, the *Castle Courant*, 1726–27, *Dublin Mercury: or, Impartial Weekly News-Letter*, 1726–32?, and the *Dublin Post-Boy*, 1727–34? The *Dublin Mercury* was the first Irish periodical to be printed on Irish paper, and Walsh's indifferent and often shoddy presswork made a just match. His lack of skill probably contributed as well to the decline of *Pue's Occurrences* in these years. Cornelius Carter's (q.v.) vendetta with Elizabeth Pue extended to Walsh, and twice Carter printed patent forgeries of Walsh's newspapers, the second occasion, a copy of the *Castle Courant*, actually leading to the arrest of Walsh on the charge of printing false news (*Dublin Intelligence*, 28 Mar. 1726/27). Little was heard of Walsh once Elizabeth's son, Richard Pue Jr. (q.v.), joined the business and took over the printing of the *Occurrences*. That Walsh married a woman of outspoken Tory sympathies, when such were increasingly out of fashion, certainly with the younger Richard Pue, may have contributed to Walsh's difficulties. In 1735 a benefit was held for Walsh at the Theatre Royal, apparently for his having failed in business (*Dublin Evening Post*, 26 Apr.). For some years after, he managed the

Globe Coffee House, Essex Street, and he died in 1787 remembered as the "proprietor of the Naul flour mills"! (*Waterford Chronicle*, 1 Jan. 1788).

WARE (JOHN), bookseller and publisher in Dublin, over against St. Michael's Church, High Street, 1698–1713. He was admitted free of the guild by petition in 1698, paid quarterage through 1708, served on the Council from 1708, and was elected Warden in 1712, but refused to take the oath (*Guild Records*). He was admitted free of the city in 1700 (Thrift, *Freemen*). He was also a book auctioneer, and in 1698 published the first Irish catalogue of books "To be sold . . . by way of Auction." His publications included *Succession of Spain discuss'd*, 1701, *A Timely Caveat*, 1704, Persius, 1705, a school book, and, with other stationers, the *Book of Common Prayer*, 1713. For the 1704 pamphlet he was ordered to the bar of the Lords, and the pamphlet, deemed offensive, was subsequently burned by the common hangman (*Lords' Journ. Ire.*, ii, 63, 70). He died in 1713, and his wife continued to hold book auctions, "next door to the Raven, Fishamble Street," through 1715 (*Walley's News-Letter*, 9 Feb. 1714/15).

WARE (JOHN), printer in Dublin, 1726. Sole reference: the colophon in *A Satyr. To Miss M--y W-t-n*, 1726, read "printed by John Ware one of his Majesty's Servants." (Compare John Ware above and *Dictionary 1726–75* entry.)

WARRINER (ISAAC), stationer in Dublin, 1684–86. He was apprenticed to James Malone (q.v.), but there is no record of his taking out his freedom of the guild; possibly he was a Catholic. He was listed as a journeyman to William Norman (q.v.), 1684, to William Weston (q.v.), 1685, and to Edward Cobb (q.v.), 1685–86, and he was recorded as "gon" in 1687 (*Guild Records*).

WATERS (EDWARD), bookseller, papermaker, printer, and publisher in Dublin, (1) School House Lane, near High Street (1707–9); (2) Smock Alley, next door to the Theatre Royal (1710); (3) the New Post Office Printing House, at the corner of Sycamore Alley, Essex Street (1711–22); (4) on the back of the Blind Quay, almost opposite to King George on Horseback, near Essex Bridge (1728–35); (5) Dame Street, opposite Fownes Street (1740). 1707–40. He was admitted free of the city in 1710 (Thrift, *Freemen*), admitted free of the guild in 1710, and paid quarterage through 1724 (*Guild Records*). He was a prodigious printer, an experimenter in journalism, and above all a stalwart Tory, labeled by one of his adversaries the "Protestant Printer to the late Pretender" (*Dublin Intelligence*, 3 May 1707). Much of his printing was tracts and pamphlets, which led most of his fellow stationers to consider him rather disreputable, perhaps attested in 1722 when as a candidate for the guild's Council of the House he received but one vote. From 1711 he had, with his son John Waters (q.v.), a working interest in a paper mill at Milltown Bridge, County Dublin, which he leased to Thomas Holland (q.v.) in 1723. His journalistic efforts included the starting of no fewer than seven newspapers, the most important of which was the *Flying Post: or, the Post-Master*, 1708–29, as well as printing the controversial *Lloyd's News-Letter*, 1710–14? (Munter, *Handlist*). He was the first of Dean Swift's Dublin printers, printing that author's *Conduct of the Allies*, 1712, and the famous *Proposals for the Universal Use of Irish Manufactures*, 1720. These, plus such provocative pamphlets as *The Queen's Peace; or, A New War*, 1712, led to repeated troubles with the authorities. In 1708 he was indicted for "Printing and Vending Popish Prayer-Books," in 1709 again indicted for reporting, falsely, the burning of Wicklow by the French, and in 1714 tried for a "Seditious and Scandalous Libel," *Polyphemus's Farewell*. In 1720 the government sought to make an example of him over the printing of Swift's *Proposals*, but "the Jury, although carefully packed, brought him in not guilty, but having been sent back nine times, and kept eleven hours, by Judge Whitshed, they were oblig'd to leave the matter to the mercy of the latter by special verdict" (Ball, *Correspondence of Jonathan Swift*). A wag's summation was,

> Though a printer and Dean
> Seditiously mean
> Our true Irish hearts from old England to wean
> We'll buy English silks for our wives and our daughters,
> In spite of his Deanship and journeyman Waters.

Often fined, occasionally taken into custody, but never severely punished, Waters in 1736 capped his confrontations with the authorities when he had the audacity to reprint a pamphlet whose original publication a month earlier had led to George Faulkner's (q.v.) being incarcerated in Newgate, and the House could but order "Edward Waters to be committed close prisoner to Newgate" (*Commons' Journ. Ire.*, iv, 214, 216). He was at work again by 1737, and in 1740 he printed a poem, *The Battle of the Sexes*.

WATERS (HENRY), printer in Dublin, the Bagnio Slip, Temple Bar, 1754. Sole reference: in 1754 he printed the *Secret History of the Two Last Memorial S-ss-ons of Parliament*, in which were charges that the Court party was responsible for "beating News-Boys, and burning papers." Perhaps he was a journeyman to James Carson (q.v.).

WATERS (JOHN), papermaker in Dublin, 1711–17. He was associated with his father, Edward Waters (q.v.), in the operation of a paper mill at Milltown, County Dublin, from 1711 to 1717. He had his own watermark. He died in 1717.

WATSON (JOHN), bookseller and publisher in Dublin, (1) on the Merchant's Quay, near the Old Bridge (1722–23); (2)

the Bible and Crown, in the Merchant's Quay, near the Old Bridge (1723–69). 1722–69. He was apprenticed to George Grierson (q.v.), in 1722 petitioned for freedom by marriage to the daughter of Peter Lawrence (q.v.), was admitted to the guild as a quarter brother in 1730, was admitted free in 1734, and paid quarterage through 1767 (*Guild Records*). He was the brother of William Watson (q.v.), his daughter Mary married Thomas Servant (q.v.), and his daughter Elizabeth married Samuel Watson (q.v.). He joined in partnership with his mother-in-law, Mary Lawrence (q.v.), in 1722, and they published the *Irish–English Almanack*, 1724, and the *Citizen's Almanack*, 1727, in which year Watson succeeded Lawrence in the business. From 1729, at least, he was in business on his own, and started the very successful *Gentlemen and Citizen's Almanack*, 1729–66. In 1764 his son John Watson Jr. (q.v.) joined him in partnership, and they continued the publication of the *Almanack* jointly in 1767 and 1768. John Watson senior published as well Hatton's *Irish Comes commercii, or Trader's Companion*, 1739, and, with other stationers, Hooke's *Roman History*, 1759. He died in 1769 an "eminent bookseller and compiler" (*Dublin Mercury*, 10 Jan.).

WATSON (JOHN JR.), bookseller and publisher in Dublin, the Bible and Crown, in the Merchant's Quay, near the Old Bridge, 1764–69. He was the son of John Watson (q.v.), and joined in partnership with his father in 1764. He was admitted free of the guild by birth in 1764, and paid quarterage through 1767 (*Guild Records*). He was admitted free of the city in 1764 (Thrift, *Freemen*). With his father he published the *Gentlemen and Citizen's Almanack* in 1767 and 1768, and alone in 1769. There is no further evidence of John Watson Jr., and the *Almanack* continued to be published by Samuel Watson (q.v.) and Thomas Stewart (q.v.) from 1770 to 1794, and then by James Watson Stewart to 1834.

WATSON (RALPH), stationer in Dublin, 1680. He was admitted to the guild as a quarter brother in 1680, and served as a journeyman to Samuel Helsham (q.v.) (*Guild Records*). A Ralph Watson, bookseller, was working in Bury St. Edmunds in 1686 (*Dictionary 1668–1725*).

WATSON (RICHARD), printer in Dublin, d. 1760. Sole reference: an obituary notice in 1760 read "Died on Sunday, Jane, wife of Richard Watson, printer" (*Dublin Journal*, 16 Sept.).

WATSON (SAMUEL), bookseller and publisher in Dublin, (1) at Virgil's Head, opposite Shaw's Court, Dame Street, later 48 Dame Street (1759–79); (2) 71 Grafton Street (1784–95). 1759–95. He was apprenticed to his brother Thomas Watson (q.v.), was admitted to the guild as a quarter brother in 1759, and paid quarterage, irregularly, through 1765 (*Guild Records*). He was the son-in-law of John Watson (q.v.), and in partnership with his brother-in-law Thomas Stewart (q.v.) continued to compile and publish the *Gentlemen and Citizen's Almanack* from 1770 to 1794. From 1772 to 1779 he also joined in partnership with his brother Thomas Watson (q.v.). He published, with others, Shakespeare's *Works*, 1766, and, alone, a composite edition of the *Almanack*, 1780. He died intestate in 1801 (*Dublin Grant Book*).

WATSON (THOMAS), bookbinder, bookseller, and papermaker in Dublin, (1) the Poet's Head, Capel Street (1755?–56); (2) Bridge Street (1758?–71); (3) at Virgil's Head, opposite Shaw's Court, Dame Street (1772–79); (4) Usher's Quay (1780–81); (5) Cook Street (1782–83?). 1752–83? He was apprenticed to George Risk (q.v.), was admitted free of the guild by service in 1752, paid quarterage through 1779, and was recorded as "dead" in 1781, but was still in practice in 1783 (*Guild Records*). He was admitted free of the city in 1753

(Thrift, *Freemen*). In 1758 he joined in partnership with his father-in-law, Benjamin Nun (q.v.), having married Frances Nun in 1754, in setting up a new paper mill at Millmount, near Rathfarnham, County Dublin (*Sleater's Public Gazetteer*, 19 Dec.). They had their own watermark and remained in partnership to 1771, when Thomas dropped out of papermaking and joined with his brother Samuel Watson (q.v.) in a bookselling partnership from 1772 to 1779.

WATSON (WILLIAM), bookseller and printer in Dublin, the Poet's Head, Capel Street, 1757–92. He was the brother of John Watson (q.v.), and took over the shop of Thomas Watson (q.v.), no relation, in 1757. He was admitted to the guild as a quarter brother in 1757, and paid quarterage through 1765 (*Guild Records*). He printed for the University—Typographia Academiae (q.v.)—in 1761 and 1773, and published, with other stationers, *The Way to Keep Him, A Comedy*, 1760, and, alone, Hooker's *Ecclesiastical Polity*, 1773. He died in 1792, and was succeeded by his son William Watson Jr.

WATTS (ANNE), bookseller in Dublin, Skinner Row, 1763. Sole reference: she was stated to be a bookseller in Skinner Row in 1763 (*Dictionary 1726–75*). What relation, if any, she was to Elizabeth or Richard Watts (qq.v.) is not known: she was neither wife nor daughter of Richard (will of Richard Watts: Vicars, *Index of Wills*).

WATTS (ELIZABETH), bookseller, printer, and publisher in Dublin, the Bible, Skinner Row, 1762–68? She was the widow and successor of Richard Watts (q.v.). In 1764 she advertised "New Books just published by Elizabeth Watts" (*Freeman's Journal*, 17 Nov.), in 1765 she printed and published Walpole's *Castle of Otranto* and Clarendon's *State Letters*, and in 1768 she published Shakespeare's *Romeo and Juliet*.

WATTS (JAMES), bookseller, printer, and publisher in Dublin, (1) next door to the Bull's Head, Big Ship Street (1722–24); (2) opposite the Watch House, on the north side of College Green (1725–28); (3) the corner of Sycamore Alley and Dame Street, or, Lord Carteret's Head, Dame Street (1728–30); (4) Capel Street (1730–32). 1722–32. He began business in partnership with Abraham Thiboust (q.v.), publishing the *Dublin Mercury*, 1722–24, and later joined business with William-Shaw Anburey (q.v.). The quarrelsome John Harding (q.v.) quickly characterized the partnership: "Whereas there are *three* strange Animals living next Door to the Sign of the Head with Horns in Big Ship Street; the First a Spawn of a French Refugee; the next a Runaway 'Prentice Boy and the Third the Litter of a Sow, viz. a Pig, who under the false Names of Printers, has the Impudence to Impose on the Publick with false and old News" (*Dublin Impartial News Letter*, 12 Jan. 1722/23). Working on his own, Watt's printing output included Oldham's *Satyrs upon the Jesuits*, 1725, Fenelon's *Lives . . . of the Ancient Philosophers*, 1728, and *Constitutions of the Free-Masons* and James Delacourt's *The Art of Beauing*, 1730. He died in 1732 (*St. Peter's Par. Reg.*, Dublin).

WATTS (RICHARD), bookseller and publisher in Dublin, the Bible, Skinner Row, 1754–62. He was apprenticed to Peter Wilson (q.v.), admitted free of the guild by service in 1754, and paid quarterage through 1761 (*Guild Records*). In 1749, as yet an apprentice, he was summoned to "attend the Committee inquiring into the printing of Charles Lucas' publications" (*Commons' Journ. Ire.*, v, 12–13), but what he had to do with the matter does not appear. In 1754 he started a lending library, the second in Ireland (*General Advertiser*, 10 Sept.; see James Hoey). His publications, all with other stationers, included Strange's *Reports on Adjudged Cases*, 1756, *The Way to Keep*

Him. A Comedy, 1760, and Shakespeare's *Coriolanus* and *Cymbeline*, 1762. He died in 1762, his will being proved in the Prerogative Court at Dublin, and was succeeded by his wife, Elizabeth Watts (q.v.).

WEBBER (EDWARD), bookseller in Cork, 1723. In July 1723 it was recorded by the Cork Council "That the arrears due by Mr. Webber's bond of £10 per annum to the corporation be allowed him, in consideration of said Webbers not receiving any fees for orders of Council, and supplying the Council with books and Acts of Parliament," and in November there was a similar entry "for supplying the Council with books, paper, &c." (Caulfield, *Cork Council Book*).

WEBSTER (JOHN), bookseller in Longford, 1710. Sole reference: advertisements in 1710 listed him as one of the provincial booksellers taking subscriptions to a Dublin edition of the *Tryal of Doctor Henry Sacheverell* (*Dublin Intelligence*, 23 June and 1 July).

WEBSTER (ROBERT BENJAMIN), stationer in Dublin, The Rose and Crown, Dame Street (1699–1700?). 1699–1703. He was recorded as a journeyman to William Norman (q.v.) in 1699 and 1700, not listed in 1701 and 1702, and had an apprentice registered to him in 1703 who was discharged in the same year, "his being a papist" (*Guild Records*).

WEIR (JOHN), bookbinder in Dublin, the Rose and the Crown, Dame Street (1683–89). 1683–1709. He was listed as a journeyman to William Norman (q.v.) from 1683 to 1689, as an intruder in 1694, was admitted free of the guild in 1695, and paid quarterage through 1709. There was a John Weir (senior or junior?) listed as a journeyman to John North (q.v.) in

1696, a journeyman, John Wilson (q.v.), was registered to a John Weir in 1702 (*Guild Records*), and there was also a John Weir, bookseller in Edinburgh, in 1681 (*Dictionary 1668–1725*). John Weir of Dublin died in 1709 (*Dublin Grant Book*).

WEIR (JOHN JR.), bookseller in Dublin, the Rose and Crown, Dame Street (1687). 1687–1700. He was the son of John Weir (q.v.), was listed as a journeyman to William Norman (q.v.) in 1687, and as an intruder in 1700? There was a John Weir (senior or junior?) listed as a journeyman to John North (q.v.) in 1696 (*Guild Records*). There was also a John Weir, bookseller in Edinburgh, in 1681 (*Dictionary 1668–1725*).

WELSH (ANDREW), bookseller, printer, and publisher in Dublin, the Bowling Green Printing House, on the Strand, near Bachelor's Walk (1714), and Cork, Castle Street, near the Exchange (1715–39). 1714–39. In 1714, in partnership with Thomas Cotton (q.v.), he printed the *Dublin Weekly Journal*, and by 1715 they were in Cork, where they printed *The Freeholder's Answer to the Pretender's Declaration*. Possibly they published a newspaper, the *Cork Intelligence*, in 1718 and 1719 (Caulfield, *Cork Council Book*). In 1722 Welsh printed alone a single sheet broadside, and in 1723 and 1724 Knapp's *Almanack* (see Elizabeth Sadlier). He printed two other short-lived newspapers, *Welsh's Impartial News-Letter*, 1726, and the *Serio-Jocular Medley*, 1738 (Munter, *Handlist*). In 1739 he printed a *Sermon preached in Christ's Church*. He was succeeded by his son Andrew Welsh Jr. (q.v.).

WELSH (ANDREW), printer in Limerick, at the sign of the Globe in Key-lane, 1721. Sole reference: In 1721 he printed *The encouragement of the ladies of Ireland to the woollen manufactury*. How this entry relates to the Andrew Welsh of Dublin and Cork is uncertain.

WELSH (**ANDREW JR.**), bookseller, printer, and publisher in Cork, Castle Street, opposite the Exchange (1738–39); and Limerick, above the Market House, in the Irish town, John Street (1739–69). 1738–69. Whether he was earlier in partnership with his father, Andrew Welsh (q.v.), is not clear, but he was in Limerick in February 1739, and his father's last known imprint was sometime after April 1739. Welsh Jr. printed the *Limerick Journal* from 1739 to 1749, which continued as the *Munster Journal* through 1769. In 1757 he took his son Thomas Welsh into partnership. There was a large and varied output from his press, including an edition of Bigg's *Military History of Europe*, 1749, and Ferrar's *History of Limerick*, 1767. He died in 1772 (*North Munster Arch. Journ.*, 2, no. i), and was succeeded by his son Thomas Welsh (q.v.).

WELSH (**THOMAS**), bookseller, printer, and publisher in Limerick, above the Market House, in the Irish town, John Street, 1757–87? He was admitted free of the city of Limerick in 1757, and in that year joined his father, Andrew Welsh Jr. (q.v.), in partnership. They jointly published the *Munster Journal* to 1769, and Thomas continued it through 1784. Thomas also printed O'Halloran's *Insula sacra: or, the General Utilities*, 1770, and Meagher's *The Popish Mass celebrated by Heathen Priests*, 1771. He died or left Limerick by 1797 (Herbert, *Limerick Printers and Printing*).

WEST (**CHARLES**), stationer in Dublin, the Rose and Crown, Dame Street (1684–85). 1684–88. He was recorded as a journeyman to William Norman (q.v.) in 1684 and 1685, and listed simply as a journeyman from 1686 to 1688 (*Guild Records*).

WESTON (**WILLIAM**), bookseller, printer, and publisher in Dublin, High Street, 1678–89. He was admitted free of the guild in 1678, and paid quarterage through 1698, when his name was removed from the list of free brothers (*Guild Records*). He was admitted free of the city in 1688 (Thrift, *Freemen*). Possibly a Catholic, he described himself in a 1688 colophon as "Printer & Stationer to the Ld. Deputy [Tyrconnell]" (Hudleston's *A Short and Plain way to the Faith and Church*), and some of his publications during the reign of James II were said to bear the imprimatur of Patrick Tyrrell, Catholic Bishop of Clogher (Gilbert, *History of Dublin*). He printed and published various pamphlets and Catholic religious tracts: e.g., *Psalms to be read for the King after Mass*, 1685, *Some Memorandum concerning the present times*, 1689, and the *Speech of Count D'Avaux*, 1689.

WHALLEY (JOHN), bookseller, printer, and publisher in Dublin, (1) the Blue Posts, next door to the Wheel of Fortune, on the west side of St. Stephen's Green (1691–98); (2) next door to the Fleece, St. Nicholas Street (1698–1701); (3) the Crown, St. Patrick Street (1704–5); (4) the Blue Ball, Arundel Court, just without St. Nicholas Gate, or, near St. Nicholas Street (1709–24). 1685?–1724. Apparently he began trade as a shoemaker, which some never let him forget, dabbled in medicine and medical prognostication, made and marketed a patent medicine (the "famous Golden Pills or Elixer Cardiac"), and came to style himself "Dr. John Whalley, Student of Astrology and Physick." However dubious his credentials, the city fathers saw fit to admit him free of the city as a "Chirurgeon" in 1708. He also indulged in prophesy, and in 1685 published his first almanac, *Vox Urani*, continued in 1686 as *Syderus nuncius*, by 1690 as *Mercurius Hibernicus, or, An Almanack*, and later simply as *Dr. Whalley's Almanack*. Dunton regretted not having met "the Ingenious Dr. Whaley" whose almanac "bears the bell from all the rest in Ireland" (*Dublin Scuffle*). An uncompromising Whig and a vicious anti-Catholic, Whalley saw fit to flee to

London during the Revolution (Gilbert, *History of Dublin*), but by 1689 he had returned, acquired a press, and entered the stationer's trade. He printed and published such works as *A Chronological Account of the Age of the World*, 1700, and the *Tryal and Conviction of Patrick Hurly*, 1701. In 1699, "An Information . . . against John Whalley for Printing Unlicensed Pamphlets" was registered in the guild, but Whalley ignored such complaints and remained an intruder (*Guild Records*). In 1704 he took up journalism, publishing *Whalley's Flying Post*, 1704–8, the *Dublin-Post: or the Post-Master*, 1714–19?, and *Whalley's News-Letter*, 1714–24. He also turned minor public crusader. In 1711 he successfully petitioned the city on behalf of the tenants of Arundel Court for repairs to the adjacent city wall, "much defective and decayed, and in danger of falling" (*Cal. Anc. Rec. Dublin*), and later in the same year petitioned Parliament on behalf of all citizens of Dublin against a John Mercer "for ingrossing of Coals." Mercer was subsequently ordered into custody and prosecuted as a "common and notorious Cheat" (*Commons' Journ. Ire.*, ii, 724–30). All such actions were duly reported in his newspapers and his newsy sensationalism extended even to an obituary notice: "Yesterday morning Sir Toby Butler, Chancellor at Law Departed this Life to prevent his Possessing the Chief Seat of Purgatory was proceeded the same Road this Morning by Judge Dayley" (*Whalley's News-Letter*, 12 Mar. 1720/21). Few Dublin stationers could abide Whalley; indeed, he incurred their outspoken contempt. Except for the later years of Anne's reign, however, his Whiggery never brought him into conflict with the government, and it was he who informed on the printer of Edward Lloyd's (q.v.) Tory polemics (see Daniel Thompson). With Swift's printer John Harding (q.v.), Whalley carried on a running war of invective, Harding answering in kind: "Cobbling Whalley's Awl-Language Old News-Letter continues to be impos'd on the City" (*Harding's Dublin Journal*, 29 Mar. 1722). Whalley died in 1724 (*Dublin Grant Book*), and was succeeded by his widow, Mary Whalley (q.v.).

WHALLEY (MARY), printer and publisher in Dublin, Bell Alley, off Golden Lane, 1724–28? She was the widow and successor of John Whalley (q.v.), and was described as a printer and publisher for these years (*Dictionary 1726–75*), but whether she ever printed is doubtful. In 1726 she advertised the publication of *Whalley's Successor's Almanack* (probably compiled by Isaac Butler [q.v.]), stating "if any other Almanack . . . should be published in the Name of any Person, as successor of Dr. John Whalley . . . the same is spurious and stolen" (*Dublin Weekly Journal*, 8 Oct.), and possibly published this in 1727 and 1728 as well. By 1727 the rights to the almanac were held by George Faulkner (q.v.), who denounced a rival—*Whalley Reviv'd: or an Almanack for the Year of Christ 1730*—as "botchingly patched up" (*Dublin Journal*, 31 Jan. 1729/30), and subsequently added "beware of Counterfeits . . . with the Name of Whalley to it . . . without the consent of John Whalley, only Son and Successor of the late Doctor" (*Dublin Journal*, 27 Oct. 1730). By 1731 Isaac Butler had acquired the rights to the title from Mary or John Jr. or both, which he exercised to 1756. Mary continued to market the "famous Golden Pills and Elixir Cardiac . . . now made by John's widow" from her "Lodgings at Mr. Rummels's Baker, in Golden Lane" (*Dublin Intelligence*, 15 Feb. 1723/24) to at least 1748 (*Dublin Weekly Journal*, 6 Feb.).

WHEATLEY (SAMUEL), engraver and publisher in Dublin, (1) Salutation Alley, opposite Crane Lane, Cork Hill (1745); (2) Mr. Costigan's, ironmonger, at the Frying Pan, Anglesea Street, opposite Cope Street (1763). 1744–63? He engraved maps for Faulkner's (q.v.) edition of Sale's *Universal*

History, 1744, and Smith's *History of Waterford*, 1746, and a Map of Lough Neagh for Barton's *Lectures on Natural Philosophy*, 1751. In 1748, with Andrew Miller (q.v.) and Halhed Garland (q.v.), he published a *Speech* by Lord Chesterfield, with engraved borders and a bust of Chesterfield (*Dublin Gazette*, 19 May), and, alone, he published a mezzotint of the Earl of Halifax, 1763. He died in 1771.

WHITE (?), papermaker in Dublin, 1773. Sole reference: in 1773 he signed, as Daniel (q.v.) and White, a petition to the Irish House of Commons from papermakers, objecting to the removal of duties on foreign paper (BL, 1890.e.5. (232)).

WHITE (HENRY), stationer in Dublin, 1767. He was apprenticed to Henry Saunders (q.v.), and admitted free of the guild by service in 1767, but there are no other guild references to him (*Guild Records*).

WHITE (JACOB), stationer in Dublin, 1768–87. He was apprenticed to Josiah Sheppard (q.v.), his indentures transferred to William Whitestone (q.v.), admitted free of the guild by service in 1768, not sworn to 1780, and then paid quarterage through 1787 (*Guild Records*). He was admitted free of the city in 1780 (Thrift, *Freemen*).

WHITE (THOMAS), bookseller, printer, and publisher in Cork, (1) 55, opposite the West Gate of the Exchange (1778–80); (2) 4, New Buildings, Carth Street (1798–1803). 1758?–1803. A Thomas White was admitted free of the Dublin guild in 1758, but there are no other references to him (*Guild Records*). By 1773 he was a bookseller in Cork, where he was listed in the colophon as subscribing to the *Merchants' Directory*, and in advertisements as the seller of Poulson's *Divine Emblems* and O'Dwyer's *English Grammar Abridged* (*Cork Evening Post*,

15 Mar. and 11 Oct.). He printed and published many works, including school books, *A new Roman History by Question and Answer*, 1744, and the *Complete English Spelling Book*, 1783, as well as Robertson's *History of America*, 1778, Hannah More's *Works*, 1778 (with Patrick Byrne of Dublin), a short-lived newspaper, the *Cork Journal*, published by "Thomas White and Co.," 1778, Priestly's *Miscellaneous Observations relating to Education*, 1780, and, with others, *Thoughts on a Union*, 1798. From 1780 to 1798 he did considerable printing for the Cork Council, and in 1797 was admitted free of that city (Caulfield, *Cork Council Book*). He died in 1803 (*New Cork Evening Post*, 18 Apr.); shortly afterward was advertised "A most elegant Establishment in the Bookselling and Stationery Line to be disposed of, i.e. the entire stock of the late Mr. Thomas White" (*New Cork Evening Post*, 21 Apr. 1803).

WHITEHOUSE (JOSHUA), bookseller and publisher in Dublin, (1) the State Lottery Office, St. Nicholas Street (1758–65); (2) Parliament Street (?); (3) James Street (1785). 1758–85? He was the son of Thomas Whitehouse (q.v.) and the brother and partner of Thomas Whitehouse Jr. (q.v.). He had an apprentice indentured to him and his brother in 1758, but apparently did not take out his freedom of the guild or of the city (*Guild Records*). With his brother he published Shakespeare's *Henry VIII*, 1761, and *Arden of Feversham*, 1763, and a *Law Grammar*, 1763. He died in 1793.

WHITEHOUSE (THOMAS), bookbinder and bookseller in Dublin, under the Free Mason's Coffee House, on Essex Bridge (1723), or, later, under the Cocoa Tree Coffee House, on the eastern side of Essex Bridge, near the Custom House (1726). 1723–53. He was apprenticed to George Grierson (q.v.), admitted to the guild as a quarter brother in 1723, admitted free by service in 1726, and paid quarterage through 1753 (*Guild Records*). He was admitted free of the city in 1726 (Thrift, *Freemen*). He was the brother-in-law of Joseph Leathley (q.v.), and was succeeded by his sons, Joshua and Thomas Whitehouse Jr. (qq.v.).

WHITEHOUSE (THOMAS JR.), bookbinder, bookseller, and publisher in Dublin, (1) at the State Lottery Office, St. Nicholas Street (1758–65); (2) Parliament Street (?). 1758–83? He had an apprentice indentured to him and his brother Joshua Whitehouse (q.v.) in 1758, was admitted free of the guild by birth in 1759, paid quarterage through 1772, and was listed on the Clerk's list to 1783 (*Guild Records*). He was admitted free of the city in 1759 (Thrift, *Freemen*). He was the son of Thomas Whitehouse (q.v.), and in partnership with his brother Joshua he published Shakespeare's *Henry VIII*, 1761, and *Arden of Feversham*, 1763, and a *Law Grammar*, 1763. He died in 1783.

WHITEHOUSE (WILLIAM), stationer and publisher in Dublin, 1758–61. A W. Whitehouse paid a fine for not riding the franchise in 1761, although this may have been an error for William Whitestone (q.v.); there are no other guild references to William Whitehouse (*Guild Records*). In 1759, with others, he published Dodsley's *Cleone, A Tragedy* (*Sleater's Public Gazetteer*, 23 Dec.).

WHITESTONE (WILLIAM), bookseller and publisher in Dublin, (1) at Addison's Head, Dame Street (1753–55); (2) opposite Dick's Coffee House, Skinner Row, or, at Shakespeare's Head, Skinner Row (1755); (3) 29 Capel Street (1775–92). 1753–92. He was apprenticed to George Ewing (q.v.), admitted free of the guild by service in 1754, paid quarterage through

1792, and throughout was an active guild member (*Guild Records*). In 1753, before he took out his freedom of the guild, he entered into a brief partnership with Edmund Brice (q.v.), but by 1755 he was in business for himself, and in 1755 took over the shop of Thomas Ewing (q.v.). He published a good deal, including Shakespeare's *Macbeth*, 1760, and, with Richard Watts (q.v.), *Coriolanus* and *Cymbeline*, 1762, the *Tatler*, vol. 3, 1777, the *Spectator*, vol. 2, 1778, and Young's *Tour of Ireland*, 1780. He died in 1792, and was succeeded by his son Henry Whitestone, who had joined his father in partnership in 1780.

WIGHT (**WILLIAM**), bookbinder in Dublin, 1607–24? Possibly he worked for John Francton (q.v.) for a period. In 1607 he was paid for some bookbinding for the government (*Cal. S. P. Ire.*, 1607). In 1618 the Privy Council in England became aware that to "Verdyn [Andrew Verdon (q.v.)] an English man, and to one Wight a Scotchman that dwell there in Ireland" had been granted a reversion of John Francton's patent as King's Printer in Ireland by James I, and, believing the two men "insufficient," worked successfully to set aside the reversion and have the patent passed instead to three representatives of the English Company of Stationers (BL, Sloan MS 4765, fol. 153). In 1624 John Gillam (q.v.) was admitted free of the city of Dublin, having completed his apprenticeship with Wight (*Cal. Anc. Rec. Dublin*; Thrift, *Freemen*).

WILCOX (**JAMES**), printer and publisher in Dublin, Dame Street, 1749. In 1749 he printed and published a short-lived, anti-Lucas newspaper, the *Apologist: or, the Alderman's Journal*.

WILD (**ABRAHAM**), stationer in Dublin, 1681–1700. He was admitted free of the city by service in 1681 (Thrift, *Freemen*), free of the guild in 1681, paid quarterage through 1700, and was listed as "dead" in 1701 (*Guild Records*).

WILDE or WILD (JOSEPH), bookseller and publisher in Dublin, Castle Street, 1670?–85. He was recorded as in business in 1670 (Gilbert, *History of Dublin*), and admitted free of the city in 1672 (Thrift, *Freemen*). He was admitted free of the guild in 1673, paid quarterage through 1684, served on the Council from 1676, as Warden in 1676 and 1680, and as Master in 1685 (*Guild Records*). Among his publications were Loftus' *Exposition of Dionysius Syrus*, 1672, and *To His Excellency Richard Earl of Arran. A Poem*, 1682, and he printed a *Sermon upon Epiphany*, 1672, de Sales's *Introduction to a Devout Life*, 1673, and *Anthologia Latina*, 1674. A Joseph Wild was buried at St. John the Evangelist Church in 1718 (*St. John's Par. Reg.*, Dublin).

WILDE or WILD (RICHARD), bookseller, printer, and publisher in London (1689–90; 1696–97), and Dublin, (1) Skinner Row (1694); (2) Cork Exchange, Cork Hill (1694–95); (3) the Drumcondra Castle, Arran Street (1710–11). 1698–1715? He was apprenticed to George Sawbridge, London, and was in business in Dublin in 1694, admitted free of the Dublin guild in 1695, and paid quarterage through 1715 (*Guild Records*). In his first Dublin stay he printed and published an *Answer to the Rector's Libel*, 1694, William Sherlock's *Sermon Preached at Temple Church*, 1695, and *Dr. Whalley's New Almanack*, 1695. Three years later he again came to Dublin with John Dunton to manage the latter's book auctions, Dunton writing of him that "There are very few Book-sellers in England (if any) that understand Books better than Richard Wilde" (*Dublin Scuffle*). Wilde appears to have confined himself to auctioneering following 1698, advertising in 1710 as an auctioneer of land as well as books (*Dublin Post Man*, 20 Jan.). He died intestate in 1715 (*Dublin Grant Book*).

WILKINS (**Richard**), bookseller in Limerick, 1660?–80? He is stated to have been a bookseller in Limerick in the 1660s and 1670s (*Dictionary 1668–1725*), to have moved to Boston, Massachusetts about 1680, where he was Dunton's landlord in 1686 (Dunton, *Life and Errors*), and he was listed as a householder in Boston in 1689 and a former bookseller in Limerick (Maginnis' *Irish Contributions to American Independence*).

WILKINSON (**Mr.**), bookbinder in Dublin, 1762. Sole reference: an obituary notice in 1762 read, "Died in High street, Mrs. Wilkinson, wife of Mr. Wilkinson, bookbinder" (*Pue's Occurrences*, 5 Jan.).

WILKINSON (**Thomas**), printer and publisher in Dublin, (1) the Picture Shop, Chequer Lane (1728–29); (2) at the Toyshop, Castle Street (1755). 1728–55. He was possibly a relative and partner of William Wilkinson (q.v.). In 1728 he published Thomas Beard's mezzotint print of Captain Macheath and Polly Peacham (*Dublin Weekly Journal*, 7 Dec.), and years later advertised for sale Beard's prints of William King, Bishop of Dublin and of Richard Helsham (*Universal Advertiser*, 26 Mar. 1754/55).

WILKINSON (**Thomas**), bookseller, printer, and publisher in Dublin, (1) Winetavern Street, at the corner of Cook Street (1764–74), later, 40 Winetavern Street (1775–95); (2) 30 Winetavern Street (1796–1802). 1764–1802. In 1758 a Thomas Wilkinson married an Anne Crooke (q.v.) (*Dublin Grant Book*). He was listed as a quarter brother of the guild and paid franchise fines in 1764 and 1770, but there are no other guild references to him (*Guild Records*). He was listed in the colophon as the seller of Fielding's *The Intriguing Chamber-maid*, 1760, he published Shakespeare's *Richard III*, 1773 or 1774, and O'Keefe's *She-Gallant; or, square toes outwitted*, 1767, and he printed and published Addison's *Cato, A Tragedy*, 1780. In 1773 he signed a memorial to the Irish House of Commons against additional duties on foreign paper (BL, 1890. e.5. (239)). He died in 1802, his will being proved in the Prerogative Court at Dublin.

WILKINSON (**WILLIAM**), printer in Dublin, Chequer Lane, 1729–73. He was possibly a relative and partner of Thomas Wilkinson (q.v.). He was listed in the colophons as the seller of Richard Purcell's (q.v.) prints of "William III at the Siege of Namur," 1748, of Michael Boyle, Bishop of Armagh, n.d., and of Samuel Madden, n.d. He died intestate in 1789 (*Dublin Grant Book*).

WILLIAMS (**JAMES**), bookbinder in Dublin, 1730–34. He was admitted free of the guild in 1730, paid quarterage through 1734, but there are no other guild references to him (*Guild Records*). He died intestate in 1770 (*Dublin Grant Book*).

WILLIAMS (**JAMES**), bookbinder, bookseller, printer, and publisher in Dublin, (1) The Book, Paper, and Parchment Warehouse, Skinner Row (1764); (2) 5 Skinner Row (1771–1780); (3) Dame Street (?). 1764–86. He was admitted free of the guild by special grace in 1764, paid quarterage through 1785 (*Guild Records*), and was admitted free of the city in 1764 (Thrift, *Freemen*). He printed and published many titles, including Pope's edition of Homer's *Odyssey*, 1766, many of Goldsmith's writings—e.g., *Essays, Moral and Literary*, 1767, and *Roman History*, 1773—Smollett's *Humphrey Clinker*, 1771, and Hume's *History of England*, 1780. He also published the *Merchant's Directory* and a newspaper, the *General Evening*

Post, 1774, which failed to survive the implementation of the Stamp Tax. In 1785 he tendered for the binding of the Parliamentary *Journals* (Craig, *Bookbinding*). In his early years he employed the usual bookseller's sideline of selling patent drugs, "The Pure Inspissated Juice of Liquorice," but by his death he had amassed considerable wealth as a lottery broker. He died in 1786, his will being proved in the Prerogative Court at Dublin, and was succeeded by his widow, Dorothea Williams, and later by a son William Williams, 1796–1828.

WILLIAMS (**Matthew**), printer in Dublin, Dame Street, 1755. Sole reference: in 1755 he was listed as taking subscriptions for Charles Spooner's (q.v.) print of Anthony Malone (*Universal Advertiser*, 26 Mar.). A Matthew Williams, "Printer," died in 1799 (Vicars, *Index of Wills*).

WILLIAMS (**William**), stationer in Dublin, the Rose and Crown, Dame Street, 1678. He was registered as a journeyman to William Norman (q.v.) in 1678 (*Guild Records*). A W. Williams was a bookseller in London in 1677 (*Dictionary 1668–1725*).

WILLIAMS (**William**), bookbinder in Dublin, 1773. He was apprenticed to David Gibson (q.v.), was admitted free of the guild by service in 1773, but there are no other guild references to him (*Guild Records*).

WILLIAMSON (**Matthew**), bookseller, printer, and publisher in Dublin, the Golden Bell, over against Sycamore Alley, Dame Street, 1751–72. He was apprenticed to George Faulkner (q.v.), admitted free of the guild by service in 1751, and paid quarterage through 1772 (*Guild Records*). He was admitted free of the city in 1755 (Thrift, *Freemen*). He printed many pamphlets and short tracts—e.g., *An Essay on the Liberty* *of the Press*, 1754—with other Dublin stationers, Fielding's *Amelia*, 1752, alone, Shakespeare's *Coriolanus*, 1757, and he was one of the undertakers and the printer of the *Universal Advertiser*, 1753–66 (see Larry Dunn). He quit business in 1772 (*Dublin Mercury*, 3 Mar.), and died in 1794, his will being proved in the Prerogative Court at Dublin.

WILLIAMSON (**William**), bookseller, printer, and publisher in Dublin, at Maecenas' Head, Bridge Street, 1750–76. He was apprenticed to Richard Norris (q.v.), admitted to the guild as a quarter brother by petition in 1750, paid quarterage through 1764, and paid a franchise fine in 1770 (*Guild Records*). He printed and published a *Modern History*, 1755, the *Shepherd Calendar*, 1763, and took over the printing of the *Freeman's Journal* from 1766 to 1776 (see Alexander McCulloh).

WILLS (**Mathew**), printer in Dublin, Coles Alley, 1711?–29. He was apprenticed to John Forster (q.v.), summoned as an intruder in 1711, admitted free of the guild by service in 1725, and paid quarterage through 1729 (*Guild Records*). He was admitted free of the city in 1714 (Thrift, *Freemen*).

WILMOT (**John**), printer in Dublin, d. 1746. Sole reference: in 1746 he was listed as a printer in his will (*Dublin Grant Book*). A John Wilmot was married in Dublin in 1728 (*St. John's Par. Reg.*, Dublin), and again in 1732 (*St. Luke's Par. Reg.*, Dublin).

WILMOT (**William**), printer and publisher in Dublin, on the Blind Quay, near Fishamble Street, 1724?–27. A William Wilmot was married in Dublin in 1721 (*St. Andrew's Par. Reg.*, Dublin). He printed various pamphlets—e.g., *An Elegy on the much-Lamented Death of Aaron Crossly*, 1725, and the *Whole Institutions of Free-Masons Opened*, 1725—printed and published *John Knapp's Almanack*, 1725 and 1726, printed *Whalley's Successor's Almanack*, and reprinted the *Ladies Journal*, 1727. He died intestate in 1727 (*Dublin Grant Book*).

WILSON (Mr.), bookbinder in Cork, 1723. Sole reference: in 1723 George Bennett (q.v.) and a Mr. Wilson bound 234 copies of the Bible for the city of Cork (Caulfield, *Cork Council Book*).

WILSON (BRYAN), printer in Dublin, 1698. Sole reference: perhaps he was a journeyman to Cornelius Carter (q.v.), for with the latter in 1698 he printed 400 copies of the New Testament, which was subsequently claimed to be laden with errors and thus ordered suppressed by the guild (*Guild Records*), and the sheets confiscated by the Lords Justice and Council before it could be published (*State of the Case of Thomas Somervell, Merchant*, King MS Z 3.1.1; see Cornelius Carter and Thomas Somervill).

WILSON (G.), printer in Waterford, 1735. Sole reference: he was stated to have printed "one very small book" in 1735 (*Dictionary 1726–75*).

WILSON (G.), bookseller in Dublin, 1751. Sole reference: he was stated to have been a bookseller in 1751 (*Dictionary 1726–75*), possibly an error for John Wilson (q.v.).

WILSON (JOHN), printer in Dublin, Skinner Row (1711), 1702–32. He was registered as a journeyman to John Weir (q.v.) in 1702, summoned for intrusion in 1710 but "desired that he might be forborne with til next Quarter Day," listed as an intruder in 1711, admitted free of the guild by petition in 1713, paid quarterage through 1732, and served as Beadle from 1729 to 1732 (*Guild Records*). He was admitted free of the city in 1713 (Thrift, *Freemen*). He died in 1732.

WILSON (JOHN), bookseller and publisher in Dublin, Trinity Lane, 1741–53? He was admitted free of the guild in 1741, but there are no other guild references to him (*Guild Records*). In 1750 he published the *R—d Mr. M—ke D—s's* [Marmaduke Dallas] *Case submitted to the unprejudiced* (which presented the Bishop of Cork, Jennett Brown's, side in his controversy with Dallas), and in 1753 he was married in Dublin (*St. Andrew's Par. Reg.*, Dublin).

WILSON (JOSEPH), printer in Dublin, 1765–88. He was a nephew of Peter Wilson (q.v.), apprenticed to Alice Reilly (q.v.), admitted free of the guild by service in 1765, paid quarterage through 1767, and again in 1787 and 1788 (*Guild Records*). He was admitted free of the city in 1765 (Thrift, *Freemen*).

WILSON (PETER), bookseller and publisher in Dublin, (1) at Gay's Head, near Fownes Street, Dame Street (1739–47); (2) at the corner of Castle Lane, opposite the Old Horse Guard, Dame Street (1748–66); (3) on the upper Blind Quay (1766–67); (4) 6 Dame Street (1767–71). 1739–71. He was apprenticed to George Risk (q.v.), admitted to the guild as a quarter brother in 1743, "it being inconvenient for him to become a free brother," admitted free of the guild by service in 1748, paid quarterage through 1774, served as Warden in 1756, as Master in 1764, and on the Council from 1764 (*Guild Records*). He was admitted free of the city in 1748 (Thrift, *Freemen*). He began business by publishing the vocal score for a comic opera, Carey's *Dragon of Wantley, a burlesque opera*, 1743, acquired some of the stock of William Heatly (q.v.) upon the latter's death in 1742, and from that date began to prosper and soon became one of Dublin's leading booksellers and publishers. He published broadly—pamphlets, plays, schoolbooks, and music—including Cervantes' *Don Quixote*, 1747, Shakespeare's *Hamlet*,

1750, *Othello*, 1751, and the collected *Plays*, 1766, Fielding's *Amelia*, 1752, Ossian's *Works*, 1763, and Homer's *Iliad*, 1770. He started a short-lived essay journal, the *Meddler*, 1744, published the *Dublin Magazine*, 1763, for which he suffered a month's imprisonment over a paragraph unkindly reflecting on a member of Parliament, several editions of the *Spectator*, and compiled and published the famous *Dublin Directory* from 1751. In 1751 he was admitted free by fine of the prestigious Holy Trinity Guild of Merchants, the first Dublin stationer to be so honored. He was a party to the notorious squabble over *Sir Charles Grandison* when he joined John Exshaw (q.v.) and Henry Saunders (q.v.) in pirating Richardson's London publication in 1753 (see George Faulkner), Wilson having the audacity to word his version's colophon "London: Printed for S. Richardson; Dublin: Reprinted for Peter Wilson"! He was the first to publish a book catalogue in Ireland, 1760, and the first to publish poll books, 1768. In 1768 he took his son William Wilson (q.v.) into partnership, and they jointly published the *Directory* from 1769 to 1771, when he retired and turned the business over to William, although he remained active in the guild for some years. William's bankruptcy in 1781 forced Peter to assert his rights to the copyright of the *Directory*, and when William died in 1801, and again the *Directory* was in jeopardy, Peter, aged 82, came out of retirement to edit the work one more year. Shortly after, in 1802, he died (Vicars, *Index of Wills*).

WILSON (**PETER**), bookbinder and bookseller in Dublin, (1) at Addison's Head, Dame Street (1771); (2) under Dick's Coffee House, 3 Skinner Row (1774–75); (3) 30 Skinner Row (1776–78). 1771–78. He was apprenticed to John Fleming (q.v.), but there are no other guild references to him (*Guild Records*). He was listed as a bookseller at Addison's Head in

1771 (Gilbert, *History of Dublin*), was married in 1772 (*Dublin Grant Book*), and in 1774 advertised "Lottery Tickets" and "a fresh Parcel of Dr. Anderson's Scotch Pills with all kinds of Books and stationary ware" as well as "bindings in the neatest and best manner" (*Hibernian Journal*, 30 Nov.). He died in 1778, "a Young Man of an Amiable Disposition" (*Dublin Evening Post*, 5 Sept.).

WILSON (**RICHARD**), bookseller in Waterford, 1710. Sole reference: in 1710 he was listed in advertisements as one of the provincial booksellers taking subscriptions to a Dublin edition of the *Tryal of Doctor Henry Sacheverell* (*Dublin Intelligence*, 24 June and 1 July).

WILSON (**RICHARD**), printer in Dublin, 1751–53. He was admitted to the guild as a quarter brother in 1751 and paid quarterage through 1753 (*Guild Records*). He was married in 1751 (*St. Michan's Par. Reg.*, Dublin).

WILSON (**RICHARD**), printer in Dublin, 1775–78. He was apprenticed to Hugh Boulter Primrose Grierson (q.v.), admitted free of the guild by service in 1775, paid quarterage through 1778 (*Guild Records*), and was admitted free of the city in 1775 (Thrift, *Freemen*). He was married in 1776 and died in 1778 (*Dublin Grant Book*).

WILSON (**ROBERT or Rt. W.**), printer in Dublin, Cook Street, 1753. Sole reference: in 1753 he was stated to have printed an *Elegy on Capt. Spencer* (*Dictionary 1726–75*).

WILSON (**SAMUEL**), bookbinder and bookseller in Cork, 1720–23. In 1720 an advertisement listed him as one of the provincial booksellers of Crooke's *Irish Statutes* (*Dublin Cour-*

ant, 30 July), and in 1723 a Mr. Wilson worked with George Bennett (q.v.) in binding 243 Bibles for the city of Cork (Caulfield, *Cork Council Book*).

WILSON (SAMUEL), bookseller, printer, and publisher in Belfast, near the Four Corners, Bridge Street, 1736–44. He was in partnership with James Magee (q.v.), and together they printed and published various plays and sermons as well as a translation of Bossuet's *Introduction to Universal History*, and took subscriptions for many Dublin publications, including Tilotson's *Sermons*, 1738, Rollin's *Ancient History*, 1740, and Sale's *Universal History*, 1744.

WILSON (WILLIAM), printer in Monaghan, 1770. Sole reference: he was the first printer in Monaghan and is known for a single imprint, *A Sermon preached . . . at Newbliss*, 1770.

WILSON (WILLIAM), bookseller and publisher in Dublin, (1) 6 Dame Street (1768–95); (2) 6 Exchange Street (1796); (3) 1 Exchange Street (1797–98); (4) 36 Grafton Street (1799); (5) 16 Cork Hill, opposite the Royal Exchange (1800–1). 1768–1801. He was apprenticed to his father, Peter Wilson (q.v.), never took out his freedom of the guild (*Guild Records*), but was admitted free of the city by birth in 1774 (Thrift, *Freemen*). He joined his father in partnership in 1768 (*Freeman's Journal*, 23 Apr.), jointly published with him the *Dublin Directory* in 1769 and 1770, and when his father retired in 1771, continued the family business and the publication of the *Directory*. Alone, and with other Dublin stationers, he published a good deal, including Smollett's *Humphrey Clinker*, 1771, Young's *Tour of Ireland*, 1780, Defoe's *Robinson Crusoe*, 1781, Gibbon's *Decline and Fall of the Roman Empire*, 1784, and he produced Ireland's first road book, *Post-Chaise Companion: or,*

Traveller's Directory through Ireland, 1784. In 1781 he went bankrupt and his creditors disposed of the copyright to the *Directory* by auction, William being rescued by his father who asserted ownership rights and got his son back on his feet, while admitting that William "was possessed of a spirit beyond his income" (*Dublin Directory*, 1802). William died in 1801.

WINDSLOW (HENRY), stationer in Dublin, Essex Street, over against Essex Bridge, 1698–1700? He was registered as a journeyman to Jacob Milner (q.v.) from 1698 to 1700, and was recorded as "dead" in 1718 (*Guild Records*).

WINDSOR (JOSIAH), printer in Dublin, Castle Street, 1667–69. He is known for three imprints, an *Oratio in inauguratione*, 1667, a *Welcome in a Poem to His Excellency John Lord Roberts*, 1669, and *The Pattern of Grace and Glory*, 1669. He died in 1681 (*St. John's Par. Reg.*, Dublin).

WINNETT (WILLIAM), bookseller in Waterford (1738). 1735–38. He was apprenticed to William Smith (q.v.) and admitted free of the guild by service in 1735, but there are no other guild references to him (*Guild Records*). He was admitted free of the city in 1735 (Thrift, *Freemen*). In 1738 he was in Waterford, and in that year took subscriptions for several Dublin publications, including *A Paraphrase and Notes on the Epistles of St. Paul*, Rollin's *Ancient History*, and Clarke's *Sermons*.

WINSLEY (GEORGE) *see* George Winslow

WINSLOW (GABRIEL), bookseller in Dublin, 1749–52. He was apprenticed to his father, George Winslow (q.v.), admitted free of the guild by service in 1749, and paid quarterage through 1752 (*Guild Records*).

WINSLOW or WINSLEY (George), bookseller in Dublin, Darby Square, 1711–49? He was apprenticed to John Rogers (q.v.), listed as an intruder in 1711, admitted free of the guild by service in 1715, paid quarterage irregularly through 1742, and was dead by 1758 when his daughter Rachael Winslow was put on the Poor List (*Guild Records*). He was admitted free of the city in 1715 (Thrift, *Freemen*).

WINTER or WYNTER (William), bookseller and publisher in Dublin, (1) the Wandering Jew, Castle Street (1681); (2) the Primate's Head, Castle Street (1682); (3) the Primate's Head, College Green (1685). 1672–1722? There was only one William Winter, bookseller in Dublin (see *Dictionary 1668–1725* and *1726–75*). He was admitted free of the guild in 1672, served on the Council from 1676, as Warden in 1683, as Clerk from 1696 to 1706, was listed as a brother through 1722, and his name was scored out in 1723 (*Guild Records*). He was admitted free of the city in 1672 (Thrift, *Freemen*). He was the brother-in-law of John Ray (q.v.), having married his sister, Mary Ray, in 1679 (*Dublin Grant Book*). He published a few short tracts in 1681—e.g., the *Count of Hanlan's Downfall, Rules for a Grand Juror*, and *Some Passages in the Life and Death of the Right Honourable John Earl of Rochester*. By the 1720s he had failed in business; in 1720 he petitioned for "the city's charity" and received £10, and in 1722 petitioned again, "setting forth that by several misfortunes he is reduced to poverty," and received a further £6 (*Cal. Anc. Rec. Dublin*). He died in 1727, his will being proved in the Diocesan Court at Dublin.

WOGAN (Patrick), bookbinder, bookseller, printer, and publisher in Dublin, (1) Church Street (1771); (2) Merchant's Quay (1774); (3) 23 Old Bridge Street (1775–1810). 1771–1810. He became the principal Catholic stationer in Dublin by the 1780s. He printed and bound Catholic missals and ritual books—e.g., *Ordo Sacramentorum*, 1785, and *Pious Christian*, 1789. He was admitted free of the guild by fine in 1793 (*Guild Records*). His list of publications, alone and with other Dublin stationers, included Young's *Tour of Ireland*, 1780, Shakespeare's *Richard III*, 1790, and *Works*, 1791, and Goldsmith's *Roman History*, 1798. In 1794 he purchased the rights to *Jackson's Almanack* (see Robert Jackson), which, under various titles, he continued to 1810.

WORRALL or WORRELL (JOSIAH), bookseller in Dublin, on the Blind Quay opposite the Swan Tavern, 1726–27. He was listed as a bookseller on the Blind Quay in 1726 (Gilbert, *History of Dublin*), served his apprenticeship to Henry Shaw (q.v.), and was admitted free of the guild by service in 1727, but there are no other guild references to him (*Guild Records*). He was admitted free of the city in 1727 (Thrift, *Freemen*).

WORTH (JOSEPH), papermaker in Dublin, 1704. In 1704 he was fined by the guild for intrusion as a papermaker "on the Poddle" (*Guild Records*).

WYNNE (CHRISTOPHER), printer and publisher in Newry, 1770–74. He was in partnership with Wood Gibson Jones (q.v.), and they published the *Newry Journal*, 1770–74.

WYNNE (CORNELIUS), bookseller and publisher in Dublin, the Parrot, Capel Street, 1733–79. He was admitted free of the city by special grace in 1733 (Thrift, *Freemen*). He was admitted free of the guild by fine in 1734, paid quarterage through 1778, served as Warden in 1754, as Master in 1758, on the Council from 1758, and served as Treasurer from 1766 to 1769 (*Guild Records*). He became one of the leading booksellers in

Dublin. He was responsible for many publications, alone and with other stationers, including Ware's *Works*, 1739, one of the rival translations of Prévost d'Exiles' *Dean of Coleraine*, 1742 (see Thomas Bacon), Fielding's *Amelia*, 1752, and Shakespeare's collected *Plays*, 1766. He died in 1779, his will being proved in the Prerogative Court at Dublin.

WYNTER (WILLIAM) *see* William Winter

YOUNG (ROBERT), printer in Dublin (1624–?), London (1625–43), and Oxford (1640). 1624–43. He was admitted, as a printer, free of the city of Dublin by special grace in 1624 (Thrift, *Freemen*). He apparently acted as a factor, managing the Irish privileges of the London Company of Stationers, but for how long is not known. Some of his London publications bear the imprint "For the Partners of the Irish Stock" (see Society of Stationers; William Bladen; *Dictionary 1641–67*).

BIBLIOGRAPHY

MANUSCRIPT MATERIAL

Bagwell MS, Library of the Representative Church Body, Dublin.

Bentham, Sir William. Genealogical Abstracts of Prerogative Wills, Public Record Office, Ireland.

Charles Maddocks and James Belcher. *Account of Secret Service Money, 1723,* MS Z 3.1.1 (xli), Marsh's Library, Dublin.

Copies of Prerogative Wills, made by Phillip Crosslé, RIA, Dublin.

A further collection of original papers relating to the United Irishmen, with some later correspondence of Dr. R. R. Madden, MS 1496, Library of Trinity College, Dublin.

Harris, Walter. *Collectanea de rebus Hibernicis,* x (MS 10), National Library of Ireland, Dublin.

Letters of William King, 1690–1715 (MS 2055), National Library of Ireland, Dublin.

Madden, R. R. Notes for a third volume of the history of Irish periodical literature, Madden (I.P.L.) MSS, Public Library, Pearse Street, Dublin.

Prendergast, MS Commonwealth Council Books, King's Inns, Dublin.

Records of the Guild of St. Luke the Evangelist. 13 vols., Sidthorpe and Sons, 33 Molesworth Street, Dublin.

Sloane MS 4756, British Museum Library, London.

Forster Collection MSS 48E6 (82) and 48E9 (45-8), Victoria and Albert Museum, London.

OFFICIAL PAPERS

Calendar of state papers, domestic series, 1689–1704. 13 vols., London, 1895–1938.

Debates Relative to the Affairs of Ireland, in the Years 1763 and 1764. Taken by a Military Officer. 2 vols., London, 1766.

Fourteenth Report of the Deputy Keeper of Records . . . in Ireland, app. ii. Dublin, 1882.

House of commons accounts and papers, vii.

House of commons sessional papers. London, 1831–1832.

Journals of the house of commons of Ireland. Dublin, 1796.

Journals of the house of lords of Ireland. Dublin, 1779.

Notestein, W., F. H. Relf, and H. Simpson. *Commons Debates 1621.* 7 vols., New Haven, 1935.

Statutes at large passed in the parliaments held in Ireland. 13 vols., Dublin, 1899.

HISTORICAL MANUSCRIPTS COMMISSION
PUBLICATIONS

Second report, app. (King correspondence), 1871.

Seventh report, app., 1879.

Eighth report, app. part i (O'Conor MSS), 1881.

Eleventh report, app. iv (Townshend MSS); part v (Dartmouth MSS), 1887.

Fourteenth report, app. ii (Portland MSS), 1894.

Report on the manuscripts of the Earl of Bathurst, 1923.

Report on the manuscripts of the Earl of Egmont, i, 1905.

Report on the manuscripts of the late Reginald Rawdon Hastings, Esq., iii, 1934.

PARISH REGISTERS

Parish Register Society of Dublin:

Bernard, J. H. (ed.). *Registers of baptisms, marriages, and burials . . . Church of St. Patrick . . . 1677–1800.* Dublin, 1907.

Berry, H. F. (ed.). *Registers of the Church of St. Michan, 1636–1700.* Dublin, 1907–1909.

Chart, D. A. (ed.). *Marriage entries from the registers of the Parishes of St. Andrew, St. Anne, St. Audoen, and St. Bride, Dublin, 1632–1800.* Dublin, 1913.

Guinness, H. S. (ed.). *The Register of the Union of Monkstown, Co. Dublin.* Dublin, 1908.

Langman, A. E. (ed.). *Marriage entries in the registers of the Parishes of S. Marie, S. Luke, S. Catherine, and S. Werburgh, 1627–1800.* Dublin, 1915.

Mills, J. (ed.). *Registers of the Parish of St. John the Evangelist, 1619–1699.* Dublin, 1906.

Mills, J. (ed.). *Register of the Parish of St. Nicholas Without, 1694–1739.* Dublin, 1912.

Thrift, G. (ed.). *Register of the Parish of St. Peter and St. Kevin, 1669–1761.* Dublin, 1911.

Wood, H. (ed.). *Register of the Parish of St. Catherine, 1636–1715.* Dublin, 1908.

Huguenot Society of London Publications:

La Touche, J. J. D. (ed.). *Registers of the French Conformed Churches of St. Patrick and St. Mary, Dublin.* Dublin, 1893.

LeFanu, T. P. (ed.). *Registers of the French Non-Conformist Churches of Lucy Lane and Peter Street.* Aberdeen, 1901.

"Burials at St. Audoen's Dublin, 1672–1692," *Parish Register Irish Memorial Association,* 12, app. i. Dublin, 1926–31.

J. T. G. (ed.). *Register of the Abbey of St. Thomas, Dublin.* London, 1889.

"Parish Register, St. Nicholas Within, Dublin," *Irish Builder,* 31 (1 Aug. 1889) and 32 (15 June 1890).

"St. Audoen's Church—Extracts from Registers, 1672–1887," *Irish Builder,* 39 (1 Feb. 1887–15 Dec. 1887).

TOWN BOOKS, ETC.

Caulfield, R. *The Council Book of the Corporation of the City of Cork.* Guildford, 1876.

Gilbert, J. T. *Calendar of the Ancient Records of Dublin.* 19 vols., Dublin, 1889.

Minutes of the Grand Lodge of Freemasons of England, 1723–39, x. London, 1713.

Steele, R. (ed.). *Tudor and Stuart Proclamations.* Oxford, 1910.

A Transcript of the Registers of the Worshipful Company of Stationers: from 1640–1708 A.D. 3 vols., London, 1913–1914.

Thrift, G. *Roll of Freemen City of Dublin 1468–1485; 1575–1770.* 4 vols., Dublin, 1919.

Young, R. N. (ed.). *Town Book of the Corporation of Belfast, 1613–1816.* Belfast, 1892.

CORRESPONDENCE

Ball, F. E. (ed.). *Correspondence of Jonathan Swift.* 6 vols., London, 1910–1914.

Barbauld, A. L. *The Correspondence of Samuel Richardson.* 6 vols., London, 1804.

Boulter, H. *Letters written by . . . Hugh Boulter, D.D., lord primate of Ireland.* 2 vols., Dublin, 1770.

Bradshaw, J. (ed.). *Chesterfield's Letters.* London, 1892.

Hill, G. B. (ed.). *Letters of David Hume and William Strahan.* Oxford, 1888.

King, C. S. (ed.). *A Great Archbishop of Dublin: William King, 1650–1729, his autobiography, family, and a selection from his correspondence.* London, 1906.

Samuels, A. E. *The Early Life, Correspondence and Writings of the Rt. Hon. Edmund Burke.* Cambridge, 1923.

BIBLIOGRAPHIES AND CATALOGUES

Anderson, John. *A Catalogue of Early Belfast Printed Books 1694–1830.* Belfast, 1890.

———. *Catalogue of Early Belfast Printed Books 1694–1830. Supplementary.* Belfast, 1902.

Bibliotheca Lindesiana: Catalogue of Printed Books preserved in Haigh Hall, Wigan County, Pal. Lancaster. 4 vols., 1910.

Bingham, C. S. "Check List of Newspapers of the British Isles, 1665–1800," *American Antiquarian Society,* 65 (Oct. 1955), 237–51.

Buckley, James. "The First Irish Newspaper: The Irish Monthly Mercury," *Journal of the Cork Historical and Archaeological Society,* 3 (1894), 136–43.

———. "Irish Provincial Printing Prior to 1701," *Library,* 2nd ser., ii (1901), 341–48.

———. "Some Account of the Earliest Limerick Printing," *Cork Archaeological Society,* ser. 2, vii (1902), 195–200.

Catalogue of the Literary Collections . . . of William Monck Mason, Esq. London, 1858.

Darlow, T. H., and H. F. Moule. *Historical Catalogue of the printed editions of the English Bible, 1525–1961.* New York, 1968.

Dennan, Joseph. "The First Hundred Years of the Dublin Directory," *Bibliographical Society of Ireland Publications,* 1, no. 7 (1920), 91–108.

Dix, E. R. McC. *Books, Tracts, etc., Printed in Dublin in the 17th Century, 1626–1650.* Dublin, 1900.

———. *Catalogue of Early Dublin Printed Books, 1601–1700.* Dublin, 1889–1912.

———. "Dates of the Earliest Printing in Irish Towns," *Irish Book Lover,* 7, no. 6 (1915–16), 110–11.

Dix, E. R. McC. (cont'd), "Dublin Printing in the Seventeenth Century," *Bibliographical Society of Ireland Publications*, 2, no. 5 (1923), 93–95.

———. "The Earliest Belfast Printing," *Irish Book Lover*, 6, no. 10 (1915), 157–58.

———. *The Earliest Dublin Printing with List of Books, Proclamations, etc. Printed in Dublin Prior to 1601*. Dublin, 1901.

———. "Earliest Loughrea Printing," *Galway Archaeological and Historical Journal*, 5 (1908), 194–95.

———. "The Earliest Periodical Journals published in Dublin," *Proceedings of the Royal Irish Academy*, 6, 3rd ser., no. 1 (Oct. 1900), 33–35.

———. "Earliest Printing in Athlone," *Irish Book Lover*, 2, no. 6 (1911), 84–85.

———. "Earliest Printing in County Louth," *County Louth Archaeological Society*, 1, no. 1 (1904), 52–53.

———. "The Earliest Printing in Dublin in the Irish, Latin, Greek, Hebrew, French, Italian, Saxon, Welsh, Syriac, Armenian, and Arabic Languages," *Proceedings of the Royal Irish Academy*, 28, sec. c, no. 8 (1910), 149–56.

———. "Earliest Printing of Shakespeare's Plays in Ireland," *Bibliographical Society of Ireland Publications*, 2, no. 1 (1923), 18–20.

———. "Earliest Printing in the Town of Sligo," *Irish Book Lover*, 2, no. 2 (1910), 21–24.

———. "Early Almanacs Printed in Ireland," *Irish Book Lover*, 18, no. 2 (1930), 38.

———. "Early Belfast Printing," *Ulster Journal of Archaeology*, 12 (1906), 40–45.

———. "Early Loughrea Printing," *Galway Archaeological and Historical Journal*, 4 (1906), 110–12.

———. "Early Printing in Carrick-on-Suir," *Journal of the Waterford and South-east of Ireland Archaeological Society*, 13 (Jan.–Mar. 1910), 69–70.

———. "Early Printing in Limerick," *Journal of the North Munster Archaeological Society*, 1 (July 1910), 194–95.

———. "Early Printing in Munster Town," *Cork Historical and Archaeological Society Journal*, 10 (1904), 122–25.

———. "Early Printing in Roscrea—supplementary note," *Journal of the Waterford and South-east of Ireland Archaeological Society*, 12 (Jan.–Mar. 1909), 110–11.

———. "Early Printing in the South-east of Ireland," *Journal of the Waterford and South-east of Ireland Archaeological Society*, 9 (1906), 45–48, 112–19, 217–27.

———. "Early Printing in the South-east of Ireland, Roscrea," *Journal of the*

Dix, E. R. McC. (cont'd)

Waterford and South-east of Ireland Archaeological Society, 11 (1908), 236–37.

———. "Early printing in the South-east of Ireland. Part. I, Carlow," *Journal of the Waterford and South-east of Ireland Archaeological Society*, 14 (Jan.–Mar. 1911), 108–12.

———. "Irish Provincial Printing Prior to 1701," *Library*, 2nd ser., ii (1901), 341–48.

———. "Irish Song Books in the Royal Irish Academy," *Irish Book Lover*, 2, no. 6 (1911), 81–83.

———. "Kilkenny Printing in the Eighteenth Century," *Irish Book Lover*, 16, no. 1 (1928), 6–9, 40–41, 55–58.

———. "List of all Pamphlets, Books, etc., Printed in Cork during the Seventeenth Century," *Proceedings of the Royal Irish Academy*, 30, sec. c, no. 3 (1912), 71–82.

———. "List of Books and Tracts Printed in Belfast in the Seventeenth Century," *Proceedings of the Royal Irish Academy*, 33, sec. c, no. 4 (1916), 73–79.

———. *List of Books and Pamphlets printed in Armagh in the Eighteenth Century.* Irish Bibliographical Pamphlets no. 2, 1906.

———. *List of Books and Pamphlets Printed in Armagh in the Eighteenth Century.* Irish Bibliographical Pamphlets no. 4, 1910.

———. "List of Books, etc., Printed in Cork prior to 1801," *Cork Historical and Archaeological Society Journal*, 16 (1910), 64–66.

———. "List of Books, Pamphlets, etc., Printed at Cork in the 17th and 18th Centuries," *Cork Historical and Archaeological Society Journal*, 9 (1900), 27–32, 97–105, 264–68.

———. "List of Books, Pamphlets, etc., Printed at Cork in the 17th and 18th Centuries," *Cork Historical and Archaeological Society Journal*, 15 (1909), 111–14.

———. *List of Books, Pamphlets, and Newspapers Printed in Drogheda from the Earliest Period to the End of the Eighteenth Century.* Dundalk, 1911.

———. *List of Books, Newspapers and Pamphlets Printed in Ennis, Co. Clare, in the Eighteenth Century.* Irish Bibliographical Pamphlets no. 8, 1912.

———. *List of Books, Pamphlets, and Newspapers Printed in Limerick from the Earliest Period to 1800.* Irish Bibliographical Pamphlets no. 5, 1910.

———. *List of Books, Pamphlets, Newspapers, etc. Printed in Londonderry to 1801.* Irish Bibliographical Pamphlets no. 7, 1911.

———. *List of Books, Pamphlets, and Newspapers Printed in Monaghan in the Eighteenth Century.* Irish Bibliographical Pamphlets no. 3, 1906.

Dix, E. R. McC. (cont'd), "List of Books, Pamphlets, Newspapers, etc., printed in Newry from 1764," *Ulster Journal of Archaeology*, 13 (1907), 116–19, 170–75.

———. "List of Books, Pamphlets, Newspapers, etc., Printed in Newry from 1764–1810," *Ulster Journal of Archaeology*, 14 (1908), 95–96.

———. "List of Books, Pamphlets, Newspapers, etc., Printed in Newry from 1764–1810," *Ulster Journal of Archaeology*, 15 (1909), 19.

———. *List of Books, Tracts, etc., Printed in Dublin in the 17th Century. Part III, 1651–1675.* Dublin, 1902.

———. "List of Newspapers, Pamphlets, etc., Printed in the Town of Tralee from Earliest Date to 1820," *Kerry Archaeological Magazine* (1909), 280–84.

———. "A List of the 17th and 18th Century Cork-Printed Books, etc.," *Cork Historical and Archaeological Society Journal*, 6, no. 97 (July–Sept. 1900), 168–74, 233–40.

———. "A List of the 17th and 18th Century Cork-Printed Books, etc.," *Cork Historical and Archaeological Society Journal*, 7, no. 50 (Apr.–June 1901), 104–10, 233–38.

———. "Pamphlets, Books, etc., Printed in Cork in the Seventeenth Century," *Proceedings of the Royal Irish Academy*, 30, sec. c, no. 3 (1912), 71–82.

———. "Plays Printed in Ireland before 1701," *Irish Book Lover*, 17, no. 2 (1929), 36–37.

———. "Printing in Carlow in the Eighteenth Century," *Irish Book Lover*, 11, no. 8 (1920), 75–76.

———. "Printing in Cork in the First Quarter of the Eighteenth Century (1701–1725)," *Proceedings of the Royal Irish Academy*, 36, sec. c, no. 2 (1915), 10–15.

———. "Printing in Galway, 1754–1820," *Irish Book Lover*, 2, no. 4 (1910), 50–54.

———. "Printing in Limerick Prior to 1801," *Journal of the North Munster Archaeological Society*, 1 (Jan. 1911), 269–71.

———. "Printing in Loughrea, 1766–1825," *Irish Book Lover*, 2, no. 10 (1911), 151–52.

———. "Printing in Mullingar, 1773–1825," *Irish Book Lover*, 2, no. 8 (1911), 120–22.

———. "Printing in Tuam," *Irish Book Lover*, 2, no. 7 (1911), 101–2.

———. "Printing in Youghal," *Irish Book Lover*, 4, no. 2 (1912), 24–25.

———. "School Books Printed in Dublin from the Earliest Period to 1717," *Bibliographical Society of Ireland Publications*, 3, no. 1 (1926), [no pagination].

Dix, E. R. McC. (cont'd), "Some Dublin Music Printers and Music Sellers of the Eighteenth Century," *Irish Book Lover*, 18, no. 1 (1930), 26–28.

Doran, C. G. "Local Bibliography, Early Irish Literature," *Cork Historical and Archaeological Society Journal*, 1 (1892), 82–84.

The Eighteenth-Century Short Title Catalogue. The online database.

Evans, Charles. *American Bibliography: a chronological dictionary of all books, pamphlets, and periodicals published . . . 1639 down to . . . 1820.* 1941–59.

Flood, Chevalier Grattan. "Dublin Music Printing from 1750–1790," *Bibliographical Society of Ireland Publications*, 2, no. 5 (1923), 101–5.

Flood, W. H. Grattan. "Dublin Music Printing from 1685–1750," *Bibliographical Society of Ireland Publications*, 2, no. 1 (1923), 7–12.

———. "Music-Printing in Dublin from 1700 to 1750," *Royal Society of Antiquaries of Ireland Journal*, 8, no. 3 (1908), 236–40.

Fordham, Sir Herbert G. "Road-Books and Itineraries of Ireland, 1647 to 1850," *Bibliographical Society of Ireland Publications*, 2, no. 4 (1923), 63–76.

Foxon, David F. *English Verse 1701–1750: A Catalogue of Separately Printed Poems.* Cambridge, 1975.

Guinness, H. S. "Dublin Directories, 1751–1760," *Irish Book Lover*, 14, no. 6 (1924), 84–86.

Herbert, Robert. *Limerick Printers and Printing. Part one of the catalogue of the local collection in the City of Limerick Public Library.* Limerick, 1942.

Jaggard, William. *Shakespeare Bibliography.* Stratford-on-Avon, 1911.

Kernohan, J. W. "Blow's Books and Bibles," *Irish Book Lover*, 6, no. 12 (1915), 197–98.

Kirkpatrick, T. P. C. "Early Dublin Printing," *Irish Book Lover*, 20, no. 2 (1932), 40–41.

———. "Periodical Publications of Science in Ireland," *Bibliographical Society of Ireland Publications*, 2, no. 3 (1921), 33–58.

Munter, Robert. *A Hand-list of Irish Newspapers, 1685–1750.* Cambridge Bibliographical Society Monograph no. 4. London, 1960.

O Casaide, Séamus. "Bibliography of Local Printing," *Irish Book Lover*, 2, no. 1 (1909), 4–6.

———. "Cork Printing in the Seventeenth Century," *Irish Book Lover*, 21, no. 4 (1933), 90.

———. "Early Dublin Song Books," *Irish Book Lover*, 23, no. 4 (1935), 92.

———. "Kilkenny Printing in the Seventeenth Century," *Irish Book Lover*, 21, no. 4 (1933), 91.

O'Hegarty, P. S. "Some Irish Eighteenth Century Editions of Shakespeare, not recorded by Jaggard, Stockwell or Ford," *Irish Book Lover*, 32, no. 1 (1952), 4–7.

O'Kelley, Francis. "The First Dublin Directory (1757) and its Immediate Successors," *Irish Book Lover*, 16, nos. 1–2 (1928), 19–22, 29–32, 52–54.

———. "Irish Book-Sale Catalogues before 1801," *Bibliographical Society of Ireland Publications*, 6, no. 3 (1953), [offprint, 55 pp.].

Peddie, R. A. "Bibliography of Irish Printing," *Irish Book Lover*, 3, no. 4 (1911), 51–53.

Pollard, A. W., and G. R. Redgrave. *Short-title Catalogue of Books Printed in England, Scotland and Ireland . . . 1475–1640*. London, 1926.

Ryan, M. J. "A Preliminary List of Greek and Latin Classics Printed in Dublin down to 1800," *Bibliographical Society of Ireland Publications*, 3, no. 2 (1926), [no pagination].

Stewart, Powell. *A Descriptive Catalogue of a Collection at the University of Texas: British Newspapers and Periodicals 1632–1800*. University of Texas. Austin, 1950.

Stockwell, LaTourette. "Handlist of the Editions of Shakespeare Printed in Ireland in the 18th Century," *Dublin Magazine*, n.s. 4 (July–Sept. 1929), 33–45.

Teerink, H. *A Bibliography of the Writings of Jonathan Swift*. Philadelphia, 1963.

White, N. B. "Elizabethan Dublin Printing," *Irish Book Lover*, 21, no. 4 (1933), 113.

Wing, Donald. *Short-title Catalogue of Books Printed in England, Scotland, Ireland . . . 1641–1700*. Charlottesville, 1955.

Young, R. M. "An Account of some Notable Books Printed in Belfast," *Library*, 7 (1895), 135–44.

PERIODICALS

The Irish Monthly Mercury. Monthly communicating all true intelligence within the Dominion of Ireland. London, 1649.

Irish Mercury. London, 1650.

The News-Letter. Dublin, 1685–1686.

The Dublin Intelligence. Dublin, 1690–1693.

Votes of the House of Commons. Dublin, 1690, 1707, 1713, 1715–1737.

The Flying Post: or, The Post Master. Dublin, 1699–1714.

The London Gazette. A Dublin reprint, 1700–1703.

The London Intelligence. A Dublin reprint, 1701.

BIBLIOGRAPHY

The Dublin Intelligence. Dublin, 1702–1732.

The Dublin Castle. Dublin, 1702, 1708.

Impartial Occurrences (continued as *Pue's Occurrences*). Dublin, 1704–1775.

Whalley's Flying Post. Dublin, 1704–1713.

Whitehall. A Dublin reprint, 1704, 1706.

The Paris Gazette Englished. A Dublin reprint, 1705.

The Dublin Courant or, The Diverting Post. Dublin, 1705.

The Dublin Mercury. Dublin, 1706, 1722–1724.

The Dublin Gazette. Dublin, 1706–1775.

The Post-Man and The Historical Account. Dublin, 1707–1713.

The London-Postman, or The Historical Account. Dublin, 1707.

Dublin. Dublin, 1708.

Edward Waters The Dublin Intelligence. Dublin, 1708–1709.

The Diverting Post. Dublin, 1709, 1725.

The Dublin Weekly Intelligence. Dublin, 1710.

The Medley. A Dublin reprint, 1710–1711.

The Tatler. A Dublin reprint, 1710.

The Examiner. A Dublin reprint, 1710–1712.

The Protestant Post-Boy. Dublin, 1712.

The Post Boy. Dublin, 1712–1716.

The Post Man. Dublin, 1712.

The Evening Post. Dublin, 1713.

Lloyd's News-Letter. Dublin, 1713–1714.

The Dublin Post-Man: and The Historical Account. Dublin, 1714 (and, with title variations) to 1727.

The Impartial & Historical Weekly Mercury. Dublin, 1714.

Whalley's News-Letter. Dublin, 1714–1723.

The Dublin-Post; or the Post-Master. Dublin, 1714 (and, with title variations) to 1719.

The Dublin News-Letter. Dublin, 1714–1716.

The Freeholder. A Dublin reprint, 1715–1716.

Englishman. A Dublin reprint, 1715.

The Flying Post: or, The Post-Boy. Dublin, 1715–1729.

The London Post Boy. A Dublin reprint, 1715.

The Limerick News Letter. Limerick, 1716.

Thomas Hume's The Dublin Intelligence. Dublin, 1716–1729.

The Free-Holder. A Cork reprint, 1716.

The Post-Man: and The Historical Account. Dublin, 1716–1726.

The Daily Courant. A Dublin reprint, 1716.

Harding's Impartial News Letter. Dublin, 1718–1725.

The Post-Boy. Dublin, 1718–1724.

Thomas Toulmin The Dublin Evening-Post. Dublin, 1719.

The St. James's Evening-Post. Dublin, 1719–1726.

The Weekly Pacquet, or The Impartial Post-Boy. Dublin, 1720.

Irish News-Tatler. Dublin, 1720.

James Carson The Dublin Intelligence. Dublin, 1720–1724.

The New Dublin Mercury: or Irish Gazetteer. Dublin, 1721.

The London Post-Man. Dublin, 1722–1724, 1727.

The Dublin Journal. Dublin, 1724–1775.

The Dublin Weekly Journal. Dublin, 1725–1765.

Faulkner's Dublin Post Boy. Dublin, 1725–1734.

The Dublin Mercury: or, Impartial Weekly News-Letter. Dublin, 1726–1732.

The Castle Courant. Dublin, 1726.

The Dublin Gazetteer. Dublin, 1726.

The Flying Post-Man. Dublin, 1726.

The Dublin Postman. Dublin, 1726.

The White-hall Gazette. Dublin, 1727.

The Ladies Journal. A Dublin reprint, 1727.

Anburey's Weekly Journal. Dublin, 1727.

Walsh's Dublin Post-Boy. Dublin, 1727–1732.

Christopher Dickson The Dublin Gazette. Dublin, 1727.

Christopher Dickson The Flying-Post. Dublin, 1727.

The Temple-Oge Intelligence. Dublin, 1728.

R. Dickson The Silver Court Gazette. Dublin, 1728.

The Intelligencer. Dublin, 1728.

The Plain Dealer. Dublin, 1728.

Nicholas Hussey The Dublin Post Boy. Dublin, 1729.

The Flying Post, or, the Dublin Post-Man. Dublin, 1729.

The Flying Post. Dublin, 1729, 1744.

Edward Water's The Flying Post. Dublin, 1729.

The Tribune. Dublin, 1729.

James Hoey The Dublin Journal. Dublin, 1730–1737.

The Dublin Packet. Dublin, 1730.

The Dublin Post-Boy. Dublin, 1732–1734.

The Dublin Evening Post. Dublin, 1732–1739.

The Correspondent. Dublin, 1733.

The Weekly Miscellany. A Dublin reprint, 1734–1735.

Dalton's Dublin Impartial News Letter. Dublin, 1734.

The Prompter. A Dublin reprint, 1735.

The Weekly Amusement: or Universal Magazine. A Dublin reprint, 1735.

The Weekly Oracle: or, Universal Library. Dublin, 1735–1736.

The Country Journal. Dublin, 1735–1736.

James Hamilton and Company. The Dublin Daily Advertiser. Dublin, 1736–1738.

Richard Reilly The Dublin News-Letter. Dublin, 1737–1741.

The General Advertiser. Dublin, 1737.

Francis Joy The Belfast News-Letter, and General Advertiser. Belfast, 1738–1775.

Ebenezer Rider The Dublin Daily Post, and General Advertiser. Dublin, 1739–1740.

The Craftsman. A Dublin reprint, 1739.

The General Post Office Advertiser. Dublin, 1741.

Andrew Welsh The Limerick Journal. Limerick, 1741 (and, with title variations) to 1769.

Thomas Bacon The Dublin Mercury. Dublin, 1741–1742.

The Meddler. Dublin, 1743–1744.

J. Gowan A Supplement to the Dublin News-Letter. Dublin, 1743.

Literary Journal. Dublin, 1744–1749.

The Dublin Courant. Dublin, 1744–1775.

James Esdall The General News-Letter. Dublin, 1744–1755.

The Universal Journal. Dublin, 1747.

The Reformer. Dublin, 1748.

The Tickler. Dublin, 1748–1749.

The Patriot. Dublin, 1748.

The Censor: or, the Citizen's Journal. Dublin, 1749–1750.

The Censor Extraordinary. Dublin, 1749.

The Apologist; or, the Alderman's Journal. Dublin, 1749.

The Political Manager; or, The Invasion of the Music-Hall. Dublin, 1749.

A Breakfast for the Freeman. Dublin, 1749.

The Church-Monitor. Dublin, 1749.

The Play-House Journal. Dublin, 1750.

Patriot. Dublin, 1753.

Dublin Spy. Dublin, 1753–1754.

The Universal Advertiser. Dublin, 1753–1754.

Public Register: or, the Freeman's Journal. Dublin, 1760–1775.

SALES CATALOGUES

A Catalogue of Books in several Faculties and Languages . . . To be sold . . . by John Ware. Dublin, 1698.

A Catalogue of Books in several Faculties and Languages . . . To be sold by way of Auction, by John Ware. Dublin, 1710.

A Catalogue of Books, newly arrived from England, Holland, and France. To be sold by Smiths [sic] *and Bruce, Booksellers.* Dublin, 1726.

A Catalogue of Books. Sold by John Smith and William Bruce, Booksellers. Dublin, 1728.

A Catalogue of Books, to be sold by the Administrators of the Reverend John Nicolson [sic]. Dublin, 1729.

A Catalogue of Books, to be sold by Auction, for the Benefit of the Poor. . . . The Sale will begin . . . at Mr. Bailli's Auction Room in Abby-Street. . . . Dublin, 1729.

A Catalogue of Books, to be sold by Auction . . . at Thomas Thornton's, Bookseller, in College Green. . . . Dublin, 1729.

A Catalogue of a choice Collection of valuable Books in most Faculties . . . By Richard Norris, Bookseller. . . . Dublin, 1729.

A Catalogue of a choice Collection of valuable Books . . . the Library of the judicious Sir Henry Echlin. . . . Dublin, 1729.

A Catalogue of choice Physick Books, etc. of an eminent Physician deceased. Dublin, 1731.

Catalogus librorum in omni facultate praestantissimorum . . . which will begin to be sold cheap . . . at Tho. Green's Ware-House. . . . Dublin, 1731.

Catalogus librorum . . . nuper ex Anglia, Gallia et Hollandia advectorum. Being a large and curious Collection . . . to be sold cheap. . . . Dublin, 1731.

A Catalogue of a choice collection of Valuable Books . . . The Library of the late Reverend Doctor Nicholas Knight . . . [to be sold by auction]. Dublin, 1732.

A choice Collection of Books, the Library of John Huson, Esq.: To be sold at Auction. Dublin, 1737.

A Catalogue of Books the Library of the Rev. Dr. Thomas Sheridan, deceased. To be sold by Auction. . . . Dublin, 1739.

A Catalogue of Books, the Library of the late Rev. Dr. Swift, Dean of St. Patrick's Dublin. To be sold by Auction. . . . Dublin, 1745.

. . . The Library of Samuel Card, Esq. . . . To be sold by Auction. . . . Dublin, 1755.

. . . The Library of Doctor Thomas Lloyd, deceased . . . To be sold by Auction. Dublin, 1758.

. . . The Bound Stock of John Smith, Bookseller, on the Blind-Quay, which will be sold by Auction. . . . Dublin, 1758.

Catalogue of Books [to be sold by auction, ca. 1758; title page missing but no books dated later than 1757]. Dublin, 1758?

... *The Shop-Stock of Mr. Richard Gunn, Bookseller, deceas'd, which will begin selling by Auction.* ... Dublin, 1758.

Catalogue of Books (with their prices) printed for, and sold by, Peter Wilson, in Dame-street. Dublin, 1760.

... *The Collections of H. Cunningham, Esq.; and a Member of Parliament, deceased. To be sold by Auction.* ... Dublin, 1760.

... *The Library of the late Revd. John Lawson ... which will begin selling by Auction.* ... Dublin, 1760.

A Catalogue ... of books ... Printed and sold by Peter Wilson of Dame Street. Dublin, 1760.

Flin's Sale Catalogue of Books. For the Years 1761 and 62 ... Which will begin selling ... at ... The lowest Price. ... Dublin, 1761.

... *The Library of Howard Parry, Esq.; deceased ... Which will be sold by Auction by Robert Bell, Bookseller and Auctioneer.* ... Dublin, 1762.

Flin's Sale Catalogue of Books for the Year 1763 ... which will begin selling ... on Wednesday the 10th of November. ... Dublin, 1762.

A Supplement to Flin's Sale Catalogue of Books for the Year 1763 ... which will begin selling on Monday May 16th. ... Dublin, 1763.

Flin's Sale Catalogue of Books for the Year 1764 ... being the Libraries of ... Charles Delafaye ... Ralph Thoresby ... both Deceased ... Which begins Selling ... October 31st. ... Dublin, 1763.

... *The entire Library of the Right Reverend Father in God, Robert Downes. To be sold by Auction.* Dublin, 1764.

The Second Part of Flin's Sale Catalogue of Books for the Year 1764 ... which will begin selling on Wednesday, January 25th, 1764. ... Dublin, 1764.

Part I of Flin's Sale Catalogue of Books for the Year 1766 ... The sale to begin on Wednesday the 6th of November 1765. ... Dublin, 1765.

... *The Library of the Late ingenious Phillip Doyne, Esq.; To be sold by Auction.* ... Dublin, 1766.

A Catalogue of the Library of the late Right Revd. Dr. Richard Pococke, Lord Bishop of Meath, deceased ... which will be sold by Auction. ... Dublin, 1766.

... *The Shop-Stock of the late William Ross, Bookseller ... which will be sold by Auction.* ... Dublin, 1766.

A Catalogue of Books, belonging to a Gentleman going abroad which will begin selling by Auction on Wednesday the 18th of June 1766. ... Dublin, 1766.

A Catalogue of Books ... to be sold by Auction by Michael Duggan. ... Dublin, 1766.

A Catalogue of Books which will begin to be sold by Auction . . . being the bound Stock in Trade of Mr. Robt. Bell, Bookseller. . . . Dublin, 1767.

Flin's Sale Catalogue of Books for the Year 1767. . . . Dublin, 1767.

Part II of Flin's Sale Catalogue of Books, for the Years 1767 and 1768. Dublin, 1767.

Catalogue of Books [to be sold by auction, ca. 1768; title page missing but no books dated later than 1767]. Dublin, 1768?

A Catalogue of the Libraries of Richard Terry, Francis Dindon, Esqrs: and Part of the Library of a late . . . Prelate . . . [to be sold by auction]. Dublin, 1768.

Flin's Sale Catalogue of Books, for the Year, 1769. . . . Dublin, 1769.

Flin's Sale Catalogue of Books for the Year 1770. . . . Dublin, 1770.

. . . The Libraries of the Rev. Mr. Burgh, and an Eminent Physician Deceased . . . to be sold by Auction. . . . Dublin, 1769.

A Catalogue of a valuable Library, collected by the late Chancellor Cox . . . which will be sold by Auction. . . . Dublin, 1772.

A Complete Catalogue of Modern Books from 1700 [to be sold by auction]. . . . Dublin, 1774.

Complete Catalogue of Modern Books printed in Ireland from the beginning of the Century [to be sold by auction]. . . . Dublin, 1774.

The Dublin catalogue of books, in all arts and sciences . . . to be sold by auction . . . by Christopher Talbot. Dublin, 1779.

The Complete Dublin catalogue of books . . . from the beginning of the century to the present time [to be sold by auction]. . . . Dublin, 1786.

. . . The Library of the late Christopher Robinson, Esq. . . . Will be sold by Auction by James Vallance. . . . Dublin, 1787.

A general catalogue of books . . . that have been printed in Ireland, and published in Dublin, from the year 1700 to the present time [to be sold by auction]. Dublin, 1791.

A Catalogue of the Library of the late Right Honourable Denis Daly. Which will be sold by Auction. . . . Dublin, 1792.

Archer's Catalogue of Books for 1793 . . . with the prices affixed to each. . . . The sale begins on Wednesday the 3rd of April 1793. . . . Dublin, 1793.

Catalogue des Livres françois, italiens, etc. de Antoine Gerna, Libraire à Dublin [to be sold by auction]. Dublin, 1793.

. . . The Libraries of the late Dr. Henry Ware and another Gentleman . . . to be sold by Auction. Dublin, 1793.

A Collection of Books, Prints and Drawings, being the Collection of the late Honourable Judge Hellen . . . to be sold by Auction. . . . Dublin, 1794.

Catalogue of Books, being the Libraries of Two Gentlemen who are going abroad . . . to be sold by Auction. . . . Dublin, 1796.

Catalogue of Books, Prints, and Book[s] of Print[s] being the Libraries of the late Rev. Doctor Usher, F.T.C.D., Mr. Clarence, and another Gentleman . . . to be sold on Wednesday the 22nd of June 1796. . . . Dublin, 1796.

. . . The remaining part of the Library of the late Richard Baldwin, Esq., . . . to be sold on Thursday the 18th of February, 1796. Dublin, 1796.

Catalogue of Books, Prints and Books of Prints; being the Collection of a Gentleman of Distinguished Taste . . . to be sold by Auction. . . . Dublin, 1799.

A Catalogue of Books and Manuscripts of the late Mrs. Walcott . . . to be sold by Auction. . . . Dublin, 1800.

A Catalogue of the Library of the late Rev. Richard Murray, D.D., Provost of Trinity College, Dublin . . . to be sold by auction. . . . Dublin, 1800.

. . . The Library of an Antiquarian . . . to be sold by auction. . . . Dublin, 1800.

. . . The Library of the late Most Rev. Dr. William Newcombe, Archbishop of Armagh . . . to be sold by Auction. . . . Dublin, 1800.

. . . The Library of the late Rev. Doctor Wilson . . . to be sold by Auction. . . . Dublin, 1800.

Catalogue of the Valuable Library of the late Dr. R. R. Madden to be sold at Auction. . . . Dublin, 1886.

OTHER CONTEMPORARY OR NEAR-
CONTEMPORARY WORKS

Anon. "Authentic Memoirs of the late George Faulkner, Esq.," *The Hibernian Magazine*, 5 (Sept.–Oct. 1775), 68–72.

——. *A Collection of Letters and Essays on Several Subjects Lately Publish'd in the Dublin Journal*. Dublin, 1729.

——. *The Lucubrations of Salmanazer Histrum, Esq., together with the Plain Dealer*. Dublin, 1730.

——. "Memoirs of Thomas Rider," *Sequin's Hibernian Magazine* (Jan. 1773), 91–101.

——. "Table Talk," *European Magazine and London Review*, 25 (Feb. 1794), 110–15; 25 (Mar. 1794), 179–84.

Baker, D. E. *Biographia dramatica, or a Companion to the Playhouse*. 2 vols., London, 1764.

Budgell, Eustace. *Memoirs of the Lives and Characters of the Illustrious Family of the Boyles*. Dublin, 1755.

Carson, James. *Jemmy Carson's Collections*. Dublin, 1759.

Chetwood, W. R. *A General History of the Stage, from its origin in Greece down to the present time.* Dublin, 1749.

——. *A Tour through Ireland.* Dublin, 1746.

Davis, Thomas. *Memoirs of the Life of David Garrick.* Dublin, 1780.

Dunton, John. *The Dublin Scuffle.* London, 1699.

——. *Life and Errors.* 2 vols., London, 1818.

Fitzgerald, John. *Cork Remembrances.* Cork, 1783.

Gent, Thomas. *The Life of Thomas Gent, Printer, of York, written by himself.* London, 1832.

Harris, Walter. *Hibernica.* Dublin, 1747.

——. *A History of Dublin.* London, 1766.

O'Keefe, J. *Recollections of the Life of J. O'Keefe, written by himself.* 2 vols., London, 1826.

Nichols, John. *Literary Anecdotes of the Eighteenth Century.* 9 vols., London, 1812–1815.

Palmer, S. [George Psalmanazar]. *A General History of Printing. . . .* London, 1734.

——. *Memoirs of **** Commonly known by the Name of George Psalmanazar.* London, 1765.

Petty, Sir William. *The Political Anatomy of Ireland.* London, 1691.

Ralph, James. *The Case of Authors by Profession or Trade Stated.* London, 1758.

Smith, Charles. *The Ancient and Present State of the County and City of Cork.* 2 vols., Dublin, 1750.

Towers, Joseph. *Observations on the Rights and Duties of Juries in Trials of Libels.* Dublin, 1785.

Watson, James. *The History of the Art of Printing.* Edinburgh, 1713.

SECONDARY WORKS

Alden, John. "Pills and Publishing: Some Notes on the English Book Trade, 1660–1715," *Library*, 5th ser., vii (1952), 20–37.

Aldis, H. G., et al. *A Dictionary of Printers and Booksellers in England, Scotland and Ireland, and of Foreign Printers of English Books 1557–1640.* London, 1910.

Aspinall, A. *Politics and the Press, 1780–1850.* London, 1949.

Barrington, Sir Jonah. *Personal Sketches of His Own Time.* London, 1827.

Benn, G. *The History of the Town of Belfast.* Belfast, 1823.

Berry, H. E. *A History of the Royal Dublin Society.* Dublin, 1915.

Blagen, Cyprian. *The Stationers' Company: A History, 1703–1959*. London, 1960.

———. "Book Trade Control in 1566," *Library*, 5th ser., xiii (1958), 28–39.

———. "The Stationers' Company in the Civil War Period," *Library*, 5th ser., xiii (1958), 21–26.

———. "The 'Company' of Printers," *Studies in Bibliography*, 13 (1960), 68–70.

———. "The Stationers' Company in the Eighteenth Century," *Guildhall Miscellany*, 10 (1959), 28–32.

Bourne, H. R. F. *English Newspapers*. 2 vols., London, 1887.

Brady, John. "Government Printing in Waterford," *Irish Book Lover*, 31, no. 1 (1949), 12.

Brown, R. "The Stationers, Booksellers and Printers of Chester to about 1800," *Historical Society of Lancashire and Cheshire Journal*, 83 (1931), 118.

Burch, R. M. "Some Notes on Irish Paper Trade History," *World's Paper Trade Review*, 52, no. 4 (23 July 1909, 26 Nov. 1909, and 25 Feb. 1910), 137–39, 905–7, 305–9.

Burke, W. P. *History of Clonmel*. Waterford, 1909.

Burton, K. G. *The Early Newspaper Press in Berkshire, 1723–1855*. Reading, 1954.

Campbell, A. Albert. "Belfast Politics," *Irish Book Lover*, 11, nos. 6–7 (1915–16), 64.

Campbell, A. H. *Belfast Newspapers Past and Present*. Belfast, 1921.

Carroll, F. "Dublin Music Sellers, etc., 18th Century," *Irish Book Lover*, 31, no. 6 (1951), 129–30.

———. "Shakespeare in the Theatre," *Irish Book Lover*, 32, no. 1 (1952), 7–11.

Caulfield, J. "Dr. Caulfield's Antiquarian and Historical Notes," *Cork Historical and Archaeological Society Journal*, 2nd ser., x (1904), 261–65.

———. "Dr. Caulfield's Antiquarian and Historical Notes," *Cork Historical and Archaeological Society Journal*, 2nd ser., xi (1905), 93–94.

Chart, D. A. *The Story of Dublin*. London, 1932.

Clarke, W. J. *Early Nottingham Printers and Printing*. Nottingham, 1942.

Collins, A. S. *Authorship in the Days of Johnson*. London, 1927.

Collins, A. S. "Growth of the Reading Public during the 18th Century," *Review of English Studies*, 2 (1926), 285.

Collins, James. *Life in Old Dublin*. Dublin, 1913.

Collins, J. T. "Gleanings from Old Cork Papers," *Cork Historical and Archaeological Society Journal*, 52, no. 196 (July–Dec. 1957), 95–101.

Cotton, Henry (ed.). *A Typographical Gazetteer*. Oxford, 1866.

Craig, Maurice. "Eighteenth-Century Irish Bookbinding," *The Burlington Magazine* (May 1952), 132–36.

——. *Irish Bookbinding, 1680–1800.* London, 1954.

Crane, J. S. *A Concise Dictionary of Irish Biography.* Dublin, 1937.

Crane, R. S., and F. B. Kaye. *A Census of British Newspapers and Periodicals.* Chapel Hill, 1927.

Davies, Robert. *A Memoir of the York Press.* Westminster, 1868.

Day, Robert. "The Business Cards of Printers, Publishers, and Booksellers," *Cork Historical and Archaeological Society Journal*, 8 (1902), 95–103.

de Buitléir, Maittú. "The Waterford Flying Post," *Irish Book Lover*, 29, no. 3 (1944), 18.

Dennen, R. "The Dublin Directory," *Bibliographical Society of Ireland Publications*, 1, no. 7 (1918–20), 91–108.

Dickins, Bruce. "The Irish Broadside of 1571 and Queen Elizabeth's Types," *Transactions of the Cambridge Bibliographical Society*, 1 (1949–53), 48–60.

Dix, E. R. McC. "Another Private Press (Drogheda)," *Bibliographical Society of Ireland Publications*, 3, no. 7 (1928), 75–76.

——. "The Case of Ireland's Being Bound by Acts of Parliament in England Stated, by William Molyneux, List of Editions compiled by E. R. McC. Dix," *Irish Book Lover*, 5, no. 7 (1913), 116–18.

——. "The Crooke Family—Printers in Dublin in the 17th Century," *Bibliographical Society of Ireland Publications*, 2, no. 1 (1923), 16–17.

——. "A Dublin Almanac of 1612," *Proceedings of the Royal Irish Academy*, 30, sec. c, no. 12 (1913), 62–63.

——. *Dublin Printers between 1619 and 1700.* Dublin, n.d.

——. "Dublin 17th Century Printing: a new item," *Irish Book Lover*, 17, no. 1 (1929), 12.

——. "The Earliest Dublin Printers and the Company of Stationers of London," *Transactions of the Bibliographical Society of London*, 7 (1904), 75–85.

——. "The Earliest Limerick Newspaper," *Journal of the Limerick Field Club*, 3 (1908), 248–50.

——. "The Earliest Periodical Journals Published in Dublin," *Proceedings of the Royal Irish Academy*, 6, 3rd ser. (1900–1902), 35.

——. "An Early Dublin Almanack," *Proceedings of the Royal Irish Academy*, 33, sec. c, no. 8 (1916), 115–19.

——. "The First Irish Papers," *Irish Book Lover*, 4, no. 4 (1912), 97–98.

——. "The First Printing of the New Testament in English at Dublin," *Proceedings of the Royal Irish Academy*, 29, sec. c, no. 6 (1911), 84.

Dix, E. R. McC. (cont'd), "The First Printing Presses in Armagh and Newry," *Ulster Journal of Archaeology*, 16, 2nd ser. (1910), 46.

——. "French Prayer Book Printed in Dublin in 1731," *Bibliographical Society of Ireland Publications*, 2, no. 5 (1923), 96–97.

——. "Initial Letters used by J. Francton, printer in Dublin," *Irish Book Lover*, 3, no. 4 (1911), 109.

——. "Humphrey Powell, Dublin's First Printer," *Bibliographical Society of Ireland Publications*, 3, no. 7 (1928), 77–79.

——. "Humphrey Powell, The First Dublin Printer," *Proceedings of the Royal Irish Society*, 27, no. 7 (1908), 213–20.

——. "Irish Book-Binding, Primary Introduction to its Study," *Dublin Penny Journal* (1902), 344–46.

——. "Irish Chap Books," *Bibliographical Society of Ireland Publications*, 2, no. 5 (1923), 85–87.

——. "Irish Pirated Editions," *Journal of the Irish Library Association*, 2 (1906), 67–77.

——. "John Francton, an Early Dublin Printer and His Work," *The New Ireland Review*, 9 (Mar.–Aug. 1898), 36–42.

——. "The Law as to Printing in Ireland before the Act of Union," *Irish Book Lover*, 22, no. 5 (1934), 110–13.

——. *A List of Irish Towns and Dates of Earliest Printing in Each*. London, 1909.

——. "Municipal Records as Sources of Information about Early Printers," *Bibliographical Society of Ireland Publications*, 3, no. 7 (1928), 73–74.

——. "A New Speciman of Early Limerick Printing: The Drapier Letter," *Irish Book Lover*, 21, no. 4 (1933), 110.

——. "Note on the Dickson Family, Eighteenth Century Dublin Printers," *Irish Book Lover*, 17 (Mar.–Apr. 1929), 45–47.

——. "Notes of Some Early Dublin Newspapers (1707–1708)," *Bibliographical Society of Ireland Publications*, 2, no. 5 (1923), 87–91.

——. "Notes on the Will of John North, Stationer of Dublin," *Irish Book Lover*, 17, no. 3 (1929), 64.

——. "Notes on the Will of Peter Lawrence, Bookseller, Dublin (1706–1709)," *Irish Book Lover*, 17, no. 2 (1929), 47.

——. "Notes on the Will of Samuel Fuller, an Eighteenth Century Dublin Printer," *Irish Book Lover*, 17, no. 2 (1929), 48.

——. "Notes Upon the Leaves of the First Book Printed in Dublin Discovered in the Academy," *Proceedings of the Royal Irish Academy*, 27, no. 18 (1908), 404–6.

Dix, E. R. McC. (cont'd), "The Ornaments used by John Francton," *Transactions of the Bibliographical Society of London*, 8 (1904–1906), 221–28.

———. "The Pamphlet: Its Rise, Development and Use," *Bibliographical Society of Ireland Publications*, 2, no. 5 (1923), 91–93.

———. "Pepyat v. King and the Office of King's Stationer in Ireland (1721?)," *Irish Book Lover*, 19, no. 3 (1931), 82–87.

———. "The Powell Family," *Bibliographical Society of Ireland Publications*, 2, no. 5 (1923), 85–87.

———. "Printing Restrictions in Ireland," *Ireland* (Feb. 1905), 589–99.

———. "Rare Ephemeral Magazines of the Eighteenth Century," *Irish Book Lover*, 1, no. 6 (1914), 71–73.

———. "Ray Family," *Bibliographical Society of Ireland Publications*, 2, no. 5 (1923), 85–87.

———. "Short Papers," *Bibliographical Society of Ireland Publications*, 3, no. 7 (1928), 73–81.

———. "Some Rare Magazines of the Eighteenth Century," *Irish Book Lover*, 8, nos. 1–2 (1916), 1–3.

———. "Some Rare Magazines of the Eighteenth Century," *Irish Book Lover*, 8, nos. 3–4 (1916), 25–28.

———. "Three Dispositions of Dublin Printers, etc., in 1712," *Irish Book Lover*, 17, no. 1 (1929), 33–35.

———. "A Very Rare Kilkenny-Printed Proclamation, and William Smith, its Printer," *Proceedings of the Royal Irish Society*, 27, sec. c, no. 18 (1908), 200–12.

———. "A Waterford Bookseller's Advt. of Books, etc., Sold by Him in 1750," *Journal of the Waterford and South-east of Ireland Archaeological Society*, 13 (1910), 5–7.

———. "Who Printed 'Hibernia Dominicana'?" *Irish Book Lover*, 14, nos. 9–10 (1924), 116–17.

———. "Will of a Limerick Printer of the 18th Century," *Journal of the North Munster Archaeological Society*, 2 (July 1911), 44–46.

———. "Will of Andrew Welsh," *Journal of the North Munster Archaeological Society*, 2, no. 1 (July 1911), 34.

———. "William Kearney, the Second Earliest Known Printer in Dublin," *Proceedings of the Royal Irish Academy*, 28, sec. c, no. 8 (1909), 57–59.

———. "Works of Oliver Goldsmith," *Bibliographical Society of Ireland Publications*, 3, no. 9 (1928), 93–101.

Duff, E. Gordon. *A Century of the English Book Trade.* London, 1905.

Falkiner, C. L. *Studies in Irish History and Biography, mainly in the 18th Century.* Dublin, 1902.

Flood, Chevalier Grattan. "Aria di Camera, Oldest Printed Collection of Irish Music," *Bibliographical Society of Ireland Publications*, 2, no. 5 (1923), 97–101.

———. "John and William Neale, Music Printers," *Bibliographical Society of Ireland Publications*, 3, no. 8 (1928), 83–89.

Froude, J. A. *The English in Ireland in the Eighteenth Century.* 3 vols., London, 1881.

Gale, Peter. *An Inquiry into the Ancient Corporate System of Ireland.* Dublin, 1834.

Gilbert, J. T. *A History of the City of Dublin.* 3 vols., Dublin, 1861.

———. "Streets of Dublin," *Irish Quarterly Review*, 2 (1852), 1–75.

Hamlyn, H. M. "Eighteenth Century Circulating Libraries in England," *Library*, 5th ser., i, nos. 3–4 (Dec. 1946, Mar. 1947), 197–222.

Hammond, J. W. "The Dublin Gazette (1705–1922)," *Dublin Historical Records*, 13, nos. 3–4 (1953), 108–17.

———. "The King's Printers in Ireland 1551–1919," *Dublin Historical Records*, nos. 1, 2, 3 (1949–50), 149–50.

Handcock, W. D. *The History and Antiquities of Tallacht, County Dublin.* Dublin, 1887.

Hardiman, James. *The History of the Town and County of Galway.* Galway, 1926.

Hennig, John. "German Script in Irish Printing," *Irish Book Lover*, 30, no. 4 (1948), 89–91.

Herbert, J. D. *Irish Varieties for the Last 50 Years.* London, 1836.

Higgins, F. R. *Progress in Irish Printing.* Dublin, 1936.

Hill, Joseph. *The Book Makers of Old Birmingham. Authors, Printers and Book Sellers.* New York, 1907.

Hodgson, R., and C. Blagden. *The Notebook of Thomas Bennet and Henry Clements.* Oxford, 1956.

Inglis, Brian. *The Freedom of the Press in Ireland 1784–1841.* London, 1954.

Jerdan, William. *Autobiography.* 4 vols., London, 1852–1853.

Kavanaugh, Peter. *The Irish Theatre.* Tralee, 1946.

Keatinge, C. T. "The Guild of Cutlers, Painter-Stainers and Stationers, Better known as the Guild of St. Luke the Evangelist, Dublin," *Royal Society of Antiquaries of Ireland*, 10, 5th ser. (1900), 28–31.

Kirkpatrick, T. P. C. *The History of Doctor Stevens' Hospital, Dublin, 1720–1920.* Dublin, 1924.

————. *Notes on the Printers in Dublin during the 17th Century*. Dublin, 1939.

Knight, C. *Shadows of the Old Booksellers*. London, 1865.

Lawrence, W. J. "Some Old Dublin Theatrical Journals," *Irish Book Lover*, 14, nos. 11–12 (1924), 130–32.

Latimer, Rev. W. T. "Armagh," *Ulster Journal of Archaeology*, 7 (1901), 57.

Lecky, W. E. H. *A History of Ireland in the Eighteenth Century*. 5 vols., London, 1892.

Lenihan, Maurice. *Limerick: Its History and Antiquities*. Cork, n.d.

Lepper, J. H., and Philip Crosslé. *History of the Grand Lodge of Free and Accepted Masons of Ireland*. Dublin, 1925.

Levinge, Sir R. G. A. *Jottings of the Levinge Family*. Dublin, 1877.

Lynch, P., and J. Vaizey. *Guinness's Brewery in the Irish Economy, 1759–1876*. Cambridge, 1960.

McCracken, J. L. "The Conflict between the Irish Administration and Parliament, 1753–6," *Irish Historical Studies*, 3 (1942), 159–79.

McDowell, R. B. *Irish Public Opinion, 1750–1800*. London, 1944.

McGovern, J. B. "Dublin Publishers in 1720," *Irish Book Lover*, 2, no. 6 (1911), 93.

MacLochlainn, Alf. "Bagnells and Knights: Publishers and Papermakers in Cork," *Irish Book Lover*, 1, no. 3, new ser. (1956), 21–23.

MacManus, M. J. "The First Limerick Newspaper," *Irish Book Lover*, 24 (May–June 1936), 53–55.

————. "A Rare Waterford-Printed Book (1647) and its Printer, Peter de Pienne," *Irish Book Lover*, 24, no. 4 (1936), 75–77.

MacWilliam, A. "The Lying-in Hospital Library," *Bibliographical Society of Ireland Publications*, 2, no. 5 (1923), 106–7.

Madden, R. R. *Irish Periodical Literature from the End of the 17th Century to the Middle of the 19th Century*. 2 vols., London, 1867.

Maffett, R. S. "Printing in Newry," *Irish Book Lover*, 6, no. 2 (1914), 17–18.

Maginniss, T. H. Jr. *The Irish Contribution to America's Independence*. Philadelphia, 1913.

Malcolm, A. G. *History of the General Hospital*. Belfast, 1851.

Mossner, E. C. *The Life of David Hume*. Edinburgh, 1954.

————, and H. Ransom. "Hume and the Conspiracy of Booksellers: The Publication and Early Fortunes of the *History of England*," *Studies in English*, 29 (1950), 162–82.

Moxon, Joseph. *Mechanick Exercises on the Art of Printing (1683–4)*. Oxford, 1958.

Munter, Robert. *The History of the Irish Newspaper 1685–1760*. Cambridge, 1967.

O'Brien, R. B. (ed.). *Two Centuries of Irish History, 1691–1870*. London, 1907.

Ó Casaide, Séamus. "A Drogheda Printer," *Irish Book Lover*, 17, no. 4 (1929), 120.

———. "A Dublin Catholic Bookseller in the Penal Days," *Irish Book Lover*, 17, no. 4 (1929), 77–78.

———. "Fictitious Imprints on Books Printed in Ireland," *Bibliographical Society of Ireland Publications*, 3, no. 4 (1926), 31–35.

———. "A Kilkenny Printer's Will," *Irish Book Lover*, 24, no. 2 (1936), 40.

———. "A Limerick Bookseller-Poet," *Irish Book Lover*, 18, no. 2 (1930), 58.

———. "A Loughrea Printer," *Irish Book Lover*, 17, no. 4 (1929), 120.

———. "Myles Swinney, Letter Founder," *Irish Book Lover*, 17, no. 4 (1929), 93.

———. "An Old Limerick Printer," *Irish Book Lover*, 22, no. 1 (1934), 7.

———. "Patrick Lord," *Irish Book Lover*, 17, no. 4 (1929), 120.

———. "Printing in Athlone," *Irish Book Lover*, 23, no. 4 (1935), 93.

———. "A Rare Book of Irish and Scottish Gaelic Verse," *Bibliographical Society of Ireland Publications*, 3, no. 6 (1927), 59–70.

———. "A Sligo Printer," *Irish Book Lover*, 17, no. 4 (1929), 120.

———. "An Unrecorded Irish Book of 1716," *Irish Book Lover*, 28, nos. 5–6 (1942), 131–33.

O'Hegarty, P. S. "Dublin Printed Classics," *Irish Book Lover*, 27, no. 2 (1940), 184.

O'Kelley, Francis. "Early Alphabetical Lists of Dublin Streets," *Irish Book Lover*, 16, nos. 4, 5, 6 (1928), 77–79.

———. "The Early Manx Printers," *Journal of the Manx Museum*, 3 (Dec. 1937), 138–40.

———. "An Early Youghal Bookbinder," *Irish Book Lover*, 18, no. 6 (1930), 173.

Petrie, George. "The Old Bridge of Mill Town, County of Dublin," *The Irish Penny Journal*, 1, no. 36 (6 Mar. 1841), 43–44.

Phillips, James W. "A Trial List of Papermakers, 1690–1800," *Library*, 5th ser., xiii, no. 1 (1958), 59–62.

Plomer, H. R. "Dermo'd O'Connor and Keating's *History*," *Irish Book Lover*, 3, no. 8 (1912), 125–27.

———. *A Dictionary of the Booksellers and Printers who were at work in England, Scotland and Ireland 1641–1667*. London, 1907.

———. *A Dictionary of the Printers and Booksellers who were at work in England, Scotland and Ireland, from 1668–1725.* Oxford, 1922.

———, G. H. Bushell, and E. R. McC. Dix. *A Dictionary of the Printers who were at work in England, Scotland, and Ireland from 1726–1775.* Oxford, 1932.

Plomer, H. R. "John Francton and his Successors," *Irish Book Lover*, 3, no. 7 (1911), 109–10.

———. "The Protestant Press in the Reign of Queen Anne," *Library*, 3rd ser., i (1910), 54–67.

———. "Some Notes on the Latin and Irish Stocks of the Company of Stationers," *Library*, 2nd ser., viii (1907), 38–47.

Plowden, Francis. *A Historical Review of the State of Ireland.* 2 vols., London, 1803.

Pollard, Graham. "The Size of the Sheet," *Library*, 4th ser., xxii (1942), 85–93.

Quinn, R. B. "Government Printing and the Publication of Irish Statutes in the Sixteenth Century," *Proceedings of the Royal Irish Academy*, 49, sec. c, no. 60 (1943), 100–11.

———. "Information about Dublin Printers, 1556–1573, in English Financial Records," *Irish Book Lover*, 27 (1942), 112–15.

Rothschild, Lord. "The Publication of the First Drapier Letter," *Library*, 4th ser., xix, no. 1 (1938), 111–13.

Ryland, R. H. *History, Topography, and Antiquities of the County and City of Waterford.* Waterford, 1824.

Sale, W. M. *Samuel Richardson, Master Printer.* Ithaca, N.Y., 1950.

Sampson, H. *History of Advertising.* London, 1874.

Stockwell, LaTourette. "The Dublin Pirates and the English Laws of Copyright, 1710–1801," *The Dublin Magazine*, 12, no. 4 (Oct.–Dec. 1937), 30–40.

Sullivan, Sir Edward. *Decorative Book-Binding in Ireland.* Letchworth, 1914.

———. "Ornamental Bookbinding in Ireland in the Eighteenth Century," *The Studio* (Oct. 1905), 52–59.

———. "The Parliamentary Journals of Ireland, 1613–1800," *Country Life* (5 Sept. 1908), 313–17.

Ward, Isaac W. "Old Belfast Signboards," *Ulster Journal of Archaeology*, 12 (1906), 10–17.

Welsh, C. *A Bookseller of the last Century.* London, 1885.

Williams, Harold. "Gulliver's Travels: Further Notes," *Library*, 4th ser., ix, no. 2 (1928), 187–96.

Williams, J. B. "Henry Crossgrove, Jacobite, Journalist and Printer," *Library*, 3rd ser., v (1914), 82–89.

Windele, John. *Historical and Descriptive Notices of the City of Cork*. Cork, 1848.

Wise, M. J. "Birmingham and its Trade Relations in the Early 18th Century," *University of Birmingham Historical Journal*, 2, no. 1 (1949), 86–94.

Wood, H. "The Court of Castle Chamber," *Proceedings of the Royal Irish Academy*, 32, sec. c, no. 8 (1913–16), 152.

Wright, W. B. *The Ussher Memoirs*. Dublin, 1889.

Robert Munter's *Dictionary of the Print Trade in Ireland, 1550–1775*, has been set in Caslon, a face cut by William Caslon in London in 1734, who modeled it on seventeenth-century Dutch typefaces. The revival used in this book was based on Caslon's original matrices and cut for the Mergenthaler Linotype Corporation in 1913. The book was composed and printed from the type by Heritage Printers in Charlotte, North Carolina. One thousand copies have been printed on Warren's Olde Style paper.